A MILLENNIUM OF
CULTURAL CONTACT

For Jennifer, Ruby, Esther, and George

A MILLENNIUM OF CULTURAL CONTACT

by
Alistair Paterson

Routledge
Taylor & Francis Group

LONDON AND NEW YORK

First published 2011 by Left Coast Press, Inc.

Published 2016 by Routledge
2 Park Square, Milton Park, Abingdon, Oxon OX14 4RN
711 Third Avenue, New York, NY 10017, USA

Routledge is an imprint of the Taylor & Francis Group, an informa business

Library of Congress Cataloging-in-Publication Data:

Paterson, Alistair, 1968-

A millennium of cultural contact / Alistair Paterson.

p. cm.

Includes bibliographical references.

ISBN 978-1-59874-492-7 (hardcover : alk. paper) —

ISBN 978-1-59874-493-4 (pbk. : alk. paper)

1. Culture diffusion—History. 2. Culture conflict—History. 3. Archaeology and history.

4. Europe—Territorial expansion. 5. Indians—First contact

Design and production services: Leyba Associates, Santa Fe, NM

ISBN 978–1–59874–492–7 hardcover
ISBN 978–1–59874–493–4 paperback

CONTENTS

ILLUSTRATIONS

TABLES

FIGURES

PREFACE

Cultural contacts between different societies have occurred throughout human history and prehistory. This book is interested in the evidence for culture contact that occurred between aboriginal Europeans and indigenous groups living outside of Europe. My interest is the second millennium AD, and accordingly, I take as a starting point the Norse settlement of the Americas and Greenland, around 1000 AD, and the contact across cultures that possibly ensued.

When initially planning this book, I was prompted by colleagues to cover ancient culture contact, such as between the Classical Romans and others. I have not done so. I chose instead to focus on the second millennium with its great breadth of topic, as it was at this time that a truly global network of societies in contact emerged, encompassing both Old and New Worlds. A consideration of the ways that historical culture contact compares with more ancient forms of culture contact is a different topic, one that has been pursued in recent literature on colonialism in ancient times as compared with colonialism as we more commonly comprehend it, as something rooted in culture contacts that came to be central to European activities across the globe over the last five centuries.[1]

This book intends to contribute to an interdisciplinary topic from an archaeological and historical anthropological perspective. Given the size of the topic, it is hardly surprising that there are few attempts to provide a global overview of culture contact. Certainly, in terms of archaeology there exist more global overviews for human prehistory than for historical eras. Historical archaeologists, whose area of archaeological expertise is often defined as being about the results of European contacts with other societies, have conducted much of the work I refer to.[2] Their interest is in what the material record tells us, combined with data from historical sources where appropriate.

There are three issues to consider initially that flow from the "big picture" approach to this topic.

1. First is the issue of speaking about any one culture in a homogeneous way. This clearly masks the diversity of human actions. For example, throughout this book I consider how different aboriginal groups respond to the change

that occurred when Europeans arrived with their various agendas of exploration, conquest, colonization, redemption, conversion, capitalization, dictation, avoidance, and control. To say that any group "resisted" or "collaborated" is clearly a generalization, one that possibly speaks only to the actions of a few. One of the most famous culture contacts was between Cortez and Moctezuma: yet different Mesoamerican communities responded differently to the Spaniards, who themselves were driven by internal differences.

The core of this problem is of identity: can we easily speak of a society's identity when we consider histories of culture contact? Part of the problem explored in this book concerns the available data: often historical accounts of societies give insight into past identity and action, but often from a European perspective and not from an indigenous one. This book tries to explore how other lines of evidence, particularly archaeological evidence, can help us to understand the complexity of human actions.

2. Another important issue concerns how and whether certain aboriginal societies have survived the events of the last millennium. Cultural survival is very important, extending to the survival of languages, cultural practices, beliefs, and attachments to places. The survival of culture is important, the loss of culture a tragedy. In exploring the archaeology of culture contact in this book, I include some examples of how cultures change as much as they survive, or indeed how change heralds survival. When reading literature on this topic, survival seems to be something that indigenous societies do, while European-descended cultures are rarely viewed as being threatened.

3. Finally, by talking about continents I clearly am making generalizations, and not all indigenous communities of any one continent should be considered alike. I use large regions as zones from which to extract examples of culture contact. Where possible, I hone in on more meaningful smaller regions.

I will provide both a general overview to culture contact and more in-depth detail garnered from selected archaeological studies. To provide a sense both of the local and global, I move from the big picture to the level of site and encounter to illuminate local–global connections. I attempt to provide context for the archaeological studies of individuals, households, communities, and societies in contact. This follows a position advocated by archaeologist Charles E. Orser, who writes, "it is clear that microhistory, though focused on the small, must be contextualized enough to provide a framework for understanding the sociohistorical milieu in which the subject of the microhistory lived."[3]

I accept and apologize for any factual errors that may arise. Those who wish to engage with the debates can do so through the literature cited here. The review is intended both for the general public and for students of culture contact; accordingly, I have provided additional references for each topic.

MILLENNIUM'S HINGE

Across the world, at least in terms of eventual implications, there is a great hinge exactly in the middle of the second millennium: this hinge is the 21 years between 1492 and 1513. Before this time, medieval Europe's tastes and demands were pushing toward greater involvement and knowledge of the broader world, but with few geographical, economic, or social influences on the world beyond Europe. After this time, the scene was set for the great post-medieval expansion of European influence and the creation of a global network that would reach every corner of the world. The year 1492 saw the voyages of Christopher Columbus and Vasco da Gama. In 1513, Portuguese ships slid into the waters of the Moluccas, the "Spice Islands" and source of nutmeg and mace, a discovery that marked the end for medieval limits on knowledge of the foreign sources of these materials.

For centuries, spices had been bundled into boats in Asian and African ports and then sold to traders before being shipped or overlanded to the markets of West Asia. From these markets, goods were sold to Italian merchants to be redistributed from the storehouses of Genoa and Venice. These arrangements changed after 1513, as Europeans increasingly *directly* accessed Asian markets. This, together with the events in the New World, transformed Europe and the world. Eventually, people across the world were enveloped in colonial and imperial systems commonly directed by European societies. The story of the multitude of culture contacts that arose, from "first contact" through to colonial times, is a core part of this history.

History books similar to this one start with Columbus. I start earlier, for the events and forms of culture contact prior to 1492 are relevant to what happens afterward. To take one example, plantations were central institutions in the colonization of the Americas. Labor for plantations largely derived from the transatlantic trade of millions of enslaved people, and this underlay the modern societies of the Caribbean and parts of the Americas. The concept of plantations, however, was developed well before 1492—in fact, from the thirteenth century onward on islands in the Mediterranean and the eastern Atlantic.

Similarly, the response of native peoples to European outsiders deserves a longer-term perspective, as encounters were set within their own cultures and were rooted in existing sociopolitical, ideological, and technical parameters.

11

THE SCOPE OF THE BOOK

The book is organized by geographical region but with some attention to chronology as well. The book begins with the earliest contacts after AD 1000 between medieval Norse settlers and people indigenous to eastern Canada and Greenland (chapter 3). I then move on in time and outward from Europe in space to consider culture contact in the peripheries of Europe (chapter 4), Africa (chapter 5), post-1492 America (chapters 6 and 7), East Asia and Oceania (chapter 8), and Australia (chapter 9).

This covers various historical periods from a European perspective, the Medieval period or Middle Ages—or at least the later centuries of these—and a period sometimes termed the "Early Modern period," meaning the period from 1300 to the Industrial Revolution. This millennium saw the Renaissance, Reformation, Age of Discovery, Industrial era, and other convenient categories. However, beyond Europe, of course, existed many other meaningful periods from other people's viewpoints.

This book is not intended to be an absolute compendium of culture contact studies. There is much missing here, especially in the Americas, about which there has been a large amount of work on culture contact studies. South America and South and Central Asia are not focused on, in the name of brevity.

This is not meant to be primarily a "world history," although I have been influenced by the attempts of authors such as Gordon Childe, Eric Wolf, Immanuel Wallerstein, Alfred Crosby, and others.[4] As a series of case studies and regional overviews taken from across the planet, it is global to that degree. The literature allows me to explore how culture contact came about, how we can learn from past studies, what data are available to understand culture contact, and how scholarly and public opinions have informed debates over time. There is no attempt here to provide a new theoretical model for culture contact; rather, this is a survey of archaeological studies.

An overview covering a millennium of almost innumerable cross-cultural encounters necessarily requires generalizations. I wish to stress, however, that I am not terribly attracted to universal generalizations about human behavior. They often reek of the perceived inevitability of certain modes of living—such as the shift toward social complexity and intensive food production, or of the inevitable victory of imperial powers.

There were many similarities in how humans dealt with cross-cultural encounters, but I hope to draw out the individual and local idiosyncratic aspects as well. For this reason, I try to burrow into the "local" and move beyond the "global": my approach is intended to give emphasis to cultural differences. One significant pitfall of global universals as they relate to humans in contact in the second millennium is that similar ideologies characterized colonial and imperial events. Ideas of racial, cultural, and religious superiority were used as tools to justify the invasion or colonization of native peoples' country, as well as the removal of the natives themselves and the usurpation of their traditional rights.

This is a story equally about the present, and not necessarily esoteric knowledge. Past culture contact is important for many people today. For many Indigenous societies, lives, languages, culture, land, and rights were lost. While culture contact has always occurred, after 1492 the rates of culture contact increased dramatically and were typically part of processes whereby indigenous peoples' rights were truncated or obliterated. From these beginnings, cultures and individuals were enmeshed in cross-cultural processes.

In Australia, for example, the process of culture contact between various Aboriginal Australian societies and Europeans followed the arrival of the British in 1788. Some Australians now call this "invasion," others prefer "colonization." Today many Aboriginal Australians face specific challenges. To understand why in some communities some Aboriginal people die decades earlier than average Australians, why the murder rate is ten times the national average, why incarceration rates are so high, why some Aboriginal students perform worse, why there is extensive alcohol and drug abuse, high unemployment, and systemic violence is to understand a longer journey in addition to current policies and practices. The year 1788 is a key date in the journey. Culture contact is part of the story, with both negative and positive dimensions.

Australians want answers to these difficulties; the past is part of the answer. Knowledge of difficult histories, of hidden histories, is thus important in understanding the past.

To take another regional example, University of California archaeologist Kent Lightfoot has spent his career working in California. His long-term study tries to understand how colonial process and cultural engagements between native Californians and various outsiders (Spaniards, Mexicans, Anglo-Americans, and Russians) and their institutions explain contemporary peoples' cultural survival.[5] Exploring difficult histories like those around culture contact allows meaningful engagements with the past that tell us more about who we are today.

We face several challenges in our attempts to disentangle cross-cultural interactions, some of which I map out in chapter 2. One boundary I need to acknowledge initially is the one made between Europe and the rest of the world. This is obviously problematic, yet the division lies at the center of this book. Can one really group all European cultures together in this way? Most of these historical societies would not have recognized the idea of "Europe" as we do today. The aim here is not to be Eurocentric: I am trying to explore cross-cultural events following the presence of Europeans. So, this is not so much *about* Europeans, as defined by a period of European events. Nor it is all about indigenous *responses* to European *deeds*, as much earlier literature seems to imply. This division is about a basic chronological fact: after AD 1000 and increasingly from the fifteenth century, certain Europeans, acting on behalf of chiefs, families, kingdoms, states, churches, companies, and as individuals, voyaged from Europe to other continents whereupon culture contacts ensued as a two-sided process, at least before becoming increasingly more complex, with genes and tensions between European and non-European centers coming into play.

This topic, then, is "European" insofar as representatives of what we now know as distinct European nations or societies—the Norse, Catalans, Portuguese, Spaniards, Basques, French, British, Belgians, Swedes, Danes, Germans, Italians—went out into the world. This was not new. There had already been established diasporic and migratory communities based on trade, colonialism, and migration throughout the globe. It is the scale of movement in the second millennium that is unique.

Nor was it just Europeans on the move. For example, in chapter 3 we consider Greenland, where, in the early second millennium, *both* of the societies that were to be in contact with each other for centuries to follow arrived *together*—the Norse in the south and the Thule in the north. The Norse arrived in Greenland from Iceland in the west, the Thule from the east, from the cauldron of the Bering Strait. The Norse represented the great arc of Scandinavians, while the Thule represented an Arctic society with roots in both the Asian and Canadian Arctic realms. Both represented the furthest arc of each of their peoples, their most isolated examples.

Yet it is mistake to think of Greenland at the turn of the second millennium as remote—goods and ideas poured in and out of Greenland for centuries, both east and west. In this sense, Greenland at this time was not remote but the center of the world. Perhaps this is true for all of the places discussed here, an increasingly "world" system, but with many centers, depending on one's perspective.

I have written a gazetteer of the archaeology of culture contact, the book I would have found useful a few years ago when I started looking at this topic in detail. It is a guidebook for the intellectual tourist—it lists places I found good to visit. I hope the reader finds this guide useful to their journey.

ACKNOWLEDGMENTS

This book was written in Copenhagen while I was a visiting fellow at the Department of Cross Cultural & Regional Studies at Copenhagen University, and it was made possible by the University of Western Australia.

In Denmark, I thank Bjarne Grønnow, Head of the Greenland Research Center at the National Museum of Denmark, for allowing access to the ethnographic library and collection, and my participation in the International Polar Year workshop, "Climate, Environment and the Thule Culture in the Holocene Arctic." I appreciated the support of museum researchers Martin Appelt, Hans Christian Gulløv, Ditlev L. Mahler, Peter Andreas Toft, and Mikkel Sørensen, and members of the Scandinavian archaeological community, particularly Poul Otto Nielsen (National Museum of Denmark). At Copenhagen University, I thank Ingolf Thuesen, Alan Walmsley, Susanne Kerner, Rachel Dann, Stephen McPhillips, Hanne Nymann, and Pia Møller.

I am grateful to Mitch Allen for encouraging this book. Along the way I have had to deal with many new topics and have appreciated information from many experts, including Sarah Colley, Kristoffer Damgaard, Pierre M. Desrosiers, M. Dores Cruz, Hilary Du Cros, Wendy van Duivenvoorde, Max Friesen, Daryl Guse, Rodney Harrison, Judith Johnston, Susan Lawrence, Paul Lane, Matthew Liebmann, Kent Lightfoot, Jane Lydon, Andrew Lynch, Jo McDonald, Sally May, Wayne Mullen, Michael S. Nassaney, Charles Orser, June Ross, Uzma Rizvi, Stephen Silliman, Claire Smith, Mike Smith, Enrique Rodriguez-Alegria, Patricia Rubertone, Corioli Souter, Matthew Spriggs, Ann Stahl, Paul Taçon, Barbara Voss, Steve Wernke, Andrew Wilson, and James Woollett. Many of these people and National Museum of Denmark archaeologists read chapter drafts. I am extremely grateful to them—though, of course, despite their efforts, any shortcomings are mine. Much of this book I developed while teaching students, and I appreciate the input from students at the University of Western Australia and University of Copenhagen.

As always, I appreciate the support at the University of Western Australia from Dianne Anstey, Jane Balme, Liam Brady, Sandra Bowdler, Annie Carson, Kate Morse, Martin Porr, and Liam Brady. Jane Fyfe has been a valuable research assistant.

In terms of Australian research, I discuss in chapter 9 work conducted as part of the Picturing Change project, with specific reference to results from the Pilbara and Arnhem Land. I wish to thank Stephen Dhu, Andrew Dowding, and other Ngarluma. I acknowledge Ronald Lamilami as traditional owner of the Wellington Range rock art sites.

During the writing of this book, several meetings were useful: Maxine Oland and Siobhan Hart chaired "Lost in Transition: Decolonizing Indigenous Histories at the 'Prehistoric/Colonial' Intersection in Archaeology" at the American Anthropological Association 2008 meeting in San Francisco, and Neal Ferris and Andrew Martindale organized "Beyond Conceptual 'Borders': The Contribution of the Archaeology of Indigenous-Lived Colonialisms to Archaeological Theory" for the Society for Historical Archaeology meeting in Toronto, January 2009, which the global recession rudely intruded upon so that my paper was read by Rodney Harrison. A session in October 2009 at the Royal Asiatic Society (London) on the Indian Ocean was very useful: thanks to J. D. Hill, Mark Horton, and Stephanie Wynne-Jones.

CHAPTER 1

THE WORLD AFTER AD 1000

Even for an archaeologist, a millennium seems vast. Only fourteen generations of seventy years stacked end to end separate us today from AD 1000, yet the world around a thousand years ago was very different from the global community of which we are a part of today.[1] The lives of our ancestors of that time were more similar to our very distant relatives in preceding millennia than to ours. Although Europe was a relative backwater, it is where, in coming centuries, momentous events were to occur which would form the basis for our modern world. Voyages, discoveries, and cross-cultural encounters would transform humanity's understanding of the world and its occupants.

At the heart of this millennium were billions of encounters between individuals of different cultures—that is what this book is about. The descendants of these encounters have many legitimate questions about these events, as do historians, archaeologists, anthropologists, geographers, biologists, and theologians—the list is long. What do we know about past culture contact in this period? How do we know about it? What types of encounters occurred? How do we understand the results of these events, since most of them occurred beyond the chroniclers of history?

These are relevant questions to us today for two reasons. First, many believe (I am one, Henry Ford was not) we can learn from the past to act properly in the present. Second, the legacy of these events remains with us today in the form of the great human accomplishments as well as the great inequalities and injustices that make the second millennium *the* greatest millennium of culture contact.

One thousand years ago, there was no global community as we understand it today. The sun rose over an extensively peopled world, but its population was probably only half a billion. On 1 January AD 1000, in jungle, desert, and tundra, in farms, villages, and cities, humanity awoke to the day ahead. People traveled over land and water to explore, trade, and migrate. Farmers went to their animals and their plants to tend them in the constant cycle of husbandry, pushing individual species of plants and animals along their own journeys of gradual change. Most of our modern diet had been domesticated—except some later domesticates like strawberry. Most people were farmers, yet hunters and foragers were to be found everywhere—in far greater numbers and landscapes than today—and they too began their day with the individual and group responsibilities that ensured everyone's survival.

The great difference between 1000 and today was the level of knowledge individuals held of the other humans with whom they shared a planet. Most humans, probably all humans, were connected to other people, beginning with their neighbors and then beyond to more distant and unfamiliar places. Travelers, traders, slaves, migrants, and refugees ensured that people were always aware of distant places. Written or oral histories were common to most people; these provided a catalog of each community's knowledge of others. But essentially, the world was far more dissected and compartmentalized than it is today and was broken up into regional networks.

Some networks were massive, extending over oceans and continents, such as the network of Arctic communities across the North American Arctic through to Greenland. Maritime networks linked Asian and African trading communities through the heart of the Indian Ocean. The main overland link across Asia was the Silk Road, joining West Asia and India with China through hubs of long-distance commerce across Central Asia, while ships sailed to Southeast Asia, known to Arab seafarers as "the land below the wind."

Barriers between these geographical compartments—best envisaged at an island, continental, or ocean level—effectively restricted the movement of species, including those with whom humans had developed symbiotic relationships. Accordingly, the ancient soils of Australia had yet to feel a hoof, America had no large beasts of burden, and the islands of Polynesia were in the process of adjusting to the recent introduction of the Polynesian "trinity" of dog, pig, and chicken, along with garden crops. The great reworking of species globally after 1492, known as the "Columbian Exchange," lay a few centuries in the future.[2]

Today we mainly live in urban societies, while in 1000 people lived closer to primary food production or food gathering. Cities existed, some of the largest being in Asia (in China, Chang'an, modern Xian, had reached a population of one million), while in Mexico, Teotihuacan, near modern Mexico City, reached 100,000. Work by Khmer hydraulic engineers was underway at Angkor Wat in Cambodia that would see it become the world's largest urban center within a century. Large cities in West Asia were Baghdad (perhaps 500,000) and Constantinople (now Istanbul, 400,000), while Córdoba in Spain and Cairo in Egypt were also large.

Yet, many of today's large cities were small communities of a few thousand people. Some, like New York, did not exist. Few of the large urban centers were in Europe.

A millennium ago, the sunrise over North and South America lit places undreamed of by the rest of the planet—these places would, after 1492, become a "New World." This is despite America's having already entered European networks of knowledge, trade, and communication with the arrival of Vikings there at the very end of the first millennium.

The people of the New World were diverse, extending from the Arctic realms to the tip of Tierra del Fuego. Hunters and foragers occupied many environments, from the very cold regions to tropical jungles. Hunting was part of most native peoples' lives, as hunted foods contributed to many peoples' quest for food, whether they were farmers or not. Farming was prevalent in many regions, built on millennia of independent domestication in several places in the Americas (the Eastern Woodlands, Mexico, and South America), and by this time farmers were successful with their maize, bean, and squash triumvirate, with potato and other crops significant in South America.

Shifts toward more complicated and hierarchical societies, as well as village and urban forms of settlement, had occurred in many parts of the Americas over preceding millennia. In the woodlands of eastern North America, along the Mississippi River's course, this was the time of the Mississippian cultures, also to become known as "mound builders" after their earth and wooden monuments. These farming communities would come to trade widely and to build urban regional centers, the largest known being Cahokia (near modern St. Louis).

In Mesoamerica, complex societies had been rising and falling for thousands of years, and the ruins of Teotihuacan, Moche, and Chavín cultures were a familiar part of the landscape (just like ancient monuments stood over Cairo, Rome, and Baghdad). One thousand years ago, the Mayans were in a slow decline—Tikal already lay abandoned for over a century; however, other major Mayan settlements like Chichén Itzá and Tula remained vibrant, yet would also be abandoned. The rise of the Aztecs in central Mexico lay in the future, as did their momentous encounters with the Spanish conquistadors. However, these futures were still undreamed of.

A millennium ago in Mesoamerica, characteristic aspects of state societies were to be found: urban communities; writing; grand architecture; elaborate social and political structures; and specialization of artists, craftworkers, engineers, and others. Despite these complex communities, most people were farmers and were required to provide some of their output to the aristocratic rulers and their entourage.

Similar complexity existed in South America, where for thousands of years many small and larger states had flourished: a millennium ago, Andean centers of the Tiwanaku, Huari, and Chimú were significant complex societies, and in many ways the predecessors of the Inca Empire of the 1400s.

In summary, the millions of Native Americans in 1000 lived amid great diversity. Many lived in permanent villages of farmers, while in some resource-rich locations like modern British Columbia, year-round villages of intensive food collectors existed without requiring farming. There also were small and large urban settlements. Many of the staples of our world were growing in American gardens and fields: tobacco, tomato, corn, coca, and coffee. These would not be known of by the rest of the globe for many centuries to come. (It seems incredible to imagine Italian cuisine without tomatoes, beans, polenta, espresso, or indeed tobacco!)

Across the Americas, there was no knowledge of the other continents, despite possible contacts between Polynesians and some coastal South American peoples, suggested by the Polynesian people's use of sweet potato, an American domesticate. Additionally, in the far Northwest, people of the Bering Strait probably maintained contacts across the Arctic world.

As we follow the sunrise westward, the Pacific Ocean world meets the new millennium. The islands of Oceania, too, were utterly outside European knowledge—this was another "New World" in the wings. The more remote corners of this massive oceanic region were still in the process of being discovered at 1000; the colonization of New Zealand (Maori: *Aotearoa*) and neighboring islands still lay centuries ahead.[3] Islands such as the Society Islands, Hawaii, the Marquesas, and the Cook Islands were newly populated by people with a shared Polynesian heritage, with links back toward distant relations in Fiji, Tonga, and Samoa.

When Europeans arrived in Polynesia, they would marvel at the massive geographical spread of Polynesian societies. The Polynesian elite man Tupaiai who joined Captain James Cook's crew in April 1769 profoundly demonstrated these links by being able to communicate with disparate Polynesians whom Cook met, as far distant as the Maori in New Zealand. In fact, this instance of culture contact brought together two great maritime navigators: the renowned Captain Cook and Tupaiai, who produced a map of Polynesian navigational knowledge covering 2,500 miles of ocean!

Pacific people had specialized to life on diverse islands, some large and relatively resource-rich as compared with small islands like atolls. Humans tended to rely heavily on gardening, marine resources, and introduced animals such as rat, pig, chicken, and dog. Societies varied in complexity; however, in certain islands in Micronesia and Polynesia, stratified societies with specialization of trades and careers developed, matched by great efforts of terra-forming and monumental construction, most popularly known today in the stone heads of Easter Island (Rapa Nui). These were a continuation of established Polynesian practices, albeit grown large.

Expert navigators and boat builders maintained links between islands, such as in the Kingdom of Tonga, or among the disparate Caroline islands of Micronesia; these were maritime empires based on trade with neighbors.

Farther west, in Near Oceania, people of Papua New Guinea, the Solomon Islands, Vanuatu, and New Caledonia were descended from the ancient colonists of the region who came millennia earlier: Asian farmers, known as Lapita people, after the archaeological site of Lapita in New Caledonia where their distinctive and widespread pottery with human face decorations was first found, as well as from the Pleistocene populations who first reached the Pacific islands at least 40,000 years ago.

Consequently, a diverse range of farmers and hunter-foragers filled Melanesian islands. In the highlands of Papua New Guinea (PNG), an independent shift to gardening had occurred thousands of years earlier, and a vast population existed in these isolated mountain valleys. These would be some of the last indigenous populations on earth "discovered" by Europeans. First contact in the "highlands" of PNG occurred in the 1930s when Australian gold prospectors led expeditions into the mountainous inland.

The continent of Australia, like the Americas, lay outside the knowledge of Europeans at the millennium. The diverse Australian environment—from the tropics of the north to the cold climate of the island of Tasmania—sustained societies of hunter-foragers with expertise in landscape management, most dramatically through the use of fire.

People had arrived in Australia at least 50,000 years ago and quickly colonized the corners of the continent. Later, contact with people in Southeast Asia occurred during the Holocene, when the dog (dingo) was introduced. Yet, in 1000, sustained contacts with Asian traders lay centuries ahead, as did the arrival of Europeans. Australia would be the last inhabited continent discovered in the European "Age of Discoveries."

Island Southeast Asia at 1000 was characterized by great diversity, from hunter-foragers of Borneo to the religious states on islands like Java. These islands were all in contact, often mercantile in nature, and linked to continental Asia, where great religions and states had long been established. In East Asia, Hinduism and Buddhism, as well as Taoism, Confucism, and animism, were all significant.

While not influential east of the Indus River until after 1000, Islam would eventually become significant in southern Asia and China, as well as in Indonesia, today the largest Muslim nation in the world.

The key regional power in Asia at 1000, as today, was China. The Song Dynasty controlled a society as advanced as, or perhaps more advanced than, any found anywhere else. While ancient trade routes enabled a trickle of trade from China to the west, Europeans knew little directly of Asians, except those of West Asia.

Trade across Asia was built on long-lasting connections. The main movement of goods at that time out of Canton was in Arab vessels, or through seafarers in the southern China seas. It would be centuries before Europeans followed the trade routes over Central Asia to meet the Chinese, although a thousand years earlier the Chinese and Roman civilizations had been in contact through trade.

As the regional superpower, China strongly influenced its neighbors in Korea, Japan, and Vietnam. Disturbance to this situation seemed impossible: the years of Mongol control of China lay centuries ahead at this time.

Key Hindu Asian states were in Java and in Cambodia with the Khmer Empire, although the development of Angkor Wat, a massive medieval-era urban settlement based on a massive water management network, lay a century ahead. This low-density settlement would cover nearly 3,000 square kilometers—the world's largest preindustrial urban settlement. Yet, the vigorous jungle would claim the city back in its decline: Angkor Wat was abandoned by the time the French discovered its ruins many centuries later.[4]

In 1000, a stable civilization in Japan under an aristocratic government was adjusting to new developments, such as the advance of script to write Japanese with freedom, and the rise of samurai in rural provinces. The "opening up" of Japan by European powers lay many centuries ahead.

In India, the ancient cities of the Indus valleys lay long abandoned—at 1000, the sequence of kingdoms that characterized southern Asia were about to see the establishment of a series of Muslim states in the northwest. Along the coast, active trade ports allowed local and Arab traders access to the products of South Asia.

West Asia had for millennia been the setting for various human "firsts": from farming to writing. The region was the very center of the Old World: the coffee table around which Asia, Africa, and Europe sat. This was a great time for the Islamic civilization, itself made up of many different cultures in contact through a common ideology. The height of the Islamic world at 1000 extended from the western Mediterranean regions of the Iberian Peninsula, across northern Africa, the Gulf of Arabia, and to the Indus River. This vast region was linked by trade routes. The maritime route via the Persian Gulf had allowed Islamic merchants to be active from India, Sri Lanka, and the Southeast Asia archipelago, and in East Asia. Shipping routes extended from Zanzibar to Java. Other goods moved overland via the ancient trade routes.

In 1000, the Eurasian trade network was similar to that formed in the Roman era, with trading ports in the eastern Mediterranean as intercontinental depots for the movement of goods between Africa, Asia, and Europe. Trade relationships would change dramatically at the end of the medieval period, when European powers would take over much of the trade from the Italian merchants in the Mediterranean, and from the Arabs, Asian, Chinese, and Gujerati traders in the Indian Ocean and Southeast Asia.

Constantinople and Baghdad were key cities in West Asia, one Christian, the other Islamic. In the Muslim world, the arts and sciences were encouraged, and key developments occurred in astronomy, mathematics, literature, and philosophy. These would soon be important in the revitalization of Europe. Constantinople would also protect older knowledge, in its role as the eastern center of the Holy Roman Empire.

Trade networks linked the Islamic world not only to Asia but to Africa. Arab traders were active along the east coast of Africa and in West Africa. In Africa, the trans-Saharan trade route moved goods—such as gold, slaves, and salt—across the Saharan barrier to North African ports such as Tangier, Algiers, Tunis, and Alexandria, all of which had long been significant locations for trade and interregional contacts. Islam thus spread to West Africa through trade.

East Africa too became enfolded in trade networks managed by Muslims. In East Africa, trade societies, such as that of the Swahili, merged African, Arabic, and Indian influences.

In central and southern Africa, culture contacts were occurring along a broad front, as people were on the move. For example, Bantu people were moving their herds south, coming into contact with hunter-foragers, many of whom would still be present when Europeans arrived in southern Africa in the fifteenth century.

By 1 January 1000, we arrive in Europe—offering some light at the end of the "Dark Ages," as it was once popularly known. The sun rose over a Europe that was largely Christian. There is debate about how many Christians were expecting the world's end at the eve of the millennium, although the numbers appear not to have been significant. Still, these were years of social change, probably accompanied by the general state of apocalyptic expectation that characterized Christianity then.[5]

While Europe largely marked the extent of Christendom (with some exceptions, such as Ethiopia), not all Europe was Christian. Folk religion remained important.

In northern Europe, older religions prevailed, despite ongoing military and political campaigns to convert groups like the Wends in northern Germany from their old belief to Christianity. In 1000, the Danes were only recently adjusting to their King Harald Bluetooth's conversion to Christianity a few years earlier, a pragmatic conversion more than an ideological realization. Other Scandinavian countries would follow later, and only slowly. Significant Islamic settlements existed in Europe alongside Christian and Jewish communities, notably on the Iberian Peninsula, where Muslim armies had arrived in 711 and would remain until the surrender of Granada in 1492 after centuries of the *Reconquista*.

From this peninsula and its various kingdoms would emerge the nations of Portugal and Spain. Both of these regions were key instruments in the European expansion out of Europe after the fifteenth century.

As in the Americas, most people in Europe were farmers, living in small rural communities. The clearing of the forests of Europe was intensifying, and the increased agricultural land supported a population boom. The medieval towns were more populous, creating more urban communities. Those urban centers that existed tended to be as large as those elsewhere.

At the turn of the millennium, towns had been in a long decline since the end of the Roman Empire. However, things were changing, and the next few centuries would see towns start to fill old Roman-era city walls—where they existed—and spill beyond them. Some urban renewal happened around ecclesiastical institutions like cathedrals and abbeys, some near fortified castles of the knightly elite. Larger towns developed to handle trade and hold markets, for either regional or even international trade. For example, records from London ca. 1000 indicate the various locations in continental Europe where trade goods originated; the archaeological record suggests embankments and jetties were built to handle the growing trade. In Seville, Spain, precious goods from Africa were traded for Andalusian produce. And, from ca. 1000, the power of merchants from northern Italian cities was soon to be ascendant; their power came through trade and monetary developments.

Trade was being reactivated following a dire period in the early Middles Ages. Maritime routes were hazardous—the Mediterranean was dominated by Arab ships, the northern seas by Vikings. Bandits threatened overland routes, and ancient roadways had fallen into disrepair. Merchants were drawn to the protection of growing urban settlements, and the origins of a bourgeoisie can be tracked to this period, with its merchants and moneylenders.

Money was rare, and barter was king. Gold and silver coins were hoarded or melted down, currency was frozen, and would remain so until the effects of Italian trade cities and the fairs of Champagne and Flanders were felt and the florins and ducats of merchants started to flow through hands and into pockets.

A third of the largest and most vibrant urban centers were in Muslim al-Andalus in Spain, with Córdoba and its neighboring royal town, Madinat al-Zahra, the largest and home to a large bureaucracy housed in terrace houses.[6] Most European towns were small, and rural life prevailed at 1000, yet by 1300 one-tenth of Europe would live in towns. The largest centers outside of Islamic Spain and Constantinople would develop in northern Italy (Venice, Genoa, Milan, and Florence) and elsewhere in key cities such as London, Bruges, Ghent, Paris, Cologne, Lübeck, Vienna, and Prague. Only the Italian and Iberian cities had reached populations of 100,000 by millennial's end.

The larger towns were those involved in trade and manufacturing, with textiles and metal products being particularly profitable. Venice stood out even at 1000, by trading such commodities as wine, grain, salt, and slaves (though illegal) to the Eastern Roman Empire in Byzantine Constantinople. Their fleets returned to Venice with precious goods available in the wondrous Byzantine markets, including spices from Asia.

The European demand for Asian and African imported products is of utmost significance to an understanding of the world of the early second millennium. The demand for profitable products along with urban and economic renewal and social changes was central to the movement of European influence beyond Europe. Eventually the Italian merchants would be bypassed by the other European centers of power, whose search for trade routes, technology, and labor to provide these and other commodities would be one of the key stories of the millennium.

As the sun sets in the west over the Atlantic Ocean, we leave the first day of the millennium to its watery conclusion. While many of the changes that we explore in this book lay in the centuries ahead, there was much in place in 1000 that would change relatively soon. In some places, the eventual changes would be dramatic and reach forward across the millennium to become part of our present.

There have been several points at which humanity has shifted dramatically as a species—developments in tool making, language, and symbolic behavior, the colonization of new environments and continents, the shift toward farming, and the development of complex societies. The second millennium saw humanity emerge as a truly global species. This millennium saw the appearance of new societies deriving from differing degrees and forms of cross-cultural engagement, from New Zealand to Iceland, from Newfoundland to Cape Town. A truly global network was formed. New societies would form, old societies would change, and some aspects of various cultures were resilient and survived. This is the legacy of culture contact.

CHAPTER 2

OUR ATTEMPTS TO UNDERSTAND CULTURE CONTACT

Archaeologists have often pointed out that culture contact is endemic to human existence. This is a key point, for given its ubiquity, there are many potential forms of interaction and exchange among societies in contact. Culture contacts have involved trade and exchange, warfare, cooperation, competition, and imitation. A core problem with the concept "culture contact" is that it is deployed to describe very different circumstances, from "first contact" to long-established and complicated cultural entanglements such as colonialism. People have, over time, proposed various approaches to detect and explain culture contact. The earliest dominant model of culture change is acculturation, which came to extensive use in the twentieth century; however, there are other explanatory models and emphases (some summarized in Table 2.1).

There are many challenges in our quest to interpret past cultural interactions using archaeological evidence, even in contexts where oral histories and historical sources exist. In this chapter, I consider (1) definitions of contact, (2) the available evidence, (3) the issue of descendant communities, and (4) and interpretive models.

WHAT IS CONTACT?

"Culture contact" describes how different cultures meet. It is used by anthropologists and archaeologists in a professional sense to describe these interactions, but is also used popularly, as seen in the film and book *Contact,* which portrays first contact with intelligent aliens.[1] For our purposes in this book, I use the term largely to denote contacts between cultures that had been basically unaware of each other. Perhaps the most renowned examples of first contacts are of the Spaniards meeting Aztecs and Incans—the latter both representing large states initially unable to effectively repel small numbers of conquistadors.

Is culture contact a moment or a process? The term "first contact" reminds us of the gulf between foreigners at their first encounter. Archaeologist Carmel

Schrire, working in southern Africa where Europeans initiated first contact with the Khoisan from the 1400s onward, describes a flawed perception of these events: "Scholars imagine themselves standing on the interface of past and present, watching former hunters teetering on the cusp as they hurtle into modernity with no previous experience of change."[2] Even today, some tour operators offer tourists a chance to meet "uncontacted people" in remote corners of the globe on "First Contact" tours; this controversial activity has occurred in places like Papua New Guinea and Irian Jaya, Brazil, Peru, and Colombia.

However, the term "culture contact" has also come to describe ongoing interactions over time beyond "first contact," and that is the approach taken here. Many studies of culture contact typically focus on the first generation or two following initial culture contact.

In many places around the world, the arrival of Europeans heralded permanent European colonization and forms of colonialism. Some studies explored in this book examine how indigenous groups became enmeshed in colonial power structures. For example, in Australia and the Americas, we look at archaeological studies of missions and other institutions established to restructure or preserve the location and nature of indigenous societies.

Colonialism encompasses a large field of study of historical power relations whose legacies are sometimes apparent in the contemporary world. Boston University archaeologist Stephen Silliman challenges us to think of culture contacts in terms of colonialism, arguing that power relations between Europeans and indigenous people cannot be ignored.[3] So defining an end point for culture contact may be harder than defining when it begins.

Are culture contact studies historical studies? Clearly, many contacts are described in historical sources. One of the issues this question raises concerns history versus prehistory, and the problems that have arisen from the creation of an artificial boundary between the two. For the non-archaeologist, it is sometimes surprising that archaeologists are interested in recent centuries, given that these are periods for which historical sources exist. However, this is also true of more ancient periods, such as Babylonia and Old Kingdom Egypt, yet we require archaeology to understand these cultures.

Even in historical settings, archaeology has an important role to play. It is true that in recent centuries the amount of written material has increased dramatically; and the study of these sources by archaeologists has led to the development of the subfield of "historical archaeology." In many places, historical archaeologists initially studied the archaeology of Europeans, which meant, for example, the Americas after Columbus, southern Africa after da Gama, New Zealand and Australia after the arrival of the British. I mention these locations in particular as they were the original foci of historical archaeology, but today historical archaeologists are more far-reaching. Despite the availability of historical evidence, time and time again archaeology reveals how much "new" information comes from archaeological studies of contexts for which historical documents exist.

A broad distinction arose between historical and prehistoric archaeologists in some places, resulting in different professional associations, conferences, journals, and even legislation. To oversimplify the problem, in many places prehistorians dealt with indigenous archaeology, historical archaeologists with European legacies. I use the term "prehistorian" in the context of these debates: "prehistory" is a term sometimes rejected by indigenous people as implying "without history" rather than "before written sources."

Kent Lightfoot summarized his concerns "that the current separation of prehistoric and historical archaeology detracts greatly from the study of long-term culture change, especially in multi-ethnic contexts." In his call for an "archaeology of pluralism," Lightfoot reminds us that rather than culture contact occurring between two monolithic cultures—one European, one "native"—colonial contexts were often more complicated.[4] His work in California at the colonial site of Fort Ross, for example, studied a historical population of Russians, native Californians, and migrant workers from Alaska, Siberia, and Hawaii (see discussion in chapter 7). Add to this the complexity within societies, concerning class structures, status, gender, age differentials, and work opportunities, and contact can be visualized as an inherently complex process. Lightfoot argues that "one cannot undertake comparative analyses of cultural transformations that took place before, during, and after European contact and colonialism" without considering what happened prior to "contact"—a period of "prehistory."[5]

Similarly, when considering the Australian situation in 1992, Sydney-based archaeologists Sarah Colley and Anne Bickford argued that "the traditional division of Australian archaeology into categories such as historical archaeology, prehistory, cultural heritage management, and ethnoarchaeology, is in part a product of Australia's colonial history and has mitigated against the archaeological study of Aboriginal historic places, which do not fall neatly into one 'camp.'" They went on to highlight a related problem posed by archaeological deposits that extend over the period of culture contact: "Even today, Aboriginal people sometimes use 'traditional' places (e.g. rock shelters, waterholes, campsites) without leaving any 'European' materials behind. To label these Aboriginal sites as 'prehistoric' because they contain no exotic materials is to render post-contact Aboriginal places, and the people who use them, invisible."[6]

The archaeology of cross-cultural interactions, then, bridges the subdisciplinary interests and practices of prehistory and historical archaeology and invites a long-term perspective often favored by archaeologists.[7]

In this book, I focus on early phases of culture contacts; however, in this regard I am limited by the availability of research. Some regions have had very little work into early phases of contact, or such work is constrained by being based only on historical accounts. Thankfully, as we move around the globe in this text, we will see that there are many settings where archaeologists have worked on culture contact arising from the arrival of Europeans. Sometimes they focus on the short term and sometimes conduct studies of the longer term to provide greater context to culture contact. For example, we will see that in Ghana, archaeologist Ann Stahl has developed an understanding of the "big picture" over time in which various contacts have occurred (chapter 5) within parts of West Africa. And, on St. Catherines Island off the Georgia coast, extensive studies by the American Museum of Natural History reveal Guale contacts with Spanish missionaries after 1570 within a 5,000-year picture of island life (chapter 6).

THE AVAILABLE EVIDENCE

How do archaeologists bring together the available evidence for culture contact in a critical way? This book uses examples to introduce the variety of evidence. In brief, data may include archaeological material, firsthand accounts, secondary sources, pictorial information (ranging from the sixteenth-century Mayan codices to twentieth-century photographs of first contact in Papua New Guinea), environmental records, and oral histories. Many of the projects I detail in this book use a historical anthropological/archaeological approach that enables dealing with multiple lines of evidence.

Since we are dealing with historical events, one challenge of these studies is to use historical *and* archaeological sources—for each is different. Archaeological data referred to throughout this book tend to provide an insight about aggregated behavior, the accumulated detritus of many individual events. To take an example: imagine a hut used for a generation or two and then abandoned. The archaeological record in and around the hut will typically derive from repeated practices of daily life—cooking, eating, organizing activities around the home. The more frequently an event occurred, the greater for its potential to be in the archeological record. In this sense, much archaeological evidence is quite different from primary historical accounts, which are often time-specific and relate to an individual (the author or the person observed).

In some historical cases there are historical written sources available, but not always. In Australia, I often work on historical sites that are not described in historical sources: in fact, I am drawn to the places and people who lived beyond the eyes and pens of Europeans.

In those instances where there are historical sources, their internal biases need to be critically considered. A challenge of "contact" studies—like historical archaeology, but more broadly so—is to develop methods to critically deal with historical documents, given they are often biased, having been created by Europeans with limited understanding of the indigenous people encountered.

We are well familiar with the adage of history being written by the winners. Considering colonial Australia, anthropologist Deborah Bird Rose describes colonial histories of Aboriginal peoples as "hidden" in her book *Hidden Histories: Black Stories from Victoria River Downs, Humbert River and Wave Hill Stations*. She is alerting us to the fact that in addition to dominant histories created by colonial whites, there existed histories of other events that remained hidden, which we need to find, perhaps in oral accounts or archaeological records. This echoes efforts to write "history from below" and "people's history." Similarly, historical anthropologist Eric Wolf wrote of "Europe and the people without history," in his book of that title, referring to non-Western nonliterate societies. These all are reminders that historical sources are created in a power differential of colonial encounters, and were often created by literate whites in positions of power. There is nothing new in history; the Egyptian hieroglyphs similarly were created by elites in powerful positions, as were accounts from colonial frontiers such as New Spain, New Zealand, or Capetown.

CONTACT DEMOGRAPHY

Since historical sources document instances of culture contact, we need to ask: given the changes that culture contact with Europeans heralded for many indigenous people, how accurate is our perception of these societies in reality?

This problem is best demonstrated by thinking about the demographic changes potentially resulting from diseases introduced at contact. This sometimes meant significant indigenous mortality and sickness. There are debates regarding the size of precontact indigenous populations across the globe. To determine population size in the past, archaeologists typically extrapolate from data such as human remains, settlement information, and some absolute dates to predict past population demography. Archaeology then provides an important means to critique historical accounts of populations at contact.[8]

In some instances, archaeological evidence suggests significant population decreases following contact. For example, based on their extensive archaeological work on Melanesian islands in the Western Pacific—on New Caledonia and Vanuatu, respectively—archaeologists Christopher Sands and Matthew Spriggs suggest that the archaeological evidence for the extent of farming and number of villages in the period leading up to contact with Europeans would indicate a much more sizable population than suggested in a reading of European observations of contact-era populations.[9] The archaeology here, as in other places, suggests a strong demographic decline in the period around first contact, presumably driven by disease and warfare.

We should not be surprised by this, for new diseases would have traveled in advance of the white men's pens. Some explorers observed the impact of diseases. British explorer Charles Sturt, who led several expeditions into the inland reaches of Southeastern Australia, met Aboriginal people who were afflicted by a disease he thought to be introduced smallpox.[10] Similarly, in other regions some early explorers observed the impacts of new pathogens on native peoples.

The study of historical demography has undergone a massive shake-up in recent decades, fueled by work into the "Columbian exchange." This scholarship reveals that in some places the decrease in population through disease vectors was high. This means that the societies observed by Europeans had already undergone dramatic change in their recent past.

The term "protohistory" is sometimes used to describe the period when the effects resulting from contact move in advance of the new settlers or invaders themselves. To take an example from chapter 7, Plains Indians in North America had access to guns and horses, yet most never met the Spaniards or French who originally supplied them. It is a useful concept, but may have a similar problem to "prehistory," suggesting that indigenous people had no history.

Historical observations prompt us to question the historical observer's perspective: Was the observer a reliable and suitably competent witness? Was he or she able to make sensible observations across the gulf of cultural difference? Some early historical observers were misguided, wrong, or unable to understand the society they encountered.

The historical accounts made at contact are termed "ethnohistory." This history is sometimes used to extrapolate backward in time to understand prehistoric communities. Thus, knowing whether a society was populous or not is essential. Other aspects of a society are available through ethnohistory. Was the observer able to detect nuances within a society, such as levels of stratification, gender and other roles, economic subsistence, or religious practices? Did the observer speak

32

the language? This is very significant, given that the contact period is often considered the ethnographic present and is used to understand earlier periods of time, or even other cultures in the deeper, nonhistorical or prehistoric past.

DESCENDANTS OF CONTACT

Not surprisingly, many indigenous people today, when tracking their history back, focus in on the changes heralded by contact with Europeans. These were times of great change, much of which was negative. Often the colonization by Europeans meant invasion, and laid the basis for colonial relationships.

Since colonialism is largely about power differentials, it highlights differences between a colonizing culture and indigenous people, although other forced migrants, such as slaves, or voluntary migrants were similarly part of colonial-era power relationships. Some historical archaeologists deliberately seek these groups out—the powerless—in their work.

A key issue today, at least in some countries, is the rights of indigenous descendants. These may extend to the right of access to land occupied by their ancestors, the right to practice activities considered "traditional," the right to actively manage one's own cultural heritage and environment, the right to access profits from resources extracted from "traditional" lands, and the right to actively participate in investigations of one's own culture—examining everything from skeletal remains of ancestors to one's own DNA.

Issues of culture heritage are not restricted to the legacy of non-European people's contacts with Europeans. One of the most well-known cultural property debates is the Greek demand for the British to return the Elgin (or Parthenon) Marbles. These statues were removed from the Acropolis in Athens by the British Lord Elgin in the early 1800s and are on display in London. "Who owns the Elgin Margins?" is a question posed to heritage studies students.

Indigenous peoples too found their cultural heritage removed by various colonial actors—not only objects, but also human skeletal material that often ended up distributed all around the world in museums, universities, and private collections. In my home state of Tasmania, for example, the remains of Aboriginal people were illicitly removed from graves and ended up in museums and medical institutions in Europe. The skeleton of one woman, Truganini, was displayed in a Hobart museum until recently. She has been returned to the community and her remains properly dealt with. The demands for repatriation of indigenous peoples' remains and cultural property from institutions around the world are only strengthened by understanding the specific events of culture contact that saw them initially removed.

When we explore the issues surrounding descendant indigenous communities, we realize that knowledge of the past is not esoteric knowledge. The past is being used in the present to determine ownership and rights pertaining to land, property, cultural materials, and human rights. Archaeologists and anthropologists are involved in demonstrating the relationships between living communities today and communities as they were in the past, particularly prior to the arrival of Europeans in recent centuries. In some places, the rise of land rights (such as in Canada, Australia, and New Zealand) has driven this development. The (re)acquisition of land rights requires being able to prove that one's ancestors occupied a particular place and often that practices and beliefs continue from the precontact era across time into the present.

Traditional practices have been part of indigenous revival or continuities. For example, some indigenous groups claim the right to hunt animal species considered protected. In Northern Australia, only Aboriginal people have the right to hunt dugong (sea cow). Similarly, many countries today support a ban on whale hunting, yet exemptions exist for communities in North America, the Faroe Islands, on Bequia (Caribbean), and Lamalera (Indonesia) to hunt small numbers in order to continue long-existing indigenous practices.

One final observation regarding descendant communities should be made: increasingly, contemporary archaeology has opened a place for indigenous involvement. In some countries, there has been a rise of community involvement into research of past societies, not only as participant workers but as principal researchers and collaborators. This derives from indigenous activism as well as from the broader understanding of the legacies of colonialism.

MODELS OF CULTURE CONTACT

Models to interpret and explain culture contact and cultural change in cross-cultural settings have developed over the last century. Early models reported the evidence for contact: these are the "when" and "what" questions about culture contact. Today archaeologists are equally interested in "why" questions. University of New Mexico archaeologist Ann Ramenofsky[11] argues for questions that ask why societies changed in the ways they did, rather than merely describing that they did change (or not).

So, how can we attempt to understand culture contact? This question is not just relevant to studying historical culture contact but, more widely, for examining any cultures in contact at any stage in the past. As our focus will be historical culture contact, we need to keep in mind two important questions.

1. *How does the important work into colonialism relate to studies of culture contact?* There has been a growing interest in colonialism in archaeological studies of culture contact, as should be clear in this book. This is due to the fact that colonialism is essentially a structure of power and difference played out in both social and material worlds. In a materialist rethinking of colonialism, objects and built places are direct lines of evidence into colonial-era behavior, not just on the side of the colonists, but on the part of indigenous people too, in the ways they interpreted, accepted, and resisted those behaviors.[12]

Also under scrutiny are the distinctly colonial ways of much archaeological research itself—with investigations by white researchers (such as myself) and little involvement from indigenous stakeholders. Today in many countries, there is a greater collaboration between indigenous communities and professional archaeology, although there are still clear problems to address.

In recent years, postcolonial theory has provided a critique of ideas that were inherent to colonial viewpoints. To take a famous example, the scholar Edward Said critiqued the validity of the idea of the "Orient" by exploring how the notion of the "East" was created by the Western world for its own purposes, such as sustaining and justifying imperial and colonial ambitions. Postcolonial thinking helps make problematic simple notions such as East and West.

Archaeologists influenced by this thinking have begun the task of writing archaeology as a counterpoint to colonizers' histories and have embraced the idea of material culture and social practice demonstrating more complex scenarios. Certainly an understanding of local efforts to deal with colonialism provides an important critique of popular histories.

2. *What theoretical models best explain what happens when cultural engagements occur?* Specifically, given the fact that we know that simple models are unlikely to be correct—say, of Europeans happening upon a bounded society who have never encountered contact before—what is the appropriate way to understand the complexity of culture entanglements? To begin to answer this, I first consider a brief history of explanation of culture contact.

Over time, it is hardly surprising that as our thinking in the present changes, so does the way we perceive of the past. Take colonialism. Much early work in archaeology was essentially rusted onto the colonial order. Today we are more aware of issues of power that are relevant to doing archaeology, and we no longer ascribe to the view popular in the last few centuries that indigenous cultures must give way to modernity (represented by Western social forces). Thus, over time, anthropologists and archaeologists have changed how they visualize and analyze forms of culture contact and how they comprehend its role in the past.

The idea of culture contact as invoking change is not new. In ancient Greece, Plato argued in 348 BC that acculturation should be minimized but not to the extent of cultural isolation: "The intercourse of cities with one another is apt to create a confusion of manners; strangers are always suggesting novelties to strangers."[13] Plato went on to suggest that only men over forty should travel to foreign places, and that foreigners should be kept in isolation from the general population.

Plato's ideas would have been appreciated in other situations of culture contact, especially where there has been a strong regulating government, such as in many Asian cultures. Both Japan and China attempted to restrict foreign traders to dedicated ports (see chapter 8). Even after centuries of European contact with China, when in the 1800s American clippers started to access the Chinese trade, the Americans found themselves restricted to places such as Canton, where they were confined to factories to trade with government-appointed traders. These policies recognize the potential for foreign influence. These fears were sometimes well founded; the British eventually forced open the Chinese market to their goods, eventuating in the Opium Wars.

These examples reveal attempts to regulate culture contact, with varying efficacy. Culture contact can thus be part of both local and national-level power plays. The British attempt to break Chinese regulations led to the Opium Wars. Despite the ruler Moctezuma's attempts to control the arrival of the Spanish conquistadors, the subsequent fall of the Aztecs in 1521 to Cortez and his allies is clearly the story of competing powers.

In some conquest scenarios, differences in technology are significant. Europeans tended to have the upper hand with technology, particularly guns and cannon, which they had been perfecting since the fifteenth century, following the discovery of gunpowder in China many centuries earlier. This meant the demise of the mounted armored knight, once the most formidable military force. In Europe, the heart of the military became infantry with munitions. Outside of Europe, when facing native peoples without guns, however, "old technology" remained effective. The fall of Mexico is telling, with the horses and armor of the Spanish allowing a very small group of Spaniards to defeat larger numbers of Aztecs, in both open combat and street fighting in Tenochtitlan.

One popular model for culture change focuses on the destruction of indigenous society, a model we could call the "Fatal Impact" model, as typified in Alan Moorehead's 1966 book, *The Fatal Impact: The Invasion of the South Pacific 1769–1840*. Moorehead cited three regional studies as examples of "Fatal Contact": Tahiti, Eastern Australia, and islands in polar regions. His interest was "the moment when a social capsule is broken open, when primitive creatures, beasts as well as men, are confronted for the first time with civilization."[14] His study focused on population demise in Tahiti, the essential "passing of the Aborigines" (the name of a popular book of the twentieth century on Aboriginal people) in Australia, and the enterprise of key European individuals. Aboriginal survival only occurred through acclimatization. Moorehead followed approaches that naturalized the destruction of indigenous societies, by citing Charles Darwin: "Wherever the European has trod, death seems to pursue the aboriginal. We may look to the wide extent of the Americas, Polynesia, the Cape of Good Hope and Australia, and we find the same result."[15] A similar fate was reserved for animals, such as whales and seals, in his study of polar islands.

For Moorehead, "fatal impact" was fueled by many factors, and sometimes inherited strength from social evolutionary ideas regarding the ascent of humanity from barbaric to civilized states. The origin of these ideas can be traced back to theories increasingly popular in the nineteenth century, fed by a solid basis in secular reasoning and driven by the increased number of reports of encounters with non-European cultures across the globe. It is true that many indigenous populations were almost utterly reduced; however, we need other explanatory models to better explain cultural survival.

For a long time, encounters between cultures were considered simply in terms of diffusion, invasion, exchange, and acculturation. For archaeologists, diffusion described the ways that practices move over space and time—whether a pottery style or agriculture—and may result from population movement, trade, or the popularity of an idea. Diffusion, then, is a very broad term and not useful in analyzing the mechanisms of culture contacts. Invasion and exchange are similarly useful broad descriptions, but are not really analytical.

Acculturation arose as a central concept in culture contact studies. The first usage of the concept arose in the 1880s, being employed by J. W. Powell, an anthropologist in the Bureau of American Ethnology.[16] He explained that the term referred to the psychological changes experienced during cross-cultural imitation. At the same time, W. J. McGee, also employed at the Bureau of American Ethnology, defined acculturation as a process of exchange and improvement. His thinking was evolutionary, seeing acculturation as a means for societies to move forward from savagery, to barbarism, to civilized enlightened beings. McGee argued that "Human development is essentially social, and may be measured by the degree in which devices and ideas are interchanged and fertilized in the process of transfer, i.e., by the degree of acculturation."[17]

Most of the work on acculturation from the 1930s onward was more interested in classifying types of acculturation than exploring the consequences of culture contact. For archaeologists, this involved measuring material culture—in the form of artifacts and their manufacture, composition, and use—as a proxy for social change. These measurements provided indices of the type and degree of acculturation.

The concept of acculturation became core to social scientists in North America, so that in 1936, "A Memorandum for the Study of Acculturation" was published in the journal *American Anthropologist*. Their definition of acculturation is interesting: "Acculturation comprehends those phenomena which result when groups of individuals having different cultures come into continuous first-hand contact, with subsequent changes in the original cultural patterns of either or both groups."[18] This definition describes a two-way process of mutual change. Yet, in reality, most researchers became more interested in Native American responses and not in European acculturation.

A key figure in North American archaeology at this time was Edward Spicer, whose research into the impact of Europeans on people in northern Mexico and the American Southwest made important refinements to the measurement of acculturation.[19] Spicer defined different types of contact communities and types of acculturation processes: incorporation, assimilation, fusion, and compartmentalization. A theme of his work asked why native peoples were not like other Americans, why the melting pot had not worked, and why some Native American groups like the Yaquis (originally of the Mexican state of Sonora) strongly maintained their culture and resisted Spanish and Mexican incursions. In a period when few archaeologists were interested in the flipside of culture contact, Spicer considered "persistent cultural systems," such as the Yaquis in the Americas, and compared them with the survival of Basque, Irish, and Welsh societies in Europe, who themselves had survived periods of great oppression.

It is perhaps not surprising that the indigenous side of culture contact was the focus of inquiry—it was easier to observe small peasant societies rather than the complexity of European societies with global reach. However, culture contact saw great change across all cultures involved, as observed in 1945 by seminal British anthropologist Bronislaw Malinowski:

> There is an impinging culture and one that receives. There are, therefore, two cultures to deal with instead of one; the modifications wrought on the recipients by the aggressors, and also *vice versa*. Not only that. There is always the formation of an aggressive or conquering community *in situ* (i.e. White set-

tlers). Thus community is by no means a direct replica of its mother community at home.[20]

However, the acculturation model was often still being applied unidirectionally: the recipient culture changing through contact with the donor culture. Malinowski, though, saw the role of potential other groups: "The interaction between Native and European communities offers opportunities for the introduction of third parties, such as Indians, Syrians, and Arabs in Africa; at times, the growth of a mixed population, such as Cape Colored in South Africa."[21]

Despite the popularity of this concept, there were some problems, which would in turn lead to a decline in the use of acculturation as an explanation. One problem was that it came to focus on the ideas of "donor" and "recipient" groups, where most change is experienced by the weaker (indigenous) recipient group.

Over time, models that were unidirectional, such as acculturation, had largely fallen out of favor, particularly in the Americas, so that by the 1970s they were being replaced by either more refined versions of acculturation or by other models altogether. A key driver was the five-hundredth anniversary of contact in 1492. The Quincentenary inspired research across the contact zones of the Caribbean and the Americas, and resulted in a florescence of new thinking, as stated by Rogers and Wilson in their 1993 edited volume, *Ethnohistory and Archaeology: Approaches to Postcontact Change in the Americas.*

> Culture change . . . was neither one-sided nor solely governed by European intentions and strategies. Rather it is evident . . . that [indigenous peoples'] attitudes and actions . . . played a large part in determining the impact of contact.[22]

Another interpretive challenge that archaeologists faced was a focus on individuals, as archaeology often best reflects past group behavior. This required new thinking that allowed for the agency of individuals to be studied. Also, researchers were increasingly interested in dominance and resistance.

Finally, acculturation relied heavily on looking at the ways that indigenous people adopted "European" material culture, so that lists of material provided a quantification of the degree of acculturation. This rude measure avoids the issues related to the *meaning* of material culture, which are not locked down but change depending on the circumstances.

For example, in the 1680s in north-central New Mexico, Pueblo people revolted against colonial Spaniards, successfully expelling them from their region (see chapter 6). The "Pueblo Revolt" was driven in part as a revitalization movement in which a charismatic holy man and his followers exhorted revolt and a return to pre-Spanish ways. Churches were destroyed, settlements abandoned, and new pueblos (villages) established. The archaeological record indicates that at a center of indigenous resistance in the Jemez province, people chose to stop making the once-ubiquitous pre-Hispanic "Jemez Black-on-white" decorated ceramics.

This seems surprising, given that the revolt saw a broad shift away from Spanish ways back toward earlier cultural practices. It appears, however, that this ceramic type had become associated with the Spanish, with the form being appropriated by Franciscan missionaries to produce ceramics in Spanish forms, such as candlestick holders. If so, it appears the indigenous perception of this ceramic type had shifted, and it no longer just meant the past but also aspects of Spanish dominance. Thus, it fell from favor.

A simple acculturation measure may see this as the loss of an indigenous form of ceramic production; however, the complexities of meaning of material culture in this cross-cultural and colonial context instead saw a specific shift in the meaning of this ware. Archaeologists have become increasingly sensitive to the complex shifting meanings of material culture in cross-cultural contexts.[23]

Today, a range of models exist to interpret and explain culture contact. In archaeology, these have included theories related to acculturation, assimilation, cores (or centers) and peripheries, resistance and dominance, accommodation, optimal foraging, ethnogenesis, creolization, frontiers, and agency, to name some. I will not review them here, although there are several key sources provided in the reference list for students of archaeological theory. There are, however, many different variables that get taken into account (see summary in Table 2.2).

The four forms of cultural encounter defined by historian Philip Curtin, with attention to the form of European enterprise and historical contingencies, are worth quickly reviewing here to introduce the subsequent culture contacts that we consider in this book.[24]

Curtin first defined "merchant diasporas." These are typically outposts established along nodes in trade networks. The fur trade companies of North America are examples of this form, which sees the establishment of isolated enclaves of Europeans within a territory not held by Europeans. In ancient times, similar diasporas were seen, such as when populations from metropolitan powers were sent out to culturally different areas, usually for the purposes of trade (although other reasons may have existed, such as military possession, overpopulation, an attempt to control a local resource, or religious conversion). Similar examples exist in the historical era: for instance, the Portuguese in East Asia held isolated ports for the purposes of trade. The Dutch followed this practice as well, although eventually they moved from a merchant diaspora to Curtin's second form—"true empire."

"True" or "territorial empire" sees the control of new territory, where typically the European population is small (say, 5 percent) and the indigenous population obviously far more substantial. Examples of this can been seen with the Spanish in the New World, where in New Spain/Mexico and Peru, the Spanish Empire was maintained despite the population ratios in favor of native populations. This required a combination of technological/military superiority and the assistance of indigenous partners, and was characterized by the rise of a mixed-descent population.

The third type is "settlement empire" or "true colonization." In this form, colonization by Europeans dwarfs the indigenous population, who constitute a minority population. This is seen in the so-called settler societies such as Australia, New Zealand, Argentina, Uruguay, and Canada, as well as the United States and Siberia. Typically, the large European population arises from a large number of migrating Europeans, while the large number of Europeans relative to the indigenous population is increased by a large population decline in the native population, typically through the impact of disease, but also through warfare.

Curtin's final form is the "plantation complex," where the native population is conquered and then replaced by a non-European population. This was seen in the Caribbean, where local people died in large numbers and African slaves were brought in by Europeans to provide a labor force (chapter 6).

These examples are simplifications. Obviously, there are several steps in each of these forms; for example, "true colonization" and "territorial empire" normally begin with tiny isolated European outposts, many of which fail; however, the general arc of history leads to these forms. These model forms, as described here, do not really portray the plural societies that arise, as we will see in several examples in this book. Similarly, many of the archaeological studies detailed identify the sometimes fuzzy borders between native people and outsiders that characterize the places of culture contact.

It was never the aim of this book to present a new model for cross-culture contact, but rather a brief overview of the topic in a restricted sense. Are there any generalities that can be observed? In Table 2.2, I attempt to summarize some of the variables that the review provided in this book demonstrate can be considered in the study of culture contact. The timing of contacts is summarized in Figure 2.1.

Table 2.1. Summary of key concepts in the study of culture contact

CONCEPT	VARIABLE	EVIDENCE
Assimilation		
Typically describes how a minority group becomes part of the dominant culture through contact. (Essentially opposite of *multiculturalism,* where minorities maintain ethnic traits.)	Minority becomes indistinguishable from the whole. Cultural features of minority groups may contribute to the greater society.	Reflected in gradual changes in all aspects of life of the minority population.
Acculturation		
"Acculturation comprehends those phenomena which result when groups of individuals having different cultures come into continuous first-hand contact, with subsequent changes in the original culture patterns of either or both groups" (Redman, Linton, and Herskovits 1936: 149). This model was particularly popular in the first half of the 20th century in North America, although it has been substantially modified since that time.	Most uses have focused on the changes in minorities, although it could be employed in two directions. Acculturation is a measure of the extent and direction of culture change.	Measured in degree of loss, maintenance, and adoption of aspects of life (these typically measured using a proxy of artifact types).
Enculturation		
Term describes the process by which an individual learns culture.	Individuals reflect culture in which they are immersed. May depend on context, such as indigenous children raised in a religious mission may reflect mission culture more than parent culture.	In contact scenarios enculturation is reflected in evidence for how individuals adopt ways of the dominant culture, whether indigenous or non-indigenous.

Table 2.1. Summary of key concepts in the study of culture contact (continued)

CONCEPT	VARIABLE	EVIDENCE
Westernization		
Where societies adopt Western culture, practices, technologies, and values. Sometimes, but not always, driven by the Western culture's intention to oversee the process (also termed "occidentalization").	Indigenous societies reflect adoption of Western traits, although traits may not be exactly the same and reflect cultural fusions.	Reflected in the extent and degree non-European indigenous society adopted Western language, behavior, laws, and customs.
Ethnocide		
The destruction of a culture. Often accompanied by the loss of language, and massive acculturation. Related to "genocide": the destruction of a people.	Abandonment of sites and landscapes, loss of language and culture.	Reflected in the cessation of cultural practices, abandonment of sites (or replacement of population). Possibly reflected in sites of warfare, imprisonment, increased burials, etc.
Resistance		
Where a population resists the presence of another society. May extend from open warfare to extremely subtle acts of resistance.	Cultural survival is maintained through active resistance. May keep conflicts between cultures at the fore. Resisting population perceived of as active, not passive agents.	Reflected in sites of resistance such as war, terrorism, symbols of cultural resistance, and survival.
Dominance		
Where a population attempts to dominate another society. May extend from open warfare to more subtle attempts to dominate including many potential acts designed to "win hearts and minds."	Outcome depends on the degree of resistance and program of domination.	Reflected in sites of domination, such as war, symbols of cultural dominance, and many possible programs to "win over" or dominate others.

Table 2.1. Summary of key concepts in the study of culture contact (continued)

CONCEPT	VARIABLE	EVIDENCE
Accommodation		
Describes the ways a culture actively adopts aspects of another culture. Model stresses active decisions.	In cross-cultural settings where differences in power exist, accommodation reflects pragmatic decisions that illustrate what is important and which aspects of life are deemed changeable (and conversely, what continuities in practice exist).	Reflected across the spectrum of cultural practices through continuities and changes.
Mimesis		
The process by which a culture adopts (imitates/mimics) the forms of another culture.	The immediate outcome would be forms of mimicry; however, interpretation requires understanding the relationship between what is being mimicked and its meaning in both the original cultural context and the one in which it's being mimicked.	Reflected in evidence for mimicked aspects of another culture, ranging from material forms and cultural practices to organization of lifeways.
Ethnogenesis		
The process by which a group becomes aware of its cultural distinctiveness. With culture contact, once-isolated societies may see a radical shift in their conceptualization of their own ethnicity.	A greater sense of group ethnicity.	May be reflected in practices deemed to be significant in the maintenance of ethnicity.
Creolization		
(See also *pidgin*) In linguistics, describes a new language created through fusion of parent languages—in colonial contexts, one dominant and one indigenous. In archaeology, the term similarly describes how a new culture is created through fusion.	In cross-cultural settings, new cultural practices in part reflecting earlier practices come into existence.	Typically reflected in daily practices such as foodways, organization of houses and settlements, and other creole practices such as music.

Table 2.1. Summary of key concepts in the study of culture contact (continued)

CONCEPT	VARIABLE	EVIDENCE
Colonization		
The process of establishing colonies from another origin. Can be temporary or permanent. May involve culture contact, if an indigenous group is present.	Establishment of a society in a new setting.	Evidence for presence of a new culture and associated plants and animals, as well as new practices (economic, agricultural, cultural etc.)
Frontier		
Frontiers most simply describe the geographical extremity of a culture, and often where two cultures meet. Frontier theory as proposed by Frederick Jackson Turner in the 1890s described how aspects typical of frontiers forged American cultural identity (namely, innovative, aggressive, democratic, and egalitarian) (related to *Manifest Destiny*).	Focuses attention on the peripheries of dominant and expansionist Western societies, and how they responded to a range of factors, including indigenous cultures.	May be reflected in sites related to frontiers, such as outposts. Conversely, western frontiers were often homelands for indigenous societies and thus not "remote."
Colonialism		
Colonialism describes how one people builds colonies in another people's territory and claim sovereignty and deploy their cultural institutions there. Unequal power relations tend to exist between the colonists and the local indigenous population, as well as between the colony and the parent country (related to *Imperialism*).	Establishment of new societies with different strength attachments to parent colony, parallel to "sibling" societies, and typified by varying relationships with indigenous populations.	Power relationships reflected in establishment of institutions (e.g., reserves, missions). Evidence of cross-cultural relationships depends on their course and nature.

Table 2.1. Summary of key concepts in the study of culture contact (continued)

CONCEPT	VARIABLE	EVIDENCE
Imperialism		
Describes an unequal power relationship between states based on domination and extending into cultural, economic, territorial, and social aspects, typified in the form of empires.	A dominant core should extend dominance to peripheries, both territorial and toward people/ resources characterized by not being part of a given imperial power.	Material culture reflects participation (or not) in imperial domain and reaction to imperial presence (e.g., resistance, mimicry, accommodation, etc.
Annales School		
Historiographic tradition focused on all levels of past societies and the collective nature of communities as well as individuals. Interested in social, economic, cultural, and environmental histories over short, middle, and long time scales.	Main outcome is the implication for historians to shift from a focus on prominent individuals to a focus on relationships between past societies and their historical trajectories.	Has been adopted by some archaeologists to interpret archaeological evidence, which is well suited to considering the short- and long-term together.
World System Theory		
Focuses on global divisions between core and peripheral countries in terms of labor, manufacturing, and provision of resources. Immanuel Wallerstein described how European nations gained control of much of the world's economy through industrialization and capitalist economy after the fifteenth century.	A clear difference exists between core and peripheral countries related to skills, production, etc. A theoretical focus on systems between polities and not on individual nation-states.	Reflected in diverse potential ways; material evidence reflects participation (or not) in the world system.

Table 2.2. Variables of culture contact

VARIABLE	KEY ATTRIBUTES	IMPLICATIONS
Demography		
Social-cultural institutions	Society and cultural institutions involved: egalitarian to more complex structures.	Importance of one or a few in decision-making processes.
Population density/ forms of settlement	From low to high (i.e., dispersed population to urban).	Population numbers and locations of contact; spread of disease; effectiveness in communication;
Demographic population after early contact	Ranging from undisturbed to "neutron bomb" scenario where colonists find abandoned native settlements and landscape.	Degree of resistance and collaboration; availability of labor and knowledge.
Pathogens	The role of pathogens (i.e. timing in relation to contact, impact).	Population health; size; retention of corporate information; ability to resist.
Whose home?	Homeland: Did contact occur within a group's homeland, or was relocation involved?	Setting for contact.
Changes in demography	Changes in demography: location (forced and voluntary migration), settlement patterns, economy and subsistence, types of residence.	Setting for contact; population size and density.
Movement of populations	None to some movement (forced and voluntary).	Degree of impact on societies; levels of local knowledge; supply chains.
Levels of intermarriage and mixed descent	From rare to common; from condoned to prohibited.	Identity of descent population; roles for men and women in cultural negotiations.
Form of contact (Curtin)	- Merchant Diasporas - Territorial Empire - Settlement Empire - Plantation Complex	Impact on relative ratios of native to non-native population, and organization of contacts.

Table 2.2. Variables of culture contact (continued)

VARIABLE	KEY ATTRIBUTES	IMPLICATIONS
Environment		
Environment	Climate, soils, vegetation, water, wild foods, wild animals, minerals, other resources (e.g., timber)	Food production levels; range of possible activities (hunting, farming, mining, etc.).
Environmental change	Enhancement or degradation?	Upper/lower limits on activities over time; change in landscape and location of resources.
Technology, Economy, and Logistics		
Economy	Forms of subsistence (hunter-foragers, fishers, farmers, etc.)	Population size and organization; ability to collect surplus; ability to handle stress.
Food storage ability	From immediate to multi-seasonal.	Measured by how long farmers could be away from farming; ability to sustain additional population.
The role of exchange and trade	What goods were exchanged and why?	Reflected in material remains; supply and demand issues.
Isolation/distance	Degrees of isolation (ability for alliances, reinforcements, supplies); distance to travel for support; type of transport technology.	Degree of contact; supply chains; communication.
Regularity	Were meetings seasonal, regular or irregular? Were they predictable?	Setting and predictability of contact.
Proximity	Did societies live with each other, near each other, or distant?	Disease, conflict, awareness of others.
Loss of own land	Degree of loss and restriction to traditional country/resources/routes.	Impact on identity, economy, movement.
Technology	What level of technology existed, and what role did technology play?	Ability to resist superior technology; technological material and information as commodity.

Table 2.2. Variables of culture contact (continued)

VARIABLE	KEY ATTRIBUTES	IMPLICATIONS
Technology, Economy, and Logistics		
Commercial interests	What were the commercial interests over time?	Location of contacts; labor and knowledge demands; environmental change.
Power and Agency		
Context of encounters	Settings for contact: whether on ships, land, trading posts, on traditional land, etc.	Power differences; local knowledge.
Intention	Was contact accidental, unplanned, or intentional and sought after?	Ability to understand contact; degree of preparedness for encounter.
Demands	What did each different agent desire and could these be provided? (including labor).	Degree of need for other culture.
Coercion and change	Attempts at coercion and change.	Leads to issues of resistance and acceptance of others.
Cultural survival	Degrees of cultural survival: survival in traditional lands, loss of cultures, language survival.	Demography and survival of cultural information; and ability to muster long-term perspective on culture contacts.
Role of war and violence	From peaceful coexistence to war; role of violence; degrees of resistance.	Weaponry; role of separate events in long-term, local knowledge; military ability.
Ideology and Knowledge		
Comprehension and language	Role of interpreters and intermediaries.	Transfer of information.
Role of religious ideology	Role of missionaries and religion.	Evidence for missions and religious paraphernalia; impact on traditional belief.
Colonialism (and nationalism)	Degree of attempt to create colonial system; forge and protect a national identity.	Degrees of resistance and acceptance; presence of implements of colonialism and/or nationalism.

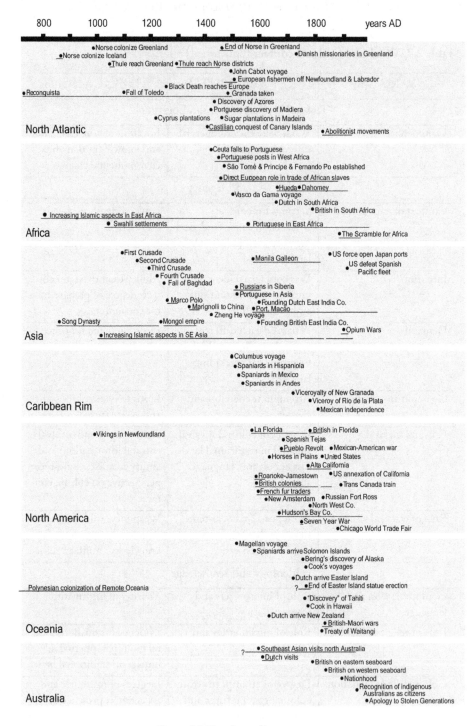

Figure 2.1. Timeline of key events.

CHAPTER 3

ENCOUNTERS IN THE NORTHWEST ATLANTIC

THE NORTHWEST ATLANTIC AD 1000

The 1893 World Trade Fair showcased Chicago to the world and marked four centuries since Columbus's 1492 voyage to the New World—the event was badged the "World's Columbian Exposition." Among the many exhibits were replicas of Columbus's Spanish fleet: the *Santa Maria*, *Pinta*, and *Nina*. However, these were not the only replicas of historic boats. Moored alongside the Norway Pavilion was *Viking*, a striking single-mast sailing ship, with vivid disk-like shields along the sheer. How did the Norwegians determine what their replica should look like? A few years earlier, the excavators of a ninth-century burial mound in Gokstad, Norway, had—incredibly—discovered a complete boat, and *Viking* was a replica. The crew had sailed *Viking* across the Atlantic to Newfoundland to remind the World Trade Fair that Columbus was not the first European to arrive in the Americas (Figure 3.1).[1]

The crew of the *Viking's* ancestors had arrived in Newfoundland nine centuries earlier, being the final settlement in an arc of Norse outposts across the northern Atlantic. The story of the Viking-era settlements in the North Atlantic risks being overshadowed by their attempted settlement in North America—the farthest limit of their sequence of migration, colonization, and culture contact.[2] The Norse dominated the North Atlantic with settlements in France, Ireland, Scotland, and Britain, as well as with colonies in the tenth century in the Faroe Islands, Iceland, Greenland, and finally continental North America/Vinland. Settlers tried to colonize these places with everything required for Norse living.

A key aspect to consider with these colonies was contact between the Norse and other societies. The Vikings found Britain, Ireland,[3] Scotland,[4] The Orkneys and Shetlands occupied, as they would Greenland and North America.[5]

In this chapter, we consider the Norse settlement of the Northwestern Atlantic and the evidence for culture contacts in the period ca. 1000 onward. The

Figure 3.1. *Viking*, a replica of the Gokstad ship, at the Chicago World Trade Fair in 1893.

main cultures we consider are the Norse, the Dorset people (Palaeo-Eskimo), and the Thule (ancestral Inuit).

PEOPLE IN GREENLAND IN AD 1000

Greenland and the Arctic are challenging places for humans. Greenland is vast, extending from sub-Arctic to high Arctic conditions. The freezing waters are rich in food, but hazardous. Sea ice and ice sheets restrict travel in boats, although sleds over ice are less problematic. The fjords and coast host seal, fish, walrus, whale, and narwhal.

The Vikings arrived around 1000, when the climate was warmer, making sailing from Iceland possible. They established their farms in protected fjords in southern Greenland and hunted along the west coast where waters were more suitable for boats. The weather would change: by the fourteenth century, it was colder, meaning more sea ice, and increasingly hazardous travel.

When the Norse arrived, they would not have known that Greenland was already occupied, as the populations did not overlap. However, as they set up farms, the Norse would have seen the remains of ancient settlements. These were the sites of ancient Americans of the Arctic who came through the "Gateway to Greenland" across the Smith Strait from Ellesmere Island (Figure 3.2). The earliest were Palaeo-Eskimos who lived from the mid-third until the first millennium BC.[6] There followed an extended period when Greenland was abandoned. Then people returned in the late first millennium AD; these were Dorset people from the Canadian Arctic.

Figure 3.2. Map of Greenland and northeastern North America.

Dorset

Thus, Dorset people were in northern Greenland when the Vikings arrived in the far south. Dorset favored coastal and tundra regions and lived around Hudson

53

Bay, on the Labrador coast, and on Greenland. Their small settlements consisted of houses of skin, sod, or snow. They built distinctive longhouses as summer gathering places; some may have functioned as ceremonial places, being megalithic structures, with a central section with a colonnade of standing stones.[7] These structures are of a complexity rare for hunter-foragers. Their seasonal migrations followed bird, fish, seals, and walrus, as well as terrestrial animals such as polar bear and caribou.

Their massive network extended across eastern Canada to Greenland. For example, chert from Labrador is found in sites in the Arctic and on the eastern Atlantic seaboard. Meteorite iron from Cape York in Greenland and copper from Coronation Gulf were exchanged widely. The disparate Dorset communities have a similar material culture: carved sculptures of animals and human figures in ivory, wood, and soapstone evoke shamanistic and religious aspects of their society.

Thule

The Dorset were in contact with a new Arctic people, the Thule. Thule culture exploded across the Arctic Circle around the turn of the millennium. There was a period of overlap between the Dorset and Thule in Greenland during the thirteenth century.

It is not clear how culture contact between these two groups worked. However, after the thirteenth century, the Dorset population in Greenland was gone, and the Thule were using many of the resources and exchange networks that the Dorset had earlier established.[8]

There is little to suggest what type of contact existed between these groups during the 1200s. Did the Thule learn of the Norse from the Dorset? This seems likely. Was there friction between these groups? Were the Dorset driven out of Greenland, as has been suggested by some? This is still not clear.

Thule oral traditions describe the Tunit, an ancient people, strong and large, who once occupied the land and left, although some of the Tunit women married Inuit men. Perhaps the Tunit are the Dorset, remembered seven centuries later, and the end of the Dorset in Greenland is explained by intermarriage and migration. There was contact and exchange, as indicated by Dorset practices adopted by the Thule, such as oil lamps, harpoon heads, and ice knives to make igloos.

The Thule were a high Arctic people, their culture derived from Bering Strait and Alaska around one thousand years ago, becoming widespread across the Arctic, Labrador, and Greenland. The Thule moved across the high Arctic quickly: a warmer climate saw the sea ice pull back, and the Thule followed their prey, such as bowhead whales.

The Thule entered Greenland after the mid-eleventh century and reached Disko Bay halfway down the west coast of Greenland in around 1250.[9] They reached the Norse settlements between 1295 (Western Settlement) and 1400 (Eastern Settlement) (Figure 3.2).[10] They remained in contact within the broader Thule circumpolar network, as suggested by the presence of ceramics imported from Alaska in a Thule site in Greenland ca. 1400.[11]

Like the Dorset, Thule society was very well adapted to Arctic life, being based on the hunting of wild animals, with harpoons and skin kayaks allowing hunting over water, and sleds for travel over ice. Kayaks were used for hunting, while larger umiaks could carry up to twenty people. Skin was used for boats and clothing. Dogs and reindeer (the latter in Eurasia, not America and Greenland) pulled their sleds.

They had advantages over other Arctic peoples, who did not have dogs, bows and arrows, or sophisticated boats. Thule hunters used larger boats and waterproof clothing to hunt whales for food, bone, and fuel for heating and lighting.

Where whale was not available, Thule people relied heavily on other animals, particularly seals, setting up villages on the sea ice as hunting bases. Their winter pithouses of stone, earth, driftwood, and whalebone contained heat effectively.

The idea of building igloos in these places may have come to the Thule from the Dorset. However, unlike the Dorset, who lived in quite small groups, the Thule economy allowed for occasionally larger settlements of up to hundreds of people.

The Norse described meeting indigenous people. Who were they? Thule or Dorset? If contact was in the 1000–1200 period, they may well have been Dorset people, either in Northern Greenland, or on Baffin Island. After 1200–1300, contacts were probably with the Thule. To solve this requires looking at the archaeological evidence.

THE NORSE SETTLEMENT IN GREENLAND

We have two main lines of evidence for the Norse in the Atlantic: the archaeology, and Norse sagas. The archaeology often supports the sagas, but also provides details not in the historical sources.

The sagas were written long after the events they describe occurred, and were biased toward elite individuals, functioning as a form of familial propaganda. The sagas say that Erik Thorvaldsson established settlements in Greenland fifteen winters before 1000, the year Iceland converted to Christianity.[12] The archaeology supports this, suggesting colonization around 960–970.

Norse settlement occurred in two locations, the Western Settlement and the larger Eastern Settlement (Figure 3.2). Both were limited to protective fjords suitable for animal farming. Here, up to six thousand European farmers were able to find a niche for their animals and families, sitting between the icecap of the interior of Greenland and the coast.

These medieval European settlements would last for half a millennium before being abandoned, the causes for which are still debated. We now know something of Norse life in Greenland, although questions remain about why Norse settlements in Greenland were abandoned. Did culture contact play a role in the end of the Greenland Norse?

Norse hierarchical society ranged from slaves (often captured during raids) to commoners and chiefs. In Greenland, far from Europe, chiefs would have remained the most significant level of governance, along with the Church.

The earliest settlers got the best grazing land. Erik and his wife Þjódhild established their farm at Brattahlíð. Archaeological excavations indicate which farms were elite, as these had a greater proportion of cattle than sheep and goats, and possibly a church and assembly hall.[13] Smaller farms were simpler, with less high-status material culture.

The Norse relied on cattle, sheep, and goats. Archaeological sites include summer herding locations in landscapes remote from the main farms.[14] The extreme climate required that stock were brought indoors during winter, and food had to be harvested and stored. Pig, highly valued by the Norse, fared poorly in Greenland. Cattle did better, sheep and goat best. The archaeological food remains also demonstrate the importance of hunted animals in the Norse diet, particularly seals and caribou. It is less clear what contribution fish made, possibly due to poor preservation of fish bones or inappropriate excavation methodologies at key sites.

Seal remains indicate the Norse left the protective areas of the inner fjords to hunt the seas. Oxygen isotope analysis of Norse burials suggests marine species became more important to the Norse diet over time in Greenland.[15] Was diet the reason settlements were abandoned? Other explanations for the dietary shift include religious dietary proscriptions, environmental degradation, and vegetation change resulting from stock raising, colder climatic conditions, and socio-economic marginalization of some settlers.[16]

The Greenland Norse were not utterly isolated. They remained in contact with Iceland and Europe, with whom they traded sheep, cattle, seal, and walrus products for iron and timber, and other commodities found by archaeologists such as ringed pins, armlets, finger rings, and bronze church bells.

Christianity was important, with churches constructed from the earliest years of settlement. The arrival of Christianity may have built on existing chiefly power, part religious already. The establishment of a bishop's seat at Garðar in 1125 demonstrates the maintenance of links with Europe. The Church would grow to be the largest landowner in Greenland.

The Greenland Norse became part of the Norwegian Kingdom in 1261 and of the Danish Kingdom in 1380. This ensured that ships arrived and maintained connections with Europe. Walrus tusk exports were particularly important, since tusks were used in northern Europe in the eleventh and twelfth centuries to create precious white royal and sacred objects, although demand diminished in the mid-thirteenth century as elephant ivory became more accessible.[17]

The Norse describe contacts with indigenous Greenlanders, whom they described as "Skrællingar." The most likely setting for early culture contact between the Norse and Skrællingar was along the western coast of Greenland when Norse hunted walrus, polar bear, and narwhal in expeditions called the "Nordrsetur" voyages.

Objects move between cultures: archaeologists have found Early Thule artifacts in Eastern Settlement farms, and Norse artifacts in Thule houses and middens in northwestern Greenland and on Ellesmere Island.[18]

The Norse abandonment of the Western Settlement probably occurred, according to historical records, in the mid-fourteenth century, and for the Eastern Settlement, by the early fifteenth century. The last historic account is of a wedding in the Hvalseyfjord Church in 1408. The archaeology supports abandonment after the mid-fifteenth century.

There were probably several factors behind the Norse abandonment of Greenland. Contact with Europe was essential for the Greenlanders' access to European goods, yet the frequency of voyages seems to have declined over time, particularly when European demand for walrus ivory fell in the fourteenth century. "Metal poverty" in Greenland is suggested by bone substitutes for metal: for example, a bone battle-ax, belt buckles, and even a bone padlock.[19]

Conditions in Norway were also a contributing factor, and the impact of plague in Norway in 1349 appears to have caused a decline in Atlantic voyaging and trade.[20]

Another factor may have been environmental, if centuries of farming had led to deforestation and increased soil erosion. This may have reduced the viability of farming in the Greenland settlements, yet some abandoned farms suffered little environmental degradation, such as the Farm Beneath the Sand, abandoned with the Western Settlement in the mid-1300s.

Another environmental factor may have been a period of cooling after 1300, with colder temperatures and stormier seas dominated by drifting ice increasing in the early fifteenth century.[21] Colder weather may have caused advancing ice to reduce available grazing land. The reliance of the Greenland Norse on farming made their position particularly precarious.

Whether the last Norse died in the Eastern Settlement, or traveled to Iceland, then greatly depopulated after the plague, remains unknown.[22] What role, if any, did culture contact between the Norse and the Skrællingar have?[23] To answer that, we need to know more of culture contacts in the region: the Norse first met Skrællingar not in Greenland but in another land—Vinland.

NORSE VOYAGES TO VINLAND

They had built their settlements up above the lake. And some of the dwellings were well within the land, but some were near the lake. Now they remained there that winter. They had no snow whatever, and all their cattle went out to graze without keepers.

Now when spring began, they beheld one morning early, that a fleet of hide-canoes was rowing from the south off the headland; so many were they as if the sea were strewn with pieces of charcoal, and there was also the brandishing of staves as before from each boat. Then they held shields up, and a market was formed between them; and this people in their purchases preferred red cloth; in exchange they had furs to give, and skins quite grey. They wished also to buy swords and lances, but Karlsefni and Snorri forbad it. They offered for the cloth dark hides, and took in exchange a span long of cloth, and bound it round their heads; and so matters went on for a while. But when the stock of cloth began to grow small, then they split it asunder, so that it was not more than a finger's breadth. The Skrælingar (Esquimaux) gave for it still quite as much, or more than before.

– Erik the Red's Saga[24]

We've found a land of fine resources, though we'll hardly enjoy much of them.

–Thorvald, having been fatally pierced by an arrow

The sagas describing the Norse settlement in continental North America are *The Saga of Erik the Red* and *The Saga of the Greenlanders*: these are the only pre-Columbian documentary accounts of Native Americans. Despite being written long after the events occurred, there are many elements that indicate the Norse successfully voyaged from Greenland to North America. The portrayal of animals and vegetation is consistent in both accounts, with descriptions of fox, bear, salmon, and halibut, as well as of the pastures, timbered forests, and grapes from which the name Vinland appears to derive.[25] The archaeological discovery in the 1960s of Norse settlement in Newfoundland confirmed the sagas, although this does not mean the details therein are necessarily reliable.

According to the sagas, Vinland was initially discovered when a ship was blown off course, a not uncommon event in Norse annals. Given the prestige associated with the discovery of new lands, the sagas disagree over whether it was an individual named Bjarni or Leif the Lucky (son of Erik) who discovered Vinland. There were at least two to four expeditions to Vinland. Several lands are described in the sagas, namely Vinland (wine land), Markland (wood land), and Helluland (stone land). These are, respectively, parts of Newfoundland, Labrador, and Baffin Island in the Canadian Arctic.[26]

The term "Vinland" is felt to refer to Newfoundland and regions farther south and west in the Gulf of St. Lawrence, the New Brunswick and Nova Scotia area, and possibly as far south as the coast of New England to New York.

Archaeological evidence provides firm evidence for the Norse in America at the Norse settlement L'Anse aux Meadows, Newfoundland. The site's significance was immediately clear, becoming the first UNESCO World Heritage Site.[27] Radiocarbon dates suggest an eleventh-century occupation. The sagas agree, describing voyages in 1000 and the years thereafter.[28] The buildings were substantial enough to have been intended for year-round use, suggesting this was a winter base from which the Norse could explore (Figure 3.3).

The settlement includes eight buildings overlooking a bay and the Atlantic Ocean. The structures were made of turf walls in a style typical of eleventh-century Iceland. The settlement could have supported 70 to 90 people, most within the two largest halls. Working areas were for forging iron, cooking, and some domestic labor.

It is an unusual place. The Vikings rarely built small villages like this, and there are no byre, corrals, or pens for animals as on Norse farms. This supports the idea that L'Anse aux Meadows was never intended to be a colonizing farm. Its location on an exposed coast, and its arrangement, suggest an outpost of a quite specific nature. The archaeological evidence of equipment and differing building sizes supports the presence of a diverse community of elites, crews, women, and slaves—as stated in the sagas.

It is likely this was not the only settlement in America, given that the sagas describe several camps in Vinland. L'Anse aux Meadows was presumably a base for further expeditions to the south. The sagas describe Vinland as having grapes,

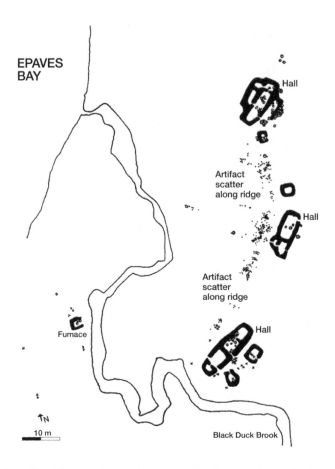

Figure 3.3. Plan of the Norse settlement L'Anse aux Meadows on the north of Newfoundland.

seemingly referring to warmer regions farther south, such as in the Gulf of St. Lawrence.[29] The discovery of butternut shells at L'Anse aux Meadows indicates the settlers traveled south, where this plant grew wild. [30]

Timber and metals were valuable to impoverished Greenland Norse; however, a singular attempt to smelt iron at L'Anse aux Meadows appears to have resulted in poor-quality metal.

The Norse found America already occupied, and they deployed the term "Skrællingar" to describe the people they met. The sagas agree that the reaction of the locals to the Norse was eventually hostile. These people were probably ancestors of the Innu and Inuit in Labrador, and the Beothuk on Newfoundland, while along the coasts of Baffin Island and Labrador they may have met Dorset people.[31]

Along the Atlantic coast, ancestral Innu people moved from coastal resources in summer to the forested interior. They also moved widely along the coast, traveling north into northern Labrador to get Ramah chert, a stone used for tool making and traded far afield. They made use of small boats, possibly skin- or bark-covered, and lived in small settlements close to the forest they exploited to make their tipis.

Innu would have observed the Norse landfalls and coastal voyages, and news of their large boats and strangeness may have traveled far. If Norse explorations extended farther south and east from Newfoundland, then they could have met various Native Americans along the New England coast or along the margins of the Gulf of St. Lawrence, such as Mi'kmaq and Maliseet.[32]

The warmer climate around the Gulf of St. Lawrence allowed for greater numbers of fish and shellfish, and the possible use of garden crops. Around the bays and along the rivers, the Norse would have found villages of people. Traveling farther up the St. Lawrence River, they may have encountered the Iroquois, at that time expanding eastward toward the coast. They do not describe farmers, who at that time were present only south of central Maine.

The archaeological evidence suggests that no culture contact occurred at L'Anse aux Meadows, despite the probability that ancestral Beothuk people were present in Newfoundland.[33] The saga of Erik the Red describes their settlement at a place called Hóp, where after a month, native peoples visited them. The natives were seemingly offended by a bellowing cow. They returned in a large group of boats to trade, with red cloth being deemed valuable (as in Erik's saga). For these transactions, the Vikings placed value on the bales of furs the native people provided. Since the Skrællingar had skin boats, this suggests contacts occurred north of central Maine, possibly in New Brunswick or in the Gulf of St. Lawrence.[34]

Of the seasons spent in America, the sagas describe various types of cross-cultural interaction, from hostility on both sides, incomprehension, and more sustained interactions and knowledge transfer—for example, about neighboring native peoples. There was certainly violence between the Vikings and natives. In one location, the leader Thorvald was struck by an arrow and died. There are several descriptions of encounters where Skrællingar died, both at Hóp and Markland. In one account, captives are taken from Markland and baptized.[35] Hostility seems to have been an essential aspect of culture contact in Vinland, and the Vikings' inability to defend their small settlements against indigenous resistance may have been sufficient reason to abandon colonization.

Was the settlement at L'Anse aux Meadows deliberately abandoned? The archaeological record suggests that the settlement was stripped of anything of value, and researchers believe the Norse left deliberately. Most experts feel that despite the suitability of the region for Norse farmers, the distance from other Norse settlements, combined with the Skrællingar resistance to them, made permanent settlement impossible. These voyages were being sustained solely from Norse settlements in Greenland, themselves a tiny population with presumably little in the way of a surplus to maintain a faraway outpost, despite the resources and potential of these new lands. This was not necessarily a failed colonization attempt, but rather a period of exploration, after which it was decided not to proceed with permanent Norse colonies. Or like NASA's lunar missions, maybe it was felt they would one day return.

These small numbers of Native Americans, then, in deterring Norse colonization, had a great impact on, and ramifications for, world history. A single artifact found in the Western Settlement in Greenland is seemingly a souvenir of their visits to Vinland, this is a chipped-stone arrowhead contemporary in style with those used in Newfoundland and Labrador around 1000. However, this is not the only archaeological evidence for links to the Americas: at the Farm Beneath the Sands in Greenland, hairs from nonlocal animals, including musk ox and brown bear, were found.[36]

This is only the first part of the story of culture contact with the Norse. It appears the culture contacts in the northwest Atlantic continued long after the time that, according to the sagas, the voyages to Vinland had finished.

CULTURE CONTACT AFTER L'ANSE AUX MEADOWS

The first culture contact the Norse experienced occurred during the voyages to Vinland and possibly during any return voyages to Markland (Labrador) and Helluland (Baffin Island). However, the greater sum of culture contact between the Norse and others probably involved people met in and near Greenland: possibly with ancestral Innu in Canada, and Dorset and Thule in Greenland and around the margins of the Davis Strait. Unlike the relatively short time of contact described in the sagas for Vinland, there are nearly five centuries during which further contact occurred between the Norse and native peoples. Lacking written histories, we turn to archaeology.

Despite the abandonment of permanent settlement in Vinland in the eleventh century, the Norse continued to travel, along the Nordrsetur (the central west coast) and possibly farther. Labrador timber may have held great value for the Norse, especially if supplies of driftwood declined in areas near Norse settlements. A description in the mid-fourteenth century refers in an offhand manner to a Norse voyage to "Markland" to collect timber, as if it were not unusual.[37] That said, these would be long journeys through hazardous waters and not undertaken lightly. This one reference is the sum of the documentary evidence for later Norse voyages to North America.

The archaeological evidence, however, does indicate that contacts occurred throughout the Middle Ages. For a time, the proposal that Vinland was in Maine was seemingly supported by the discovery of an eleventh-century Norwegian coin at Penobscot Bay, Maine; however, this isolated item could easily have moved south by exchange, as suggested by the presence of stone artifacts from Labrador found at the same site. Importantly, the coin was minted many years after the Vinland voyages described in the sagas. If it is evidence of anything, it is of indigenous trade networks, not southern voyages of Vikings.[38]

In the Arctic, there are other sites containing Norse-era objects postdating the adventures in Vinland, in addition to the Norse coin in Maine. For example, a pendant made from Norse copper was found on the east coast of Hudson Bay in a twelfth-century Dorset site. These items suggest direct contact, although such material may have come from shipwrecks, from raids, or through indigenous networks of trade that extended from people in more regular contact with the Norse in Greenland. If direct contact is indicated, the Norse may have been more active across the Eastern Arctic, and more in contact with indigenous people, than previously thought from a reading of documentary sources.

The discovery in a late Dorset hut on North Baffin Island of seemingly Norse-spun yarn of Arctic hare fur with traces of goat (only found at Greenland Norse farms) suggests more complex encounters and perhaps trade. The yarn was found in a hut with pine timber fragments that once held square iron nails; the wood is from the late thirteenth or early fourteenth century. This suggests that a range of materials, not just iron, were exchanged.[39] Other evidence in support of direct contact between the Norse and Dorset is less conclusive—specifically, several small native-made figurines that appear to depict Europeans.[40]

There is the clear evidence that the Norse traveled north from their settlements into regions where they may have encountered native people. The evidence for trips undertaken to the north from their southern settlements includes historical accounts, archaeology, and environmental information. These expeditions could date to the whole period of Norse settlement. While the earliest written description dates from 1170, voyages may have occurred as early as the first century of settlement. The evidence for this is northern musk ox pelts found in an early Norse farm, and whetstones originally from Disko Bay—to the north—in an eleventh-century hall.[41]

Northern animal species occur in the southern Norse farms, such as musk ox at the Farm Beneath the Sand archaeological site. Carcasses of seals, walrus, and bear were found in Norse rubbish. Polar bear and walrus occur with greater frequencies at the Western Settlement, given its closer proximity to the northern hunting regions.[42]

This fits with the historical references to northern voyages to get ivory, hides, and presumably meat. The hunters wanted walrus ivory, polar bears, seals, and driftwood. The trade of items to Europe included polar bear skins as well as the occasional live polar bear, which made at least one importer wealthy overnight by delivering the bear to the Danish king.[43] None of these products were essential for survival in Greenland, but were high-status, low-bulk materials valued in Europe which the Norse could, in turn, trade for the metal and other European goods they desired. Their own place at the margins of the European world thus depended on the Nordrsetur.

Most of the animals sought in the Nordrsetur hunt were found north of the Western Settlement, around the vicinity of Disko Bay and farther north. The walrus were probably hunted on the beaches where they gathered in summer. This was a dangerous yet potentially profitable activity, given that many walrus could be killed in such locations. Needless to say, the hunt for polar bear was also dangerous.

There is archaeological evidence of their bases in the north, most tellingly from the island of Kingigtorssuaq, where one season Norse hunters erected several stone cairns and an inscription that stated they were built by Erling Sigvatsson, Bjarni Thordarsson, and Eindridi Oddsson in April, probably between 1250 and 1300, based on the runic style. This suggests a winter camp when the sea ice would not have yet opened up.[44] One can imagine that sitting idle out in a winter's camp would allow time for leaving calling cards.

While this suggests that these men spent the winter in the north, other Norse hunters presumably sailed north for the summer hunting season and then returned during winter. Depending on whether they were sailing from the closer Western Settlement or not, they would have had two to three months in the north. These may have been rushed voyages: the remains of walrus and polar bears in the Norse settlements suggest a hurried butchery occurred during the hunt, and the remains were further processed once they returned to the settlements.

NORSE CONTACT WITH DORSET OR THULE?

The Nordrsetur provides a setting for culture contact between Norse hunters and Dorset Culture people (up until 1300) and Thule/Inuit (after 1100) in northern Greenland. The Norse accounts do not indicate which people they met, just that when meeting a new group of people for the first time, the Norse tellingly denoted them by the term their ancestors used nearly two centuries earlier: the Skrællingar. The Inuit had a universal term for Europeans when they encountered the British in the 1600s, and may have similarly described the Norse in these earlier times: *qadlunat.*[45]

One Norse account of contact in Greenland is vivid:

> Beyond the Greenlanders some manikins have been found by hunters, who call them Skrælings. Weapon-wounds inflicted on them from which they will survive grow white without bleeding, but if they are mortal the blood hardly ceases flowing. But they lack iron completely: they use whales' teeth for missiles, sharp stones for knives.[46]

This probably referred to the Dorset people, given the time period. The material culture fits with either the Dorset or Thule people. There is no mention of Thule-specific elements such as dogs or bows and arrows in this account, items that may have given the Thule an advantage over the Dorset people when facing down the Norse. The description indicates that bloodshed occurred between the Europeans and Eskimos.

Another piece of evidence for early Norse contact with the Dorset comes from L'Anse aux Meadows, where an oval soapstone lamp was found sitting atop the final cultural layers in one of the sod buildings. It appears to be a Dorset lamp, which the Norse may have acquired before arriving in Vinland, presumably in Markland or Helluland.[47]

Farther north, there is evidence for culture contact between Norse and Thule: Norse material occurs in sites around the Smith Sound. On Ellesmere Island, the largest concentration of Norse metal objects was found in the houses of a village from the Skræling Island archaeological sites.[48] These include chain-mail fragments (Figure 3.4), ship rivets, fragments of knives and spikes, bone game pieces, a comb, pieces of copper, and Norse woolen cloth cut into squares.

Figure 3.4. Norse Medieval metal chain-mail found in two indigenous sites in Greenland (*Gulløv et al. 2005: 291*).

Some finds in separate locations may derive from the same object; for example, the woven woolen cloth and the chain-mail sections were found on both Ruin Island and Skræling Island. The chain-mail was also found in Greenland, at Kap Seddon. It is interesting to conjecture on who separated it—Norse traders or Thule—as this may imply one instance of contact or several. Another explanation suggests no direct contact: perhaps this was a Norse shipwreck later plundered.

As only a very small amount of material entered into Thule hands over time, was it traded or acquired through raiding? If trading, the Thule would have been able to provide the pelts and other animal products the Norse valued. The metals were clearly desirable to the Thule—the only other local source of metal was from the Cape York meteorite in northern Greenland, and this may have attracted the Thule to the eastern Arctic in the first place. Even scraps of iron, less desired by the Norse, may have been of value. Perhaps it was the opportunity for trade with the Norse that encouraged the Thule to migrate farther down the western coast of Greenland and into the homelands of the Greenland Norse.

If they were in cross-cultural trade, a valuable commodity for the Norse may have been walrus tusks. In Northwestern Greenland, a Dorset longhouse has a large number of walrus crania with the tusks removed, which, together with the presence of Norse metal in another Dorset house, hints at a complex of trade with perhaps Late Dorset people also involved in trade.

While Norse material moved into indigenous people's hands, the amount of material is very small, especially considering the time span. The handful of indigenous objects found in Norse settlements are trivial, probably curios.[49] This has led at least one archaeologist to propose that the largest collection of Norse artifacts in one locality, on Skræling Island, resulted either from Norse use of a Thule hut, or from Norse explorers stranded in the far north and spending time with the Thule. However, further cross-cultural trade is suggested by evidence for Norsemen's access to Thule trade networks, with the presence of brown bear and buffalo fibers at the Farm Beneath the Sand. These are North American species and either indicate further Norse voyages to America in the Middle Ages, or the movement of these skins into Thule trade networks and then on to the Norse.

Altogether, it seems very possible that contact occurred between the Norse and the Dorset and/or the Thule. Some Norse material made its way to these people, most notably the Thule. Norse metal presumably moved through existing networks in the same way that other regionally specific valuable materials, like the Cape York meteorite iron, did. Thus, the Norse need not have traveled to all the locations where Norse-derived metal is found.

Several explanations could account for the movement of material from Norse to indigenous groups: (1) being pillaged from a Norse shipwreck, (2) being taken through raiding, or (3) deriving from some form of exchange or trade occurring in a low-level fashion over time. Some objects hint at direct contact, such as carved images—one from Baffin Island of a human figure suggested to be a priest, a missionary, or even a Teutonic knight.[50] Other figures are strong candidates for carved images of Europeans, some possibly by the Norse, others possibly Thule.[51]

Another line of evidence for culture contact is settlement patterns. Simply, when the Thule finally arrived in the more southern regions of Greenland, they lived near the Norse. At the Western Settlement, Thule sites at nearby Kangeq date to 1295–1435, overlapping with Norse occupation for up to fifty years, assuming Norse abandonment after the mid-fifteenth century. The Thule were close, yet occupied a different environmental niche. Their interests were in hunting whale, a resource the Norse did not pursue, sticking instead to caring for their imported domesticated animals and the animals they hunted, such as caribou, walrus, and seals.

So, the potential for overlap of Thule and Norse in the same landscape *finally* existed. After the Norse were gone, the Thule were certainly happy to use the inner regions of the fjords where the Norse farmers had been established. While both communities were present, it seems a policy of avoidance existed, peppered with a little bit of trade. There was no sustained attempt by the Norse to convert the people they met into an indigenous workforce.

We can ask why the Norse did not adopt Inuit ways. The Inuit were great survivors in the Arctic, yet many aspects of Thule technology and economy that the Norse could have adopted and adapted, such as whale and seal hunting with harpoons, they did not. Since it is not clear what happened to the Norse settlers, some have suggested that their failure was in part due to their decision not to take up indigenous lifeways. Certainly, Viking avoidance of the Thule suggests a fairly conservative society, which is perhaps hardly surprising, given their increasing remoteness from their European links as fewer ships arrived.

Did the Thule help the last Norse to depart? The archaeological record seems to suggest not; there is no major shift to increased fortification, nor evidence for traumatic deaths, although the Thule would have seen the diminished population and certainly took up the territorial advantages that abandonment offered. The archaeological record suggests that abandoned Norse settlements were later pressed into service by native people, who made use of some buildings and modified them for their own purposes.[52] Presumably, the remains and detritus of settlement were worked over for any useful material, particularly metal.[53] The world of Europe receded from the shores of Greenland for a couple of centuries or so, when a very new and very different set of culture contacts began.

LATER EUROPEAN CONTACTS WITH INUIT

The icy waters of southern Greenland were free from Europeans for a time, and safe in Inuit hands. After this hiatus, a new suite of culture contact occurred with European explorers, whalers, traders, and missionaries. The pattern of contact shifted from avoidance to greater engagement.

The northwest Atlantic became a setting for European competitiveness. The main European visitors to the northwest Atlantic and the coastline of America were fishers and whalers, and explorers. Perhaps by the late 1400s, English and Portuguese ships explored the northeast.[54] By the early sixteenth century, French, Spanish, and Portuguese vessels plied the Newfoundland waters for cod, while Basque whalers hunted here and farther north off Labrador. Presumably, few contacts occurred with Innu and Inuit in Labrador, or with the Beothuk and Mi'kmaq on Newfoundland, although landfalls were limited, perhaps driven by the need for provisions and possibly fuel for try pots on whaling vessels. Few accounts of contact with native peoples prior to the nineteenth century exist. Clearly these were seasonal visits, and there was little intention for permanent colonization, so relations with indigenous people were thus limited until more permanent European settlements were formed in Newfoundland and Labrador in the nineteenth century.

The fate of the Norse in Greenland must have been a question in Scandinavia, for the kings of Denmark and Norway sent missions to Greenland expecting to find the descendants of the Norse. However, these missions report a Greenland solely occupied by Inuit. A Danish expedition in 1605 abducted five Inuit and brought them back to Copenhagen. (Several years later, another boat returned to Greenland; the Inuit recognized a crew member as an abductor, and killed him.)

European powers were increasingly interested in the waters off west Greenland. When English explorers were there in the late sixteenth century, they saw Basque whalers trading with the Inuit.

Northern waters increasingly came under European attention, in part fueled by desire to find a route (the Northwest Passage) to Asia and the valuable spice markets. A century after the disappearance of the Greenland Norse, Martin Frobisher reached Baffin Island in 1576 and met Inuit people, capturing some to take to Queen Elizabeth I in England, where they all died through exposure to disease. The people he met were willing to trade with the British, perhaps recalling older patterns of culture contact established by their ancestors with the Norse. Dutch traders were also actively trading with Inuit in west Greenland in the 1600s. Ice-edge exchanges regularly occurred with Dutch whalers and traders, where Inuit demanded needles, cooking pots, knives, and flintlocks.[55] By the mid-1650s, whalers from various European countries hunted at least one thousand whales a year.[56]

Permanent European colonial settlements in Greenland were reestablished after 1721, first with the small settlement of Danish missionary Hans Egede. There followed the first voluntary Inuit visitors to Europe, arriving in 1724 and forced to understand the world within their own cultural frame of reference. One Greenlander, Pooq (Figure 3.5), described the white Royal Palace that stood where Christiansborg castle was built: "It was like a big, chalk-white iceberg. In the great hall there was room for 20 tents and on both sides there were a group of armed men dressed in fine clothing."[57] The story of distinctive buildings in Copenhagen remained in Inuit oral traditions for centuries.

Colonial settlement from 1800 first focused on central western Greenland, and then the south. It comprised mainly Danish trade stations and Moravian (German) missions. With colonial settlement in Greenland came disease. At least two smallpox epidemics, in 1733 and 1800, killed many in Nuuk and Disko Bay, respectively.[58]

In Greenland, the historical period saw cultural developments within Inuit communities that suggest the maintenance of long-range communication and changes within settlement patterns and residential organization, notably the popularity of large communal residential buildings after the late seventeenth century. These buildings were located in coastal settings and apparently were used in winter. Their size required either bone or timber supports and may have originated in southern Greenland, where timber was available as driftwood. They suggest a shift from single-family to multi-family residences. These occur in western, southern, and eastern Greenland.

The use of communal houses is not restricted to Greenland. In Inuit communities along the coast of Labrador, similar changes occur in the contact period.[59] There have been multiple proposals for this shift, including responses to climate change, a shift in hunting behavior, the organization of labor, responses to contact trade opportunities by Inuit entrepreneurs, and as attempts to build alliances by ambitious kin heads.

In West Greenland, the distribution of communal houses derived initially from the seasonal migration north of southern Inuit, until the cessation of these voyages. In East Greenland, certain artifacts in these and other residences suggest that these settlements, remote from whalers and traders, had some access to European materials, possibly supplied by the southern gathering sites such as at Aluk. Additionally, the presence of metal fragments from Norse bells suggests how abandoned Norse rubbish heaps and settlements were stripped of useful objects.

Inuit people continued to conduct themselves in traditional ways even with the arrival of traders and whalers. In summer, people moved around the coasts of

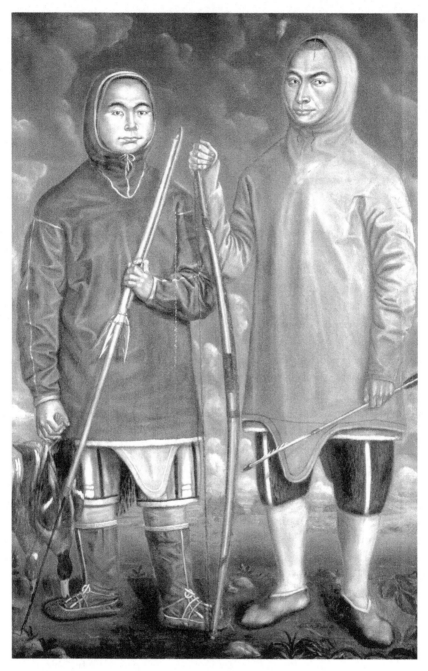

Figure 3.5. The Greenlanders Pooq and Qiperoq in Copenhagen, 1724.
(*Permission National Museum of Denmark.*)

Greenland to avail themselves of hunting opportunities. Some large groups gathered at *aasivik* (meaning "summer places") that offered opportunities for trade and communal and social activities. *Aasivik* are characterized by the remains of many tent rings—the stone bases for the residential structures —and a location close to a suitable seasonal resource such as fish or seal. These gatherings were observed in the earliest European records from the sixteenth century. A German missionary compared the activities at the Taseralik *aasivik* to the Leipziger Fair in Germany.[60]

A key aspect of *aasivik* was the trade of valuable materials from different Greenland regions. The presence of Europeans appears to have amplified trade opportunities, with Inuit providing baleen and furs to traders. *Aasivik* were held close to whalers, merchants, and missionaries, all of whom may have been drawn to the presence of Inuit (at least for merchants and missionaries, who required people to trade with and convert). Thus, the contact period did not stop the movement of people and gatherings such as *aasivik*, at least initially. Eventually, however, under colonization the pattern became one of bringing trade goods to the Inuit, and thus the seasonal regional movement of people stopped. The south of Greenland became a focus of settlement for people from other regions, as characterized by the nineteenth-century movement of the *uiarnerit*—East Greenlanders who settled in southwest Greenland.[61]

Greenlanders recovered from demographic decline, but were changed. The annual expeditions from the south along the coasts to meet, trade, and hunt were cut back, with many people staying year-round closer to the colonial settlements and Moravian missions. The traditional Inuit exchange system closed down, in part because of the items provided by the Europeans. Most contact now occurred in the Cape Farewell District, with ten main settlements. The movement of Inuit from the east coast of Greenland led to depopulation there. The tension between the European traders and missionaries created changes in nineteenth- and twentieth-century settlement patterns: traders wanted people to be able to access useful resources across the landscape, while missionaries preferred to have people residing close to their stations. The historical records and archaeology in southwest Greenland presumably reflect Inuit decisions regarding affiliations with the Europeans. Colonial Danish policy agreed with the traders—people were best making use of available resources and thus in a dispersed pattern of settlement.

AASIVISSUIT: A HISTORICAL INUIT SUMMER GATHERING PLACE

The seasons, decades, and centuries rolled by to form the archaeological record at Aasivissuit, a place where in summer, herds of caribou made their way from the interior of Greenland toward the coast. Historical sources report that Inuit families would travel inland from the coast and fjords to Aasivissuit, a natural choke point where the caribou were forced together between a rocky ridge and a lake. After a long winter surviving on seal, the Inuit would have fondly anticipated caribou meat, and their other products, especially their skin.[62]

In the fifteenth and sixteenth centuries, the summer camp was used every few years. Around 1700, some massive hunts occurred, leaving piles of caribou bones. The community hunted together, some scaring deer forward to waiting hunters who used

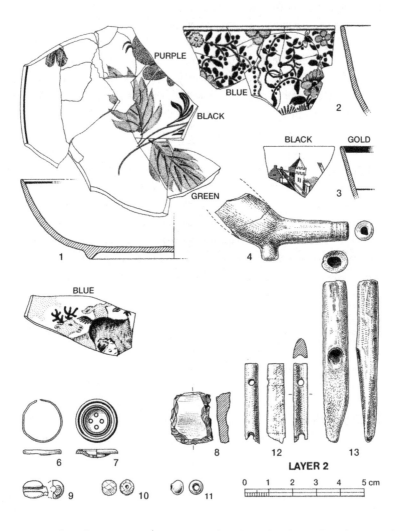

Figure 3.6. Artifacts from Aasivissuit: European beads traded for caribou hides in the sixteenth and seventeenth centuries, and trade goods from the colonial period including faience sherds (one with caribou motif), clay pipe, and gunflints (*from Grønnow et al. 1983: figs. 69–71*).

bows and arrows to fell animals, or used kayaks and lances to pursue those that entered the lake. People built cairns and stone walls to make the joint hunt even more successful. These were bountiful years, and at the end of the hunting season, the women's boats and kayaks would have returned loaded with meat, fat, bone, and skins.

We discuss Aasivissuit not as a place of direct culture contact, but one of *indirect* culture contact. The presence of Dutch glass beads is proof they were in contact with whalers or traders who were active along the coast; however, no Dutch would ever have come this far inland at this time.

Then the camp is abandoned for nearly a century, until after 1800, mirroring the impact on the Inuit population of smallpox and other disease.

The caribou population increased in the nineteenth century, and people began to return every summer to Aasivissuit. But things had changed. Now they came with flintlock guns obtained from the colonial trading stations, presumably in return for caribou skins. The guns changed the way people hunted, the joint hunt replaced by stalking and shooting from hidden, fixed positions. Again the animals were brought back to camp for butchery, but not in the same numbers as a century earlier. Their rubbish heaps indicate access to a greater range of European manufactured goods, entering their society from traders and missionaries. Ceramic bowls, clay pipes, buttons, and metal knifes demonstrate how new practices and objects were taken up by the Inuit (Figure 3.6). An ancient meeting place and hunting practice reflect both continuity and change in the colonial era. One fragment of pottery reveals how Europeans were targeting Arctic consumers in this trading process: it shows the head of a woman and caribou, an attempt at anticipating an indigenous market demand. The caribou-decorated sherd from the factories of Europe lay discarded among the butchered caribou bones of Aasivissuit.

USEFUL SOURCES

Museums and online resources: See The Greenland National Museum, the National Museum in Denmark, the National Museum of the American Indian (NMAI) at the Smithsonian, and the Canadian Museum of Civilization.

Key journals: Arctic Archaeology, Canadian Archaeology, and North American archaeology journals.

CHAPTER 4

EUROPE AND
ITS NEIGHBORS

Everyone calls barbarity what he is not accustomed to.

–Montaigne[1]

Mysterious are the works of the Creator, the author of all things! When one comes to recount cases regarding the Franks, he cannot but glorify Allah (exalted is he!) and sanctify him, for he sees them as animals possessing the virtues of courage and fighting, but nothing else; just as animals have only the virtues of strength and carrying loads. I shall now give some instances of their doings and their curious mentality.

–Usmah Ibn Munqidh (1095–1188): *Autobiography*, excerpts on the Franks[2]

It may be hard for most people reading this book to comprehend being as isolated as communities were in past eras, where goods from anywhere else were rare and restricted to elites, where very few people knew much of the world beyond their own communities, and where most people had very little power in political and fiscal terms. Yet, this describes much of Western Europe at the turn of the millennium: remote and not particularly influential, as it had once been (Figure 4.1).

In the early centuries of the second millennium, the control of contacts between Europe and its neighbors was largely in the hands of merchants in the eastern Mediterranean. The trade networks that linked Europe to the earlier world trade systems of Asia and Africa lay outside of European control and variously in the hands of Arabs, Turks, Indians, Mongols, Chinese, Malays, and Africans.

Despite being a relative latecomer to intercontinental networks—or a return customer, given that contact had once existed between the Roman Empire and China—developments in medieval Europe after the eleventh century set the scene

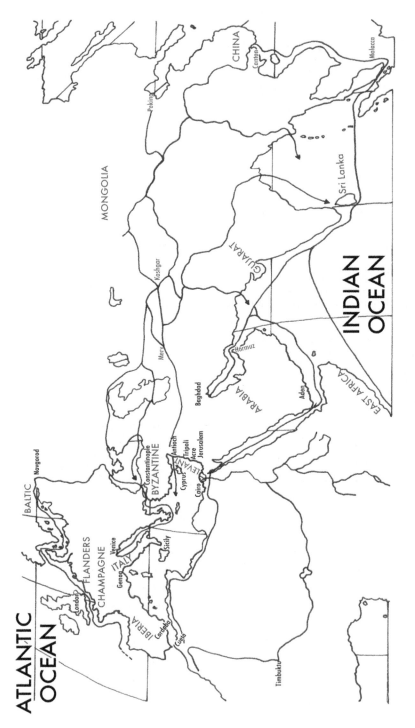

Figure 4.1. Map of Europe and its neighbors, ca. 1000–1400.

for the episodes of European colonization and contact around the globe after the fourteenth century, which we deal with in the remainder of this book.

Let us initially move forward in time to the end of the medieval era. Heralding eventual European influences around the world, three events in the first and last decades of the fifteenth century mark the beginnings of our modern "global" world. In 1402, Castilians from Spain established a colony in the Canary Islands where they conquered a native people previously unknown to Europeans. For the indigenous Canary Islanders, the results would be disastrous, for after many decades of resistance, they were effectively crushed by the Spanish. So began the century. At the end of the century, two dates stand out: Columbus's voyages of 1492 to the "New World" of the Americas, and Vasco da Gama's voyage to India around the southern extent of Africa in 1497. The multitude of cross-cultural exchanges in Asia, the Americas, Oceania, and Sub-Saharan Africa that derive from these events are considered in later chapters. But first we need to consider the centuries leading up to these dates. That is the intention of this chapter: how did Europe go from being a backwater in intercontinental trade to becoming the source of key protagonists in global commerce?

I want to begin by observing that by "medieval Europeans," I am specifically referring to Europeans of the Middle Ages after AD 1000 and up to the Renaissance, which began in Italy in the fourteenth century. The Renaissance, a renowned period of cultural florescence which heralded the end of the medieval era, was preceded by an earlier period of social revitalization in the eleventh to thirteenth centuries which marked some of the high achievements of the Middle Ages. These developments were due in part to culture contacts, as they were fueled by increasing contacts with the Islamic world and Byzantium that provided access to Greek and Arabic literature and various social and scientific developments.

The second point I must make is that there was no concept of "Europe" in these years; this was a region with vastly different societies, where the most important distinction was between Christendom and rest of the world. So, I speak here of "Europeans" as a geographical convenience.

CULTURE CONTACTS WITH MEDIEVAL EUROPE AFTER AD 1000

Given their limited geographical knowledge, medieval Europeans had vastly different ideas about the world outside of Europe than later generations would. To take an example from the dying days of the medieval period, Columbus's library included relatively informed accounts of Asia (Marco Polo's *Description of the World*, published in 1300) and quite fantastic accounts (John Mandeville's popular, derivative and apparently fictitious travel account, published after ca. 1357–1371). While in the Caribbean, believing himself to be in the West Indies or eastern Asia, Columbus wrote of his expectation, from Polo's account, to see the golden roofs of Japanese temples and to meet the Great Khan (although unbeknown to Columbus, by 1492 the Mongols had been replaced by the Ming Dynasty).

At the same time traveling toward Asia, but from the west, Vasco da Gama carried with him to India a letter from the Portuguese king to Prester John, a mythical Christian king who would have had to be several centuries old by 1497. My point is underscore how different perceptions of the world were from a medieval mind-set, something we need to take into account when considering how they interacted with other societies.

In this chapter, I examine aspects of culture contact in the early centuries of the millennium, including contact with the Islamic world, intercontinental trade, the origins of the form of plantation economy familiar in later centuries on other continents, and the colonization and conquest of the islands of the eastern Atlantic Ocean.

I briefly consider how Europeans encountered the broader world—that is, how Christendom defined itself in relation to its neighbors. At the start of the second millennium, there were several settings in which Europeans were in contact with others: the north Atlantic (chapter 3), the Iberian Peninsula (modern Portugal and Spain), Eastern Europe, and West Asia, where, from a European perspective, a "Latin East" was recreated during the Crusades.

After 1095, thousands of Europeans moved by foot, hoof, and sail to the eastern Mediterranean to create a great cross-cultural frontier between Europe and West Asia. The numbers in each of these episodes are very different: the Norse Atlantic colonists were measured in mere thousands; the Latins (also termed Franks) in Asia may have exceeded 200,000.

However, a focus on the Crusades potentially distorts the picture, for Europeans were rarely in control of these interactions. The bigger picture is of centuries of trade directed variously through Near Eastern, Egyptian, Turkish, Arab, and Mongol traders. From a European perspective, Islamic control of trade was particularly important, through Islamic Spain and other Muslim possessions in the Mediterranean. At times, the networks across the Muslim world would reach from Spain to the Malay Peninsula and into Central Asia, as shown in Muhammad al-Idrisi's *Tabula Rogeriana,* drawn for the Norman King Roger II in the mid-twelfth century (the name means "Book of Roger"). Roger's court in Palermo, Sicily, was inherently cross-cultural, bringing together a range of religions, nations, and ethnicities. The map reflects contemporary knowledge collected by the geographer and followed conventions laid down in Roman times by Ptolemy (Figure 4.2).

Today we may be more aware of past wars between Europe and parts of the Muslim world than of successful trade and exchange. The various campaigns

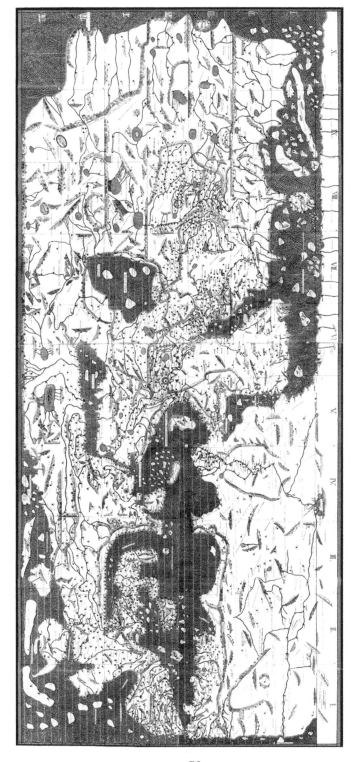

Figure 4.2. Muhammad al-Idrisi's *Tabula Rogeriana* (1154) drawn for King Roger II of Sicily, showing Arab knowledge of East and South Asia, Africa, and Europe.

waged by Europe against Muslims in these centuries include the Reconquista (reconquest) of the Iberian Peninsula by north Spanish and west European kingdoms, and the Crusades in the Near East which were a response to the arrival of the Seljuk Turks in West Asia and resulted in the establishment of feudal states in Asian Minor (modern Turkey and Syria) and the Levant (modern Israel and Palestine regions) for short periods in the twelfth and thirteenth centuries.[3] The Crusades, however, were also Church-sanctioned campaigns directed at various groups—Jews, slaves, Mongols, or, indeed, any enemies or perceived heretics.

For most Muslim and other non-European medieval-era societies, the rather localized Crusades were not a concern. Of far greater import was the rise of the Mongol Empire in the thirteenth century, extending from China to Russia and into southern and western Asia.

There are several issues raised in this chapter.

1. Most contact was not with foreigners but with foreign goods. High-value imports, such as spices, entered Europe through West Asia and Africa, similar to the ways they once had in ancient times.

2. From a European perspective, the idea of "otherness" was largely created along religious lines, as exemplified by the Crusades.

3. Much control of contact and trade lay outside of European hands. Intercontinental trade routes linking the Middle East to Africa and Asia were only accessible to Europeans (mainly Venetian and Genoese merchants) in settings in the Near East, Constantinople, and Cairo markets. This remained the case until the discoveries of alternate routes to Asia in the late fifteenth century. Trade and exchange mechanisms improved in the late twelfth century, and Europe and Asia were in contact, creating in the thirteenth century a greater "world economy" (really, Old World economy) that flourished for a century. This window was due to the period of Mongol dominance, termed "Pax Mongolica" by some scholars. This stability ended with the disintegration of Mongol rule and the impact of the bubonic plague (the Black Death) originating in Asia in the mid-fourteenth century.

4. Many medieval accomplishments occurred first in the Arab world or China, and eventually through contact contributed to European agriculture, architecture, the arts and sciences, medicine, navigation, and mathematics.

5. High-value monocrops came to be grown in the Mediterranean in the medieval era, such as sugar, which established the plantation model of produc-

tion in Europe. This mode of production and labor relationship was new, and laid the basis for European colonization/invasion of a range of inhabited and uninhabited places, from Atlantic islands to Africa and the Caribbean.

6. Of some significance was the growth in the use of slaves, an ancient practice of inequity, to work in plantations and assist colonization episodes.

7. In the fifteenth century, there were other theaters of European colonization on islands of the eastern Atlantic and on the North African coast. In the colonization of the Canary Islands, we see the conquest of indigenous islanders by Castilians; thus, the eastern Atlantic islands, both occupied and unoccupied, offer us an early example of biological and cultural consequences of colonization predating the colonization of the Americas.

DEFINING AND DESCRIBING EUROPE

What was Europe in these centuries? Perhaps the best way to define Europe is along cultural, rather than physical lines. There was no Europe in 1000 as we understand it today: an eventually unified set of social and cultural traditions, a set of agreements between nation-states, and agreement over certain principles of governance and politics. A more meaningful separation for much of the second millennium would be between Christendom and everyone else. Thus Latin Europe (particularly modern Italy and France) and Byzantium were very significant regions. Constantinople, as the ancient eastern capital of the Roman Empire, had maintained the idea of Christendom in the East, although there were two poles of Christianity by the thirteenth century, and the Western church was in ascendancy over Byzantium after the Latins sacked Constantinople in the Fourth Crusade.

After 1000, Europe saw new developments in relationships between the church and the populace—both elite and non-elite—and eventually a greater demarcation between secular and sacred aspects of medieval and post-medieval societies. Many people living in Europe would have identified themselves—beyond their local allegiances—as perhaps living within someone's realm, and as affiliated with the Christian church, of which there were an array of medieval variants, the dominant being the Catholic Church, although Celtic and Orthodox religions were significant.

Key developments at this time were the improved trade and manufacture of goods. The small trading emporia of the first millennium were replaced by larger settings for trade, such as regular fairs capitalizing on growing local, regional, and long-distance trade and the ability of elites to control the trade. These networks are visible archaeologically in the distribution of traded goods: for example, ceramics, distinctive stone tools (such as querns from Scandinavia), metal decorative items, and glasswares. The discovery of traded luxury goods such as Chinese porcelain reveals the reach of these networks. In addition to these, the Crusades saw greater access to silk and other exotic textiles, as described in historical sources.

Trade reunited Western Europe along its north–south axis and invigorated the European subsystem of the larger "world trade system" that incorporated East, Central, South, and West Asia, and North and East Africa—the European component was particularly vibrant leading up to 1250–1350. In this scenario, parts of Europe came into contact with one another over these centuries, as well as increasingly in contact with the East and the goods that moved through the Old World system.

The early medieval period, once popularly termed "the Dark Ages," came to pass in northwestern Europe after AD 1000, when there was a population boom and greater urbanization. Feudal territories became integrated, and the extent of trade and exchange increased. One consequence of the greater wealth was the capital to support the First Crusade at the end of the eleventh century and then later crusades.

The Dark Ages experienced in northwest Europe had not been as dim in Italy. The primary center of Europe immediately after 1000 was, as it had been for millennia, the Mediterranean, around which a history of civilized communities had long existed, and which acted as a conduit for movement of goods, people, and ideas. The Italian port cities of Venice and Genoa, and to a lesser extent Pisa, developed as merchant and naval forces to rival opponents in the "Arab Sea" and to access trade in Egypt, the Levantine coast, and the Black Sea. Their fierce competition with others and each other, and the profitability of their trade, were accompanied by innovations in business, the movement and management of capital, maritime technology, navigation, and warfare.

In the early millennium, we can think of trade and contacts along east–west and north–south axes. Venice and Genoa were the key southern centers for trade: their ships moved goods from east to west from their trade particularly with the Levantine ports, Byzantium, and Cairo. Improved connections along Europe's north–south axis were driven by the rise of markets and manufacture in the northwest of Europe (in modern France and Belgium), as detailed below.

Europe is small compared with Asia or the Americas and was linked by overland transport routes, by rivers, and by sea travel over the challenging North Sea. Infrastructure for travel and communication was basic; most transport was by foot and horse, although dedicated infrastructure such as canals and bridges were being established—or reestablished for the first time since the Romans.[4] This met the growing demand, fueled in part by trade, for towns and ports to be in communication, and allowed the movement of people, as seen during the various Crusades.

The time of the Crusades furthered knowledge of the wider world and accompanied growth in manufacturing, agriculture, and commerce in northwestern Europe. This is described in detail in Janet Abu-Lughod's excellent *Before European Hegemony: The World System A.D. 1250–1350*. She describes a European system where the key elements occur around the Flemish cities of Bruges and Ghent; the Champagne fair towns of Lagny, Provins, Troyes, of Bar-sur-Aube; and the Italian ports of Venice and Genoa. In France, regular market fairs increased contacts with the East and demand for goods; in Flanders, this continued in increasingly urban settings as a focus of commerce and industrial manufacture.

The ability to move goods by sea improved in the early second millennium. Dock facilities also allowed for more efficient movement of goods, as seen in harbors at London, Lübeck, Bergen, Venice, Genoa, and Pisa. Additionally, while there are written accounts of this, there is also archaeological evidence. In Scandinavia, for example, archaeologically investigated ships give us evidence of larger cargo vessels, such as the Skuldev I ship (ca. AD 1030, 24 tons of cargo), the Hedeby 3 (ca. 1025) and Lynæs I (ca. 1140, both 60 tons of cargo), and the Bergen ship (ca. 1187, 120 tons of cargo). This substantial improvement resulted from better shipbuilding and use of wind propulsion by a variety of maritime traders, particularly the Italians, as such vessels allowed for ocean travel between the Italian ports and northern Europe.[5] Larger vessels were also built in response to the increased amount of trade made possible following the establishment of colonial outposts in the Levant after the Crusades.

From the start of the millennium, and indeed earlier, the Mediterranean world was engaged in constant naval warfare. The piracy that characterized sea travel plagued shipping from the Italian city ports. To travel safely meant to travel in convoy. In the Mediterranean, a combination of small and larger sailing vessels moved most trade; these ships appeared to have been rigged to allow for greater maneuverability in skirmishes.

Transport was possibly a key factor in the success of the Flemish: in France, the sites of trading emporia and associated manufacturing declined after the mid-fourteenth century, yet the North Sea ports of Flanders fared better. Flemish merchants imported English wool to manufacture textiles for trade, along with iron and bronze. Italian merchants were increasingly able to sail the North Sea to access these ports, thus linking Flanders effectively into wider trade networks.

As economic activity grew, so did the money market; local mints grew up, with coinage being a key line of material evidence for commerce and its spatial organization. It is in the international trade, however, that we see long-distance exchange of valuable commodities clearly.

One of the largest impacts on this era was the massive demographic collapse of the mid-fourteenth century. Trade meant contact: one key aspect of cultures in contact is the effect of diseases. The most significant disease of these centuries in Europe was the Black Death (1347–1351, and then recurring in various plagues), which was apparently a direct result of trade between Europe and Asia, as the bubonic plague possibly arrived in the bodies of fleas on rats on merchant vessels. The disease appears to have arisen in East Asia, and epidemics ripped through the trade towns and cities engaged in international trade between China and Europe. Somewhere over a third of Europeans were killed, and the disease changed the course of European demography.

Similarly, Europe was also a biological zone where key pathogens developed, particularly in urban environments. As Alfred Crosby demonstrates in his book *Ecological Imperialism: The Biological Expansion of Europe, 900–1900*, as happened with the Black Death, when people left Europe they took not only their plants and animals, but also their diseases unwittingly concocted in the laboratories of medieval urban settlements.

THE USES AND ORIGINS OF IMPORTED LUXURIES

As we can see, there was in medieval Europe from 1000 increased demand for luxuries made exotic by distance and unfamiliarity, and the means through trade to access these goods. Some items were possibly more familiar, such as textiles, and others less so—the narwhal's tusk from Arctic waters was thought to be of a unicorn. Mummified corpses from Egypt were crushed down for their medicinal values. Ambergris from the heads of sperm whales came from mythical ocean animals.

The trade of items from foreign lands was well organized, and a wide range of goods moved through trade networks. In 1192, King Richard captured a merchant caravan while on Crusade in the Holy Land, reporting "mules loaded with spices of different kinds, and of great value; gold and silver; cloaks of silk; purple and scarlet robes, arms and weapons; coats of mail, . . . a large quantity of conserves and medicines; basins, bladders, chess-boards; silver dishes and candle sticks; pepper, cinnamon, sugar, and wax; . . . an immense sum of money, and an incalculable quantity of goods."[6]

From Africa came ivory, timber, slaves, exotic animals and their products such as feathers, and sub-Saharan gold. Silver coins, slaves, furs, and amber flowed down rivers from Russia to Constantinople. From East and Central Asia came spices, silk, textiles, and ceramics, porcelain being particularly valuable. From India, the region of Gujarat traded textiles, metals, raw materials (silk and cotton), horses, and some foodstuffs; while the eastern Malabar coastal ports were also active in international trade. India was a source of spices, dyes, oils, honey, ivory, and narcotics, and acted as intermediary in traded goods from elsewhere.

Spices were valued for their flavor, perfume, and medicinal values. The aromatic value of spices alleviated the many intruding odors of medieval Europe, emanating from sewage, sweat, animals, and smoke.[7] Herbs, too, had medical values and were used in food, yet being available in Europe, were not as expensive and valuable as imported spices.

Some information about the uses of spices comes from descriptions of meals and recipes. A recipe for spiced wine from *Curye on Inglysch* required cinnamon, ginger, grains of paradise, long pepper (not related to black pepper), cloves, nutmeg, caraway, spikenard, galangale, and sugar or honey.[8] Recipes between the thirteenth and fifteenth centuries nearly all contain spices, with typically twenty spices used.

Medieval concepts of spices encompassed a wide range of imported aromatic substances, not all technically spices by our contemporary understanding. Being expensive, they were typically sold in small amounts. Sugar, while not an aromatic, was considered a spice, at least until plantations increased production to make it more available. A Florentine commercial manual of spices produced in 1340 by Francesco Pegolotti lists 193 substances; however, many of these were nonperishable imports such as wax.[9] Even so, the wide range of substances included common spices: black pepper, cinnamon, ginger, saffron, nutmeg, cloves, as well as galangale, zedoary, and grains of paradise (a West African plant).

Spices were an essential part of medieval life, and not merely for elites. When the flagship of Henry VIII's navy, the *Mary Rose*, sank in 1545 while engaging the French, nearly 400 crew died. When rediscovered by archaeologists, some were shown to have carried private supplies of peppercorns, possibly for flavoring as well as for their commercial value.

In medieval Europe, spices were a means of visible consumption across social classes. There were quite strict ideas of food and status, so that some foods (uncooked fruit, root vegetables) were not high-status foods, while game, meat, and elaborate confectionaries were. Medieval concepts of health also involved spices: certain substances were considered either hot and dry, or warm and wet, and were suitable for different types of people and their ailments.

Spices had medicinal value. Licorice, for example, was used for coughs. Pegolotti lists quite exotic substances, such as the scrapings of chimneys from Alexandria (*tutty*), and *momia* from the heads and spines of mummified corpses (preferably foul-smelling), used to prevent bleeding. Frankincense, ambergris, musk, and civet were fragrant perfumes with medicinal properties. During the horror of the Black Death, aromatic substances were used for protection, ambergris apparently being particularly effective.[10] Others substances were valued as aphrodisiacs.

EUROPEAN KNOWLEDGE OF FOREIGN REGIONS

The spice trade was ancient and its products highly valued. This value underlay the intercontinental trade networks. For most Europeans, the sources of spices remained vague. In medieval Christian thinking, spices were thought to originate from, or grow near, Paradise; in many accounts, the Garden of Eden was located outside of Europe, often in the East. Rivers were considered to flow from Paradise, requiring some tricky hydrography and geography as knowledge of the Nile, Tigris, Euphrates, and Indian rivers developed. This idea was reinforced by the fact that most gems at this time came from Indian rivers, while it was believed that aloe wood fell into rivers in Paradise to be transported downstream for collection.[11] The real story behind this very mystical geography is that India sat in the middle of the Eurasian trade network that linked peripheries such as Europe indirectly to key Asian spice producers.

The harvesters of pepper, mace, nutmeg, and other goods in Asia remained largely beyond the medieval world. Perhaps they would have diminished the attraction of exotic substances, in the same way accounts of the human suffering behind some African diamonds detracts from the satisfaction of purchasing expensive jewelry. The accounts of Marco Polo's travels, and of other travelers, were exceptions, providing gripping stories of the Orient for Europe until the links were again closed in the fifteenth century.

Marco Polo's father and uncle, Venetian merchants too, had previously traveled to the court of the Mongol Emperor of the recently conquered China. The Italians set off to return to China in 1271, this time with Marco, who would later describe his travels in *Description of the World*. Their route followed a key overland trade road from Palestine, through Iran and Afghanistan, into China, to the capital near modern Beijing. His return, decades later, was by the sea route, visiting the Malay Peninsula, modern Indonesia, Sri Lanka, India, the Persian Gulf, and then overland to the Black Sea and Constantinople.

Marco Polo is not famous for being the first to travel these routes but for his published account, which he dictated to a cell-mate while in an Italian jail. Not everyone initially believed his account of the Mongol dynasty and seventeen years spent in the court of the Khubilai Khan. In fact, when Marco Polo eventually returned to Italy, children on the street mocked him as a liar, and his accounts were only widely accepted later.

As with China, European knowledge of India improved by the fourteenth century, but it too remained a largely mystical location, perceived as the source of spices, precious gems, gold, and fantastic animals.

The medieval European concepts of the occupants of exotic lands are significant, serving as a baseline for eventual culture contact. Ideas of people in the East were particularly influenced by Pliny's *Natural History*, whose fantastic human and other creatures are found in medieval accounts. These include humans such as pygmies and cannibals, and more fantastic creatures such as those with the heads of dogs, or only one leg, or lacking a head.[12]

While peculiar to us today, these were important ideas, for early travelers felt they would meet these creatures. The idea of headless humans, for example, dated to Pliny but was still perpetuated by Sir Walter Raleigh in his accounts of South America in the sixteenth century. Maps of the late medieval period are populated with fantastic creatures, such as monsters and Amazons (Figure 4.3).[13]

Fascination with cannibalism has been particularly enduring. Even in the European Enlightenment, cannibalism remained a significant issue in cross-cultural encounters. In the late 1700s, the issue of whether Maoris and other Pacific peoples were cannibals would plague James Cook and his crew in the Pacific. Many nineteenth- and twentieth-century accounts of native peoples included—as a necessary marketing tool!—references to cannibals (along with head hunters).[14]

Clearly, given the importance of religion in medieval Europe, most foreign lands were perceived as home to infidels or pagans, but with such exceptions as the legend of a great Christian King named Prester John who ruled many minor kings, originating in the eleventh century. Initially Prester John was located in India, then Ethiopia; however, the location of both these places was inexactly understood by medieval Europeans. His kingdom was said to be occupied by riches, spices, and exotic things, including a range of semi-human creatures as well as Amazons and centaurs. These were fantastic yet powerful ideas—perhaps now it seems easier to comprehend why da Gama carried a letter to Prester John with him to India.[15]

However, not all accounts were sensational. When the Franciscan missionary John of Marignolli visited India and China ca. 1353, he describes the Indian pepper harvest quite sensibly.[16]

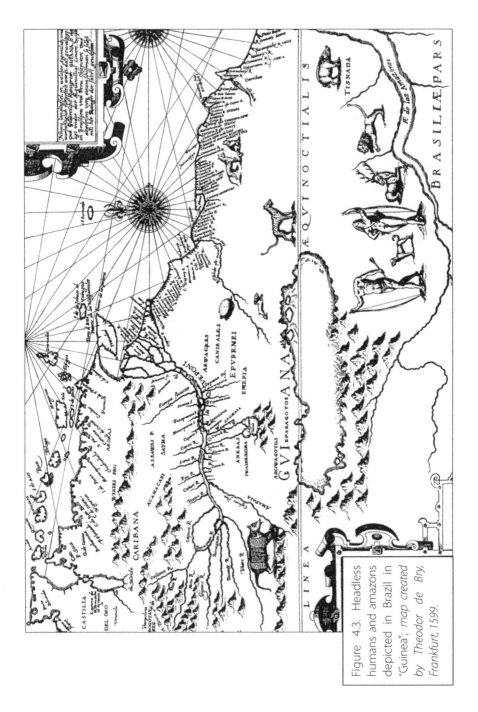

Figure 4.3. Headless humans and amazons depicted in Brazil in "Guinea"; map created by Theodor de Bry, Frankfurt, 1599.

EUROPEAN TRADE

Goods from China and India, Southeast Asia, and Africa moved through the entrepôts of the eastern Mediterranean, particularly Constantinople, Alexandria, and the Levant. Inasmuch as imports derived from Middle Eastern markets, these were the primary intermediaries between Europe and the rest of the world.

The key European entry points were through the Italian merchants, who reigned supreme until sidelined by the Portuguese discovery of a sea route to the Indian Ocean and the Spanish discovery of America.

The Italians traded through the Crusader sites, Egypt, and Constantinople. With the successful military campaigns of the Seljuk Turks in the late twelfth century, the Crusaders were increasingly forced from the Levantine region, and eventually the extraordinary leader Saladin retook Jerusalem in 1187. Only a few European colonies survived, at least for a time, and Constantinople and Cairo became a greater focus for trade, along with Crete, Cyprus, and Rhodes.

The second half of the thirteenth century saw the Mongols sweep out of Central Asia (ca. 1240–1360). Using their horses for rapid warfare, they seized northern China, attacked Muslim centers, destroying Baghdad (1258), and invaded Russia and Eastern Europe in the 1240s. Europe was not as attractive as China, the greatest civilization in the medieval world; thus, the threat receded from Europe. Negotiations to form an alliance between Europe and the Mongols against Muslim polities, and expectations for Christian conversion of Mongols, never went anywhere.

With the nodal city Baghdad destroyed, the caravan trade between Baghdad and the Levant largely collapsed. Egyptian forces prevented the further expansion of Mongol forces and provided Cairo the means to dominate the Indian Ocean trade—and forever frustrate any Italian ambition to expand beyond the Mediterranean. Under "Pax Mongolica," the Silk Road westward into Crimean and Black Sea ports where Italian merchants were established was improved, and trade intensified.

During these years, a handful of European merchants and adventurers came to visit and reside in Persia, Central Asia, China, and India, such as Marco Polo. Improved knowledge of Asia was revolutionary, the most important aspect being geographical (particularly the location of India and China), the existence of the islands in Southeast Asia that were the source of spices, and the organization of the trade routes. Thus, two routes rose to dominance: the Central Asia overland route ending at the Black Sea and Constantinople, and the sea route across the Indian Ocean ending in the Red Sea/Arabian Peninsula and delivering goods to Cairo.

Abu-Lughod describes these various routes of the medieval trade network.[17] The northern route opened by the Mongols in 1250 across Central Asia was closed at the end of the fourteenth century, making a repeat of Polo's journey impossible. A "middle route" continued from Baghdad across Persia (Iran) via Samarkand to China or into northern India. This route was quickest by boat down the Persian Gulf into the Indian Ocean and along the coast to Gujarat (an Indian state) where the main trade ports were located. This route, however, was partially sundered with the fall of Baghdad in 1258. The third route was a southern course across the Indian Ocean, the western terminus being controlled by Egypt at the throat of the Red Sea—this route saw Cairo prosper, particularly from the thirteenth to the fifteenth century.

Historical sources describe voyages within the Mediterranean from European to African and Levantine ports. The archaeological finds of ships in Mediterranean waters illustrate that coastal routes were favored between these ports and Italy. Maritime archaeological finds detail individual voyages rudely terminated. For example, the Serçe Limani vessel sank in ca. 1024 off Turkey with a cargo of scrap glass to be recycled; this vessel suggests trade between the Byzantine Empire and the Fatimid Caliphate in Egypt.[18]

As is the case in parts of the East African coast today, the threat of piracy was real and expensive. As fleets were required to offset the risk, a large part of the cost of trade (and thus goods) was from carrying arms and sufficient men to fight, as well as through lost cargoes and vessels.

A lost ship is a potential boon for archaeologists: we know of trade through archaeological shipwrecks, and through the discovery of traded items that survive, such as coins and pottery. The distribution of containers used to transport goods demonstrates the ways that items such as wine were traded. Indirect evidence suggests the use of more archaeologically invisible materials, such as metal ores, salt, sugar, spices, textiles, wood, wines, and meat. For example, infrastructures like salt works, and sugar plantations indicate market demand for specific products—salt was, like spices, very valuable, and few places existed for its easy production.

With the decline of the Crusader Latin states along the Levantine coast in modern Syria, Turkey, Lebanon, Israel, and Cyprus, Byzantium remained a significant interface between Europe and Asia. The well-traveled twelfth-century pilgrim Benjamin of Tudela described Constantinople and Baghdad—until it fell to the Mongols (below)—as the two greatest commercial centers in the world. Other contemporary trade cities were Córdoba in Spain and Cairo in Egypt.

With the demise of the Mongol Empire, the opportunity for international travel by Europeans receded, and the heavy curtain fell between Europe and Asia, only to be lifted again by the Portuguese when they arrived in India at the end of the fifteenth century. I say "arrived" rather than "discovered" because they already knew of India; what they discovered was that you can get there via a southern route and that the Indian Ocean was open and not a landlocked sea, as suggested in earlier medieval maps.

Interestingly, they arrived at a time when any potential resistance was diminished, at least as compared with the previous century: Indian maritime power had waned, and the withdrawal of the navy of the Chinese superpower was complete by 1430, leaving a small fleet of Mamluk and Gujarati boats to protect Arab-Indian interests and deal with a Portuguese fleet whose program of violence and forced compulsion heralded a new way of doing business in the Indian Ocean.[19]

EUROPE AND THE MUSLIM WORLD

Medieval Islam stretched from the Iberian Peninsula to Southeast Asia along the axis of northern Africa, Arabia, and India. Being at the center of Old World trade networks, its cities acted as markets for goods from Asia, India, Africa, and Europe. A shared language, religion, and currency underlay intercontinental commerce networks that existed at the periphery of Europe.

With the fragmentation of the Islamic world into subregions, in the tenth century Cairo increasingly became an essential city for trade, with other markets in West Asia (Damascus and Aleppo), the western Mediterranean (Tunis, Seville, and Córdoba), and the Middle East (Baghdad).

Here I consider the evidence in Spain, and then sites related to the Crusades; these have been subject to archaeological study for over a century. I return to the topic in chapter 8 when I consider the archaeology of Islam in island Southeast Asia.

Iberian Peninsula Contacts

Islam on the Iberian Peninsula dates back to the eighth century: its Arabic name was al-Andalus. In the ninth century, al-Andalus was established as an emirate rivaling Baghdad. Migrants to al-Andalus comprised Arabs from northern and southern Arabia and Syria, as well as North Africans, particularly Berbers. These ethnic groups were characterized by tribalism, although in al-Andalus this trait appears to have diminished in importance by the turn of the millennium.[20]

Archaeological analyses of Islamic contexts have compared the Iberian Peninsula with nearby Morocco. Evidence comes from analyzed historic structures, archaeological ceramics, fortified settlements, evidence for water infrastructure, and urban settlements.[21] Córdoba was particularly important as the greatest center for learning and commerce.

Al-Andalus was in conflict with Christian kingdoms from its inception, and sporadic warfare characterized the subsequent centuries. The recapture of the peninsula involved a complicated series of battles—with some times of peace—known as the Reconquista, a process that took on much of the ideology of the Crusades. Further pressure saw the fall of Toledo (in 1085), triggering the involvement of North African Muslims in an Iberian war that became increasingly religious. Al-Andalus broke into smaller Muslim kingdoms (*taifas*) following the capture of Córdoba and the disintegration of the caliphate there in 1236. Lacking central authority, the *taifas* paid tribute to Christian kingdoms to the north, notably of León and Castile. After the capture of Córdoba, only the Emirate of Granada remained, until it surrendered in 1492.

Not surprisingly, then, fortifications were an important part of the cross-cultural landscape, and hilltop fortifications (*husun*) were increasingly popular from the eleventh century.[22] In a survey of castles, villages, and irrigation in Al-Andalus, it appears that fortified habitation played a role in the social stability and organization of the local landholders, in both Muslim and Christian eras.[23]

As migrants to al-Andalus were Arabs and North Africans, this led to regional differences across al-Andalus, which also included Christian and Jewish communities. The transition toward Arabic lifeways seems to have occurred more quickly than conversion to Islam, which appears to have been a slower process until the tenth century.[24] There were many significant developments in al-Andalus, in philosophy and learning, medicine, the sciences, geography, economics, agriculture, technical infrastructure (wind and water mills), and water supply.

The popular monuments of these times are found in architecture, particularly religious buildings. In 786, the first congregational mosque in al-Andalus was erected in Córdoba and became especially renowned. Before that, Christians and Muslims had worshiped in the existing cathedral, with Christians to the east and Muslims to the south. Other large mosques were built in Seville, Toledo, and Saragossa, while smaller mosques were attached to castles and villages. Most required conversion of an existing church to a mosque by "changing the axis and direction of prayer."[25]

House design derives from social differences. Muslim houses tended to be closed off and very private. The only openings onto the street were through doors, not windows, while light was offered through a central courtyard (*patio*) as a central space. Muslim houses appear to have had a separate kitchen.[26] The hearths of Muslim houses tended to be more varied and substantial than in Christian houses in al-Andalus.

In addition to architecture, culture change and practice are measurable through foodways—for example, through archaeological food remains and ceramics, food preparation and consumption are illustrated. In al-Andalus, differences between Muslim and Christian contexts are detectable. Certainly both ate domesticated animals, popularly cattle, sheep, goat, and pig for Christians, and sheep and goat, cattle, and bird species for Muslims. Christians, particularly elites, preferred game. Bone remains reflect different cultural practices, for the way they were cut derives from religious and social preferences. Vegetable foods seem to have been consumed in similar ways across Christian and Muslim communities. Prepared food highlights various preferences—for example, elites had more elaborate and varied meals and greater access to spices. For most people, the popular stew *olla* served.

Water in Iberia was precious. Clean water was prepared through disinfecting red ocher earth (*almagra*). Structures were used to collect, route, and store water: these irrigation and distribution systems were similar to those throughout the Islamic world and would be used by later Spanish colonists in the Canary Islands and the Americas.

Interestingly, the evidence from various sources, including detailed land registers called the *Llibres del Repartiment* (which, like the *Domesday Book*, documented the cross-cultural transfer of landscape in a medieval setting), allows us to interpret the transition from Muslim to Christian worlds in Spain. There are iconic transitions, the most commonly referenced being the conversion of mosques to churches. However, even as the social landscape changed, some things remained—the extraordinary system of irrigation and water allocation was, perhaps unsurprisingly, left in place. Spanish culture today reflects these diverse cultural influences.

The Crusades

In Asia, the decline of Byzantine Constantinople and centuries of friction between Arab Muslims was the setting for the Crusades. These were a series of military campaigns waged by medieval Christian polities in Europe against Muslims, as well as communities both "internal" and "external" to the Church, including Jews, Cathars, various Christians including Greek and Russian Orthodox faiths, and Mongols.

The First Crusade was initiated in 1097 to "redeem" Christianity in the East—drawing umbrage from 1009 when the Church of the Holy Sepulcher in Jerusalem was destroyed. The forces of the First Crusade were able to establish Crusader Latin states; however, these were relatively short-lived.

The Crusades were configured as religious, but enveloped territorial and commercial ambitions, as expressed by early twentieth-century archaeologist C. N. Johns: "Yet in the Holy Land itself the actual result was colonization on lines that anticipated the settlement of more remote parts of the globe in later centuries by merchant venturers, landless aristocrats, or chartered companies."[27] Many of the migrating population for colonies were French, while the Second Crusade was dominated by Normans. In Arabic, their name meant "European."[28]

The First Crusade was particularly significant for the Siege of Antioch, which eventually fell to the Lombards (1098). The non-Christian population was murdered or fled, and the mosques destroyed. Similarly, Jerusalem fell in 1099. These events cast a sharp relief between Christian and Muslim and Jewish communities. This distinction, however, masks the multi-ethnic qualities of these settings, where it may not have been clear to people on the street who was (or was not) "European"—in fact, they may not have thought of identity in these terms at all. Islamic and other historical sources describe the complexity of cross-cultural contacts. The following account by Usmah Ibn Munqidh distinguishes between Franks who acclimatized to Palestine and more recent arrivals.

[W]e came to the home of a knight who belonged to the old category of knights who came with the early expeditions of the Franks. He had been by that time stricken off the register and exempted from service, and possessed in Antioch an estate on the income of which he lived. The knight presented an excellent table, with food extraordinarily clean and delicious. Seeing me abstaining from food, he said, "Eat, be of good cheer! I never eat Frankish dishes, but I have Egyptian women cooks and never eat except their cooking. Besides, pork never enters my home." I ate, but guardedly, and after that we departed. As I was passing in the market place, a Frankish woman all of a sudden hung to my clothes and began to mutter words in their language, and I could not understand what she was saying. This made me immediately the center of a big crowd of Franks. I was convinced that death was at hand. But all of a sudden that same knight approached. On seeing me, he came and said to that woman, "What is the matter between you and this Muslim?" She replied, "This is he who has killed my brother Hurso." This Hurso was a knight in Afiimiyah who was killed by someone of the army of Hamah. The Christian knight shouted at her, saying, "This is a bourgeois (i.e., a merchant) who neither fights nor attends a fight." He also yelled at the people who had assembled, and they all dispersed. Then he took me by the hand and went away. Thus the effect of that meal was my deliverance from certain death.[29]

The Crusader states were feudal kingdoms run by hundreds of knights over their fiefs. Castles were used to maintain their hold over the local populations and displaced rulers. Courts for the Crusader nobility, merchants, and townspeople were separated from, and maintained superiority over, indigenous populations of Muslims, Jews, and Greek Christians.

The study of the physical remnants of these events has largely focused on the Crusader castles, although for a long time there was little interest in Crusader monuments of the eleventh, twelfth, and thirteenth centuries; later European visitors were more likely to note Roman antiquities than those of Lombards.[30] Medieval sites tended to be the subject of art historians, not archaeologists, until after the mid-twentieth century.[31]

The various Crusader castles and fortifications provide some limited insight into medieval Near Eastern and European military techniques and reflect an antagonistic cross-cultural landscape, from which the European invaders were eventually repelled.[32] The Crusaders encountered fortified cities in the Holy Land, such as at Jerusalem, Tyre, and Aleppo. These places repelled the sieges for a time. The walls of Cairo were also substantially rebuilt prior to the Crusades, though not for defensive purposes.[33] Small castles (*qasr*) also existed in the Levant.

In Europe, castles were significant military installations, while also being residences, administrative centers, and physical demonstrations of power and legitimacy. Western European castles at the time of the First Crusade included motte and bailey, and enclosure castles, or used elevated parts of the natural terrain in their defense. In the East, castles were primarily military in function, the apogee represented by the Crac des Chevaliers, built from 1142 to 1271 in what is now Syria.[34] There was a wide array of Crusader sites, and most were not as elaborate as Crac. Many other fortifications were simple, such as a keep to control a local village, or made use of existing structures. The construction techniques in many fortified sites are a testament to the importance of these structures, many of which were under siege and changed hands more than once.

Beyond the insight into the military campaigns and activities of Europeans in the Levant, at first glance it appears these places demonstrate little about their cross-cultural aspects, other than the ambitions and security concerns of conquerors and defenders.[35] However, Oriental elements were taken up by the Crusaders, such as long, vaulted galleries in the baileys, doglegged entrance corridors, and machicolations (slots from which to drop items onto attackers) and pierced battlements.[36] Crusaders in the Levant also used existing local fortifications: some were already ancient, such as those at Antioch and Constantinople. However, many of these older forts were vast and unsuited for dealing with aspects of modern siege warfare.

Other fortifications indicate the influence of Armenians, who had been architects of fortifications for centuries—for example, the fortifications of Edessa. The Armenians tended to build castles on rocky ridges or outcrops, with a curtain wall making use of any cliffs, and round towers along the wall with arrow slots to allow projectile fire along the face of the walls.[37]

Some medieval sites regularly changed hands. To take an example from modern Lebanon, the Franks captured the fortifications at Qal'at al-Shaqif in 1139 and renamed the castle Beaufort (Figure 4.4). They built a castle of masonry and defensive elements typical of Crusader style, including a donjon (keep), a bailey with a cut-masonry arched entrance protected by a machicolation. Covered areas were intended to provide protection from the projectiles hurled during attacks, while a trench was cut to create a reservoir to keep siege engines back. In 1190, Beaufort was captured by Muslims, recaptured by the Franks in 1240, and then taken by Muslims in 1268.[38] (More recently, the castle has been separately held by the Palestine Liberation Organization and the Israeli Defense Forces, and has been damaged by shelling and rocket fire in modern battles.)

Muslim defenses were built in response to the Crusades. These included improved existing fortifications at Antioch and Aleppo as well as new castles, such as Ajlun in northern Jordan.[39] Muslim fortifications often deliberately lacked the large round towers seen in Crusader castles like Margat and Crac; likewise absent were the concentric castle design and use of inner and outer walls. The purpose of this design was to keep engineers and catapults away from the inner defenses. Another difference is that Crusader castles were designed as residences for knights, with halls, chambers, and chapels. By contrast, the Muslims fortified urban settlements that were used during sieges; otherwise the defenders probably lived in the surrounding town.

In addition to fortified sites, ecclesiastical sites have been carefully studied. Churches and cathedrals were rebuilt along styles then dominant in Italy. If buildings were not redesigned, they were redecorated: the basilica of the Nativity at Bethlehem was decorated with images of Western saints such as St. George and King Canute, St. Anthony of Egypt, and St. Leonard of France. Reflecting a moment of compromise between the Roman and Greek churches, the inscriptions were in Greek and Latin.[40] Other infrastructure existed to safeguard traveling pilgrims: hospices, monasteries, stables, and houses.

One focus of research has been the sites of various military orders that were active defenders of the Latin States—the Hospitallers, Templars, Teutonic Knights, Leper Knights of St. Lazarus, and the Knights of St. Thomas. These orders were responsible for fortifications, hospitals (in Jerusalem and Acre), trade, urban developments and administration, small industries such as glassworks, and rural properties, including sugar plantations, particularly during the twelfth and thirteenth centuries.

In urban settings like Acre and Jerusalem, Jews and Muslims would have used the hospitals, while rural infrastructure like mills remained in use in post-Crusader times.[41] Continuity in such circumstances should be expected, as seen with the adoption of many Islamic innovations in the Mediterranean and the Iberian Peninsula.

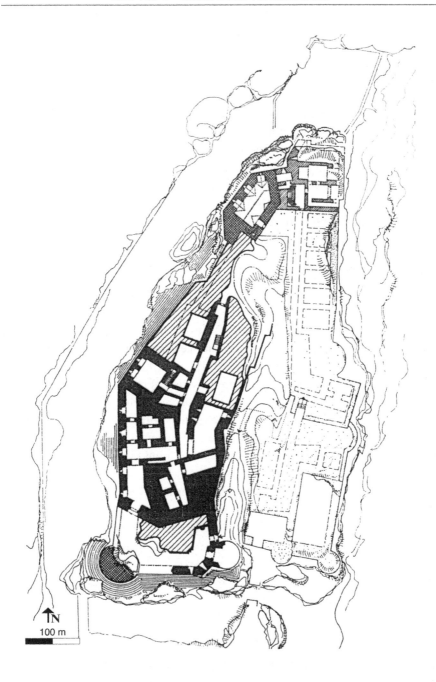

Figure 4.4. Beaufort: plan. Crusader work is in black, Arab work crosshatched (*adapted from Kennedy 1994: fig. 3*).

Later Crusades

The Second Crusade began with Christian successes, such as the capture of Lisbon from Muslims in 1147, and ended with the failed Frankish attempt to take Damascus in 1148. There were several other crusades. The Third Crusade (1189–1192) responded to the recapture of Jerusalem from the Crusaders by Saladin (in 1187). Cyprus was taken from the Byzantines to become a major base for later Crusader settlement and military operations. Jerusalem remained in Muslim control, although Richard I negotiated access for Christian pilgrims.

The Fourth Crusade (1202–1204) was designed to consolidate Christian control in Palestine, yet instead sacked Constantinople.

Crusades in the thirteenth century were conducted in Spain, in the Baltic, as well as in the eastern Mediterranean where, at the end of the century, many Crusader strongholds fell to the Muslims.

These activities allow us to make a final observation regarding the Crusades—namely, that they influenced the European explorations in Africa and the Americas during the fifteenth century. This is clear when considering Prince Henry the Navigator, a key figure in fifteenth-century Portuguese exploration and colonization who directed Portuguese efforts toward Africa and beyond. Henry backed explorations of Africa for many reasons, expressing his desire to locate Christian settlements, assess Muslim strengths, and rout Muslim traders. The Muslim city of Ceuta was a North African trading port conquered in 1415 under Henry's urging. Today it is a Spanish city (a souvenir from 1580 when the Spanish seized the Portuguese throne) and a European Union outpost in North African Morocco.

The idea of being conquerors for Christ certainly characterized Spanish and Portuguese colonization and invasion, even though the colonization of the New World was not an official crusade. While religion was important to the Spanish and Portuguese, it would be less so for powers from northern Europe, such as the Dutch and English whose interests were more singularly focused on profit, nationalism, and territory. This becomes clear when considering differences in European colonization in the Americas (chapters 6 and 7).

SLAVE LABOR

I introduce the topic of slave labor here because slavery and unfree labor were a significant element of culture contact in medieval and early modern times. Slavery is a practice with ancient roots that continues into the present. Slavery is perhaps best known today from the transatlantic slave trade when, over a period between the fifteenth and twentieth centuries, at least eleven million enslaved Africans were transported to the New World by European societies (see chapter 5).

In terms of the formation of a global interrelated community, one of the most significant issues to European activities in this millennium is organized slavery. While regional networks of trade had existed prior to the Atlantic trade, the world had never seen anything on this scale before. It is impossible to consider issues of culture contact without taking into account the growth of the organized trade, with particular relevance to American, European, and African histories.

Slavery existed in most complex societies in the past. There were slaves in Europe in the first and second millennia, with domestic slaves being particularly pervasive as a labor force. There were reportedly captured German slaves with the Vikings when they landed in North America in 1000. Slaves constituted a disempowered and often forcibly mobile group. They were not alone in their powerlessness, however; many people in the Middle Ages were in positions of servitude, such as peasants and serfs, who were essentially agricultural workers or artisans tied to land owned by elites.

Very few historical sources exist for medieval slavery, and archaeological evidence is equally rare. One rare line of evidence is shackles, which have been found in medieval Europe. However, the invisibility of slavery has made its study a great challenge for historians and archaeologists.

The Islamic trade in slaves built on and amplified earlier slave networks, particularly those dealing with African slaves, a practice predating the Romans. For centuries prior to the Atlantic slave trade, slave caravans moved captives into Islamic lands in northern Africa, and via the Red Sea into Asia. While Muslims captured some slaves in Spain, the center of this trade was East Africa, the Red Sea, and West Asia.

With increased contact with West Asia in the twelfth century, and a growing demand for slaves, captured European slaves moved through Islamic slave markets. During the Crusades, both Muslim and Christians enslaved war captives.

Slaves were used on sugar plantations in the Mediterranean from the eleventh century, in combination with free workers. By the fifteenth century, outside of the Mediterranean plantation workers, Europe had only a small demand for slaves, given the work provided by serfs.[42] Slaves then were present in small numbers, but a significant phase in plantation production had been reached that would structure events in the fifteenth century and later around the world.

MEDIEVAL PLANTATIONS

One distinctive element of the Europeans in the Americas after the fifteenth century would be the use of plantations for agricultural production of crops such as sugar, cotton, and tobacco. Plantations were intensively used in the New World tropical regions, and the story of these places is a significant part of the history of the New World in economic, political, and social realms (chapters 6 and 7). That history is best known from its role in the Atlantic trade in slaves and associated production enterprises termed by prominent American historian Philip Curtin as the "plantation complex." He was describing an institution of intensive production that had its roots in the first half of the second millennium, and not in America but in the Mediterranean, the eastern Atlantic and, eventually, Africa.[43]

One of the key crops in the growth of plantations was sugar. In the medieval diet, sugar was a luxury spice, with medicinal properties and common to many dishes, such as sweetening sauces for meats. It fattened people after illness. Prior to sugar, the main medieval sweetener had been honey. In the late seventeenth century, sugar shifted to a role as a specific staple, used in sweetening beverages and certain foods (deserts, chocolate). Sugar consumption increased thereafter and is now consumed in levels that constitute a health crisis.

Europeans encountered sugarcane from the time of Crusades, as Muslim sugar production was already established in the Levant. Sugar production required a local factory to produce sugar and molasses, products of suitable value for long-distance trade. Various players in the Near East from the early twelfth century attempted sugar production, including Venetians (at Tyre), Baldwin II (Acre), and Teutonic Knights and Knights Templar (Acre, Galilee). Archaeological excavations at Acre have located the remains of refining processes.[44]

Despite these attempts, European production moved to the Mediterranean and, by the thirteenth century, Cyprus had become the main producer for Europe.[45]

Philip Curtin observes how sugar production in this period can be seen as developing a distinctive plantation complex. First, unlike in parts of Europe where many of the Crusaders came from, in the Mediterranean slaves had remained from the Roman era; while slaves were not a large part of the workforce on Cyprus, they were present. Second, in northern Europe, the feudal elite was a military class that had little involvement in agricultural production, this being handled by villagers who were beholden to their overlords. Crusaders found that as conquerors of lands in the East, they could manage land and began to develop as agricultural managers. Some managers, particularly Italians, were from commercial and merchant backgrounds, and brought these skills to bear to develop a more capitalist approach to production. They used slaves to boost the workforce, and built capital works such as irrigation and invested in the refining technology.

Increasingly sugar was grown throughout the Mediterranean as Cyprus was overshadowed by sugar production on Crete,[46] Rhodes,[47] and Sicily. Normans took over sugar production with their capture of territory in southern Italy and Sicily. Islamic Spain also grew sugar for export. In the fifteenth century, from these origins the plantation complex was moved out of Europe to the islands of the eastern Atlantic.

Entering the Atlantic

Island groups in the eastern half of the mid-Atlantic Ocean include, from the north to the south, the Azores, Madeira, the Canary Islands, and Cape Verde Islands, and then in the southern Atlantic, Ascension Island and St. Helena Island. The climates vary from Mediterranean to semiarid to tropical. Most were unoccupied when discovered, the exception being the Canary Islands, which were occupied by the indigenous Guanche. Each offered different potentials for Europeans—and only the Canary Islands offered native resistance.

In 1419, the discovery of Madeira by Portuguese explorers backed by Henry the Navigator led to their settlement in the 1420s. Eventually Henry promoted sugarcane plantations, which required migrant settlers, as the Madeira Islands were unpopulated.

The Guanche people of the Canary Islands, being closer to the African coast, had possibly been in contact with outsiders previously. It has been suggested these are the Fortunate Islands referred to by Pliny in the first century AD.[48] If so, they were "forgotten," only to be visited again from the 1300s by Europeans leading up to Spanish conquest.

The Guanche were a relatively homogeneous population spread across several islands, with an economy based on fishing, cultivation of barley, and some pastoralism, raising sheep, pigs, and dog. The islands had no metals, so metal technologies were abandoned for tools of bone and stone and ceramic production. Some Canary Islanders today are descendants from Guanche, Spaniards, and others.

The Guanche came under increasing attention from Europeans. From the late 1300s, Guanche were taken as slaves, while the remaining population had to deal with invaders. The first stab at conquest was with a Castilian colony in 1402. Portuguese and other Spanish invaders followed. Certain islands resisted successfully—the Portuguese failed to get a foothold despite at least four major assaults.

The indigenous guerrilla warfare employed on Gran Canaria, La Palma, and finally Tenerife (which only fell in 1496) successfully resisted the Spanish armies, at least for a time. The capture of Tenerife required two major military campaigns with thousands of soldiers, guns, and horses. Hundreds of Spanish fell at *La Matanza de Acentejo* (the massacre of Acentejo).[49]

101

We see here the Spaniards learning the techniques they would eventually employ in the Americas, such as the use of armored horses as intimidating instruments against infantry. The numerous Guanche were able to maintain resistance, but were facing an invader backed by a nation of resources, which were only weeks away by boat. The Spaniards had superior weaponry. They had horses which, while not always suitable for the types of warfare being fought, provided great advantages in many types of fighting, as well as being imposing. The Guanche had neither armor nor boats, so each island was an isolated battleground. The Europeans were reprovisioned by their vessels (and more effectively than the European colonies in Greenland or in the Latin East had been).

Another contributing element to the fall of the Guanche was the impact of epidemics. Historic accounts are vague but suggest massive mortality, possibly from typhoid, although many other common European diseases could have had similar effect. This would have greatly restricted their ability to wage war. By the sixteenth century, few natives remained, except those transported elsewhere as slaves or in exile.

There are other aspects about the colonization of these islands that are echoed elsewhere. For instance, introduced species brought in to improve the economic potential of the land for Europeans—for example, sugarcane, sheep, cattle, and goats—had considerable impact. Some introductions had immediate effect. Rabbits introduced on the island of Porto Santo, in the Madeira Islands, resulted in a plague that the settlers could not quell and caused the temporary abandonment of the island.

New animals and plants would change the ecology of these places, with consequences both small and large for original inhabitants and settlers. The land was modified to be useful for farming. Madeira was found covered in vast forests that took seven years to burn out, presumably losing many endemic species never seen by humans.[50]

While sheep and cattle were to be significant in the Azores and Madeira island groups, the biggest earning crop was sugar. By the end of the fifteenth century, twenty thousand workers were in place, many of them slaves involved in the small island's monocrop.[51] The first slaves are thought to have included Guanche from the Canary Islands; Madeiran historical sources called for limits on the numbers of Canary Islanders.[52] As such, the first Atlantic slaves were not black Africans, but Canary Islanders.

So, medieval European colonization faced resistance and sometimes failed as a result. In the eastern Atlantic, 1402 marks the beginning of an arc of cross-cultural encounters that would run for the next six centuries. Resistance to Europeans, like that of the Guanche, would characterize those encounters: the Canary Islanders are reminiscent of many people who defended their land and lives from

European would-be conquerors. The destruction of an indigenous society would also be seen again many times.

The main action now moves south along the coast of Africa and west into the Atlantic.

USEFUL SOURCES

Museums and online resources: Spain: National Archaeological Museum of Spain. Italian ports: Start with Galata Maritime Museum (Genoa). New York: The Metropolitan Museum has organized a pathway through their collection along Marco Polo's route. Crusades: Sources compiled at *www.crusades-encyclopedia.com*.

References: A useful overview is available in David Ditchburn, Simon MacLean, and Angus MacKay, eds., *Atlas of Medieval Europe* (London: Routledge, 2007). An excellent review of trade can be found in Janet L. Abu-Lughod, *Before European Hegemony: The World System A.D. 1250–1350* (Oxford University Press, 1989) and of diseases in Alfred W. Crosby, *Ecological Imperialism: The Biological Expansion of Europe, 900–1900* (Cambridge University Press, 1986). For an introduction to the archaeology of medieval Europe, see James Graham-Campbell and Magdalena Valor, *The Archaeology of Medieval Europe* (Aarhus: Aarhus University Press, 2007). There are other key atlases and overviews to medieval Europe more broadly, such as Daniel Power, ed., *The Central Middle Ages* (Oxford University Press, 2006); and also see Timothy Insoll, *The Archaeology of Islam* (Malden, MA: Blackwell Publishers, 1999).

Key journals: Medieval Archaeology, Antiquity, World Archaeology, European Journal of Archaeology, Journal of Mediterranean Archaeology, Levant, Near Eastern Archaeology, Palestine Exploration Quarterly, Journal of Iberian Archaeology.

CHAPTER 5

SUB-SAHARAN AFRICA

Madaka ya nyamba ya zisahani
Sasa walaliye wana wa nyuni

Where once the porcelain stood in the wall niches
Now wild birds nestle their fledglings.

–Swahili poet, 1815, on the glory of Pate, an East African trading settlement[1]

AFRICAN ENCOUNTERS: 1000–1500

In the 1980s, the film *The Gods Must be Crazy* exposed many people for the first time to the African Khoisan people and language. The actor N!xau plays Xi, a Sho man of the Kalahari, who finds a Coke bottle tossed from an airplane. The Kalahari tribe is portrayed as having all they require, so that arrival of this unique object throws the tribe off balance, causing Xi to initiate a journey to the "end of the world" to destroy the bottle. On his journey, he meets white people and sees the "outside" world, at first thinking the Europeans to be gods, but then realizing they are flawed beings.

This film portrayal of first contact is clearly designed for entertainment and requires the band of hunter-foragers to apparently have no information at all about the world beyond their desert, while in reality information and goods move into even the most remote human communities. For these and other reasons, some were uncomfortable with the film. My point here is simply to observe that the idea of "first contact" is a fascinating notion for the historical imagination and popular consumption. Culture contact over time in Africa was far more complicated than the film suggests.

There is no clear arrival of Europeans in Africa such as we described for Greenland. Even the idea of "history" is fuzzy. African oral histories provide non-textual but valid records of the past. The earliest written accounts are Egyptian, while Islamic and Chinese accounts precede any European observations of Africa, at least beyond the Mediterranean fringe. And, there is a rich archaeological record of culture contacts, as introduced here.

Europeans took over existing patterns of contact in Africa: they did not invent them. The trans-Saharan slave trade has its routes deep in antiquity, while the East African trade polities existed long before the arrival of Europeans.

Leaving *The Gods Must be Crazy* behind, in reality first encounters between indigenous southern Africans and Europeans occurred in the late 1400s, when Khoisan people living along the southern coast of Africa met Portuguese explorer Bartolomeu Dias at Mossel Bay in 1488.

Despite early contacts such as these, Europeans tended to remain in coastal outposts. The widespread European control of Africa occurred only much later, in the nineteenth century—a rush described as "The Scramble—or Race—for Africa" (ca. 1880–1920s) in which European states coerced, invaded, annexed, and occupied much of Africa. The widespread abandonment of colonial powers in Africa only occurred in the second half of the twentieth century.

There are several ways one could organize this chapter: chronologically or geographically, or by such themes as slavery or colonialism.[2] Africa is clearly a massive, ethnically diverse continent—I use only a few archaeological examples of what we have learned of cross-cultural encounters.

What various strategies were employed in cross-cultural encounters? What are the material manifestations of responses to culture contact? In this chapter I focus on:

- West Africa, where white–black contact was greatest in coastal nodes, yet the impacts of slavery were felt well inland.

- Southern Africa, where cultural engagements over the last five centuries were preceded by earlier examples of cultural entanglements involving different African farmers and hunter-foragers.

- East Africa, where we find medieval coastal settlements in contact with the world via the Indian Ocean.

Along the way, I explore how archaeology provides insight into the historical and colonial past by enfolding precolonial and colonial communities within historical frameworks, an enterprise that assists our understanding of how modern Africa was created.

Many of the theoretical models raised in chapter 2 will be apparent in this discussion. European–African encounters ranged from sporadic contacts with European traders to more direct colonialism in which European powers, in "the scramble for Africa," wrangled for territory and resources. Indigenous responses vary widely in these studies, given the diversity of African societies; such responses include examples of resistance, successful control of Europeans leading to encapsulation and confinement, as well as processes of creolization. In some instances, contact led to loss of land and cultural identity.

AFRICA LEADING UP TO THE FIFTEENTH CENTURY

The three Old World continents have, of course, been "in contact" for millennia. The rise of state societies in West Asia and the Indus Valley were accompanied by African states along the Nile River, where respective polities were engaged in trade, war, and competition with powers both outside of Africa and in neighboring African states, such as Kush. The Classical-era civilizations of Greece, Phoenicia, and Rome were clearly enmeshed with North Africa and influenced African developments.

At around AD 1000, northern Africa had been long subject to historical accounts. That was not the case for Sub-Saharan Africa, which requires the use of archaeology and oral history to interpret the past.

The first millennium saw the development of great trade and exchange networks, and a range of states developed across Sudan, West Africa, and North Africa (Figure 5.1). State development may have derived from the ability to manage or monopolize trade or local production of some kind. West Africa had been in indirect contact with the broader world via Saharan trade that linked Sub-Saharan Africa with the Mediterranean, while other routes ran east–west. Trade moved both commodities and finished goods, including metals, glass, ceramics, salt, beads, and slaves.

The early second millennium saw shifts in farming communities and iron users across central, eastern, and southern Africa; the mosaic of societies included small-scale peasant communities through to kingdoms, such as the Kingdom of Congo encountered by the Portuguese in the fifteenth century.

Cattle herding became more important, although sheep and goat were also raised.

Trade was also an important element in developments along eastern Africa coasts, where wealth and presumably political power are demonstrated through access to trade goods, such as glass beads and gold and copper objects. Here the interface between coastal and hinterland communities was significant. The coastal trade communities would eventually provide the means for the Portuguese to access the gold of the interior; however, these trade communities had long histories.

Another significant network of contacts was with Islamic societies. By the turn of the second millennium, northern Africa was united under Muslim rulers,

Figure 5.1. Map of Africa ca. AD 1000–1600.

although the Fatamid territory in the eastern Mediterranean diminished during the Crusades and with the rise of Muslim Turks (chapter 4). Muslim control of the seas of the western Mediterranean and Red Sea trade generated a healthy profit and would only decline with alternate routes to Asia.

Islam's influence extended across Africa, from West Africa and into Sub-Saharan societies, as well as along the East African coast, where powerful coastal trading centers arose. The East African trading communities had Arabic, Indian, and Persian influences, and saw Muslim communities develop as a result of these international linkages. Islamic outposts sat at the very edge of the world of unbelievers. The spread of Islamic belief had many effects, one being that slaves for Islamic slave markets came from non-Muslim regions (dar el Hab). This extended the network of slave trading before European networks were developed.

The longevity of contacts with Islam led Timothy Insoll to state that "Islam is surely the leitmotif of African archaeology and history over the last millennia."[3] Christianity was less influential, although long-established in Ethiopia, and was eventually extended through European colonial structures.

Thus, Muslim–African contacts mostly predate African–European contacts, except in southern Africa, where Islam arose from contacts with the Dutch who, after 1652, brought Muslim slaves, convicts, and laborers from the Dutch East India Company colonies in Java and Malay Peninsula—these were the Cape Malay or Cape Muslims. Similarly, Muslim Indians were responsible for bringing Islam to British colonies in Kenya, Tanzania, Uganda, and Malawi.[4]

THE FIFTEENTH CENTURY ONWARD: EUROPEANS ON FRINGES, AFRICANS IN CENTERS

By the fifteenth century, Africans were in contact with diverse societies both within Africa and beyond African shores. Foreign visitors were active around Africa: the Chinese had explored the east coast with the fleets of Admiral Zheng He, abandoning the coast in 1434. However, no further Chinese expeditions reportedly occurred.

The capture of the Moroccan port of Ceuta in 1415 signified the beginning of direct Portuguese interests in Africa; the date has come to signify the beginning of Western diasporas, although, as argued in chapters 3 and 4, these actually began earlier. What drove the Portuguese? Europe's trade with Asia in the fourteenth and fifteenth centuries was dominated in Europe by the Italian agents. European interests looked toward alternate sea routes. The Portuguese attempt to outflank the Italian-Muslim monopoly of Asian trade required the diversion of trade from the existing Indian Ocean network around southern Africa to Western Europe. Voyages both accidental and exploratory had led to the discovery and colonization of the eastern Atlantic islands.

It was clear to some that at least two potential routes to the "East Indies"[5] existed. Voyages west across the Atlantic witnessed, in 1492, the Spanish arrival, via Columbus, in the Caribbean; and in 1502, Magellan's entry into the Pacific around the southern tip of South America, which secured a route across the Atlantic and Pacific to East Asia for the Spanish (chapter 6).

The second route was via the Indian Ocean. In the fifteenth century, many maps showed the southern extent of Africa as landlocked. Persistent Portuguese expeditions along the African coast, however, resulted in new cartographical knowledge and the discovery of the route around the Cape of Good Hope. This episode of exploration was not unlike the twentieth-century space program: each voyage provided more data and extended knowledge, and design changes were made to vessels as needs changed from exploration (i.e., the Apollo mission) to movement of goods (i.e., the Space Shuttle). Like a space program, these expeditions were expensive. The exploration was driven in ships of Prince Henry the Navigator, a financial backer of exploration and settlement who desired an eastern route to East Asia and the end of Muslim trade dominance.

Portuguese shipping technology developed to make regular travel in coastal waters possible. After 1440, Portuguese expeditions were fitted with caravels using new shipbuilding practices. The rudder hung from the bow rather than using a steering-oar, and they changed the design of the bow and stern. One captain said they "were able to go anywhere." These boats were lightly rigged, could sail close to the wind, and had a shallow draft useful for exploration of uncharted coasts.

In 1497, Vasco da Gama's voyage to India was equipped with a larger ship, less suited for coastal travel, more suited for transport of trade goods. This was a prototype of the oceangoing ships of the sixteenth century.

SLAVES AND THE PORTUGUESE

There was not a single burning Portuguese ambition to get around Africa; the continent was not a mere impediment on the way to Asia, but a series of potential and realized resources. European names reflect this: the Grain Coast, the Gold Coast, the Slave Coast, and the Ivory Coast. The Portuguese were interested in goods, particularly gold or spices, as well as partnerships against the Muslim world. Over time, slaves became a more significant product. Trading posts were constructed, some of which have survived to be studied in the present, places such as Elmina (Ghana) and Fort Jesus (Mombasa, Kenya).[6] A vast array of coastal outposts would be created by Europeans—only some have been studied archaeologically. By 1800, on the Gold Coast alone there were sixty forts.

A brief chronology sees early Portuguese settlement in the Azores (1430s), and then African trading posts as far-flung as Arguin in Mauritania (1445), Elmina (1482), and Axim (1503) in Ghana (Figure 5.2). In the late 1400s, Portuguese traveled into Central Africa to the Kingdom of the Congo to begin recruiting slaves—eventually the slave trade would see the disintegration of the kingdom. It appears that in the Congo (Angola) and northern Namibia trade developed quickly, as suggested by seventeenth-century glass beads in African sites well beyond the contact zone; eventually some glass beads ended up in the camps of Kalahari hunter-foragers.[7]

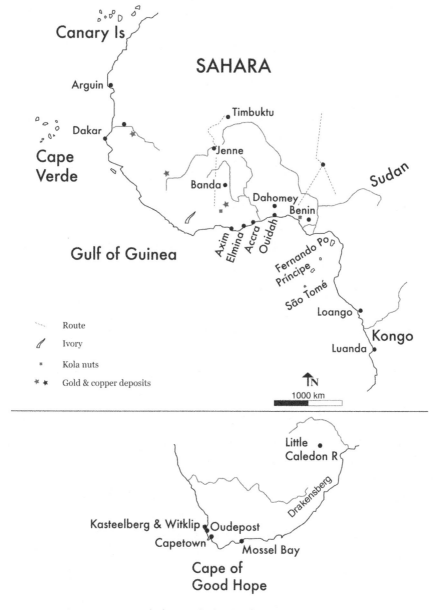

Figure 5.2. Map of Africa, with details of West and Southern Africa.

The islands of São Tomé and Príncipe in the Gulf of Guinea (discovered 1470s) and Fernando Po (1471) were to provide the basis for Portuguese plantations off the African coast.

The Portuguese slave trade initially directed African slaves to Atlantic islands and Iberia; from 1441 to 1521, over 150,000 slaves were exported, after which slaves went increasingly to the Americas, or to São Tomé, which had a large population of unfree workers and was an important sugar producer in the early 1500s prior to the rise of Portuguese sugar plantations in Brazil.[8] It was to Brazil that the Portuguese transported most African slaves.

THE SLAVE TRADE DEVELOPS

The Portuguese hold on the African coast was threatened first by the Dutch in the seventeenth century and then by the English and the French. The Dutch East India Company was founded in 1602, and the Dutch West India Company in 1621.[9] Competition with English and French interests increased after the mid-1600s and with other European nations thereafter. This is indicated in the number of African slaves transported in European vessels, with millions transported in the eighteenth century. While the abolition of slavery first by the British (in 1807) reduced the number of slaves, still in the nineteenth century, more than half a million slaves went to Spanish parts of the New World and over a million to Brazil.[10]

Thus, the most infamous trade with Africa was of slaves. The foundation of many New World societies was built on Africans. We shall explore the New World aspects of this in chapters 6 and 7, where we see that demand for slaves only ended with the emancipation movement of the first half of the nineteenth century. Much of what is known of the African slave trade in Africa derives from historical accounts by slavers and their associates. Archaeology promises a more thorough understanding, an approach that some see as as a valuable addition to text-based histories, and others as a challenge to the "hegemony of text."[11]

The Atlantic slave trade built on the existing internal African and Islamic slave trade.[12] The differences were the eventual scale of the enterprise, the fact that slaves were intended for the Americas for the first time, that the focus moved from northern and eastern Africa westward and southward, and that there was a greater demand for male slaves than previously.[13]

STUDYING SLAVERY

Why were African slaves were used in such massive numbers? Some reasons predated the Atlantic slave network, such as the rise of the Ottomans and the subsequent restricted access to Arab slave markets, and prohibitions on selling slaves in Italy (despite which, slaves were present) and elsewhere in Europe. An increased demand for slaves was fueled by new economies (derived from plantations) and new labor markets in the New World and the Atlantic.

While the first two centuries of direct contact with Africa saw trade in slaves, it is in the seventeenth and eighteenth centuries that the number of slaves increased greatly, driven by demand within the Atlantic slave network. The sites that relate to the slave trade in the Americas, Europe, and Africa invoke considerable emotional response—the effects of this trade resound into the present.[14] Much of the research into historical sources can be found in the Trans-Atlantic Slave Trade database; this details almost 35,000 voyages transporting over ten million slaves between the sixteenth and nineteenth centuries.[15]

The push to end slavery derived from several factors: the suffering of slaves in the Americas, the effects in Africa (such as depopulation and human suffering), and the potential to open up new markets based on the idea that only African elites involved in the slave trade were benefiting. To paraphrase one merchant in the mid-1850s: "the slave trade was pursued by chiefs, the palm oil trade is pursued by all."[16] If this were true, then the restricted access to European goods prior to the cessation of slaving should be visible in the archaeology.

A core area of research deals with the nature and effects of historical cross-cultural encounters in Africa. Part of this requires resolving how the slave network was organized. Was the capture of slaves typical of African societies? Or did a trade in slaves develop over time to meet the demand for slaves, as suggested by the increase in slave numbers over time?

Some regions saw large numbers of slaves captured and moved, while other regions produced small numbers, or intermittent slaves. The demographic effects are apparent, with warfare, population decline, social changes, and transformations arising from culture contacts.

A range of studies have attempted to deal with these problems and use a wide variety of evidence, from historical sources to settlement information and archaeological findings. The studies I refer to here focus on the Gulf of Benin (the modern Republic of Benin)[17] and Ghana.[18] This work is critical in providing a view of the last six hundred years of African life and departing from an idea of a "timeless" Africa interrupted by white outsiders.

Some have effectively argued that an understanding of slavery is best achieved when the focus is not slavery but the world around slavery, and within which slavery and various forms of cross-cultural encounter existed. As stated by Ann Stahl, Chair of Archaeology at the University of Victoria, Washington, and director of a major regional archaeology program in Banda, Ghana:

[E]fforts to "find slavery" will likely to be frustrated by a paucity of material traces. . . . If, however, we consider slavery as part of a broader landscape of

113

intersocial entanglements—a total social fact for the last number of centuries across wide swathes of Africa—our focus is directed instead to its implications for a range of practices: subsistence, craft production, settlement dynamics, and more. Viewed in this light, questions of slavery cease to be a special topic and need to be routinely incorporated into our research designs.[19]

This approach is described by Stahl as shifting from "the archaeology of slavery" to "the archaeology of daily life during the slavery." This ambitious direction is becoming plausible, as archaeologists build on studies of immediate sites of contact to regional, long-term, society-wide studies using all available data: historical, archaeological, geographical, and ethnographic. Other important research relates African experiences to the broader setting of the slave trade, linking Africa with the various ethnic African diasporas in the New World.

ARCHAEOLOGY OF CULTURE CONTACT IN BENIN

Coastal West African states came into intensive contact with Europeans early, with the settlement at Elmina in Ghana, established in 1482, signaling the Portuguese ambitions. The Portuguese established Elmina for the gold trade; as slaves became increasingly important in West Africa, Benin met Portuguese demand for slaves. In Benin, the Europeans traded first with the Hueda state (1660–1727) and then its successor, Dahomey (1727–late 1800s).

Archaeological studies have been conducted at Elmina, Savi (Hueda's capital), and Ouidah (Dahomey's key town). A core difference between these places of cross-cultural contacts and trade appears to have been that at Elmina, African control of trade diminished rapidly in favor of various European traders (first the Portuguese in the late 1400s, then the Dutch, and British), unlike in Savi and Ouidah, where Africans maintained control.

Archaeology at Hueda and Dahomey demonstrates how African societies responded to European demand and, in particular, how African elites were able to manipulate the Europeans and their trade. Eventually many European states became involved in the West African slave trade through these states—England, Portugal, France, and Denmark included. Archaeological research has focused not only on the coastal European and African outposts, but also on inland sites away from direct cross-cultural contact with Europeans.

The initial focus of much archaeological work was on coastal forts and trading posts, slave quarters in African and European settlements, and slave settlements on plantations.[20] However, the firmest evidence of slavery is not iron shackles or cells, but rather the evidence of European traders in contact with the African communities who provided slaves, and the study of their towns, trade routes, and societies over time.

In West Africa, the evidence suggests how Africans regulated the presence of European traders, something that is surprising to those whose ideas of cross-cultural interactions between Africans and Europeans is viewed solely from an understanding of the later colonial-era relationships characteristic of the nineteenth and twentieth centuries. In earlier centuries, Africans—specifically, African elites—regulated much culture contact, at least in Savi and Ouidah.

In Benin, the coastal Hueda people capitalized on their access to slavers, gaining power over the previously dominant interior state of Allada and becoming independent around 1660. The archaeological record indicates that the key trading settlement of Savi dates from the contact period—this suggests that the Hueda state may have risen to power as a result of its privileged access to European trade.

The profits of trade attracted the Dahomey state that conquered Hueda in 1727. This saw the relocation of Europeans from Savi to Ouidah, a few kilometers closer to the coast.

In both places, Europeans were restricted by Africans: where they were allowed to live and build, where they could travel. They were not allowed into Hueda's capital of Abomey, for instance. Several European trading nations were encouraged to be present, preventing monopolization. The eighteenth-century Hueda palace complex at Savi had lodges for the Portuguese, French, English, and Dutch representatives—all adjacent to the court accommodation and administration, and located within the area defined by defensive ditches (Figure 5.3). The Europeans at Savi were distant from any support on the coast, 10 kilometers away, and subject to easy surveillance.

The Dahomey in the 1700s took a different approach to their handling of Europeans. Rather than incorporate them into traditional settlements, as at Savi, they created new precincts for Europeans in isolation from Dahomeans. At Ouidah, forts were built for each European trading nation (Figure 5.3); these were overseen by a senior public servant and military outpost.

The situation at Elmina was different again: here the European fort dominated the town and protected ships in the bay. The different spatial arrangements in these examples suggest that very different forms of cultural interaction occurred. The archaeological record indicates that at Savi people had access to some European traded goods, such as clay pipes—smoking tobacco being a European-introduced vice. While pipes were common at Savi, only small quantities of imported ceramics, glassware, and beads were found: new goods were not radically transformative. At

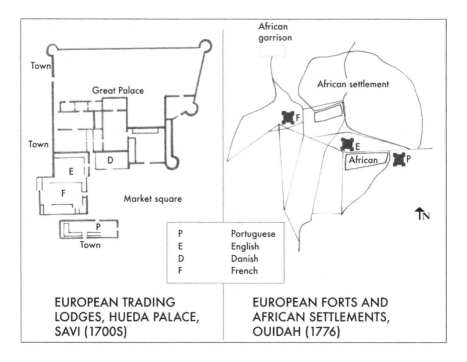

Figure 5.3. European forts and trading lodges at Hueda Palace, Savi, and Ouidah (*based on Kelly 2002: figs. 5, 9*).

Elmina, in contrast, the imports were many times more popular, making up nearly half the archaeological record.

American archaeologist Christopher DeCorse excavated Elmina; he argues that the greater amount of imported goods does not suggest a population who were less "Fanti"—the local ethnic group—but rather indicates that a process of creolization created a new society. The argument is that the new material augmented existing societal practices. This idea of augmentation is supported by the evidence of burials: people were buried under the floors of peoples' houses, as they had been in the past, but imported material culture was added to the grave goods—new things being used in old ways. But in addition, there were new developments in architecture, with flat-roofed stone buildings marking a new preference for buildings that may have looked more European.[21]

Thus, the archaeology from the West African coast indicates different approaches to and outcomes of European–African contacts. Some contacts were with one European power, some were multinational settings. In some instances things didn't change—for example, at Ouidah traditional housing design and con-

116

struction continued—yet at Elmina the architecture did change. Attempts to control cross-cultural contacts and trade are clearly evident in the different approaches toward Europeans, from isolating to enfolding them. In other locations, the muscle of forts and firepower gave Europeans strong footholds on the coast.

One important trade item was guns, which, while known to Africans, became increasingly available through slave trading. Hundreds of thousands of rifles and handguns entered West Africa during the seventeenth century, with Europeans of the mind that if they stopped trading guns, the other European powers would meet that demand.[22] African powers utilized guns extensively, and controlled their extent—for example, guns were not allowed north of Dahomey.

What of the interior away from direct contact with Europeans? One change due to culture contacts evident in communities located inland from the coast was to local African trade patterns and power, with a shift of power and influence toward those who controlled trade.

In Benin City, for example, away from the coastal contact zone, a range of imported goods—bronze and brass, European ceramics, glass beads, swords, clay pipes, buttons, cowries—demonstrate indirect connections with European trade.[23]

Other Evidence of Slavery

Significant impacts resulted from slaving; there is evidence of how communities dealt with the threat and benefits of slaving. Africans provided most of the slaves to European slavers. Most slaves were created either to settle debts or raise funds, through warfare, or as punishment for a real or perceived crime.[24] Some villages gained from controlling key parts of the trade. In other regions, whole landscapes were depopulated by slaving and by communities fleeing from capture. Earthworks in Togo, for example, demonstrate how small villages may have tried to prevent slave raiders.[25] In northern Togo, people fled to refuge areas away from slave raiders and were unable to return; this is indicated archaeologically by their potters who experimented with ceramic production because they were cut off from their customary clay sources.

These studies provide insight into local African responses to externally stimulated change. In some places, religious practices reveal the impact of slavery. Among the Diola of West Africa, for example, religious authorities seemed to have legitimized and regulated the slave trade, as evidenced by new cults and shrines to spirits. It appears that accusations of witchcraft increased as a response to the slave trade, although this practice already existed prior to contact. Secret societies arose to protect people from slavery. Ethnic and religious differences were also used to promote successful slavery.[26]

Banda, Ghana

Research in Ghana provides detailed insight into processes of cultural entanglement over a longer timeframe. Ann Stahl's study of Banda sites in west central Ghana has delineated, through the excavation of various settlements, different moments of people over the centuries of contact. Banda is well inland from coastal European–African meetings as described for Elmina or Hueda. Banda was a chieftaincy that, during the seventeenth and eighteenth centuries, was in a frontier zone where preexisting power structures associated with Saharan and Sudanic trade networks were disrupted by Atlantic slave trading. This led to the region being taken over by Asante in the eighteenth century and in the 1870s being colonized by the British after their conquest of the Asante state.

Stahl's excavations detail the multitude of changes and continuities over time in Banda villages. Some practices ended or were replaced, such as local iron smelting and pipe manufacture, while pottery and textile production continued into the present.

During the Asante phase, slaves were provided to the trade, yet few European-made goods moved into Banda hands. Local production and trade supplied goods such as pottery and metal items. Subsistence also changed with the introduction of New World crops and new methods of hunting. The nature of settlement changed due to warfare, shifting allegiances, and slavery.

In the British colonial period, villagers were required to lay out their villages in a grid fashion, reorganize cemeteries, and participate in the British colonial order. Banda settlements suggest a greater use of, and access to, European goods, as well as a greater shift toward New World crops and a corresponding decline in the growing of sorghum.

This work in West Africa allows the period of "global entanglements" to be considered in longer trajectories and to explore how West African societies were part of dynamic and complex relationships over time which were particularly influenced by varying degrees of exposure to, and involvement in, trans-Saharan trade and then, after the fifteenth century, Atlantic trade systems. In this approach, thousands of years of events across the changing mosaic of West African societies, technologies, economies, political systems, and beliefs are the subject of inquiry— of course, limited by the work done and the quality of data, particularly archaeological. The African Iron Age and the historical eras intrude upon each other, and the boundaries between them are less distinct.[27]

A Colonial African Plantation

Other archaeological research focuses on slavery in African plantations, which were also significant settings for cross-cultural contacts. The earliest plantations were established in the fifteenth century by the Portuguese. During the nineteenth century, when much of Africa was carved up into various European colonies, plantations provided produce and raw materials for European markets and were run both by Africans and Europeans.

Here, we consider a colonial-era Danish and British plantation on the Gold Coast, near Accra, Ghana, researched by Ghanaian archaeologist Yaw Bredwa-Mensah. The Danes once had the majority of slaving sites along the coast of Ghana, forming a network of trading stations, forts, castles, and lodges. Enslaved workers at agricultural sites produced sugar, tobacco, coffee, dyes, cotton, maize, and other exports. Some of the largest farms were state-run enterprises.

The early nineteenth century was a transitional time. The Danes abolished slave trading in 1803, the first European nation to do so. (Britain followed in 1807, and Holland in 1814.) For Danes, instead of exporting slaves, growing crops in Africa for export to Europe was an alternative.

Many early plantations failed, or produced only small amounts of cash crops for export. Most used enslaved workers, and the capital came from the Danish government. Danish records distinguish between unfree property/house Africans and mortgaged/pawned Africans.[28] The Danes also employed free labor, such as the invaluable canoe men (*remindors*) who moved slaves and goods to ships and along the coast; much transport in West Africa required canoes.

Very little is known of life on these plantations, with historical analysis being restricted to European documentation. An archaeological study at Fredericksgave provides additional insights.[29] Fredericksgave was one of the many Danish attempts at farming and was initiated in the 1820s to produce coffee. (It was taken over by the British, with all other Danish possessions, in Ghana in 1850.) The slaves were mainly Akan, from Ghana, with a handful from other ethnicities in northern and eastern Ghana. Initially, the vast majority were men (perhaps perceived to be better plantation workers), and then after 1850s the majority were women and children.

The archaeological recording targeted the plantation house and Djabing village for slaves. The village had two phases of use, an early phase from the 1820s to the 1850s, and a later phase from the 1850s to the 1920s, after which it was abandoned. The model was to house workers in cottages on the plantation. While the slaves were drawn from different ethnic groups, the archaeological record documents a way of life that remained distinctly "African," as suggested by the traditional design of their dwellings in wood and mud. Ethnic differences in house design and material culture were not evident, despite different ethnicities being present.

Introduced goods were evident in the archaeology. Typical European trade goods found in the village included "ceramics, kaolin smoking pipes, beads, gun parts, cowrie shells, metal objects such as hoes, knives, nails and spikes, assorted buttons and bottle glass."[30] Both European trade beads (of glass from Venice and Bohemia, and German chalcedony) and locally made stone beads were excavated. The presence of this material indicates the ways that goods produced in Europe (and elsewhere) entered into the coastal settlements of West Africa.

Local goods were important: 95 percent of the ceramics were local wares. Over half the assemblage was of African origin which, in addition to faunal remains (people ate both domesticated and hunted animals), included pottery, brass items, stone tools, and beads. The pottery appears to have been derived from a local tradition in the nearby Densu Valley, a centuries-old tradition that continued throughout the contact period and was characterized by hand-built vessels. In the twentieth century, such vessels were made by women; this may have been the case in colonial times as well.[31] The vessels had various purposes, ranging from food preparation and storage to ritual and health uses. Various new decorations and pottery forms represented major innovations dating from the nineteenth century and occurred throughout the Accra coastal communities.

The excavators of Fredericksgave believe this evidence indicates how much the coastal community changed from the early phase of European contact in the sixteenth and seventeenth centuries to later periods when the coastal community was more heterogeneous, owing to long-term entanglements with slave trading and the European trade. The combined faunal and pottery evidence suggests the slaves ate meals typical of earlier African communities—with the addition, presumably, of new introduced crops. Imported alcoholic and nonalcoholic drinks were consumed, and tobacco was popular.

Items used traditionally remained popular, even if imported, such as beads and cowrie shell. The cowrie shells were not local and functioned as cross-cultural currency. The Africans measured them in strings and units, while the Danes had set values by weight linked to both the Rigsdaler (the Danish currency) and the gold standard.[32] There may have been further noncommercial values for these shells.

This evidence can be considered in relation to research by Akin Ogundiran, Chair of Africana Studies at University of North Carolina, into cowrie shell trade.[33] Ogundiran describes how shells were collected by Europeans from the Indian Ocean and used as currency in West Africa. However, their value extended beyond currency. Cowrie shells, once rare, during the sixteenth century in Yorubaland were part of transformative processes in society. Their use in shrines suggests how successful individuals were able to demonstrate their high status.

As shells became increasingly common, they were used in novel ways and were included in ritual practices related to well-being. Shells are evidence for global linkages, cross-cultural exchanges, the slippery nature of what objects mean depending on cultural and social settings, and how innovation occurs over time.

Fredericksgave has the potential to be compared with plantations in other parts of the world where Africans were taken, as the latter have been more commonly studied by archaeologists and provide the material evidence for resistance, change, and continuities. A comparative analysis would also reveal the various social dynamics of life on plantations which, in the case of Fredericksgave, required daily contact between various colonial (Danish, then British) figures and a diverse cross section of coastal Ghanaian society.

CULTURE CONTACT IN SOUTHERN AFRICA

One of the primary areas of archaeological research into historical culture contact has occurred in southern Africa, in part a result of a strong archaeological tradition twinned with an interest in historical archaeology. The sequence from a European perspective is simple: (1) the Portuguese discoveries and occasional visits, followed by (2) the establishment of Dutch colonial settlement (1642) to support their East Indies mercantile trade, (3) the arrival of British colonists who conquered the Cape in 1795 (and again in 1806), leading to (4) British primacy as the colonial power in southern Africa and the establishment of South Africa.[34] However, culture contact did not begin with Europeans bursting bubbles of ahistorical, unchanging African societies (or alternatively, as described evocatively by Carmel Schrire, "a great glass bell jar on the very verge of shattering from a massive blow").[35] Rather, southern Africans had seen ongoing culture contact with migrations of pastoralists over recent millennia who came into contact with hunter-foragers. In fact, indigenous hunter-foragers had faced the southward movement of farmers during the African Iron Age and the northward movement of European farmers a millennium later—truly a pincer move of contact.

Existing Culture Contacts

Across southern Africa, many centuries of contact between hunter-foragers (such as the San/Xam/Bushmen) and first, African and then later, European pastoralists are evident in archaeological sites. This contact probably began in southern Africa between the first to the fifth century, depending on location, with the southward movement of various non-San people, comprised of animal-herding and millet-farming Bantu speakers, ancestors of Sotho-Tswana and Nguni people. The other migrants were pastoralists known over time as Khoekhoen, Khoi Khoi, and Hottentot.

There are debates about how these different groups interacted—for example, the degree to which hunter-foragers and pastoralists were separate in the landscape or, if in contact, whether hunter-foragers resisted, acted as client herders, were seasonal laborers, or were in total subjugation to herders.

The term "Khoisan" is used as a collective term for African farmers living at the Cape at contact. Ethnography suggests complex relationships between different groups here. The Sonqua (also Soaqua), for example, are described by the Dutch as living at the fringes of Khoikhoi society, possibly with access to non-breeding stock. (It was probably the Sonqua that the Portuguese met in the region, as they did not describe meeting pastoralists but rather "fishermen.") Dutch describe enmity and killing between herders and hunter-foragers, while some Sonqua were in clientship to the herders, being able to hunt, herd, and fight for them. The Sonqua may even have been rainmakers and healers for the Khoikhoi.

Key archaeological sites such as Kastelberg and Witklip provide evidence of hunters and herders. They indicate that groups were in long-term culture contact over two millennia, implying some stability in relationships. Items such as ostrich shell beads were traded between hunter-foragers and herders, while their respective economic foci on hunting and herding meant they lived in different parts of the landscape. Other differences in prehistoric sites suggest different stone tool traditions, differential use of ceramics (the herders used pots, the hunters did not), different diets, and different preferences for decoration. However, as interesting as these differences are the crossovers—the hunters, for example, did have some access to sheep (hunted illicitly or as payment?), kept a few pots (but probably did not make them), and wore a different size of ostrich shell beads than the herders.[36] The identification of herders in the archaeological record is possibly more difficult than it may initially seem. The telltale sign of the presence of domesticated animals may, of course, arise from hunting, not herding. The absence of animal bones may not indicate the absence of herding, but could relate to the ways a site was used or might suggest taphonomic processes.[37] It is interesting to consider, then, that with the arrival of European farmers, a long-term familiarity with this type of contact already existed.

Contact with the Dutch

With the Dutch arriving in 1652, a new and differentiated society was established in southern Africa. The Dutch needed a provisioning station—they observed the herds of sheep and cattle belonging to the local pastoralists and wanted their stock.

The Dutch realized that the Khoikhoi were nomadic herders who moved their camps and animals, although they did not initially comprehend the seasonal aspect of their transhumance, where movement was based on available water and pasture. But trade with the Dutch quickly altered existing patterns, with results seen across the mosaic of land use in the region. Change would have rippled out beyond the contact zone to affect neighboring herders and hunter-foragers.

The Dutch settlement was initially a fortress and supply depot between Europe and the East Indies. Trade ensued between the Dutch and Khoikhoi, and within a few years a struggling group of Dutch farmers was established. The small colony included the local Khoisan, the Dutch, other Africans, Indonesian slaves, Chinese convicts, and other prisoners of the Dutch.[38] This mixed society changed the language, foodways, architecture, and material culture such as ceramics—all are forms of creolization, albeit in the case of food, with strong Dutch food traditions but blended with Asian and African ingredients (i.e., spices and rice). The red earthenware vessels found in these early colonial sites looked European, but were also used by slaves (Asian and African) in colonial households.

One key archaeological study of contact between the Dutch and Khoikhoi took place at Oudepost, established in 1669 as a provisioning station and trading post. The site was excavated by University of Cape Town archaeologist Carmel Schrire. After an early battle, the fort was moved in 1732. Excavations located the remains of several buildings, material evidence of Dutch use which included items from Southeast Asia, the Cape colony, and, of course, Europe. Initially, the excavations indicated the Dutch soldiers ate wild animals, suggesting an impact on local wild foods and possibly the stock of local herders. The team later found, however, that the earliest occupants threw their rubbish into the ocean—and the bones found there were from sheep and cow.

The archaeology at Oudepost seemed to indicate local African people camped at the fort, suggesting established cross-cultural relationships. However, an alternative critique suggests material described as being Khoikhoi predated the Dutch fort, or was deposited in the years when the Dutch were absent.[39]

Resistance to Europeans by southern Africans saw Dutch–Khoikhoi wars in the seventeenth century, as local people were impacted heavily by a small but expansive group of Dutch (*freeburghers*) farmers. By the end of the second war (1670–1677), illegal trading for livestock increased—stock loss was a critical aspect of the decline of Khoikhoi power. The Dutch got involved in local politics and stopped the raiding, one of the ways that at least some groups traditionally gained stock. Some Khoikhoi came to work for the Dutch, revealing the twinned strategies of resistance *and* cooperation. Few historical sources exist for these contexts, but both survival and social disruption are indicated. In the early eighteenth century, the Dutch wandering ranchers (*trekboeren*) who moved out from the Cape also came into conflict with herders. Later the British too clashed with various groups as their colonial program developed.

For the Khoikhoi, many aspects of their traditional society were negatively impacted, the final straw being smallpox epidemics in the early 1700s. The loss of stock through trade and grazing land would have economic impacts, and would affect identity and prestige as well. Some escaped, such as those groups who headed north into the Namib Desert. The archaeological study of their settlements indicates how they eked out an existence in a harsh coastal environment. Other groups also left the Cape in the seventeenth century; some formed remote bands of raiders. Others adopted European ways: the "Griqua" were Dutch-speaking Christians of mixed Khoisan and black African descent who ended up attempting to form communities under the influence of the London Missionary Society.

As *trekboeren* headed north with their stock, intense fighting characterized their northern advance.[40] Some of this history is captured in rock art (below). By the time the British arrived in the late 1700s, the disruption to Cape people had largely occurred; thus their contact frontier was with agropastoralists in the Eastern Cape—with whom they would wage war.

Contact in Rock Art

Southern Africa is world famous for its rock art. The rock art is found in several countries in southern Africa: South Africa, Zimbabwe, Lesotho, Namibia, and Tanzania. Some of it is Pleistocene (art from a cave named Apollo XI dates to at least 19,000 BP), some postdates the arrival of African herders (over the last two millennia), and some San rock art is recent and historical, such as that from KwaZulu-Natal Drakensberg in South Africa, showing both indigenous people and their encounters with colonial European-descent settlers. Much of the painted rock art probably dates to the last millennium.[41]

Not surprisingly, there has been a dedicated effort to incorporate rock art into historical chronologies and analyses and to use the rock art to provide an alternative indigenous insight into colonial contexts.

San rock art illustrates culture contacts with pastoralists occurring well before the arrival of "historical" Europeans, indicating centuries of contact. Much of the art appears to depict symbolic aspects deriving from religious ceremonies. The analysis of the San rock art was given a major boost by work that used nineteenth-century ethnographic and historical accounts to interpret the older rock art, of which the work of David Lewis-Williams was particularly significant. He proposed that rock art was "embedded in rituals and myths, not in the narrative surface of either but in their shared metaphors and symbols." The main themes and intentions of the rock art were shamanistic. The art was also imbued with power: "The images did not merely depict things, they did things."[42] In this regard, they were political devices, embedded in cross-cultural negotiations between cattle herders and San shamans, as well as being intracultural, embedded in San cosmology, action, and experience.

What of the role of rock art in historical interactions? The work of Pieter Jolly from the Department of Archaeology, University of Cape Town, has focused on how San people's interactions and observations of Bantu-speaking pastoralists are documented in San rock art. For example, bandolier apparel worn by Bantu ritual specialists occurs in San images. The increased number of rainmaking images is believed to derive from contacts between herders and San shamans, with the herders being particularly reliant on rainfall. In a related cross-cultural process, San images of cattle became more popular over time, sometimes overlying the once popular images of eland. As resources became contested, rock art showed stock-raiding missions. Interestingly, in a take on "history being written by winners," the scenes never picture San losses in these battles (although they must have occurred), only victories.

The arrival of Europeans is depicted in San rock art, with a focus on new things, such as ox-drawn carts, European garb, horses, and equipment. Sven Ouzman describes the painted rock art in a shelter on the Little Caledon River, dominated by new imagery (Figure 5.4).

> There is very little "traditional" imagery at this site. Instead there is a fat-tailed sheep painted above a striding human figure bearing three spears and most probably representing a farmer or herder. . . . [T]here are two large human figures. The figures are shown in European dress, have their hands placed on their hips near to a powder horn, and each figure has a gun painted next to it. Horses, one with many white dots, flank these two human figures while a third human figure is shown in similar dress with a gun on its shoulder while dismounting from a striped horse.[43]

Lions with bristling manes complete the panel. The panel is interpreted as depicting power through dotted humans and horse, as well as the lions and guns, the use of dots to signify supernatural energy being an existing convention. The pigments depict a shift in rock-art conventions, with the use of new local materials to achieve a different "look" than earlier rock art. Elsewhere motifs portray hybrid creatures combining eland and horse elements, similar to the eland/cow motifs in Bantu–San contact rock art; this seemingly reflects how the experience of contact

Figure 5.4. Historical image of Europeans at Little Caledon River (*from Ouzman 2003: fig. 8b*).

with new things was incorporated into San belief and pictorial traditions in both historical (European-era) and earlier (Bantu-era) contexts.

Working out from the focus on San-produced rock art, Ouzman considers the wider production of historical rock art, which encompasses European engravings (typically names and dates), Khoikhoi rock art (hand-painted and engraved geometric and representational figures), and Bantu-speakers' rock art related to initiation. Ouzman finds rock art produced in the eighteenth and nineteenth centuries by a frontier group known as the !Kora people, and demonstrates how rock art provides a historical line of evidence missing from traditional European-created texts.

So, through rock art the exploration of identity construction in contact contexts is possible as an alternative to contemporary historical accounts.[44]

THE EAST AFRICAN COAST

When the Portuguese arrived in East Africa, they discovered firmly established coastal polities whose control of the movement of local trade items placed them between local African and international Indian Ocean trade networks. Most of the archaeological understanding of this situation derives from investigations of the coastal centers from Mozambique to Somalia, including on the islands of Pemba and Zanzibar, the Comoro islands, and the Lamu archipelago, and of settlements at Mombasa, Shanga, Gedi, Mandu, and Kilwa.[45]

Key research themes along this coast include the archaeological evidence for the origins of Swahili (the main coastal ethnic group), the arrival of Muslims and long-distance trade (dating back now to at least the ninth century), the relation-

126

ship between coastal and hinterland communities, including the impact of slave trading and the workings of African trade networks, and the results of the arrival of the Portuguese.

The East African coast had ancient interregional contacts, with evidence for limited trade contacts with the Mediterranean world predating Islam, suggested by rare finds of Roman glass. Trade increased following the rise of Islamic contacts. The evidence from distinctive material culture such as ceramics suggests early Islamic contacts were driven from the Persian Gulf and that over time the focus shifted to Red Sea connections. In Egypt, Fatamid demand for East African gold and ivory may have fueled early contacts.

There is debate about the influence of the Muslim world on East African Swahili. What is clear from sites like Shanga (Kenya) is that East African coastal Swahili communities with links to hinterland pastoralists and agriculturalists came into contact with overseas people and, as one result, converted to Islam. At Shanga, we find the earliest dated Muslim burials on the coast (800), a sequence of mosques, and ceramics from China, Persia, Arabia, and India.

Early small Islamic outposts existed for a time; then the influence of Islam increased so that after 1100, most Swahili were Muslim. The religious emphasis is very much coastal—all pre-nineteenth-century mosques and Muslim tombs are within 1 kilometer of the sea. Thus, aspects of Swahili societies in the early second millennium, such as stone buildings (houses, mosques, and tombs) and some urban settlements built between 1100 and 1500, are presumably the result of African communities engaged both with African and more distant communities. The debate about the roots of Swahili culture sees both African and Arabic influences—it is clearly the result of both, which produced an outward-looking culture at the time of European contact in the late fifteenth century.[46]

By the fifteenth century, there were also links between the African coast and India, suggested through material evidence and African-descent communities near Gujarat, India (Figure 5.5). Links between East African coastal and hinterland communities are indicated by imported goods, the most distinctive and rare being international trade items such as Chinese and Islamic ceramics found in Kenyan and Zimbabwean hinterland sites. Most famously at Great Zimbabwe, hoarded items included Near Eastern glass and Chinese ceramics.

Presumably in this trade, high-cost/high-status items were exchanged for commodities like gold, copper, iron, grains, and fish. The greatest amount of international trade goods and currency is found in coastal urban settlements, and included ceramics and glass trade beads. The Islamic trade networks grew to demand gold, copper, ivory, possibly timber, and slaves.

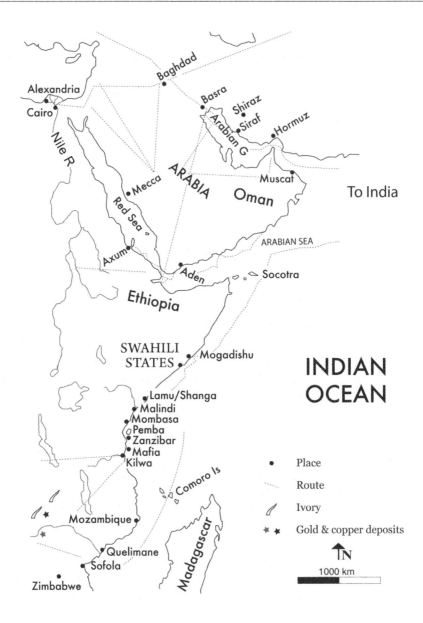

Figure 5.5. Map of the East African coast.

Archaeology of Kilwa: A Medieval East African Trading Center

Archaeological excavations have documented the important trade settlement of Kilwa located on an island off the Swahili coast. Medieval Muslim visitors describe Kilwa and other East African trading outposts. Visitors, probably merchants, would have sailed for weeks in dhows along the African coast from the Horn of Africa. Some stopped to visit other ports where a civilized merchant could find harbor. The African coast may have seemed less safe, as some observant Muslims describe the resistance sometimes put forward by neighboring communities on the African mainland. It was worth it, though, as valuable resources came from Africa, and places like Kilwa were significant intermediaries for these trade goods.

Some goods came from farther south in Africa: Kilwa was one of the southernmost links in an international trade network, as indicated by archaeological objects from Fatamid, Persian Gulf, and Far Eastern trade. Even Chinese porcelain from the ninth to the fourteenth centuries has been found in East Africa near coastal settlements.

Kilwa's heyday was long before the Portuguese arrived, as its main period of power was in the twelfth to fourteenth centuries. Its power is apparent in its architecture. As soon as visitors stepped onto the dock, they would have been impressed by the massive mosque at Kilwa and reassured by the familiar Islamic architecture.

Thus, the archaeological record at Kilwa illustrates the town's importance: it was comprised of stone-built structures, with a Great Mosque, and a distinctive, separate Husani Kubwa residential and administrative palace complex for a powerful ruler, possibly designed by an Arabian architect. The discovery of coins minted in Kilwa suggests the importance of currency in the organization of trade in the local region. The site uncovered in the archaeological work is one of the largest set of precolonial ruins in East Africa.

The Portuguese brought competition to the Swahili trade centers. A decline in East African trade following the Portuguese, however, should not be seen merely as a result of the presence of Portuguese, but rather as another layer in a complicated regional history set into deeper histories of local and international contacts. At Kilwa, for example, it is possible to see the demise of power there following the Portuguese as part of a longer issue related to the management of power and not merely as a simple result of European power and intrusion.

Portuguese on the East Coast

The Portuguese had limited settlements along the coast, with key locations being Kilwa and Mombasa, where Fort Jesus was built after 1593. Small traders were established along the Zambezi River by the 1540s. At Mtoko and Hartley, the archaeology located buildings of sun-dried brick and settlements defended by banks and ditches. The Portuguese had an uneasy presence here. Fort Jesus would be the flashpoint for resistance, being eventually taken by Omanis by the end of the sixteenth century. Such successes lay the foundations for a revival in East African trade in the seventeenth and eighteenth centuries, matched by a greater migration of Arabs. Some coastal settlements that underwent growth probably overlie earlier Portuguese structures, such as at Zanzibar.

Despite this potential, there is a tellingly small amount of material evidence for the Portuguese in East Africa, suggesting that only small numbers ever came. A couple of factories were established on Zanzibar, for tobacco processing, one of the crops introduced along with potatoes, cassava, cucumber, pawpaw, avocado, and guava. Another indirect influence included a shift in boat design to a squared stern on African dhows. The Portuguese colonial interests in the region, however, were nonetheless long-lasting, controlling Mozambique until the 1970s.

Discovering Africa: Colonialism and the Scramble for Africa

The colonial legacy is a significant aspect of Africa. The discussion here has revealed something of the roots of the partition of Africa by European colonial powers—the geography of which was laid down in the Treaty of Berlin (1885), where lines of latitude and longitude, often ignoring any reality of landscape, mapped out African futures. The retreat of European states is remarkably recent, largely occurring in the second half of the twentieth century.

The colonial era is a topic in which historical archaeology has begun to make more extensive inroads, such as seen in the work at Fredericksgave (above). There is potential to take a longer-term view of the colonial period, considering how pre-contact/precolonial communities related to the colonial period and industrialization (where it occurred) and the material aspects for these times.

A material-based approach offers tangential insights, as suggested by Andrew Reid and Paul Lane in *African Historical Archaeologies*. In one example, they refer to the ways that African architecture has changed in colonial contexts. In Tswana communities in southern Africa, houses have shifted from being built of stone, to a mud-and-dung mix, to brick with iron or tile roofs. There has also been a shift from the distinctive round houses—as the explorer Livingstone noted in 1840,[47] people "have a curious inability to make things square." When the British moved Sebele II to a new chief's residence in Molepolole (Botswana), people felt he had abandoned tradition—the British building was rectilinear with decorative gables. To regain authority, Sebele built new residences, in the form of round houses. He also came to experiment with rectangular structures—a compromise form balancing two cultural traditions. This balancing act characterized colonial contexts in Africa as the basic elements of African life and economy changed. In places such as South Africa, changes were created by industrialization or work, shifts in work and gender, as well as the role of African religious belief in response to imported religions.

USEFUL SOURCES

References: A useful comprehensive overview is UNESCO's *General History of Africa* (8 volumes; London: Heinemann Educational Books, 1981–1985). For general overviews of African archaeology, see Gilbert Pwiti and Robert Soper, eds., *Aspects of African Archaeology: Papers from the 10th Congress of the Pan African Association for Prehistory and Related Studies* (Harare: University of Zimbabwe Publications, 1996); David W. Phillipson, *African Archaeology* (Cambridge: Cambridge University Press, 1993): chap. 8 deals with AD 1000 onward); Robert B.M. Ridinger, *African Archaeology: A Selected Bibliography* (New York: G. K. Hall, 1993); Peter Mitchell, *The Archaeology of Southern Africa* (Cambridge: Cambridge University Press, 2002); Susan Kent, ed., *Ethnicity, Hunter-Gatherers, and the "Other": Association and Assimilation in Africa* (Washington, DC: Smithsonian Institution Press, 2002); Peter Mitchell, *African Connections: Archaeological Perspectives on Africa and the Wider World* (Walnut Creek, CA: AltaMira Press, 2005); Ann B. Stahl, *African Archaeology: A Critical Introduction* (Malden, MA: Blackwell, 2005).

For historical archaeology in Africa, see Peter R. Schmidt, *Historical Archaeology: A Structural Approach in an African Culture* (Westport, CT: Greenwood Press, 1978); Lisa Falk, ed., *Historical Archaeology in Global Perspective* (Washington, DC: Smithsonian Institution Press, 1991); Kit Wesler, *Historical Archaeology in Nigeria* (Trenton, NJ: World Press, 1998); Andrew M. Reid and Paul J. Lane, eds., *African Historical Archaeologies* (London: Kluwer Academic/Plenum, 2004); Peter Schmidt, *Historical Archaeology in Africa: Representation, Social Memory, and Oral Traditions* (Lanham, MD: AltaMira, 2006); Natalie Swanepoel et al., eds., *Five Hundred Years Rediscovered: Southern African Precedents and Prospects* (Johannesburg: Wits University Press, 2008); Natalie Swanepoel, "The Practice and Substance of Historical Archaeology in Sub-Saharan Africa," in Sub-Saharan Africa," in *International Handbook of Historical Archaeology*, ed. T. Majewski and D. Gaimster (New York: Springer, 2009), 565–581.

Key journals: Mainstream international archaeology journals, plus *African Archaeological Review, Journal of African Archaeology, African Studies, Journal of Southern African Studies, West African Journal of Archaeology, South African Archaeological Bulletin, The Digging Stick, Annual Review of Anthropology.* For historical studies, see *Journal of African History* and *History in Africa.* See also *The South African Archaeological Society, Goodwin Series,* and the *African Diaspora Archaeology Newsletter,* which is published quarterly online.

CHAPTER 6

THE SPANISH
IN THE AMERICAS

With the true God, the true *Dios*,
came the beginning of our misery.
It was the beginning of tribute, the beginning of church dues...
The beginning of strife by trampling on people,
The beginning of robbery with violence,
The beginning of forced debts,
The beginning of debts enforced by false testimony,
The beginning of individual strife.

–Mayan account from *Books of Chilam Bayam*[1]

The contacts that ensued between Native Americans, Europeans, and Africans after 1492 lay at the roots of our modern world. Many societies that fell, and those that arose, after the fifteenth century have Iberian, African, and Native American roots. While the trajectory toward America from a European perspective has roots in the medieval world, one imagines initially that Native Americans were caught unaware, although there was much built into indigenous world views that helped to explain the multiple encounters, at least until Europeans diverged from the script. It is easy to simplify these encounters into narratives of conquest and loss, but there is much complexity here, as expressed by historical archaeologist Kathleen Deagan:

> It cannot be characterized by any of the familiar dichotomies—conqueror/conquered, invader/invaded, resident/immigrant, trader/supplier, or European/aboriginal. It was simultaneously an invasion, a colonizing effort, a social experiment, a religious crusade, and an economic experiment.[2]

The arrival of the Spanish in the Americas in 1492 meant the world was changed forever. The event can be compared to a stone thrown into a pool, with ripples extending outward: the people of the Caribbean rim were the first to come into contact with the Spanish. Hispaniola was the first front, and within decades Florida, Mexico, Central America, and South America were the foci for European settlement or other contacts, such as slave raids. The ramifications for native peoples were often calamitous. Some people were destroyed, some maintained traditional lifeways, and in many places new societies were created from processes of culture contact.

This chapter begins with the Caribbean archipelago, being the first area of sustained culture contact, and then moves to the major foci of Spanish activity in Mexico and Central America, La Florida, the North American Southwest, and California.[3]

The focus on the Spanish in America has a long pedigree. The obvious similarities across the Spanish colonial realm invite comparisons between disparate parts of an empire that extended from the Philippines to Florida. However, this masks the variety of indigenous societies in contact with the Spanish, and each set of contacts is better explored in regional studies focusing on understanding the response of indigenous societies to colonial circumstances.

IBERIA AND THE NEW WORLD CONNECT

The Spanish story always begins with Columbus. The Genoese merchant captain Cristóbal Colón (Columbus) had spent years promoting a western route to Asia in the courts in Seville and Portugal; his brother Bartolomé sought support in France and Britain. With Spanish support achieved, the caravels *Pinta, Nina,* and *Santa María* departed, manned with crews keen to profit from their undertaking. While the theory of Asia being to the west was correct, Columbus miscalculated the distances to Asia. Arriving in the Caribbean, he believed he had reached some small islands off the Asian coast and that the courts of the Great Khan were over the horizon.[4] Thus, the people he met were "Indians," a term that came to be used for indigenous Americans.

Landing in the Bahamas, Columbus acted like other Europeans laying land claims around the Earth: he landed a party on the beach, raised the flags of his sponsors, thanked God, took possession of the land on behalf of Ferdinand and Isabella, and named the island San Salvador. While it is unclear which island this was, the local people called it *Guanahaní.*

Columbus saw native people as easy-to-control resources, capturing some to be returned to Castille for assessment by the court and to learn Spanish: "[T]hese people are very simple as regards their use of arms. . . . they can be subjugated and made to do what is required of them."[5]

The Spanish colonial domains across the Americas resulting from these discoveries were eventually expansive, as was the Portuguese realm in Brazil. Consequently, Iberian-speaking peoples today extend from the United States to the southern tip of South America. Within decades of 1492, Spaniards controlled the Caribbean; Mexico (Viceroyalty of New Spain), following the fall of Tenochtitlan (1521); the Andes (Viceroyalty of Peru), after the conquest of the Incan capital Cuzco (1533); the southeastern United States, which the Spanish termed *La Florida*—with their capital of St. Augustine (1565); and the North American Southwest to California. Later the Viceroyalty of Peru was carved into the Viceroyalty of New Granada (1717)—modern Panama, Colombia, Ecuador, and Venezuela—and the Viceroyalty of Río de la Plata (1776) encompassed modern Argentina, Bolivia, Paraguay, and Uruguay (Figure 6.1).

Spanish demands for gold dominated early culture contacts. Large numbers of native people died extracting it from mines and alluvial deposits. However, significant gold deposits would be found only in Colombia, while silver became the primary precious metal to pour from the Americas into Spanish royal coffers. Massive silver deposits were mined in Bolivia (after 1545) and Mexico (1546 onward).

Figure 6.1. Map of the Caribbean, showing key locations and some indigenous American societies referenced in the text.

Other valuable exports to Europe were dyes (cochineal and indigo) and cacao. In exchange, the Spanish poured trade goods into the Americas.

SPANISH APPROACHES TO AMERICANS

The Spanish process of conquest and colonization had several common elements, the first being warfare, sometimes accomplished by manipulating local groups as campaign partners and informants. Contact often tended to be direct, based on colonization, missionization, and exploitation of native people, coupled with a suite of expectations, including tribute, servitude, taxation, and adoption of new beliefs. Together these elements constricted the world of various indigenous people, particularly those in more direct contact.

Common Spanish modes of cultural engagement were employed, particularly *encomienda, repartimiento*, missions, and *haciendas*. The *repartimiento* (*mita* in Peru and the *cuatequil* in Mexico) allowed colonists to apply for Native Americans as forced labor: normally a percentage of a local population was required to meet the obligations of the system. In the *encomienda* system, Native Americans were assigned to Spaniards who in turn could demand tribute in the form of labor, food, or gold.

Encomienda and *repartimiento* were suited to contexts where the Spaniards required indigenous laborers in large numbers, such as for the mines and plantations common to the Caribbean, Central America, and South America. Attempts were made to end this slave labor, such as the "New Laws" of 1542 that ended the use of *encomienda,* briefly. They were less suited for contexts where labor was less important, as in La Florida, where often the mission was the core colonial strategy.

There was little differentiation between church and state, and religious institutions were a significant aspect of colonization. But it took the provision of indigenous labor and tribute to make the missions viable. In studies of the military and religious aspects of colonization, the role of the church differentiates the Spanish from other European colonizers.

Additionally, the Spanish crown granted *haciendas* for enterprises like plantations, mines, and ranches. Haciendas included the land *and* the native people on them and were particularly common in colonial South and Central America. In regions with few natural resources, the main resource was labor used to produce food and tribute. Ranches, too, mobilized labor, to raise stock for hides and meat. Labor as tribute varied from collecting water and transporting goods to domestic work, collecting nuts (in New Mexico), and mining salt—whatever was in demand.

Also significant were *presidios,* fortified bases common in frontier regions like New Mexico and California.

Spanish cities were the main focus of civic and administrative function: Native Americans provided the labor to build them, and they created ethnically diverse communities. By 1600, there were four hundred Spanish American cities. They mirrored Spanish thinking about town planning in the transition from late medieval ideas: some common elements were the basic grid pattern dictating the organization of streets and squares, and the presence of civic, religious, and administrative functions. Colonial settlements were dictated by economic factors: profitable places attracted merchants and grew; other places were more peripheral and existed to meet security and territorial needs. Since cities and towns tended to be built where Native Americans lived, the locations of the earliest colonial settlements often reflect indigenous population demographics at contact.

Archaeology demonstrates fine-grained details about the lives of the various occupants of these towns, as detailed below for Ciudad Vieja, El Salvador's first Spanish capital.

Spanish treatment of indigenous Americans varied, but was often appalling. The most famous whistle-blower about Spanish mistreatment of indigenous people was Bartolomé de las Casas who, after a period in Hispaniola as priest and running an *encomienda* with slaves, and witnessing the killing of Taíno people, became an advocate for reform, attempting to end the *encomienda* and to alert Europeans to the violence in the New World. He detailed the destruction of native societies in *A Short Account of the Destruction of the Indies.* Las Casas represented one side of a debate about conquest and appropriate treatment of native peoples. The other side felt justified that native societies were subdued and reduced because they were perceived as inferior to the Spanish.

Some Native American responses to Spanish colonialism can be briefly detailed here, varying as they did from forms of resistance and rebellion to alliances and collaborations.

Unlike in West Africa (chapter 5), control of traditional land was often wrested away from indigenous Americans, resulting in conflict. However, indigenous resistance did not necessarily mean warfare, as withholding of labor was sufficient to successfully undermine the viability of Spanish ventures. Other rebellious tactics by laborers may have included deliberately poor planting of crops, poor tending of crops and animals, hiding produce, and flight.[6]

Archaeology has often focused on cultural change from precontact baselines: others have reversed this perspective and focus on the ways that indigenous societies persisted and on the evidence for cultural survival. There is a long tradition in American archaeology of exploring the indigenous engagement with Spanish colonial institutions, some of which is briefly explored in this chapter.

DISEASE AND HEALTH

One critical issue is demography and disease, as many new diseases stalked native peoples after 1492. The analysis of skeletal material reveals there already were infectious diseases in the New World, but there was no smallpox, measles, influenza, typhus, chickenpox, cholera, plague, whooping cough, or malaria. These had developed in crowded European cities. In America, these diseases were "virgin soil" events, with high mortality levels.

Thus, in the power struggle that was culture contact across the Americas, the role of disease and demography was significant. There are several important aspects to American disease histories. First, there is debate about the degree of impact of diseases. Part of this debate concerns the size and density of populations prior to 1492, something that is calculated using archaeological and historical data. The key problem with the use of historical accounts to determine population size is that they may have been written well after a disease front, or not. For example, it has been argued that a smallpox pandemic in 1518 in the Caribbean, Mexico, and South America resulted in high numbers of fatalities and wiped out some communities. As such, historical accounts of these regions were of post-pandemic communities.

To determine population character *prior* to contact requires good archaeological evidence, such as human remains and settlement data up to regional levels: this quality of evidence does not occur everywhere. Some demography models calculate that mortality was high, extensive, and early. Other models suggest more of a tapestry of diseases, with varying degrees of population decline and a greater time period for first exposure to diseases whereby some remote populations remained unaffected by diseases until more recent times. Factors such as the nature of the infection, exposure to hosts, settlement density, and treatment of infection all relate to eventual fatality levels. Further, there is debate about which infections were present—some diseases leave no traces on skeletal remains.

Overall, it seems likely that while large numbers of people died as a result of infectious diseases after 1492, the distribution of these effects depended on these variables. The ways that people dealt with these dramatic changes varied greatly. While some indigenous societies were destroyed, survivors sometimes coalesced into new communities or moved to the colonial settlements (or vice versa). Environmental factors were also significant, as many native people in colonial settings were malnourished, overworked, and had a poor diet—increasing the impact of disease and physical stress.

Consequently, early colonial America would have often seen landscapes less densely populated than they were prior to 1492. This was due partly to population decline through disease and conflict, coupled with the small number of Spanish migrants.

THE ARCHAEOLOGY OF CONTACT

The contact period is a vibrant area of archaeological, historical, and anthropological research: some key areas can be briefly raised here. Importantly, archaeology provides, alongside analysis of indigenous accounts, some sense of indigenous people as meaningful actors in culture contact.

The legacy of contact in the Spanish colonies differs from that in the British and French colonies in the Americas (predominantly in the United States and Canada) in several keys ways. There were fewer Spanish migrants than indigenous people. Today, as a result, across Latin America the dominant ancestry is indigenous, similar to many African contexts (chapter 5). Instead of replacement populations, as seen in settler societies such as Canada, in Spanish colonies contact relied on a process of Hispanicization, where local people became enmeshed in colonial institutions. The Spanish viewed indigenous peoples as an essential element in their economic activities, something that was not always true for the British, although it was sometimes true for the French fur-traders (chapter 7). Additionally, and related to this, there were legal differences between the Spanish and the other Europeans in the New World related to slavery, intermarriage, and inheritance.

The sizable African population in the Americas was critical in the development of the Spanish Americas. Consequently, a sizable African-American population came into existence alongside others tracing descent to both Spanish and indigenous ancestors.

The Spanish were very aware of ethnic, racial, class, and gender differences, and a system—*sistema de castas*—existed in which racial identity and social position were defined. The Spanish defined "pure" races: Spanish, African, and American. These had legal consequences, defining free and unfree, colonized and colonizer. The *sistema de castas* described a multitude of mixed-descent peoples—*castas*—beyond these racial boundaries. Archaeology provides some insight into the ways such differences were lived out (Figure 6.2).

Archaeologists have explored the material remains of these different elements of Spanish colonies and the way that new communities were formed, a process described as "ethnogenesis," the most common form being creolization. A key concept is *mestizaje*, referring to the mixing of Indian and European elements, although it can be used more broadly to refer to any ethnic mixing, as in Brazil. The concept has had different meanings over time, from the *sistemas de castas* of the

Figure 6.2. Example of image showing *casta*:
"Miguel Cabrera, de español y de india, mestiza," 1763, oil on canvas. *Private collection.*

early colonial eras, through to issues of elite and non-elite in countries like Mexico in later centuries, to present-day issues of identity.

From an archaeological perspective, the work of Kathleen Deagan is important, as is that of others, such as Barbara Voss in San Francisco (below). A key strategy for archaeologists has been to focus on the evidence for mundane activities, often within households, for it is here that the evidence for multi-ethnic households and cultural fusions can be found. For example, the appearance of ceramic vessels, decisions made about food and its consumption, and other preferences of daily life and its physical trappings (e.g., clothes) can reveal much about a community.[7]

EARLY CULTURE CONTACT IN HISPANIOLA

Our Lord miraculously led me there to a point from which I could no longer proceed nor retreat with the ships, but had to unload them there and establish a settlement.

–Christopher Columbus[8]

The Caribbean archipelago includes the Greater and Lesser Antilles; at contact, Caribs occupied the Lesser Antilles, with strong links, in terms of language and contacts, to the South American mainland. In the Greater Antilles, Taíno people lived in complex chiefdoms—one of the chiefs encountered in 1492 was Guarionex who, like a handful of high chiefs on Hispaniola, ruled over tens of thousands of villagers. There were also hunter-forager groups, notably on Cuba, presumably remnant populations that predated the Taíno expansion from South America over two thousand years earlier. The Taíno world was interconnected via the sea, over which large canoes each shuttled up to one hundred people. Popular events were ball games, which acted as festivals for religious activities, trade, feasting, conflict resolution, and to meet marriage partners.

In similar ways to the early Portuguese dealings with West Africans, the Spanish targeted the chiefs like Guarionex, whom they termed *caciques*—as they needed them to maintain the tribute system whereby desired goods flowed to the small number of Spaniards. Often the Spanish resorted to force. Smaller numbers of Spaniards used their physical superiority: guns, swords, dogs, and horses worked a principle of "shock and awe." The first couple of decades of contact saw massive changes across Hispaniola in terms of the size and organization of the Taíno population faced with their destruction.

Finding remains of the very earliest colonial settings in the Americas has proved elusive, but it has been possible to find traces of the earliest period of Spanish–American contact. The key archaeological sites of early Spanish settlement and culture contact in Hispaniola are La Isabela (1493–1498),[9] Puerto Real (1503–1578), and Concepción de la Vega (1502–1562).[10]

As the earliest planned European settlement in the Americas (after the Vikings), La Isabela is a significant site, despite the fact that it lasted only four years after Columbus landed fifteen hundred men from seventeen ships. Archaeologists argue that this settlement laid the ground rules for Spanish settlements in the New World: it also laid the basis for cross-cultural contacts with local Taíno people.

The Spanish were already mistrustful when they arrived, having found out that the group of forty men Columbus had left behind at the settlement of La Navidad the previous year had been killed, and their fort destroyed. The Spanish were well equipped, but the settlement was dominated by male soldiers and adventurers, many of whom had fought in the *Reconquista* of Spain (chapter 4).

The ships were loaded with European animals and plants, including sugarcane, which would become a major cash crop in the Caribbean region. Also on board—in bodies—were the organisms that would cause devastating diseases. Illness beset the settlement, with death stalking both the Spanish and Taíno.

The early days were hard: epidemics swept away many of the settlers, while fire destroyed much of the settlement. A mutiny in the first few months was crushed, and some mutineers were hanged. Another rebellion in 1497 ended La Isabela, though new settlements continued elsewhere in Hispaniola. What does archaeology tell us of this turbulent sliver of colonial time?

La Isabela

The Spanish built La Isabela on a Taíno village site, which materially dates to the second half of the fifteenth century. It appears to have been abandoned before the Spanish arrived, who built their church, cemetery, and house for Columbus over the remains of the village. Its coastal location and concentration of net sinkers suggest it was once a fishing village. Most archaeological finds—fishing gear, ceramic bowls and bottles, midden remains, stone tools, and human burials—predate the Spaniards; however, the Spanish appear to have collected Taíno decorative and ritual objects, such as bone and shell amulets possibly associated with concepts of life and death. These objects were found in the Spanish residential quarters. Interestingly, the Spanish did not use Native American ceramics, something that would characterize other early colonial sites in the Americas.

The Spanish colonists built a fortified urban settlement at La Isabela with church, hospital, houses, warehouses, and defenses; nearby was an agricultural settlement, watermill (Las Coles), and a quarry. Neighboring Indian villages have been excavated: El Perenal and Bajabonico were farming villages only 500 meters apart; both were established by ca. 1300 and remained occupied through the early contact period, as suggested by the presence of Spanish trade goods. The different ceramics at each site indicate two different groups, one Taíno, the other the Spanish called *Macoriges*. Columbus described curious Taíno visitors to La Isabela from neighboring villages, drawn in part by the potential to trade. Popular items were tiny bells (hawk's bells) and beads.

The Spanish reports described an orderly town in a regular plan, yet the archaeology reveals a haphazard arrangement dictated by local topography. The building remains—masonry and rammed-earth buildings with lime-plastered walls and floors and tiled or thatched roofs—are the only fifteenth-century European structures in the Americas.

The military trappings of the settlement are clear, although most battles with islanders occurred away from La Isabela. By 1492, a shift from crossbows to firearms was underway—both types of weapon are found in the archaeological record. The evidence for defensive and offensive behavior extends to armor, artillery, edged weapons (swords, knives, daggers, rapiers), and horse equipment.

Beyond La Isabela

La Isabela and nearby villages provide evidence for the early phase of Spanish colonization and culture contact in Hispaniola. Later sites would differ in key ways. They would survive longer and be more elaborate. They would have more women. They operated in a rapidly changing demographic environment in which the population of Hispaniola fell from over one million to around twenty thousand in two decades. The abandonment of Native American villages is hardly surprising. In fact, it is amazing that so many aspects of aboriginal diet and design survived, not only through the early contact period but still today in the Dominican Republic.[11]

Of the other early colonial towns in Hispaniola, two others have been excavated: Puerto Real and Concepción de la Vega. The archaeology indicates many differences from La Isabela. These towns were better planned and larger, and did not require defensive walls. The changes observed by archaeologists concerned daily life, as the occupants shifted "from the medieval Andalusian material world reflected at La Isabela towards a Renaissance-inspired, mixed American and European material pattern."[12]

Food remains at Puerto Real indicate a dietary shift: people ate more local food and beef (which was rarer in Spain). Part of the new diet may relate to women—be they Spanish, Native American, or African cooks—because this trend was not seen at the all-male La Isabela. The new cuisine was very much a New World cross-cultural creation.

The presence of Native American and African women in domestic contexts is strongly suggested by the use of Native American or African pottery vessels for cooking and food storage, as well as traditional hearths and American food grinding equipment—the manos, metates, and griddle used for cooking maize and cassava. The simple pots that were found in Hispaniola and across the Spanish Caribbean are called "colono-ware" by archaeologists (Figure 6.3); they are a material manifestation of culture contact, being similar to precontact forms, but simplified, and probably used by both Americans and Africans.

The Caribbean people who lived at these and other colonial settlements were surviving Taíno, but increasingly indigenous people from across the Caribbean were brought alongside African slaves to work in mines, households, ranches, and plantations. The people of Hispaniola, as the first scene of Spanish colonization in the Americas, suffered a terrible calamity. From this base, the colonial program rolled onward and into the Americas.

Each part of the Caribbean had its own contact history. Taíno on Puerto Rico were conquered around 1500, while the colonization efforts on Cuba were initially less intense, given that there was no gold. Carib people of the Lesser Antilles were initially beyond sixteenth-century Spanish colonization—with the exception of sporadic slave raids.

Figure 6.3. Colono-ware pottery: 44KW0029.
(*Courtesy Virginia Department of Historic Resources.*)

Across the Caribbean, many African communities were established, typically at plantations dominated by slave labor. From the sixteenth century onward, settlements came to have more enslaved Africans than Native Americans. Consequently, some archaeological research has focused on the development of Creole communities, with elements of Spanish, African, and Native American societies.

In addition to the Spanish, other European nations—the British, French, Dutch, and Danes—established Caribbean and South American colonies and plantation economies that are the root of many contemporary Caribbean societies.

New Spain

> Proudly stands the city of Mexico,
> Tenochtitlán,
> Here no one fears to die in war…
> Keep this in mind, O princes…
> Who would attack Tenochtitlán?
> Who could shake the foundations of heaven?[13]

The Spanish conquest of Mexican and Andean societies followed the Caribbean. Here the Spanish encountered levels of social and political complexity equal with their own: large urban societies with strong agrarian bases, standing armies, and effective communication. How is it that the Spanish, numbering a few hundred and poorly provisioned, were able to defeat the Aztecs in their homeland? The Aztecs were around ten million people, whose capital was possibly the largest in the world. The answers are in part due to cross-cultural negotiations. The conquistadors' initial success resulted from their manipulation of local tensions and their access to important intelligence.

Aztec historical accounts describe the critical conditions leading up to conquest: that the Aztec leader Moctezuma was worried by prophecies of disasters preceding the arrival of Cortez, and that his initial impressions of the Spaniards were of their potential otherworldliness, their association with the Aztec deity Quetzalcoatl, and their brutality.

The Spanish were provided with gifts and delegations from the Mexican king, but it is clear that the Spanish accounts fail to interpret Moctezuma's messages correctly. His gifts were intended to remind the Spanish of the Mexican king's dominance and wealth, which Cortez effectively brushed aside with the help of Moctezuma's enemies.

When the Spaniards entered into Tenochtitlan-Tlatelolco, the Mexican capital with 200,000 residents, they seized Moctezuma. After the death of Moctezuma, the Spaniards laid siege to the city, which fell in August 1521. The

Spaniards destroyed the city, replacing it with a new capital for New Spain. Our understanding of these events is based on historical accounts; however, the subsequent centuries of Spanish colonialism are also available in archaeological records.

Xaltocan

Archaeology provides an important line of evidence separate from historical accounts. To take one example, a study by Enrique Rodriguez-Alegria (2008) of cutting tools in Xaltocan, in the Basin of Mexico, provides some surprises. His study considers stone tools, which in some models of contact studies are considered to fall out of favor with indigenous people, who are supposedly quickly won over by the superior metals of Europeans. This model is, at least in part, fueled by a bias toward European material and technological superiority.

However, archaeologists across the Americas have begun to detail how stone tool traditions sometimes continued after contact, despite the presence of new metals. The reasons were complex, including functional preferences, availability of material (both stone and metal), symbolic aspects of tools, gendered aspects of tools production and use, and social ranking.[14]

The evidence from Xaltocan provides a long-term perspective on indigenous decisions about tools. The evidence indicates that from at least 900, the main type of stone tool was made from flaking (chipping) obsidian, which needed to be imported: primarily, blades, projectile points, and scrapers were produced.

In 1430, Xaltocan was conquered by the Aztecs. In 1521, it became part of the Spanish realm. Under the Aztecs, tool production changed immediately: people stopped flaking tools and started buying finished tools in local Aztec-dominated markets.

The arrival of the Spanish did not see a shift toward metal tools; instead, people resumed flaking tools, a practice abandoned several generations earlier. The use of stone may have continued well into the nineteenth century, when metal tools possibly became affordable, accessible, and legitimate, as the Spanish had restricted the access to metal weapons in the early contact period.

This study reminds us that native people were already familiar with intruders with imperial ambitions long before the Spanish arrived, so that people in the Aztec and Incan empires already knew of forms of domination and appropriate responses, in a sense similar to that described for both East and West African societies in the previous chapter.

The colonial Viceroyalty of New Spain extended from the southern and western United States through to Panama (and included the Philippines and New Mexico), with Mexico as its capital, and lasted until 1821, when Mexico gained independence from Spain. Native Americans of Mesoamerica became variously enfolded into the Spanish Empire. Many survived: the descendants of Mayas, Zapotecs, Mixtecs, Aztecs, and others maintain strong links with indigenous heritage today. Some resisted for centuries; for example, Mayans of the Yucatan Peninsula were conquered after the mid-sixteenth century, yet they warred with Spanish and, later, Mexican forces until the twentieth century. The current Chiapas rebellion continues Mayan resistance today.

Contact in Cities

Spanish cities were an essential aspect of the Conquest period in Central America: "[he] who fails to settle fails to conquer properly" (Francisco López de Gómara).[15] Some cities survive as archaeological sites—for example, in El Salvador, the site of Ciudad Vieja provides evidence of one early Spanish city, Villa de San Salvador, founded in 1525 and abandoned by 1545. Here the indigenous population (Pipil and Tlaxcalan) far exceeded the number of Spaniards, and indigenous attempts to resist resulted in a brief period of settlement abandonment.

Archaeological research at Villa de San Salvador reveals the use of the grid layout consistent with Spanish planning, and the remains of dwellings, food preparation areas, ritual spaces, civic buildings, commercial and industrial buildings, warehouses, defenses, and transport infrastructure. In this city, the residences of the Spanish differed from those of indigenous people: the Spanish lived in larger multi-room structures with stone foundations and tiled roofs, while other houses were small, with earth floors and thatched roofs. There were differences, too, in how each was aligned in relation to the street and the grid.

Spanish influences in architecture were strong, and buildings used industrially produced materials like glass, iron, and brick. However, in the more mundane material culture, we see a stronger fingerprint of local people: 60,000 sherds of ceramics were of indigenous production, and other artifacts like jade objects and jewelry suggest a sizable indigenous population in the city. One interesting form of the ceramic tradition is serving plates made with Mesoamerican techniques and designs but copying European majolica shapes; these hybrid objects were daily reminders of the mixed community.

Outside of cities, rural life across Central America was a key setting for culture contact. Mines and ranches were important components of colonial economics and show heavy reliance on indigenous labor. Although colonial ventures necessarily took place in landscapes with longer traditions of agricultural production and political activities, these earlier traditions could affect the degree to which Spanish colonialism succeeded—for it was resisted successfully in many places.

Throughout Central America, we see clear differences in response, particularly when comparing a large agrarian indigenous population, a Creole population, and Spaniards and Africans.

A key interpretive issue in Central American culture contact is dominance and resistance—especially in early phases of contact. As in the African examples, however, there is much racial mixing here, certainly more than in Greenland (chapter 3) or the Pacific and East Asia (chapter 8). Beyond mere dominance and resistance, regional studies record how material culture is evidence for approaches to culture contact: the stone tools of the Xaltocan, for example, evoke Ann Stahl's study of ceramic production in Ghana, as in each, material evidence provides insight into changes and continuities in material practice reflecting *both* external forces on these respective societies as well as local preferences and decision making.

The Spanish colonization of Central America and the Caribbean was focused on gold, silver, and access to indigenous labor. In Florida, a very different pattern of culture contact unfolded.

LA FLORIDA

La Florida (modern Florida and Georgia) was peripheral to Spanish interests in the Americas but an important buffer for other European expansionary states. Culture contact was initially sporadic. Early coastal slave-raiders seeking plantation laborers were followed by official explorations in 1513 by Juan Ponce de León and in 1540 by Hernando de Soto.

There were unsuccessful attempts to explore and to colonize the Atlantic seaboard by Spanish settlers, and by the French (1562) at Charleston/Santa Elena, and the English (1565) at Roanoke (chapter 7). Add to these a handful of shipwreck survivors who lived among Native Americans.

In these contacts, diseases and information about Europeans were introduced to North America in advance of permanent colonies, of which the longest-lived settlement was St. Augustine (1565). Centuries later, the Spanish hold on Florida was lost to the British (in 1783) and then the United States (in 1821).

The consequences of early contacts were sometimes tragic. De Soto in 1539 described abandoned villages depopulated by plague and pestilence; in some cases, houses were filled with corpses.[16] Where contact was greatest, the impact of diseases would have been higher—and densely populated groups suffered more. Near St. Augustine, for example, some local communities did not survive the early Spanish presence.

As a consequence, Spanish settlement occurred when indigenous societies were responding to great change. Some Native American societies united—for example, the Yamasee Indians encountered by the Spanish in South Carolina and Georgia appeared to have coalesced as a regional polity only during the 1600s, possibly in reaction to depopulation following disease epidemics, or in response to the threat of slave raiders.

Not all Native Americans of La Florida came into direct contact with the Spanish. The key societies in contact were Apalachee, Timucua, and Guale (Figure 6.4). The primary settings for contact were missions and haciendas, where forms of cross-cultural accommodation occurred, although conflicts were also significant.

Some Native Americans were remote from the "frontline" of contact, occupying regions that were less attractive to the Spanish, such as in the interior of La Florida, along the Gulf Coast, or north of the Guale toward Chesapeake Bay.

- ■ Franciscan missions before 1606
- ★ Franciscan missions in Apalachee 1633–1650
- □ New missions in Timucua after 1656 rebellion

Figure 6.4. Map of La Florida phases of missions, Spanish settlements, and Native American people.

Missions to southern hunter-foragers were never successful, given the sparsely populated regions, nor were missions to very distant communities, such as the Creek in inland Georgia.

While there were many similarities in American societies of the southeast, differences existed, such as economic practices. Missionaries were most successful among agriculturalists and less so among hunter-foragers. Consequently, much contact was directed toward farmers living in villages and organized into chiefdoms.

The most complex societies in contact with Spaniards were the Apalachee Indians in northwest Florida: they were of the Mississippian culture, with a mound-building tradition and a densely populated chiefdom based on the farming of maize, bean, and squash. The Apalachee farmers helped the Spanish to survive in La Florida. Their food fed the Spanish, as did crops from Guale gardens.

It was more difficult for missionaries to deal with people who were not permanent village dwellers, as Father Rogel made clear in 1640: "To make conversions among the people of this province who are unaware of Christianity they must be made to come together, live in settlements, and cultivate enough food so they can live year-round in one place. After they are settled, let the preaching commence."[17]

Native American responses to the Spanish varied, but included outright resistance as demonstrated by an uprising in Apalachee (1647) that required the combined efforts of a coalition of Spanish soldiers and Timucuan warriors to suppress. Nor was resistance over quickly: the year-long Timucua Rebellion of 1656 came more than a century after Spanish contact and after a half a century of missions. The failure of the rebellion resulted in a smaller population and a readjustment of the colonial landscape, increasingly along Spanish settlement patterns. By the middle of the seventeenth century, the main elements of resistance had ended, and mission development among the surviving population continued.

If we look elsewhere, we may find comparisons with places such as southern Africa (chapter 5), where a local population was subject to invasion and colonial rule, although the colonial program there took many decades rather than occurring in a rapid demographic shift, as seen in Hispaniola. The key element to culture contact in La Florida was the Spanish missions.

THE SPANISH MISSIONS OF LA FLORIDA

Once colonization was firmly underway, the missions were an essential aspect of the Spanish presence in La Florida. By the late eighteenth century, over 150 Franciscan and Jesuit missions had been established from Florida to the Chesapeake Bay.[18] Some key archaeological sites comprise Spanish settlements and missions, including St. Augustine, Pensacola, San Luís, San Luís de Talimali (ca. 1656) in Florida, Santa Elena (South Carolina), and St. Catherines Island (1580) in Georgia (described below).

The missions were obligated to provide tribute to the Spanish, typically food (mines and plantations were unimportant in La Florida). Thus missions and Native American villages occupied the same landscape.

The location of many early missions indicates precontact patterns of settlement, as missions were often located near existing communities. Yet despite our evidence from Spanish sources and native accounts, most missions described by the Spanish are not easily matched to known archaeological sites. Archaeological traces of early Spanish-era missions are slight, and few have any above-ground permanent structures like those associated with missions in California or Texas.

This pattern had changed by the seventeenth century, however, where we see the peak of the system, with around 38 missions overseeing some 26,000 Christian Native Americans.[19]

The missions included one or two friars, the local Native Americans, and, in some instances, some soldiers. The addition of a church was often the greatest change to villages, which may have remained otherwise unchanged from precontact organization. Similarly, the society remained structurally unchanged. As the conversion process focused on the elite—the chiefs and their family—it did not attempt to change the ranked nature of these communities.

While the archaeology of these settings is very limited, it does suggest:

- Differential distribution of elite material, such as Spanish goods, to chiefly elite, indicating that indigenous status and rank structures remained unchanged.

- A shift in burial practices from the precontact use of burial mounds to Indian burials in cemeteries or churches (however, in some places mound burials continued unchanged).

- The development of new material practices that reflect the cross-cultural and creole communities that arose in places, as demonstrated at St. Augustine.

St. Augustine

The most famous archaeological site is St. Augustine, established by Jesuits in 1565. The early years at St. Augustine were a struggle; the mission was briefly abandoned in 1572 following Native American resistance. The Franciscans took over, and St. Augustine became the coastal nerve center of a network of missions and *visitas*—communities regularly visited by traveling missionaries.

From here, missions were spread in a chain to the west, to San Luís de Talimali mission in Apalachee territory, and along the coast into Guale territory, to the northern missions based at Santa Catalina de Guale on St. Catherines Island and on Amelia Island.

At St. Augustine, archaeological research has continued for over thirty years, directed by historical archaeologist Kathleen Deagan from the Florida Museum of Natural History and assisted by the city archaeologists, archaeology students, and keen volunteers. The program has provided a detailed view into life in the capital, how the Spanish adapted to the Americas, and how a *criollo* culture developed from cultural entanglements.

Kathleen Deagan's detailed analysis of St. Augustine defined a "Spanish Colonial Pattern" whereby colonists balanced their Spanish identity with life in the New World. Historical accounts describe that only a tiny number of Spanish women accompanied men to St. Augustine; consequently, a great amount of cultural mixing occurred here, as in many other settings across the Spanish colonies. Highly visible aspects of their life—clothing, tableware, religious items, and personal ornamentation—were distinctly Spanish, while other aspects of their life indicate close relations with Native Americans. Presumably this pattern mirrors male–female roles: the Spanish males and their Native American–descent partners.

The development of mixed-descent (*mestizaje*) creole communities, with African, Native American, and Spanish aspects, were documented at St. Augustine particularly at the level of household, where the union of European men and Native American women led to new cultural traditions (Figure 6.2). Deagan explored differences between *criollo* households, where Spanish traits in the New World were emphasized, and *mestizo* households, where new traditions arose from multiethnic relationships. This creolization process was seen in different parts of the Spanish Americas, such as the Caribbean and Central America.

Beyond St. Augustine

Beyond St. Augustine, other archaeological sites indicate the impact of Spanish settlement on Native American societies in La Florida. The clear finding is the association between introduced European goods and elite indigenous individuals, presumably those who were in primary contact with the Spanish. The Spanish strategy was to center contact on chiefs and their kin. Presumably, access to Spanish goods allowed chiefs to gain additional prestige and become more powerful chiefs. In turn, they organized tribute, such as labor, food, and hides for the Spanish.

To take another example, the archaeological work at San Luís de Talimali mission in Apalachee territory has provided a comprehensive view into this well-preserved site. The investigation located the plaza, blockhouse, council house, church and burial ground, and Spanish village. The information from the analysis of burials provided insight into past diet, status, and mortuary practices in both the Spanish and Native American populations. The council house is significant—this was an essential part of the precontact village, being where business was conducted, chiefs ruled, and guests stayed. They were typically large, round structures—the council house at de Talimali was 20 meters in diameter. The Spanish residences at the mission prove how the colonial town became wealthy, from its important role as a food-producing center for the wider Spanish colony.

At a mission village in the seventeenth century, one would have been likely to see both a council house and a church, reflecting the perseverance of traditional political organization as well as the new ideology. The two structures were probably equally elaborate, given that both had important decorative elements. The sound of the church bell would have defined a new ideological zone within which native practices and belief competed with the mission order.

The missionaries knew the key to teaching doctrine was literacy, so they taught reading and writing, and in some cases wrote down local languages. People learned the catechism, sang mass, and offered prayers. The feast days were taught and observed, the commandments learned, the Catholic ideology memorized—in some cases with great vigor. Christian names were used in addition to clan and village names. The mission was significant for agricultural production, with new European plant species added to the existing crop assemblage; the surplus was essential to feed the Spanish settlers and soldiers across La Florida.

ST. CATHERINES ISLAND, GEORGIA, 5000 BP TO THE SPANISH MISSION PERIOD

St. Catherines Island, south of Savannah, Georgia, sustained Native Americans for thousands of years and became the focus for cross-cultural encounters between Guale Indians of Georgia and the Spanish from the sixteenth century.[20]

A small group of Franciscans arrived in the 1570s to establish a very remote— for them—outpost. In 1605, the Spanish increased the size of the mission, presumably to meet the food demands on places such as St. Augustine. The key to their success was converting the Guale Indians and keeping good relationships with the indigenous elite.

It remained the northern stronghold for the Spanish in La Florida until it fell to British raiders from South Carolina in 1680. Soon after this, the location of the ruined mission fell from local memory, until nearly three hundred years later when it was rediscovered in the late 1970s by the American Museum of Natural History, which started looking for the site of the Franciscan mission on the island. Four years of surveys led to the discovery of the long-lost site: the archaeological investigations located the various phases of the mission, consisting of the church, friary, kitchen, wells, and Indian pueblo—*pueblo* being the Spanish word for village and town. The excavations uncovered a well-planned mission precinct around the central plaza. The cemetery (*camposanto*) was found in the church, with some 431 individuals buried in the floor.

Work has not just focused on the mission. Since the 1970s, a long-term archaeological program by the American Museum of Natural History has provided a detailed understanding of the archaeological evidence for the use of this landscape over this long period spanning both precontact and postcontact times. The archaeological research at St. Catherines Island has been very detailed, making this settlement one of the best studied on the Atlantic seaboard. This impressive work has led to many specialized reports which demonstrate resoundingly the potential of archaeological insights into these prehistoric and historical cross-cultural settings.

Background to Mission Santa Catalina de Guale

The Guale Indians lived in chiefdoms, in which the heads of small villages (100–300 people) paid allegiance to the main settlement. Significant chiefs across La Florida were referred to by the Spaniards as *caciques*, the Caribbean term. Guale villages were organized around central plazas, the council meetinghouses, and residences. The dead were stored in charnel houses.

St. Catherines Island has been occupied for five thousand years, being a location where several rich environments came together: forest, marshlands, and ocean. The hunter-foragers living in this rich environment approached sedentism, for the food they gathered was always close to hand.

In the centuries leading up to the arrival of Europeans, two major changes occurred in the Guale Islanders' world. First, around 800 they shifted from an egalitarian to a more differentiated society, as demonstrated by the way they buried their dead. This type of shift typically occurs when people become farmers, but not so here, as the shift toward the cultivation of the American mainstay, maize, happened much later, around 1300. That was the second major change.

The arrival of Europeans was the next dramatic shift in the Guale world; archaeologists call this period the Altahama (Mission) period (1580–1700). The Europeans arrived during a challenging time, as the greatest drought of the century was underway. As crop yields were low, Spanish demands for food would have been very threatening. This, combined with the impacts of disease (below), means that the earliest Spanish accounts of coastal Guale described communities at very high levels of stress. This has consequences for our archaeological interpretation: if we rely on historical accounts to interpret the archaeology, we may be misled. The Spanish accounts describe mobile communities who dispersed at different seasons, found soils infertile, and relied little on horticulture, yet the archaeological analysis convincingly demonstrates that the opposite was true—that, at contact, the people of the island were quite settled and relied heavily on maize farming.

We can identify both Spanish and Native American strategies in the early contact period. One was resistance. The Guale rebelled against the Spanish in 1597, burning down the mission buildings and forcing a Spanish retreat. Around 1604, the Spanish returned to rebuild the mission. Clearly, many Guale Indians became involved with the mission, as converts and collaborators, so another strategy was accommodation.

An important discovery was the 431 burials—the largest number of early-contact humans in North American archaeology. The analysis of their skeletons indicates that there was increased crowding and sedentism in the early colonial period, a great reliance on maize, a general decrease in health, a rise in infectious disease, and greater stress on men's and women's bodies, probably through increased manual labor.

The impact on the Guale of new diseases was probably dramatic and may have occasioned attempts to avoid Europeans. The creation of nucleated communities at the mission, however, would have increased the risk of epidemics. These were ongoing throughout the life of the mission, with epidemics reported in 1569–1570, 1582, 1649–1650, 1657, and 1659. The bioarchaeological analysis suggests that people living at the settlement became more physically diverse; it may well be that more people from the wider region came to the mission than were present in precontact periods.

Of all the archaeological findings, I want to focus on two types of material found by the archaeologists: beads and pots.

Beads

Of the many archaeological finds, the beads provide a fascinating insight. The exchange of beads with indigenous people around the world stands almost as a cliché of cross-cultural exchange . . . and of the perceived unequal nature of the exchange. The editor of Columbus's diary recounts this for 1492:

> I, he says, in order that they would be friendly to us—because I recognize that they were people who would be better freed [from error] and converted to our Holy Faith by love than by force—to some of them I gave red caps, and glass beads which they put on their chests and many other things of small value, in which they took so much pleasure and became so much our friends that it was a marvel.[21]

155

European traders could exchange inexpensive beads for local products they valued highly. The Spaniards probably valued beads as part of religious paraphernalia. During the excavation of the fifteenth-century Spanish mission on St. Catherines Island, nearly 70,000 beads were found. Each bead provides information about both the makers and users of the beads—revealing how the mission linked local Guale and Spanish people to global, transatlantic and local American networks. These, then, are tiny artifacts with the potential to tell local and global stories of cultures in contact.

Archaeologists assume that beads directly reflect the technology, belief, and ideas of the societies that made, traded, used, and disposed of them. And, given their robustness and size, they tend to survive in archaeological contexts. Guale people and their ancestors had worn beads for thousands of years, yet here we have more beads than anywhere else in Spanish America. What makes this site so rich in beads and what do they tell us about this mission?

The beads included both Native American and imported examples (Figure 6.5). The local beads were present from 5000 BP onward. Beads were valued in precontact and contact eras along the Atlantic coast. In the Northeast they were called *wampum,* and on the Middle Atlantic coast *roanoke.* They were valued as tribute, trade items, bride prices, religious objects, mortuary goods, and currency—in fact, they were legal tender in the thirteen original North American colonies.

The name of the beads on the La Florida coast is not known, but they were certainly used at St. Catherines Island. In other Atlantic colonies, *wampum* and *roanoke* were useful, particularly for the cross-cultural trade and in the absence of minted currency; however, in La Florida there were fewer free traders and there was currency in circulation.

Most beads on St. Catherine's Island were found in burials, a trend that began around 800 and continued in the mission period: 95 percent of all beads found were from mission-era burials.

The European beads were dominated by Venetian glass-beads, Spanish beads, as well beads from elsewhere in Europe and from East Asia—presumably via the Philippines and the Manila trade. They could have entered into Native American possession in several ways. Gifts were a common feature of cross-cultural relationships, especially during early phases of culture contact. Gifts were carried by explorers and colonists and were exchanged for food, information, safe passage, and trade items. They may have been intended to promote *caciques* to convert—particularly as decorative religious icons were significant in this process. Where *repartimiento* was established, beads may have been a form of compensation. Beads may have been payment, acting as currency. As St. Catherines Island was an important

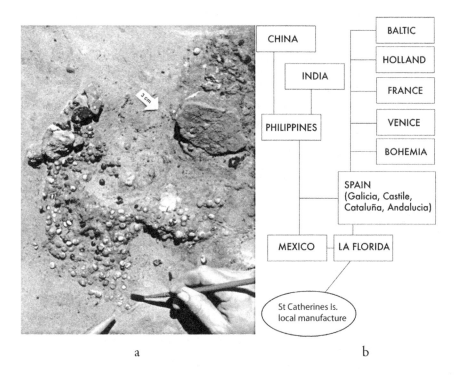

a

b

Figure 6.5. (*a*) Beads found at St. Catherines Island;
(*b*) origin and trade of beads at St. Catherines Island.

producer of corn and deerskin for St. Augustine, and the capital depended heavily on the food, this alone may explain the larger proportion of beads found here.

The beads have the potential to illuminate social differences: archaeologists feel they indicate social and political status within the mission. As such, they are a record of the missionization process. The distribution of beads was probably not conducted by the friars, but by the *caciques*, who would have redistributed Spanish goods.

How valuable were these items? Most were inexpensive to the Spanish. Only a small number were expensive—for example, the Spanish jet beads and gold beads. Yet they were valued by the Guale.

The use of beads as grave goods is interesting, suggesting the continuity of traditional behavior that the friars would have considered pagan. This probably was one phase of missionization: the early phase required winning over *caciques* through the exchange of religious and utilitarian gifts; the second phase condoned indigenous religious activities while conversion was underway; while the full secularization would have seen a decline in indigenous religious activity such as use of grave goods. In the first two phases, material culture, such as rosaries and other decorative and iconic objects, were probably particularly important. The Spanish struggled with traditional behavior—for example, allowing use of ball courts for a time and then banning them.

Another change saw women become more important as leaders, as men were absent in order to meet Spanish labor demands. This development was opposed by the Spanish, particularly given that *caciques* were permitted to be polygamous.

Beads, then, tell stories that extend in several directions, linking the local to the global.

Pots

Archaeological material often throws up surprises and new historical information not reported by Spaniards. One of the most common materials in the archaeological record is ceramics. Interestingly, following contact, one particular ceramic tradition dominates coastal sites—characterized by the use of grainier clay and "rectilinear stamping . . . and grooves of paddle stamped designs, an increase in fine-line incising, and folded, cane punctuated rims."[22] Certainly, these pots *looked* different in form and decoration.

The adoption of these new ceramics differed: in some villages old and new pots were found together, in other places the new tradition replaced the old, and in other Guale regions more remote from the contact zone, the old ceramics prevailed. Clearly the ceramics reflect something about the contact period, but what exactly?

The regional shift in pots suggests that native people from South Carolina, Georgia, and Florida interacted during the contact period in ways that are not reported in the Spanish historical sources. This alone is a significant finding.

Who or what made the new pots popular? To answer that, we need to recognize that the tradition, or the style of their tradition, predated contact. Early examples of these vessels occur in coastal Guale country and in that of their neighbors in South Carolina and Georgia from the fourteenth century—much earlier than the Spanish. Perhaps contact meant that groups who used these ceramics gained a greater interregional power base. If this is true, it may delineate the growing influence of a particular society, ethnicity, or political group following contact. Or, the pattern may reflect broader shared shifts in Native American identity and responses to Spanish impacts on ceramic production. This is a debate that needs further archaeological evidence to address it.

THE NORTHWEST FRONTIER

The Spanish were lured north of New Spain in the sixteenth century by the prospect of resources: fantastic stories of rich cities somehow percolated forth from the froth of Spanish wishfulness and cross-cultural miscommunication. They established their outposts from Texas to California.

Eventually the Mexican-American War (1846–1848) and Louisiana Purchase saw Spanish Mexican territory become part of the USA—this involved parts of Texas, Colorado, New Mexico, Arizona, Wyoming, Utah, California, and Nevada. While these are called "borderlands," the first borders here were between Spanish speakers and Native Americans.

Early contacts between Spaniards and Native Americans were often violent. For example, during Coronado's early exploring expedition of 1540, cross-cultural negotiations deteriorated and the Spanish waged violent war on many Native American settlements. Native Americans returned to damaged lives and villages, having shifted their perception of the Spanish from potential deities to threatening mortals.

Sixty years passed, and in 1598 the Spanish came to conquer lands beyond the Rio Grande. Towns were claimed for Spain, pledges of submission demanded, crosses erected, and the Spanish cautiously received. The military equipment and horses of the Spanish were powerful and threatening. At the mesa settlement of Acoma, some Spaniards were killed; consequently, the Spanish razed the town using a cannon and street fighting. Hundreds died, or were captured, mutilated, and forced into slavery. These atrocities were remembered for generations. A revolt eight decades later in 1680 saw the Spanish thrown out of New Mexico (see below) until 1602. This resistance saw Pueblo people maintain many core aspects of their society. Indigenous religion, for example, survives through to the present.

For the Spanish, these were always geographically and politically marginal areas and part of bigger geopolitical processes. The Spanish colonization of Texas (*Tejas*) after 1690 responded to perceived territorial threats to Mexico from the French (in Louisiana) and later the United States. The settlement of Spanish California too was a reaction to other nations—namely, Russians who were increasingly active along the Pacific coast.

Across these regions, the Spanish often encountered stiff aboriginal resistance and were forced to abandon areas, but overall the region became a dynamic colonial contact zone where trade was able to occur *despite* mutual differences and the Spanish disregard of indigenous society, belief, and traditions. As elsewhere in the Spanish domains, missions, ranches, and tribute (food and hides) were an essential part of the colonial program.

Studies reveal that indigenous labor changed as a result of colonization, with a tendency to focus increasingly on a more limited range of activities related to Spanish demands. Labor became increasingly organized not at a village level, but at a regional level, to match Spanish tribute demands on provincial leaders. Studies of human skeletons from precontact and postcontact populations suggest that after contact, greater work demands were made of older women, and men tended to have to work harder overall.

THE PUEBLO REVOLT OF 1680

Native American groups resisted the Spanish, not just in the early years but also later, in new ways that made use of new forms of political cohesion. The Pueblo Revolt (1680–1692) illustrates local responses to Spanish colonization. It is an example of a popular and widespread revitalization movement—an event led by a charismatic leader typically rooted in a period of stress. The people were, as one man expressed it, "tired of the work that they had to do for the Spaniards . . . because they did not allow them to plant or do other things for their own needs; and that, being weary, they had rebelled."[23]

The Pueblo Revolt was thus a regional response to Spanish colonialism. A holy man, Po'pay, had a revelation: the spirit world, through him, directed the people to return to life as it had been some eighty years earlier before the Spanish. A core group of believers spread Po'pay's message. Puebloans were to purge their world of the material presence of the colonists. The message was taken up by a variety of indigenous people in New Mexico, despite their language and cultural differences. Perhaps ironically, the Spanish had lumped together disparate farming people as "Pueblo people"; the same group was now willing to act together against the Spanish.

The revolt was carefully planned. On August 10, 1860, more than four hundred Spaniards were murdered, settlements destroyed, and Santa Fe routed. Churches and missions were destroyed, and people were ordered to destroy the Catholic icons. Some villages were abandoned for new settlements.

For example, the Jemez Pueblo built two new settlements immediately after the Revolt, the sequence documented by tree-ring dating of wooden roof beams. The architecture of the post-Revolt villages of Patowka and Boletsakwa reflects the revival message: they rejected the design of scattered, unconnected rooms they occupied in the Spanish-era town, and looked to their past by building villages of compact, connected buildings around plazas akin to pre-Spanish planning. These villages were more than mirrors to the past: each was designed around two plazas, a "new" type of planning, perhaps part of a dramatic shift toward a society and community divided into two moieties (kinship groups).

The two villages derive from the actions of the followers of Po'pay. Other post-Revolt villages were organized along different plans, and some did not destroy the churches and acted to preserve Christian faith.

The material evidence suggests further interesting trends: the Jemez people abandoned their distinctive Black-on-red pottery, despite its long use predating the Spanish. Perhaps its use in colonial contexts made it unsuitable for a revivalist movement: oral histories note that objects made for the church were abandoned after the Revolt. A new Red-ware pottery incorporating design elements of other Puebloan people was instead widely produced by the women potters. Regional similarities in material culture suggest that the unifying message of the Revolt took hold, at least among many. While the message was to look toward the past, the archaeology reveals the way people looked forward through the creation of new material forms—in these cases, material culture (pots) and settlements.

ALTA CALIFORNIA

At the end of the spectrum of Spanish colonies, around 1769, nearly three centuries after Columbus, the Spanish colonized Alta California from New Spain (Mexico), with a spine of coastal forts from Baja California to San Francisco Bay. Alta California became a Mexican state in 1821 and was annexed by the United States in 1846–1847.

In the Spanish period, their frontier institutions were missions, presidios, and pueblos. Missions were conversion machines—turning Indians into farming and herding Christians; pueblos housed the settler population, and presidios were frontier nodes of defense and administration. Ranchos expanded after Mexican independence (1821), becoming more secular and more interested in economics than religious conversion. California was not densely settled before contact, with scattered hunter-foragers living in a delicate environment. Thus, the ratio of settlers to Native Americans was higher than in other parts of the Spanish Americas.

The archaeological study of contact in California has a deep history here, dating back to the early 1960s at La Purísima Mission, where James (Jim) Deetz worked at this eighteenth-century locale of Chumash–Spanish interaction. This research has continued. Kent Lightfoot and his team at Fort Ross provide an important case study in a complex setting for culture contact, a Russian outpost in northern California.

Stephen Silliman from Boston University studied the Spanish rancho at Petaluma north of San Francisco, mapping out the archaeological evidence for hundreds of Native American laborers present there in the nineteenth century. These studies have all been critical in their own ways in the development of archaeological explanations for culture change and contact.

El Presidio de San Francisco

Another Californian culture contact research project has been directed by Barbara Voss from Stanford University, investigating the San Francisco Presidio in the heart of San Francisco.

The various colonial settlements were settings for an axis of contact between colonists from New Spain and Native Californians. The presidios and pueblos, however, were themselves complicated communities comprising various ethnic origins—coming from New Spain, they were Spanish subjects but of mixed heritage, the result of centuries of mixed descent in the Spanish New World, with African, Spanish, and Mesoamerican ancestors. Race was important, as the colonists were legally classified according to the sistemas de castas.

The colonizers were very much products of the colonial world.[24] Records from the San Francisco Presidio (founded 1776) list Español, Mestizo, Mulatto, and Indio residents. No colonists had been born in Spain; rather, the colonists included free Africans, Christianized Indians, and castas.

Gender also played a role in social distinctions, as there were different expectations for men and women. For example, men's identity was in part defined by sexual conquests, while women who had sexual relationships with lower-caste men brought shame on the broader family.

Despite this diversity, the archaeological record at this Spanish military outpost suggests homogeneity in the Presidio and very little evidence for Native Californian items or influences. Marriages across the contact divide were rare; Native Californians were commonly present as domestic workers.

Analysis of discarded material from the earliest years of the Presidio (1780–1800) suggests a homogeneous diet across the diverse population, with meals of beef, corn, peas, beans, and buckwheat; locally made ceramic vessels were used by individuals and family-sized groups for food preparation and consumption, not for large communal cooking. Typically, when people want to emphasize difference, foodways are significant—here there seems to be little attempt in this regard.

The architectural styles would have given a colonial impression, as the settlers used Mexican styles and adobe, despite the climate being unsuited to these materials. Barbara Voss, who excavated the Presidio, suggests that the absence of influences from Native Californians—wild foods, stone tools, ceramics, architecture—may be part of a reaction by the presidio population to create their own identity, one that moved beyond the facets of caste identities. The residents started describing themselves as *Californios* and refusing to disclose their *castas* identity. This is supported by historical accounts.

This suggests that the composition of the colonial population may have various implications for the outcomes of culture contact, on *both* the colonist and indigenous sides. It also makes such concepts as being "Spanish" in colonial settings very slippery and complicated, rather than simple and monolithic.

USEFUL SOURCES

Museums and online resources: North America: National Museum of the American Indian (Smithsonian); Mexico: Museo Nacional de Antropología; Spain: Museo Nacional de Antropología.

References: For American Indian tribes there are many encyclopedias, the standard reference being *The Handbook of North American Indians* (William C. Sturtevant, general editor), published by the Smithsonian Institution. These twenty planned volumes cover the archaeology, history, biology, and languages of all native peoples in North America; Volume 4 is *History of Indian-White Relations*. Most volumes take a culture-historical approach within regions, while Volume 4 is driven from European categories such as economy and policy. The three *Columbian Consequences* volumes edited by David Hurst Thomas (Washington, DC: Smithsonian Institution Press, 1989–1991) provide many archaeological studies and detail further reading related to the Spanish in the Americas and aspects of culture contact. See also J. G. Cusick, ed., *Studies in Culture Contact: Interaction, Culture Change, and Archaeology* (Carbondale: Center for Archaeological Investigations, Southern Illinois University, 1998); W. W. Fitzhugh, ed., *Cultures in Contact: The Impact of European Contacts on Native American Cultural Institutions A.D. 1000–1800* (Washington, DC: Smithsonian Institution Press, 1985).

Key journals: Historical Archaeology, International Journal of Historical Archaeology, Journal of Social Archaeology, American Anthropologist, American Antiquity, Archaeology, Current Anthropology, Journal of Anthropological Archaeology, and *National Geographic.*

CHAPTER 7

NORTH AMERICA

... to dread nothing where there is everything to be feared.
    –J. Marquette, *The Mississippi Voyage of Jolliet and Marquette,* 1673[1]

The Spanish were not alone in the Americas: contemporary with the Spanish colonies of the sixteenth century, along the Atlantic seaboard, Native North Americans started to observe the ships, crews, and tiny stockades of other Europeans.

In the sixteenth century, European fishermen were drawn to the Grand Banks off Newfoundland. Farther afield, Basque, Portuguese, French, English, and Dutch crews arrived for fish, whales, and furs. As these products entered the wharves of Europe, and seafarers became more confident, it is not surprising there was further exploration and interest in establishing colonies. These initial settlements grew, and significant populations of settlers and their descendants came to outnumber Native Americans in their own lands. As we saw for the American contacts with Spaniards in the last chapter, European diseases exacted a very heavy toll on some societies. That said, in regions remote from contact zones, it sometimes took a long time for settlers to outnumber Native Americans. Even first contacts, which began in the sixteenth century on the east coast, were still occurring over three hundred years later in the west.

The history of North America describes how, between the sixteenth and nineteenth centuries, disparate colonies of settlers and their descendants gained their own identities, land was claimed and lost and traded, wars were fought, and the modern nations of Canada and the United States arose.

Part of this complex history involved encounters and relationships between Native Americans and various European "others." Significant resistance to European takeover was posed by some Native Americans across the continent. Early encounters were often driven by the European desire for profitable trading relationships or for land. Native Americans who survived the effects of new diseases and conflict eventually faced the European settlers directly, although in many regions, direct "face-to-face" contact was rare for a long period of time. Contact often did not involve soldiers—farmers and colonial industries demanded the most land and resources. Many colonial communities were established near existing Indian communities, the densest of which, like today, were on waterways and the coast. Thus, the map of colonial North America reflects the distribution of people and resources as it was before contact.

As European settlement grew, the power differentials common to colonialism came to define cross-cultural relationships. Some surviving Native Americans were relocated as part of official policies. Some people ended up a long way from their own country—for example, Cherokee, Chickasaw, Choctaw, Creek, and Seminole Native Americans from east of the Mississippi River were moved west to Oklahoma.

In other instances, traditional land was "reserved" or rights to land recognized; however, attempts to shift the concept of land "ownership" from community to individuals reduced the efficiency of this form of ownership along Western lines.[2] Today's indigenous communities across North America represent the legacy of these events. Issues of identity, rights, discrimination, and marginalization are important for many today who view the past as a road map for modern communities.

Canada and the United States have their own archaeological traditions for the study of culture contact. In both places, archaeological and historical sources are used in collaboration with indigenous oral traditions where they have been recorded in the past or continue to the present.

Terminology used for indigenous Americans is important: over and above nation or tribal names, specific indigenous Americans in Canada are today considered in three groups: First Nations, Inuit, and Métis (a specific ethnic group with shared white and Aboriginal ancestry), and collectively as Aboriginal. In the United States, Native American, American Indian, and Amerindian are preferred terms.[3]

This chapter starts on the east coast in the sixteenth century and moves westward. Building on the Spanish–Native American contacts detailed already for La Florida, the Southwest, and California, the first topic considered is the establishment of European colonies on the eastern seaboard.

The second issue I discuss is the network of contacts that occurred as part of fur trading. We may think the Spanish plundered the New World of silver and gold, but five centuries of fur trading clearly demonstrate the extraordinary value of these resources, as deftly captured by Eric Wolf: "The development of the fur trade runs like a thread of blood and gold through the history of North America."[4] Fur trading created a massive zone of contact extending from the Hudson River, the Gulf of St. Lawrence, and the Hudson Bay westward though the Great Lakes and eventually along the Pacific seaboard. The fur trade sits behind much of the discussion in this chapter, given that intercultural relationships developed around the fur trade. These have been described as a "middle ground" by historian Richard White in his book of that title.[5] White's middle ground marked an interpretive departure in American history from a focus on the conquest of Native Americans by Europeans (exemplified in 1975 by Francis Jennings's influential book, *The Invasion of America: Indians, Colonialism, and the Cant of Conquest,*)[6] instead highlighting frontiers as settings for cross-cultural convergence over conflict.

Actually, Jennings's and White's interpretations overlap somewhat in their thinking. White illuminated those places, such as colonial towns, forts, and missions, where power differentials between cultures were more equal than in other settings. This is important, for between 1492 until the early nineteenth century, North America remained largely Native American land. Many of these settings, beyond the gaze of Europeans, are often accessible only through archaeology.

The term "protohistory" has been used particularly in North America to describe settings where the impact of Europeans was felt only indirectly. Regions of "protohistory" were where change occurred in Native American societies in advance of settlers—and thus presumably in advance of "history." However, such terms must be used carefully, recognizing, as Stephen Silliman states, that "precontact societies and lifeways on the North American continent were as varied and as full of history as any; they just did not record their histories in written words."[7]

The chapter finishes on the Pacific coast, where an early network of European trading colonies and outposts prior to Spanish and American colonization of this seaboard encountered varied Native American societies.

Contact Archaeology in North America

Clearly, this is only a brief introduction to a massive topic, when one considers the millions of Native North Americans and their diverse cultures in very diverse environments and ecosystems (Figure 7.1). To get a sense of the variety, over four hundred North American languages were spoken before the arrival of Europeans: many of these languages have been lost, although some have survived contact and colonization. My focus is the early years of culture contact and the archaeological evidence for these survivals and losses. In particular, I explore some potentials and limits of different archaeological evidence in our understanding of culture contact in North America.

Figure 7.1. Map of North America showing key sites.

An impressive amount of work has been conducted on historical sites in North America; in fact, the discipline of "historical archaeology" originated here and remains a major area of archaeological research. Historical archaeologists were for many years mainly interested in the colonists (be they French, English, Spanish, or Dutch) and African American and other non-European migrant communities. Despite some work in the 1950s and 1960s into Native Americans in historical settings, culture contacts between Native North Americans and Europeans had been a less significant research topic until recently, a situation described by historical archaeologist Patricia Rubertone: "Despite the potential to contribute to new understandings about Native peoples during and after European contact, the research commitment has been ambivalent at best."[8] That situation is changing, as demonstrated here. There are several core issues relevant to contact studies in North America that I will briefly raise here before considering our case studies.

First, as described for other places already, in North America there has been a call to bridge the gap between prehistoric archaeology and historical archaeology through the study of culture contact. The core argument is convincing, and perhaps best argued by Kent Lightfoot in his work at the Californian Russian outpost at Fort Ross (see below). Lightfoot stated that a suitable time perspective in contact studies allows one to measure what happens to indigenous societies before contact, and continuing onward—that is, not just focusing on "first contact." The trick is to use available evidence to decipher the past, rather than privilege historical text.

To put this into historical perspective, for much of the twentieth century, studies of contacts with Native Americans were largely conducted by ethnohistorians. Increasingly, archaeologists came to contact studies in two ways: through the study of certain historical sites that involved historical Native Americans, such as Spanish missions, or through the study of frontier forts.[9]

Others studied the early contact period to better understand prehistoric sites rather than the specifics of Americans embroiled in colonial-period events. This approach was critiqued by Canadian archaeologist Bruce Trigger, author of key books *Natives and Newcomers* (1985) and the *Children of Aataentsic* (1976), among others. Trigger and others were keenly aware that European historical sources—which clearly relate to events *following* initial contact—should not be uncritically used to try to understand what indigenous life was like before contact, but as evidence about the ways that indigenous people dealt with the contact world.[10]

Second, historical archaeologists became committed to studying past groups and societies who were represented unfairly and incorrectly in historical sources, or were overlooked. These huddled masses included African Americans, non-English-speaking migrants (such as the Chinese), women and children, the poor and disenfranchised—people who did not leave written records or were overlooked by those who did. Native Americans were also similarly marginalized, but were different, being people in their own land faced by the threats and opportunities of European colonization.

It is true, however, that there are fewer historical sources created by Native Americans as a counterpoint to the avalanche of historical accounts created by Europeans in America. (Later in this chapter, I examine how rock art in the Great Plains provides an example of indigenous narrative comparable to documents.)

Third, it is important not to think of Native American and settler societies as absolutes in terms of ethnic identity—although it is impossible not to use terms like, say, "the Cherokee" (which is better than generic labels like "Indian") or "the French" (which is better than "European," but even less accurate than to hone further in, say, to "French Canadian"). Ethnic identity is particularly malleable and fluid in the contact period, where we see the development of new communities and societies with both settler and indigenous roots. From a settler perspective, early communities developed into societies that understood themselves as "American." Native American societies also changed; many joined together, and new societies were formed, such as the Métis (described below). Intermarriage also occurred between Native American and African American groups, and between different Native American tribes as they came into contact in various colonial settings (see discussion of creolization in chapters 2 and 6).

The fourth point concerns the direction of archaeological thinking. The big shifts in archaeological theory and practice were particularly significant in North America: it was here that the shift in the 1960s toward a more scientific approach—often described as the "New Archaeology" or "processualism"—occurred, in part as a reaction against prevailing approaches which were often inefficient at explaining how past societies changed. There was little space for studies of culture contact in this theoretical environment, perhaps being perceived as "historical" rather than "anthropological."

The 1980s saw a reaction against perceived weaknesses in processualism, driven particularly by an interest in understanding individuals and not just seeing past societies as systems. The term "post-processual" is applied to a range of subsequent archaeological approaches and cannot be easily treated as a whole; however, in recent decades there have been several key developments:

- a recognition of the importance of power in the past and the present;

- a commitment to study people often made powerless ("archaeology from below");

- the recognition of the importance of gender; and

- a recognition of the importance of the politics of the present in the study of the past.

These probably fueled the growth in studies of culture contact in North American archaeology. The main theoretical implication involves the way in which Native American sites are studied. Some archaeologists have tried to modify the acculturation approach advocated by Quimby and Spoehr[11] and others, where indexes allowed archaeologists to measure how much a community had shifted toward an adoption of European materials and behaviors.

Other approaches have focused on the ways that the meaning of artifacts is socially constructed. Put simply, proponents argue that we should not assume that things meant the same thing to everyone. For example, as explored in chapter 6 about St. Catherines Island, the use of beads by Native Americans is best understood as part of a continuation of indigenous world views about what was important, rather than as evidence of being "duped" by new "exotic" material culture. Beads were important in contact transactions because they were already important to Native Americans.

As already detailed for Africa, the interpretation of colonialism is also important in the Americas, given that thinking about past colonialism focuses in on the various ways societies dealt with the power struggles that constituted colonial contexts. For archaeology, the relevance derives from the fact that the material world (objects, architecture, and urban design, for example) offers evidence of attempts to both dominate and resist. These forms of interpretation about past power struggles match an interest in explaining indigenous "agency"—in particular, moving away from ideas of Native Americans as somehow "passive" during the transformation of their societies, and instead acting as conscious agents. An understanding of colonial periods has been identified as a critical element in linking the lives and concerns of contemporary Native Americans to their precontact ancestors. The work of archaeologists such as Kent Lightfoot, Patricia Rubertone, and Stephen Silliman referred to in this chapter helps to demonstrate the importance of historical cultural continuity, survival, and change.

Other trends in archaeological thinking, such as a focus on feminist approaches, have been significant. To explore one example, Janet Spector and her students at the University of Minnesota responded to debates about gender in their research. They perceived this as a critical issue, for often stereotypes about men's and women's activities were projected backward onto the past uncritically. In their work at the site of *Inyan ceyake atonwan* (Little Rapids), a nineteenth-century Eastern Dakota village in Minnesota, Spector examined historical sources and the archaeological evidence, and

> challenged orthodox notions about hunting, food gathering, farming and child care, for example, which archaeologists have often treated as single, indivisible actions rather than multitask activities organized in various ways. [Their] . . . analysis also showed how men and women may have responded differently to changes in their natural or social environments depending on the tasks they performed, when they did them, and where they lived. For example, the impact of the [colonial-era] fur trade on Winnebago and Dakota men and women must have differed depending on which gender traditionally prepared skins for exchange and conducted the trade, and whose daily activities were most significantly affected by the introduction of new raw materials, tools, and ornaments.[12]

One question that arises from Spector's study concerns how changes resulting from either direct contact or forms of indirect contact such as providing furs to middlemen changed these particular Native American communities. Spector presented their research in a novel way by using a narrative centered on a single object—a bone handle for an awl—to tell a story of Wahpeton life. Rather than adopting a more familiar form of archaeological reporting and describing which artifacts originated from trade with Europeans and which did not, the story of the awl handle centered the story on the village and in particular on the work of women. The book is titled *What This Awl Means: Feminist Archaeology at a Wahpeton Dakota Village*. Part fiction, part interpretation, this is worth quoting in part:

> Ha-za win (Blueberry Woman) and Mazomani were proud of their daughter, Mazo okiye win (One who talks to Iron). One day after visiting Faribault [a European trader], they brought her a new iron awl tip and some glass beads. Even though she was still young (unmarried), she had already established a reputation among the people at Inyan cetake atonwan for hard work, creativity, and excellence through her skills in quill and bead work. Her mothers and grandmothers taught her to keep a careful record of her accomplishments, so whenever she finished quilting or beading a skin bag or pair of moccasins, she remembered to impress a small dot on the fine antler awl handle Ha-za win had made for her.[13]

This way of telling an archaeological story is more accessible than much "standard" archaeological writing, although it is still based on interpretation—and some guesswork—by the archaeologist.

Another development has been a shift in toward an interest in landscapes, a trend seen in a range of disciplines such as geography and anthropology. Landscape may seem an essential part of any archaeological study, since all sites exist in landscapes. This particular focus, however, has involved several important ideas—notably, the ways in which landscapes have both physical aspects (such as the location of resources humans use) and social aspects (for example, indigenous names for places obviously precede colonial names). One important result has been to shift attention from a focus on the specific historical sites, such as forts and towns, to a broader range of colonial sites, both indigenous and settler. As put by Brown University historical archaeologist Pat Rubertone, in her review of the historical archaeology of Native Americans, research on landscapes has "led to profoundly richer and more nuanced understandings of the role of place in Native people's lives. The insights gained about native landscapes as active and animated places steeped in names, memories, and routines have shed considerable light on why relationships to ancestral homelands have remained important despite incursions by non-Indians, dispossession, diasporas, and forced removals."[14] This is particularly significant in North America where, unlike in much of South and Central America (chapter 6), indigenous people came to be vastly outnumbered by new migrants and, as increasingly marginalized groups, many people lost access to traditional lands and were in many instances forced off country to other regions.

Fifth, and finally, there has been a change in the relationships between archaeologists and Native Americans. Janet Spector mapped the change in her research as community involvement developed. In her initial years of research at the site of Little Rapids, she did not engage the indigenous community. When the community became involved, there were profound shifts in the work methods, the research design, the interpretation of results, and—as demonstrated in the above quote—the ways the archaeological interpretation was told.

Parallel to this, the last few decades have seen a major shift in the heritage industry, much driven by changes in law, with The Native American Graves Protection and Repatriation Act (NAGPRA) passed in 1990. NAGPRA dictates how indigenous peoples' cultural material—including human remains—should be returned to American Indian groups. At the same time, collaboration has become more common in archaeology and the management of cultural resources.

THE EASTERN SEABOARD

We found the people most gentle, loving and faithfull . . . void of all guile and treason, and such as lived after the manner of the golden age. . . . [T]he earth bringeth foorth all things in aboundance, as in the first creation, without toile or labour.

–Barlowe's account of Roanoke Island[15]

The seaboard and waterways of the northeast of North America saw the earliest European colonies and resulting contacts with Native Americans. This is rich country, by 1500 sustaining permanent maize-farming villages nearly as far north as Maine, while other less sedentary groups moved between regional settlements in seasonal cycles, making use of the tapestry of coastal and woodland resources. In colder northern realms, more specialized lifeways allowed communities to rely on key marine resources and terrestrial fauna; for example, in the more extreme latitudes of Labrador, the Inuit specialized in getting and using marine species.

Of the many different indigenous societies, there were two very significant groupings: in the Northeast, from North Carolina to Maine, were large and small tribes speaking Algonquin languages. Farther north, Algonquin speakers included the Beothuk (Newfoundland), Innu (Quebec and Labrador), and Mi'kmaq (throughout St. Lawrence Gulf). Inland, the Iroquois Confederacy had formed by the late 1500s and was a significant political and military force by the time Europeans began to arrive.

Let us briefly let the Iroquois provide an insight into precontact events. Archaeology suggests that Iroquois tribes moved into the southern Great Lakes from the south between 700 and 1000, disrupting Algonquin-speaking communities. (Actually, there is a debate as to whether farmers, possibly Iroquois, arrived centuries earlier than this.) Their main farming villages comprised longhouses surrounded by defensive palisades; some villages housed up to 2,000 people, and some longhouses were over 100 meters long, although most were half this length.

In the seventeenth century, European accounts start to detail ethnohistorical information, such as how the longhouses were organized by totemic kinship, about the matriarchal nature of life, about gender roles and work, political organization, and cosmology. Much of our interpretation of the Iroquois relies on these European accounts. And yet, a century *before* contact, European trade goods start to occur in Iroquois longhouses in Ontario, exposing the long arc of contact and the ways that objects (and presumably stories and even diseases) preceded face-to-face contact. This reminds us to think very carefully about the accounts made by Europeans of these societies, especially if we expect them to provide insight into precontact lifeways.[16]

The key point here is that Native American societies were not static prior to the establishment of European coastal toeholds. Instead, they were in flux, migrating, innovating, learning, resisting, fighting, negotiating, and changing—just like the regions the Europeans set sail from.

The southern Atlantic coast was largely the setting for Spanish colonies in Florida, Georgia, and the Carolinas (chapter 6). In the Carolinas and extending northward to the sub-Arctic regions, there were numerous potentials for European activities of two broad types. First are the infrequent or seasonal activities associated with resource extraction, such as fishing off the Grand Banks, or Basque whaling in Labrador. European crews would have made occasional landfalls at places like Newfoundland in the years after John Cabot's voyage of 1497. These seasonal events were the most common European activity in the Americas in the sixteenth century.

Cross-cultural "encounters" occurred as a result of such events. For example, on Newfoundland the Beothuk initially harvested metal from abandoned European seasonal settlements to rework into awls, harpoon points, scrapers, and arrowheads. These modified items have been found in the remains of their camps. Similarly, in Labrador, the Inuit mined abandoned sixteenth-century Basque whaling stations.

The second type of European activity was colonization, which occurred increasingly after the sixteenth century, although not always successfully. For Europeans, the eastern seaboard was the primary landfall following transatlantic voyages. In addition, these were attractive lands: the farmed areas of the east coast offered cleared country, storable foodstuffs, animal diversity (particularly for furs), and good ports. However, as colonies, they required support from Europe, made expensive through shipping. As start-up investments, they promised great profits, yet many failed commercially (one need only see how French investors threw their money at the promise of New Orleans, only to watch their investments vaporize). The colonies did, however, allow for various European interests to claim territory in the Americas.

Not surprisingly, there is a fascination in the early European colonies in the Americas, and their archaeological traces. However, they often tell us little of culture contacts. The earliest English colonies were at Roanoke (1585), Jamestown (1607), Fort St. George in New England (1607), Plymouth (1620), and in Newfoundland (after 1610, for a few years at Cupers Cove and Avalon in 1621). The French settled in Nova Scotia (1605, at Port Royal) and along the St. Lawrence waterway (1603, at Quebec).[17] The Swedish and Dutch established colonies of New Amsterdam (New York, 1628) and New Sweden (New Jersey, 1638). From these origins developed an increasingly congested colonization front on the Atlantic coast and along waterways into the continent.

Colonization involved cross-cultural encounters (the land had to be taken from someone), and these encounters are sometimes (though not always) woven into the national histories that would follow and memorialize supposed origins, from the story of Thanksgiving to that of Pocahontas.

Contact allowed for shared zones, but often led to competition. To return to the Beothuk in Newfoundland, for example, with permanent French and English settlements in the seventeenth century the Beothuk suffered: they came into conflict with European crews and hunters, leading to mutual recrimination; they competed for resources with Europeans and Mi'kmaq, retreated from their coastal settlements, encountered new diseases, and were spatially constricted to a small refuge; eventually their society was destroyed. This is obviously the extreme result of contact; many Native Americans survived to participate in both the retention of traditional life and in new forms of society.

Early English Colonies

Archaeology and history provide glimpses into these early sites of colonization and encounter. The earliest English colonies were at Roanoke Island, on the North Carolina coast in Secotan country. Three colonies backed by Sir Walter Raleigh were attempted in 1585 (to be evacuated by Sir Francis Drake in 1586) and 1587.

The colonization attempts involved several stages of cross-cultural dealings: first, trade and exchange, then alliance building with the Secotan chief Pemisapan for a space and provision of food from the Secotan farmers, and finally conflict and warfare. Secotan people had been devastated by disease which, along with the English demands for food, led to tensions and conflict. The Roanoke colonies failed, found abandoned in 1590; the fate of the so-called Lost Colony in Virginia remained unknown. However, traces of archaeological evidence relating to Elizabethan-era activity have been found on Roanoke Island.[18]

From these early events, the first information about Native Americans began to filter into England. John White, one of the colonists at Roanoke, painted watercolors depicting local people (Figure 7.2). These were later reproduced and published in the 1588 illustrated edition of *A Briefe and True Report of the New Found Land of Virginia*.[19] This was published in four languages and included depictions of ancient Picts, Britons, and Adam and Eve, inviting comparisons between the newly "discovered" Americans and ancient peoples. The published images were hand-colored in Germany, and instead of the brown skin and dark hair of White's originals, the Americans were depicted as white-skinned with blond hair. This may have simply been how the printer knew people to look from his own experience.

The English returned in 1607, establishing a settlement in the Chesapeake Bay region in the country of allied Powhatan tribes led at that time by Chief Wahunsonacock (Powhatan). The Jamestown settlement was marked by intermittent hostilities and alliances between the English and Powhatan, and is popularly remembered for the cross-cultural union between Wahunsonacock's daughter Pocahontas to the Englishmen John Rolfe.

Until recently, it was thought that the 1607 fort had been destroyed by the James River, yet the site was discovered in the 1990s. Subsequent excavations have found over a million artifacts from a settlement touted as "America's Birthplace."[20] Most artifacts relate to the initial years of the struggling colony. Some indicate the Powhatan side of the encounter—such as unused arrowheads, evidence of the manufacture of copper items which were highly valued by the Powhatan, blue glass beads made in Venice and popularly traded, and American Indian–made pots for cooking and storage.

In recent years, a team of archaeologists claims to have discovered Weremocomoco, the capital of the Powhatan confederacy at the time of Jamestown. Whatever village it is, archaeological studies of American Indian settlements like these are an important portal into Native American life at contact.

A series of drawn-out wars and alliances characterized the 1600s, leading to a treaty in 1722 between the American Indian survivors and the state of Virginia. Yet a long history of interracial faultlines followed. Most of the American colonies

Figure 7.2. John White's illustration of the wife and daughter of principal chief of Pomeiooc, with freshwater shell necklaces, a drinking gourd, and English doll.

discouraged interracial marriages, and in Virginia this came to a head in 1924 with the passage of Virginia's Racial Integrity Act, which categorized Virginians as "white" or "colored" (anyone with Native American, African, southern European, or Asian heritage). Many Virginian Indians were reclassified as African, except for the descendants of Pocahontas. The law was struck down by the United States Supreme Court in 1967.

Resistance and alliances took place against a regional backdrop of disease, demographic change, war, land loss, and changes to the social fabric of Native American societies. Disease and war, in particular, hindered resistance. For example, to consider another setting, in South Carolina the English colonists arrived during the 1670s and encountered one of the largest tribes in the Cherokee nation. Epidemics of smallpox in 1697, 1730, and 1760 reduced their population to one-quarter within a century. The survivors were divided over their future: some backed the resistance leader, Dragging Canoe, who joined Shawnee fighters on the Tennessee River. The resulting "Real People" resistance movement lasted for a decade.[21] However, the future access to traditional lands for many Native Americans living east of the Mississippi River would be reduced by the density of colonial settlement along the eastern seaboard.

Narragansett Indian Cemetery and Eastern Pequot Reservation

Let us further consider what archaeology can tell us of American Indian life in colonial America. Research on Rhode Island reveals aspects of Narragansett Indian life in the turbulent years of the seventeenth century. New England Algonquin tended to be settled farmers and, consequently, more populous than peoples to their north.[22] European accounts from the early 1600s suggest the Narragansett were indeed a very populous tribe; early colonist Roger Williams stated that fewer Narragansett people died in the epidemics (1617–1618) that caused high mortality levels among neighboring tribes. However, Narragansett society was shattered in 1675–1676 during King Phillip's War when, in retaliation for providing refuge to Wampanoag people, the English attacked Narragansett settlements, killing many. Some survivors were enslaved for Caribbean plantations or for local white farmers, while others settled elsewhere in New York and Canada.

Some evidence for these years comes from burial grounds, such as that at North Kingston (known as site RI-1000) which included fifty-six seventeenth-century burials. It is rare to find such a large burial complex intact, and work at this important site involved collaboration between local Narragansett Indians, Brown University, and government authorities. The North Kingston cemetery was used in the decades after 1650 (based on the artifacts in the burials) and provides a unique window into these years, particularly when combined with ethnohistorical sources and a nearby older Narragansett burial ground (site RI-84, at West Ferry, used 1620–1660).

The burials indicate that following contact, the Narragansett were under much greater stress than they had been prior to contact. People were dying much younger—nearly a third at RI-1000 were adolescents (this had been less than 5 percent previously). The excavators feel that tuberculosis was the killer stalking the young; 30 percent had lesions consistent with that disease. TB was present in the Americas prior to contact but in very low levels; its large impact here may have been due to a shift toward farming cattle, increased exposure to wood smoke inhalation, and dietary changes.

This was not the only evidence for physical afflictions: one burial possibly suffered from venereal syphilis, others from arthritis, osteoporosis, and minor infections.

There were twice as many females as males in RI-1000, suggesting males died or were buried away from their homes, possibly as a result of colonial-era work demands—we know that many men hunted to meet English demands for animal products. Similarly, their remains indicate women also worked harder, possibly as farm laborers. Dental diseases were also much higher than they had been prior to contact, possibly resulting from sugar and molasses trade goods.

The European goods in the burials—including glass bottles, rings, metal vessels, textiles, glass beads (over 6,000!), knives, nails, lead shot, mirrors, cups, scissors, bells, buttons, and clay pipes—clearly indicate Narragansett access to goods from the nearby English trading post.

This may seem like a surprising abandonment of, or at least disruption to, traditional practices: why put these new things in people's graves? However, as much as these items were "new," the burials suggest that customs were *not* changing. In keeping with older customs, graves faced toward the southwest in the direction of the creator Cautantowwit, to whom the soul traveled after burial. People persisted in burying their kin in flexed positions.

So the burials show how new things were incorporated into, but did not necessarily replace, tradition. Despite the new, there is also continuity in the grave goods. Local objects were also present in the burials, such as shell beads (nearly 5,000), ornaments, pots, stone tools, and textiles.

Beads were already precious to the Narragansett. The explorer Giovanni da Verrazano observed in 1524 how highly valued azure beads were to the Narragansett.[23] For this reason, archaeologists often consider European-made beads as a "special case" in these types of studies of Native Americans, as the way in which they were added to existing indigenous value systems seems clear in the evidence from places like RI-1000 (and also in the study of Guale beads on St. Catherines Island discussed in chapter 6).

However, the evidence from RI-1000 should not only be used to measure ways that Narragansett people changed (or did not) in the mid-1600s as compared with the time before the English. As the number of studies of culture contact and historic Native Americans has increased, more nuanced questions are being asked, such as: Are ideas of continuity and change confining the investigation of past communities? How can we get past the trap of thinking of objects as being "European," "Native American," or hybrid? Why focus on what happened to Native Americans when *every* community in North America changed over the last few centuries?[24] Some of the answers relate to time scales: it is useful to look at change between precontact communities and the early phases of contact, but as the centuries unfold, it is less useful to compare backward to the years before contact. (This is comparable to measuring the lives of the signatories of the Declaration of Independence against a baseline of life in London in the Tudor period without reference to intervening eras.)

To explore this point, let us consider a collaborative project between the Eastern Pequot Tribal Nation and the University of Massachusetts Boston. In 1683, a reservation was established for the Eastern Pequot who, along with their once-undifferentiated relatives among the Mashantucket or Western Pequot, had lost a war with the English. Many of their ancestors had died, been enslaved, or been removed from tribal lands, before losing in war: the reservation was a place for survivors. The reservation still exists, Eastern Pequot people have remained there, and it is one of the oldest occupied reservations in North America. How did the Eastern Pequot negotiate their culture in colonial New England? The research to date has focused on the sites from the period ca. 1740–1860.

Stephen Silliman observes that for this time scale, categories of artifacts as "European" or "Native American" have little value. For example, lead-glazed red-bodied earthenwares occurred in the Eastern Pequot sites much as they did elsewhere in colonial New England. Eastern Pequot families used this ware, and other goods available in the New England market, without reference to the ceramics used by their ancestors. The earthenwares should not be used as evidence for change: this had occurred generations earlier.

Another example from this reservation is stone tools, a type of evidence used commonly in archaeology to measure change in stone-tool-using cultures. For example, do people keep making stone tools? Do stone tool technologies shift to new materials, such as glass? For the Eastern Pequot in this reservation, stone tools were not commonly used. However, in one site dating to the early nineteenth century, ancient stone tools were found in the rubbish and in an underfloor cavity. Such tools made by distant ancestors may have been collected by Eastern Pequot and of interest to them in some capacity, probably lost to us now. The point is that these stone tools are not evidence for continuity *or* change, but represent something else altogether.

The archaeological remains of houses and their contents on this reservation are essentially similar to those in contemporary colonial New England households. Silliman observes that if, as the archaeologist, he did not know they were occupied by Eastern Pequot families, he may not even interpret these colonial places as Native American (although continued work may be able to discriminate the material or spatial features that *could* distinguish them). Yet they were places where Eastern Pequot culture was maintained and produced by each generation. The question of material culture should then be, if possible, *who used this thing and how*?

People and Pelts

> On his hed a Flaundrish bever hat.
>
> —Chaucer, *Prologue* 272 (ca. 1386)

The political importance of North America escalated after Jacques Cartier's 1534 expedition to the Gulf of St. Lawrence, when he claimed the land for France. As French merchant boats arrived at Tadoussac (Quebec), Montagnais and Abenaki tribes came to trade with them—soon learning to wait until several French vessels were present and the competition drove French demand for furs up . . . along with the price. Soon, the Dutch and English became involved with the fur and hide trade.

After 1600, Europeans increasingly demanded beaver furs, in addition to other furs and hides.[25] In many parts of North America, initial contact between Europeans and Native Americans inevitably involved these transactions. The fur trade did not *necessarily* require extensive colonization by whites. Rather, the trade attempted to use indigenous people—their hunting skills, their labor, and trade and communication networks—in an economically beneficial manner, to get furs suitable for European markets, as medieval Eurasian fur stocks had been falling as forests were cleared for farms. As the trade involved cross-cultural exchange, a currency was required. The basic unit of value was a beaver pelt in good condition; this was termed "Made Beaver," to which all prices were set. The most desirable beaver skins were those that had been worn by American Indians for a period of time, as their longer hairs had been worn away through use.

By the early seventeenth century, the French were based along the St. Lawrence River valley, at Quebec and then Montreal; fur traders were present on Dutch settlements on the Hudson River (1609) and Manhattan Island (1614); and the English settlements from New England to Virginia also exported hides and furs, along with other commodities, such as tobacco from Virginia. In northern realms, the French had key advantages: the thicker furs and hides from northern species were more desirable, and they had access to regions farther west via rivers and the Great

Lakes. The Dutch and English had difficulties moving westward, with the Iroquois raising a significant barrier to the expansion of their colonies. Another difference was that the French were less committed to colonization in large numbers, while greater numbers of Dutch and English migrants fueled both demand for land and resources and rivalry with American Indians.

The colonial world was one of rivals and alliances. Rivalry existed among the Dutch, French, and English, as North America became the setting for Old World agendas. For example, the 1754–1760 Seven Year War (or French-Indian War) involved European nations, Native Americans, and American colonists. (Combined with other colonial settings in India, Southeast Asia, and Africa, which also saw incidents, truly this was a "world war.") Rivalry also existed between Europeans and American Indians, as well as between indigenous societies. This made for a complicated seventeenth century, where local events were increasingly of global significance. Some American Indian nations had great influence, such as the Iroquois nations, which tended to remain independent and often were at war with neighboring tribes.

French alliances were directed toward the sustenance of the fur trade as well as checking the Iroquois expansion. The French developed alliances with Huron and Algonquin tribes, while the English prompted Iroquois resistance to the French. Consequently, the Iroquois devastated the Huron and attacked French outposts.

The French needed a successful fur trade for geopolitical reasons. To encourage alliances with American Indian groups, they established settlements at Detroit and Louisiana, but these were not accompanied by extensive French demands for American Indian lands. French Canadians developed a system based as much on political rationales as economic ones. The French had to move their furs a great distance to get them to Montreal for shipping, and established inland outposts where they formed close alliances with various Native American tribes. The regular contacts required the French to learn American Indian languages, trade protocols, customs, routes, and watercraft technology. As a result, trade and familial relationships were formed, and a mixed descent population—termed Métis—grew. Thus, many French-speaking fur trade workers became accomplished in cross-cultural settings.

After 1670, the scale of the fur trade and nature of cultural contacts escalated: from this point, there were two broad rivers of history, whose waters mingle. One river has largely to do with the English based out of Hudson Bay, and the other with the French in the St. Lawrence River valley.

In 1670, King Charles II granted vast territory to the "Governor and Company of Adventurers of England trading into Hudson's Bay" and the Hudson's Bay Company (HBC) was born. A tract of nearly eight million square kilometers of western Canada was named Rupert's Land (after the King's cousin), and this land remained in company hands until a partial sale to the Canadian government in the late nineteenth century. The HBC remained the primary interface between Europeans and First Nations people in Canada for three centuries. Initially, the HBC model was to "sleep by the frozen sea," setting up factories or depots on Hudson Bay and waiting for indigenous middlemen to bring furs to them. This characterized the first century of the company. The middlemen provided the HBC the means to access furs from people across northwest Canada, in return for trade goods. The middlemen had great power in this system, while the English kept costs down, much to the satisfaction of shareholders in London.

So, most First Nations people in Canada at this time were not in direct contact with whites. It has been proposed that *all* American Indian people in contact with middlemen were transformed *despite* not being in direct contact with whites, as their desire for new materials (iron objects and textiles in particular) would have been transformative. This is hard to measure, as presumably desirable objects like metal cutting implements and cooking pots were highly curated and less likely to turn up in archaeological sites. Yet, it is hard to support the proposed widespread transformation, for the archaeological evidence reveals that some "protohistoric" communities had very little or no access to European trade goods, and their traditional tool kits and material culture changed little.[26] This suggests that some communities were not transformed much at all, and a more complicated process took place in the indirect trade zone, where the movement of trade goods from middlemen was organized through indigenous social networks and some communities had access to the new items and some did not. It was only with the establishment of many more trade posts across central and western Canada that access to European trade goods increased, along with the extent of direct cross-cultural contact.

For two hundred years, the fur trade would dominate cross-cultural entanglements in much of North America. Beyond towns, in much of North America there was no quick replacement of the American Indian population. Some country seemed not worth settling, as reported by early English fur trader David Thompson, whose account of central Canada weighs the potential of the environment for farming and finds it wanting.[27]

> The whole of this country may be pastoral, but except in a few places, cannot become agricultural. Even the fine Turtle Hill, gently rising, for several miles, with its Springs and Brooks of fine Water has very little wood fit for the Farmer. The principal is Aspin which soon decays: with small Oaks and Ash. The grass of these plains is so often on fire, by accident or design, and the bark of the Trees so often scorched, that their growth is contracted, or they become dry: and the whole of the great Plains are subject to these fires during the Summer and Autumn before the Snow lies on the ground. These great

Plains appear to be given by Providence to the Red Men for ever, as the wilds and sands of Africa are given to the Arabians.[28]

Contrary to this appraisal, settlers would eventually come. The period up until the 1760s favored Native American entrepreneurship and power, but the regional picture was changing. The French and their alliances with American Indian tribes had acted as a barrier to English expansion westward as well as diverting furs from Hudson Bay. However, the French-Indian War ended French control of Canada, as the English defeated the French despite their American Indian allies.

After the French surrender, the Montreal fur trade became dominated by Anglo-Scottish traders. An intense rivalry developed between the Hudson's Bay Company and the Montreal-based North West Company (NWC; established 1779) which continued the legacy of the French fur traders. The NWC was sharply differentiated by rank and ethnicity: the owners and upper management were Anglo-Scots, while the vast majority of workers were Métis, French, or Aboriginal. The NWC expanded westward, setting up forts in the regions of the HBC middlemen, and forcing the HBC to also establish trading outposts. Each company attempted to get the native trappers' furs before the other. One result was the increased use of alcohol as a trade good, with deleterious impact on Aboriginal communities.

For half a century, intense commercial rivalry would drive westward expansion. The large number of workers, for the forts and transport of furs, required feeding. In the Plains, the production of pemmican by American Indian groups grew to be a significant economic enterprise (below). This expansion occurred despite years of war, between the fall of New France and the global conflagrations of 1812. By 1812 the companies merged. By this time, many Native Americans lived close to or at trading posts and were far more economically dependent on the fur trade.

Social and Material Dimensions of the Fur Trade

As detailed, the fur trade provided a form of culture contact described by Richard White as a "middle ground" in his study of American Indians in the Great Lakes region between 1650 and 1815. This suggests some form of shared zone where different cultures—European and Native American—met for the purposes of trade and exchange (Figure 7.3). Certain items dominated trade: useful and interesting metal objects, guns, clothing, and decorative items.[29] Metal knives and axes were reworked; durable pots and kettles were very desirable. Decorative items like beads, ribbons, and bells enhanced adornment to signify fashion and prestige. Guns were perhaps no better than bows and arrows (until the late nineteenth-century improvements in munitions) yet were highly demanded—particularly as game became increasingly wary of the noise of hunters. Clothing from traders was

Figure 7.3. "Inside an Indian hut, Manitoba." A rare depiction of the inside of an Indian hut, 1824, by Peter Rindisbacher. This was from the early years of Red River Settlement. (*Library and Archives Canada, acc. no. 1981-55-73 Bushnell Collection.*)

more comfortable but expensive. The design of clothing, too, reflected responses to contact: some American Indian clothes copied European styles (such as great coats; see Figure 7.4), while others were made of traditional cuts and construction but with added trade items. Similarly, across a range of material culture, new materials were used to enhance existing practices and forms. Europeans were responsive to indigenous tastes, making specific items such as pipes to meet preferences. The English and French were keen to ensure that their goods were preferred so that they could outperform their rivals in trade negotiations, while the English were less interested in gift-giving than the French had been.

Figure 7.4. Native American–made hide coat of the mid-1800s modeled on European traded coats (*museum no. 8303, Minnesota Historical Society, St. Paul*).

In the middle ground as described by White, social relationships as part of the fur trade were as important as economic outcomes, and from cross-cultural relationships new social identities (through ethnogenesis) were formed. This immediately breaks down ideas of "Indian" and "French": for the French men were also husbands, parents, and brothers of American Indian women, men, and children. The children of French and American Indian unions often moved between both indigenous and settler communities.

The results were not only seen in American Indian settlements, but also in the French forts, such as at Fort St. Joseph near Lake Michigan, an eighteenth-century mission, trading post, and garrison. At St. Joseph, the archaeological record suggests that Native Americans resided at the fort, or the occupants adopted Native American activities, or both. There were traditional flint projectile points possibly used as flintlocks, smoking of Mi'kmaq pipes, antler gaming pieces, and tanning of hides in Aboriginal ways. This evidence complements historical sources describing how French Canadians adopted elements of American Indian life, as noted by a French priest: "many Frenchmen . . . can scarcely be distinguished from the Indians. . . . they imitate them not only in their nakedness, but even in painting their faces." In fact, natural pigment (hematite) was also found at the fort: whose faces did it paint? From the evidence, they may well have been French, American Indian, or both.[30]

The middle ground documents how Aboriginal people were active participants in trade. Trade goods may not necessarily indicate abandonment of traditional lifeways, or a form of one-way dependency (in fact, it was the Europeans who were dependent on the trade for their own economic survival). Archaeological objects actually reflect complicated historical events with social, economic, and personal dimensions. Different Native American communities and individuals were involved with the trade: working as trappers, hunters, middlemen, partners, canoeists, and guides. Over time, more outposts came to be used, and this broadened the number of "nodes" for encounters and trade.

Policies were important. For example, the Hudson's Bay Company banned married men, while the North West Company saw unions between their employees and Aboriginal people as a means to develop trading alliances. There was thus a tapestry of contacts: different tribes developed different relationships with various European societies, commercial entities, and religious orders.

French and Native American unions led to the development of a large Métis population. This is seen today in Canada by the three main groupings of indigenous people: First Nations, Métis, and Inuit. The Métis are about one-quarter of the recognized indigenous population of Canada, although their homeland extends into the United States along the Great Lakes (obviously, it predates the national border).

The Métis are best known from French–Indian unions, although there are Métis with English and Scottish ancestry. Métis ancestors include Cree, Ojibwa, Algonquin, Salteaux, Menominee, Mi'kmaq, and Maliseet, and others.

The Métis communities—with shared language and culture—originated around trade outposts and became concentrated in certain regions, such as along the Peace River and in Saskatchewan province, where they were valuable trackers, hunters, cross-cultural intermediaries, and voyageurs. After 1812 they came increasingly into conflict with new settlers, also drawn into western Canada and competing as food providers for the western fur trade.

The path to increased recognition of Métis identity and rights originated in events such as the Red River resistance to new settlers by the Métis following 1869.

In these events, political activism in mainstream society became increasingly part of the struggle for recognition and rights.

While not explored here, contact continued in the nineteenth century in the fur-trapping regions of North America. The transcontinental railway of 1885 opened up much of Canada for new settlers, who came to dominate the Great Plains. The fur trade continued into the twentieth century, having reached the Pacific coast (below) and the Arctic Sea. As the domination of the Hudson's Bay Company was undermined by the greater number of small traders, the HBC focused its efforts toward the far north and remained a significant pseudo-governmental institution actively involved in many First Nation people's lives well into the twentieth century.

THE GREAT PLAINS AND AMERICAN WEST

In the Great Plains and American West, Native Americans came into contact with Spanish to their south and French and English to their north and east. In these regions, some groups were horticulturalists, while most Plains Indians were largely hunters.

Europeans provided access first to horses and then later to guns.[31] Horses and rifles gave some Plains Indians the means to shift their hunting economy toward the largest animals on the continent—bison—to provide trade goods such as skins and pemmican. Consequently, the changes wrought by horses and guns altered power structures across the West, as societies sought advantage over their enemies, often against a broader picture of land loss and the encroachment of Europeans. The evidence from Native American imagery on rock, skin, paper, and wood provides an alternative narrative as a counterpoint to historical accounts largely produced by Europeans. In this discussion, I focus on rock art, although much more archaeological research has been conducted in these regions.

The Great Plains of North America, extending from west Texas to the central provinces of Canada, contains much rock art, including some from the contact era. The northern half of the Great Plains is better known archaeologically. Over 1,200 reported rock-art sites in the northern Great Plains from Colorado to Alberta derive from the earliest years of human occupation of North America through to the nineteenth century.[32]

Indigenous American peoples' observations of the arrival and settlement of outsiders (typically Spaniards, French, English, Canadian, Anglo-American) are depicted. Also shown are some other changes, new animals (particularly horses) and their tracks, items (guns among many others), and restrictions and opportunities.

In concert with other archaeological, historical, and oral evidence, rock art illustrates some of the changes within native society in these post-Columbian settings. Importantly, rock art records changes and continuities that essentially precede the arrival of Europeans, with the significant instruments of change being horses and guns in advance of direct European colonization.

A key element of the historical study of the Great Plains concerns the introduction of horses. Their introduction to Native Americans via Spaniards dates to the seventeenth and eighteenth centuries, depending on location, and appears to have preceded the introduction of guns.

The earliest indigenous accounts of horses occur in rock art. A striking element of early depictions is that the horses were covered by protective garb. It appears that for almost a century, from the mid-1600s until the mid-1700s, horses were protected by leather armor. The rock art illustrates this, showing armored horses and riders with lances facing infantry sometimes protected by shields.

The Spanish were reluctant to trade guns, but eventually guns were obtained from the French, and the need for leather protection ended. With guns, speed was more important than armor.

The shift to fighting from horseback in turn led to the demise of large, rounded body shields popular in precontact rock art. At the site of Verdigris Coulee, on the Milk River in Alberta, images of conflict between mounted warriors and infantry appear to portray the advantage for those tribes with horses. In these early images, the artists seem less familiar with the horse, underscoring the learning curve of early contact. These early images show the standing warriors in greater detail, perhaps signaling that the local Blackfoot were depicting their early battles with other mounted warriors from their firsthand experiences. In any event, the depiction of the short-lived phase of horse armor suggests that rock art was important in depicting aspects of "early" contact as it occurred.

Horses were introduced even earlier in the southern Great Plains. In Colorado, depictions of armored horses represent a period following access to Spanish horses ca. AD 1650, when Comanche and Apache warriors were dominant. Guns only became available by the mid-1700s, after which armor on horses was abandoned in favor of mobility. A strong tradition in the seventeenth century of using armored horses existed; however, these horses were not ridden by warriors with the large, round precontact shields, as seen in rock art in Alberta, revealing regional differences in contact-period warfare.

A site of particular significance is Writing-On-Stone on the Milk River. Research into this large rock-art complex exposes precontact and postcontact images and shows how the site continued to be used in the historical era in ways that suggest changes in indigenous life, warfare, tribal locations, and art.

Archeologist Michael Klassen observes a focus by artists on specific motifs imbued with spiritual significance and power, suggested by their choice of depiction and their relative size. In the contact era, new visual elements were added to, and replaced, precontact motifs.

Earlier motifs included large, rounded shields and bow and arrows, sometime depicted as isolated motifs or enlarged. In the contact period, guns are depicted in similar ways to these earlier motifs—that is, free of association with humans, and not necessarily involved in action. Horses—both alone and mounted—also seem to be depicted in similar isolated ways. This perhaps suggests something of the symbolic power of guns and horses.

The other type of rock art described by Klassen at Writing-On-Stone exhibits multiple motifs arranged in meaningful scenes, such as battles and horse raids. The visual shorthand in this style delineates elements like horses, weapons, and people in a very simple way, described as pictograms. In the battle scene at DgOv-81 (Figure 7.5), we see the narrative style at its most complex. The horses and guns indicate that this is a contact-period image. The three elements (left to right) depict a camp of tipis defended by warriors (shown as guns or people holding guns) with shots fired toward the central scene. There are fortifications around groups within the camp. In the central part of the scene, two armed humans are fighting, one being shot. Many other humans and guns are shown, with bullets bursting out (as a series of dots). Nearly every gun in this scene is firing. To the right are people seemingly moving to the central battle followed by horses dragging travois. Klassen has suggested that while there may be many symbolic elements, the panel may depict a real battle, possibly even the "Retreat up the Hill" battle of 1866 between Piikáni and a group of Atsina, Cree, and Crow warriors.[33] However, these may not be *merely* historical accounts, given that the rock art is located in an area of great spiritual significance for Blackfoot people.

A narrative form of rock art from the contact era has been termed the "Bibliographic Tradition" (Figure 7.6). This is found along the eastern Rockies from

Figure 7.5. Battle scene at DgOv-81 (*Keyser 1977: fig. 15, p. 70*).

190

Mexico to Alberta, as well as on non-rock surfaces, such as painted and engraved on dead trees (most long gone), and on other surfaces such as skins made into robes, tipis, and clothes (termed "Robe Tradition" and observed by Spanish visitors to the American Southwest in the early 1500s). Little Bibliographic Tradition rock art was painted; mostly it was engraved.

Another setting for images in the contact period was ledgers (after 1860s), as ledgers of paper, skin, muslin, and canvas were assembled into books. This Ledger Tradition survived into the twentieth century. Many similarities in depiction exist between the rock art and the Ledger and Robe Traditions.

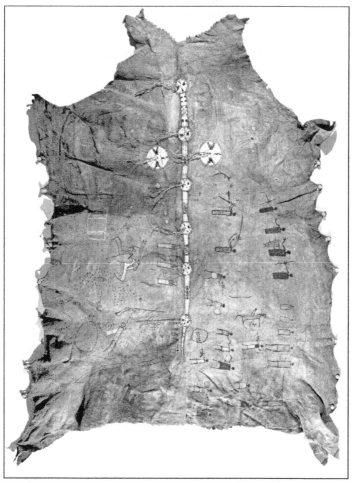

Figure 7.6. A decorated skin in the Bibliographic Tradition, ca. 1850 (*National Museum of Denmark*).

Later phases of contact-period rock art show motorcars and other twentieth-century things, but most of the Bibliographic Tradition appears to date to the eighteenth and nineteenth centuries or earlier. The absence of many scenes showing Europeans, rather than just trade items, suggests that the rock art in the Bibliographic Tradition became less pervasive following permanent European settlement after the mid-1800s, although we do find some depictions of military, wagons, motor vehicles, buildings, and men with European hats.

The fact that rock art was produced for centuries during the contact period in the Plains traditions allows us to observe indigenous pictorial and narrative traditions and to see how they shifted over time, including the shift of narrative outputs to new media in the historical ledgers. Here rock art and other contact imagery offer contemporaneous data for regional contextualized analyses of introductions, cultural continuities, shifting practices, and the various power struggles leading up to the arrival of permanent European settlement and the greater dispossession of Native Americans.[34]

THE WESTERN SEABOARD

Three centuries after contact began on the Atlantic, it occurred on the Pacific, particularly following Bering's "discovery" of Alaska in 1741. Culture contact with indigenous Americans of the Pacific seaboard largely resulted from the maritime fur trade, which involved Russians, English, and Americans. Contact between boat crews in their outposts and indigenous coastal communities characterized relationships from northern California, to Oregon, British Columbia, and Alaska. Northwest societies including the Tlingit, Haida, Tsimshian, Bella Coola, Kwakiutl, Nootka, Coast Salish, and Chinookans were the main coastal peoples of the Northwest in cross-cultural encounters and trade relationships.

Many of these communities included skilled maritime hunters. In fact, as the Russians were unable to effectively hunt seals, they engaged indigenous hunters operating from kayaks to do so, particularly the Aleut, who were most involved with the Russian traders.

Well prior to contact, there was a large volume of coastal trade as well as trade between the coast and hinterland. Contact only augmented this regional commerce, which included terrestrial and marine skins, canoes, copper items, and decorative objects. Of course, contact also brought the negative demographic and health impacts of disease, and alcohol, tobacco, and sugar. In some historical circumstances, Aboriginal people moved into new regions as part of fur-trading activities (see Fort Ross, below). The number of settlers and points of contact were fewer than, say, in California, and as a result many indigenous communities survived. A great amount of material wealth was generated for a time, which in the Northwest tended to be spent on potlatches (feasts) and possibly to increase the production of other prestige materials such as totem poles and decorated objects (which Europeans also desired as curios.)

Thompson's River Post, British Columbia

An initial period of rapid intensive resource extraction between 1780 and 1820 was followed by a shift toward other resources (inland furs, as well as timber and salmon). Inland traders did business too, including as part of Hudson's Bay Company efforts.

For example, when the HBC in ca. 1821 established the Thompson's River Post (British Columbia), local Secwepemc people built a nearby village. The archaeological record reveals several interesting aspects of this development. First, they built a new village (although there were already older, precontact villages nearby). The houses and food storage areas were the same design as they had been previously, being pithouses. There was no attempt in the early contact period to use new materials in their construction—no glass or nails. There was a shift toward particular European items, such as tools and metal dowels. Unlike in many places, European ceramics were not popular, but perhaps the robust metal cooking equipment was.

When comparing the houses in the village, some are clearly larger, yet overall the material found in each of the houses was quite similar. This suggests the egalitarian nature of this community where, unlike the chiefdoms of the coast, for example, there were no major differences in status across the village. Other evidence suggests that despite being close to the trading post, life remained relatively close to the ways of the past—the remains of food support this, with evidence for continued deer hunting and fishing.

This site suggests that European trading posts were small islands within indigenous country, presumably reliant, in this example, on the Secwepemc, not only for furs, but probably for food as well. Over time, Secwepemc society faced greater challenges, such as disease, religious conversion, population loss, and environmental change; yet, they survived.

Fort Ross, California

Long before the Cold War, the Russians arrived in America. Only 150 kilometers north of San Francisco, in 1812 in northern California at Fort Ross (from *Rus* for Russian), the Russian-America Company established a colony to supply food for their Russian American (Alaskan) fur-trapping outposts in Alaska. The Company was chartered by the tsar's family and backed by Russian nobility—although in 1812 they were clearly distracted by the French and the destruction of Moscow. (Also in 1812, the United States declared war against the British as a result of actions to defeat Napoleon.) California was part of the Viceroyalty of New Spain, yet the Spanish had settled only as far north as San Francisco (chapter 6).

The local Kashaya Pomo people met the new arrivals: a mix of Russian managers and native Alaskans from the Kodiak and Aleutian islands. Soon a stockade was built, and a multi-ethnic settlement established. The settlement was a toehold on the Pacific coast, with no further territorial aspirations.

Kent Lightfoot and his colleagues have mapped out the archaeological evidence for the various cultural engagements that defined this place. The interactions at Fort Ross seem to have been different from those described for the Spanish settlements in California, and also lacked the mixing of cultural practices we saw, for example, in La Florida (chapter 6). Like the occupants at the archaeological site of Oudepost in South Africa (chapter 5), the Kashaya Pomo chose to both avoid *and* join the fort community. That is to say, in their existing regional settlement pattern, people had the option of living close to the fort, or not. Some Kashaya Pomo, Coast Miwok, and Southern Pomo people joined the community, and Lightfoot focused on their multi-ethnic households, particularly those formed of Native Californian women and Native Alaskan men (mainly Alutiiq). The Russians were very aware of ethnic differences, categorizing these occupants in "estates" as Russians, Creoles, Aleuts, or American Indians. These estates reflected work, status, and pay. Native Californians were mostly seasonal workers, paid only in food, clothing, beads, and tobacco.

The research identified different activity areas at Fort Ross (Figure 7.7) and adherence to Californian and Alaskan cultural practices. There is some evidence for dual-ethnic households in which traditional aspects of life such as hunting and foraging activities were maintained. Food remains indicate that different dietary traditions continued, with marine foods preferred by the Alaskans, evident alongside the terrestrial foods preferred by the Native Californians.

Compared with settings elsewhere where creolization was very clear, such as at St. Augustine, Fort Ross's evidence for creolization is rather ambiguous. Despite marriages and multi-ethnic households, there is less evidence for creolization or ethnogenesis, and firmer evidence for the maintenance of existing practices but with the adoption of new materials such as ceramic, glass, and metal. This is not to exclude creolization, as Lightfoot makes the point that the ethnic categories were defined and observed by the Russian managers, and that in their daily activities, there was scope for movement across these categories. A Native Californian could, for example, dress and cook like Native Alaskan women.

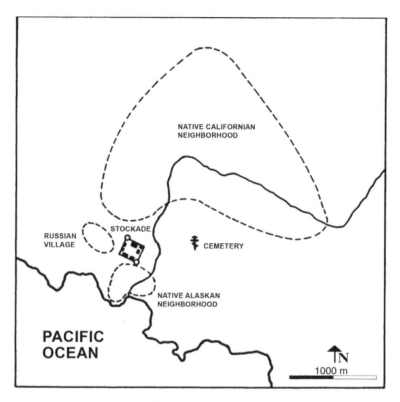

Figure 7.7. Spatial layout of Fort Ross showing the Russian stockade and village, and the Kashaya Pomo and Native Alaskan communities. (Courtesy of Kent Lightfoot.)

Considering the evidence, Lightfoot and his team describe Fort Ross in terms of pluralism, where social identities were maintained and created in inter-ethnic households. They argue that in houses where Native Californian women lived with Alaskan men, each maintained distinct identities.

CONCLUSION

This chapter has briefly introduced some key studies of culture contact and the ways that material remains through archaeology help illuminate this turbulent period of culture contacts. What becomes clear is that there are centuries where many Native Americans remained beyond the frontiers of face-to-face contact, yet we see in the early contact period a tapestry of varying degrees of access to new goods, conservatism and change, leading to a quickening in the intensity of disruptions to indigenous societies as many regions became the setting for more intensive settlement.

195

This is, of course, variable, with some regions only becoming settled by outsiders in the nineteenth century, if at all (as we see in the Arctic).

Over time, Native American and indeed all American societies developed so that comparisons with their ancestors of the fifteenth century—either in America or indeed Europe—became part of a longer-term picture, where cultural survival and creation in the colonial years exhibit cultural persistence and human agency.

The evidence for culture contact provides a new insight into "the prevailing opinion that European contact signaled the inevitable demise and disappearance of native cultures."[35] We see that, instead, our interpretations need to be set into longer histories that consider indigenous societies as they were before the arrival of outsiders and during the contact period, and how modern societies reflect the cross-cultural encounters of the last five hundred years in North America.

USEFUL SOURCES

Museums and online resources: The main national museums are the National Museum of the American Indian (NMAI) at the Smithsonian, and the Canadian Museum of Civilization. Native American records are held at the National Archives (USA) and include Bureau of Indian Affairs files; similarly, the Library and Archives Canada holds material related to Aboriginal people. The Aboriginal Canada Portal (*www.aboriginalcanada.gc.ca*) has information about First Nations, Métis, and Inuit people. An example of a community-driven institution is the tribally owned and operated Mashantucket Pequot Museum and Research Center (*http://www.pequotmuseum.org/*).

References: For American Indian tribes there are many encyclopedias, the standard reference being *The Handbook of North American Indians* (William C. Sturtevant, general editor) published by the Smithsonian Institution. The planned twenty volumes cover the archaeology, history, biology, and languages of indigenous peoples in North America; Volume 4 is *History of Indian–White Relations.* For an overview of archaeology, see F. P. McManamon, ed., *Archaeology in America: An Encyclopedia* (Westport, CT: Greenwood Press, 2008).

Key journals: Historical Archaeology, International Journal of Historical Archaeology, Canadian Journal of Archaeology, Journal of Social Archaeology, American Anthropologist, American Antiquity, Archaeology, Current Anthropology, Journal of Anthropological Archaeology, National Geographic, North American Archaeology, and publications by the Smithsonian Institute. Most regions have their own journals that may include studies of culture contact.

CHAPTER 8

EAST ASIA
AND OCEANIA

CONCERNING THE GREAT ISLAND OF JAVA. When you sail from Chamba, 1500 miles in a course between south and south-east, you come to a great Island called Java. And the experienced mariners of those Islands who know the matter well say that it is the greatest Island in the world, and has a compass of more than 3000 miles. It is subject to a great King and tributary to no one else in the world. The people are Idolaters. The Island is of surpassing wealth, producing black pepper, nutmegs, spikenard, galingale, cubebs, cloves, and all other kinds of spices. . . . This Island is also frequented by a vast amount of shipping, and by merchants who buy and sell costly goods from which they reap great profit. Indeed the treasure of this Island is so great as to be past telling. And I can assure you the Great Kaan [Khan] never could get possession of this Island, on account of its great distance, and the great expense of an expedition thither. The merchants of Zayton and Manzi [Southern China] draw annually great returns from this country.

–Marco Polo, *The Travels of Marco Polo*[1]

According to what the nations here in the East say, things in China are made out to be great, riches, pomp and state in both the land and the people, and other tales which it would be easier to believe as true of our Portugal than of China.

–Tomé Pires, 1512–1515[2]

With Asia, we reach the ultimate destination for many European intentions in the second millennium. Since antiquity, Europe had been in indirect contact with Asia: after 1500 it became direct and regular for a handful of merchants. In the islands of Southeast Asia, the fields of India, and the textile towns of China were the silks, porcelains, and spices that drew Europeans outward.

In this chapter, we consider some examples of contacts often mediated (from a European perspective) from the water, particularly in ports and on beaches. Europeans in Asia were confined to coastal ports in early phases of contact and necessarily often became involved with larger polities in the arc of the Indian Ocean and into Asian seas: from the Swahili states of East Africa, to the Mughals in India, the kingdoms and sultanates of the Indo-Malay region, to China and Japan (Figure 8.1). The restriction of Europeans to ports and coastal settlements remained unchanged for centuries, until the eighteenth century, when colonial realms such as those of the Dutch in Indonesia and the English in India, Malaysia, and Burma were established.

Figure 8.1. Map of the East Indian Ocean and Asia.

CONTACT IN EAST ASIA

The Portuguese and Spanish entered the Indian and Pacific Oceans from the end of the fifteenth century, seas where Arab, Gujerati, Malay, and Chinese merchants reigned. The Portuguese were entering a realm known vaguely to them, given indirect trade modulated by West Asian middlemen (chapter 4). A focus on the age of European expansions places Asia at a periphery, when in reality Asian polities had been at the center of Old World economic systems for millennia. From this perspective, Europe was the periphery of African-Asian developments.

Culture contact within Asia was ancient; Neolithic trade and migration throughout mainland and island Asia had been followed by the development of complex-state societies and distinctive cultures with extensive networks of influence. China had long been the largest consumer and producer of goods in East–West trade. In the millennium leading up to the arrival of Europeans, significant culture contact had resulted in the spread of Buddhist, Hindu, Chinese, and Muslim influences in Asia, and much historical understanding is from these literate traditions. With these Asian documentary traditions stretching back over two millennia, archaeologists are operating in an environment very different from many other regions discussed in this book.

Indirect Asian contacts with Europe waxed and waned over the preceding millennium as various sea and land routes linked the Mediterranean into Afro-Asian trade networks.[3] The trade routes termed "Silk Roads" linked Asia to Europe long before Europeans arrived in Asia. For the Romans, knowledge of Asia came largely secondhand, from meeting the Arab, Indian, Malay, and Persian seafarers who plied the oceans between West Asia and India and East Asia.

There was not one Silk Road. Maritime routes linked coastal ports, while ancient overland roads took various routes, the best known through the deserts of Central Asia, although others were significant, such as through Burma and those linking China to Southeast Asia.[4] Cultural influences resulted from the flow of new ideas and direct contacts along the roads of Eurasia. The roads of Eurasia were traveled by different societies over time, including the Scythians, Huns, Turks, and Mongols, to the Russians in the nineteenth century. While many Eurasians were nomads, urban settlements arose along trade routes. These routes carried goods and ideas, attested by the spread of Buddhism and Lamaism, Islam, Persian Zoroastrianism, and eventually Christian sects.

Following the fall of the Western part of the Roman Empire, international trade had continued and Chinese trade with Arabs increased, with spices, silk, and ceramics all in great demand. The Song Dynasty (960–1279) in China saw increased trade in large junks and a greater presence of Chinese traders at Asian ports. Shipyards sprung up to service the trade. Arab merchants resided in Chinese cities such as Quanzhou (the largest port, which Polo called "Zaitun") and Guangzhou (the new imperial capital). Chinese intercontinental maritime activities are most famously seen in the extraordinary efforts of Admiral Zheng He, whose expeditions in the early fifteenth century took his fleet to Sri Lanka and

India, and onward to the east coast of Africa. This flotilla of massive boats was unlike anything the world had seen, yet the Chinese policy became much more insular after Zheng Ho's death. By the time the Portuguese arrived in the following century, the Chinese were not exploratory, and trade was highly regulated and managed through direct or tributary relationships with traders across Asia.

The expansive maritime network of Arab merchants had for centuries integrated the East Asian trade networks with West Asia. From trading origins, converts to Islam in island Southeast Asia were increasing in number when the Portuguese arrived: it was this network in particular that the Portuguese sought to usurp.[5]

In Asia, Europeans were required to deal with large state societies, well organized, productive, stratified, densely populated, literate, and able to control their points of culture contact. Unlike in the Americas, there was no massive demographic collapse with the arrival of Europeans (except in Siberia; see below). Consequently, the types of cultural engagement that developed were very different from those in the New World. The Portuguese, and then the Dutch and English, could only form small centralized settlements (often termed "factories") through which trade goods moved, and the European population was contained. This remained the case for centuries.

These settlements tended to be coastal (such as Goa and Batavia) or located on islands off the coast (Macao and Japan). With few intrusions into mainland Asia until the British in the Indian subcontinent and the French invasion of Indochina, the most sustained cross-cultural interactions were in island Southeast Asia and the Malay Peninsula.

In summary, then, Europeans established coastal enclaves in South, Southeast, and East Asia, with China remaining effectively separate from European exertions for centuries, until after ca. 1830. There were exceptions to this scenario, such as the Spanish Philippines, essentially a western expression of Spain's American colonial interests and involving agents of the Catholic Church in a massive religious conversion program.

It is worthwhile distinguishing early and later phases of culture contact to determine how culture contact was organized and how it influenced Asian societies.[6] A line can be drawn between the first few centuries of European contacts with Asians and later colonial efforts, as it was only at the end of the eighteenth century that more imperial and colonial ambitions were realized in the "Orient," with the British in India and the Dutch, to a lesser degree, in island Southeast Asia. These activities were quite different from earlier patterns of culture contact enacted by European powers.

By the late nineteenth century, nations with Asian colonies included the French in Vietnam, Cambodia, Laos, and China; the United States in the Philippines; and Germany in Papua New Guinea. European powers were, of course, only part of the regional picture from the fifteenth century onward. Asian states with regional ambitions included the kingdoms of Siam, Mon, and Java, and the Chinese and Japanese empires.

The archaeological study of culture contacts between Europeans and Asians since the fifteenth century is patchier than of other places described in this book. Historical studies are restricted to historical buildings and towns. However, some examples of archaeologies of culture contact can be considered here.

This chapter first briefly considers the various culture contacts that occurred in Asia prior to the arrival of Europeans. It is very clear that while the arrival of Europeans represents a significant historical seam, these regions had been involved in ongoing culture contact and interactions for millennia: the various European nations were just the latest phase. The Banda Islands are considered as a case study of the potential value of archaeological studies to understanding contact. The chapter then considers Oceania and, in particular, looks at the archaeology of culture contact in Polynesian societies.

SIBERIA

Most of the discussion in this chapter is of culture contact and trade in ports and on offshore islands. However, before proceeding, let us briefly consider one example from inland. A setting for dramatic historical culture contact in Eurasia was Siberia which, as a neighbor of Europe, had an indigenous population of Eurasians. As in North America, fur-bearing animals attracted Europeans (Russians and others), in this case in the sixteenth century AD. Within a century, Europeans were the majority of the population. Despite being part of the Eurasian landmass, Siberia had remained isolated: when introduced, smallpox, venereal infections, measles, scarlet fever, and typhus devastated the indigenous Siberians. Smallpox was the worst, wiping out a generation in 1630 and returning in later epidemics to cut down the next survivors. This was how Russians came to exceed indigenous Siberians in number, not through massive migration.[7] Many places in Asia were less biologically isolated, although comparisons can be made between Oceanic communities and Siberia in terms of being isolated societies coming into contact with European outsiders.

PORTS OF CONTACT

The ports of South Asia (modern India, Bangladesh, Pakistan, and Sri Lanka), Southeast Asia, and East Asia have long histories of use, as documented in ancient texts and archaeological evidence for port facilities, shipping, and trade. The location of ports changed as routes developed, allegiances shifted, and the coastal landscape was altered (see Kedah, below). Some existing ports became key to European mercantile activities, notably Canton, Malacca, Galle, Diu, and Goa. Other smaller ports were built up to become international trade centers, such as Batavia, Calcutta, and Macao.

Ports tended to be places where cross-cultural contacts occurred, multiple ethnicities coexisted, international diplomacy and trade deals were hammered out, and military campaigns waged. In addition to historical sources and terrestrial archaeology, the evidence from shipwrecks provides material insight into the nature of trade over time.[8]

Galle Harbor

To take one example, in Galle Harbor, Sri Lanka, archaeological surveys have found sites from the first and second millennia, discovering anchors from Oman in the Persian Gulf, and early celadon bowls from China. These reveal a harbor at the very crossroads of the world.

While Galle Harbor had been used in ancient times, it only became more significant in the twelfth century. Zheng He's Chinese fleet arrived in Galle in 1411; a century later, the Portuguese arrived and built a small fort. This fort was part of the Portuguese network extending from Macao, Japan, the Philippines, and Malacca, to Goa. The Portuguese maintained regional dominance over Asian waters only for a time, and Galle, like many settlements, moved between various European powers.

After 1640, the Dutch East India Company (VOC) turned Galle into a keystone of their Asian network, second only to Batavia on Java. The waters of the harbor remember all these transitions, as do the streets of Galle, particularly for the Dutch period.

The archaeology of shipping promises information of the ways that goods moved between Asia and Europe, and also of regional networks. For example, the excavation of the *Avonstar*, a Dutch East Indiaman which sank in Galle Harbor, uncovered a great array of material from local Asian production and trade networks, including plant remains from India and ceramics from Thailand, India, and China. Thus, archaeology traces the complexity of contacts that existed not just between the well-known principal ports, but also among the many other smaller Asian locations of intercontinental trade.

CONTAINING CONTACT

When we consider culture contact with China from a European perspective, we encounter a heavily regulated form of culture contact, evident from the early contacts between the Portuguese and Chinese. The Chinese reactions to the early Portuguese delegations were deliberately noncommittal and probably allowed for information to be gathered by the Chinese, who kept delegations waiting for months and years in Canton. There was misinformation on both sides; for example, there existed a belief in China that the European barbarians had been buying children to eat them. (The Chinese did not call only Europeans "barbarians": this term had been long deployed to describe all foreigners.[9])

The Portuguese were pushy. An attempt to establish a coastal Chinese settlement with force was routed in 1521 by the Chinese fleet. While the Portuguese cooled their heels in Canton, Malacca had already fallen to the Portuguese cannons, and the estranged king entreated the Chinese emperor to assist in routing the Europeans. Eventually, trade transpired and led to the Portuguese establishment of Macao in 1557 as *povoação do Nome de Deos na China* (settlement of the name of God in China),[10] a port that existed only with permission from China. This continued the Chinese practice of keeping foreign influences offshore or in restricted ports.

Keep in mind that the Chinese were well prepared in developing policies for culture contact, as trade with outsiders dated back millennia to the Han Dynasty. In the Tang Dynasty, there was contact with Byzantium and West Asian powers, and a relatively greater acceptance of foreigners—diplomats, merchants, and missionaries largely—in China than would be the case in later times. Visitors from Japan, India, Greece, Arabia, Persia, and Siberia were in Ch'ang at this time, for example. The presence of foreigners was regulated in places such as Canton, where Polo encountered Jews, Zoroastrians, Christians, and Moslems.

The rise of Islam saw a significant conversion in China, as well as changes in Central Asian societies. As long-established overland routes declined, sea routes dominated by Arab ships and largely based out of Canton became very important for trade and contact.[11]

Some evidence for the Chinese trade comes from historical sources, but also from archaeological finds on shipwrecks and Chinese ceramics in archaeological contexts elsewhere in South Asia, Europe, and East Africa. It is, of course, the ceramics that survive in these contexts; nonetheless, other, less robust materials like textiles were traded alongside the ceramics.

Chinese traveled overseas, most famously with the vast expeditions of Zheng He in the fifteenth century. However, there had long been Chinese merchants and diplomatic missions in Southeast Asia, as well as to Japan and the Philippines.[12] Chinese communities across Asia are described in historical texts, detailing that Chinese immigrants married into local communities and maintained the trade bond that many polities shared with China. It is interesting to observe that while

Indian influences are clearly seen in Southeast Asia, this is less true for Chinese influences, despite their regional significance and presence.

It is, however, the tight control of points of contact with foreigners by societies like China (also Japan) that is most distinctive. In fact, the Portuguese in Macao were successful because the Ming court was closing its ports to the Japanese; consequently, the Portuguese had the franchise on trading Chinese silks and Indian textiles to Japan—a lucrative trade indeed. Additionally, from Japan they could collect items in high demand in Europe, such as lacquerware.

The Portuguese dominance was not to last. The Japanese court, too, was concerned about the influence of outsiders, viewing them as increasingly undesirable. Portuguese merchants had been in contact with Japanese elite and had introduced missionaries, resulting in conversions to Catholicism. The mix of influences grew more complicated as Dutch and British merchants joined the Portuguese and other Asian merchants in Japanese port cities. In the 1630s, the Japanese court acted to ban foreigners. Only the VOC remained, restricted to the island port of Deshima, banned from unauthorized contact with Japanese, and their employees restricted to one year's employment. Missionaries and European women were also banned, and Japanese converts to Christianity were forced to leave. Japan's attempt to restrict and regulate culture contact remained intact until 1853, when the U.S. fleet of Commodore Perry forced the Japanese to allow greater foreign presence in their ports.

Despite losing access to Japan, the Portuguese retained Macao, and Canton grew in importance as the only other open Chinese port after 1757. From Canton came ceramics, silks, tea, and various other luxuries, fine arts, and exotica. In Canton, various European traders—from Holland, England, France, Denmark, Sweden, Austria, Spain, and in the 1780s, America—were closely monitored by the port authorities (Figure 8.2). In this trade, key European institutions were the British East India Company (1600) and the Dutch East India Company (1602).

The European traders in Canton had a privileged yet restricted access to China, although the presence of Fan Kwae (foreign devils) was certainly felt. Outside of Canton, in the kilns of Shekwan, the potters produced ceramics that catered to Chinese people's anxieties about the foreigners: these depicted the Canton traders in subservient poses, symbolically upsetting the merchants' power (Figure 8.3). These were especially popular after the humiliation of the Chinese in the Opium Wars.

The Opium Wars originated in part from an imbalance in trade, as the Chinese had more to sell. The growing demand for Chinese tea in the eighteenth century only intensified the differential. Of course, there were goods the Chinese demanded: for example, Americans came loaded with ginseng grown from New

Figure 8.2. The European factories in Canton. Painting, 1749–1784
(*The National Museum of Denmark*).

Figure 8.3. Figurines of the Fan Kwae (Foreign Devils) in Canton
(*The National Museum of Denmark*).

England.[13] Furs, sandalwood, and bêche-de-mer (trepang) were also desired. Many of these commodities were extracted from the Pacific during the nineteenth century; for example, the sandalwood stands discovered in the Marquesas and Hawaiian Islands were quickly felled and shipped to China.

Overall, however, silver was pouring into China from North American and European reserves. This was relatively easy for the Spanish, who had silver mines in their American colonies; but the British had to buy silver to pay the Chinese. The British answer was to force open the Chinese market for opium, which they traded illicitly from India. The demand was, not surprisingly, high: up to 10 percent of the Chinese population became users. This led to wars beginning in 1839 and 1856, both lost by the Chinese. Consequently, after the 1840s the Chinese trade opened up for European merchants; Hong Kong, Shanghai, Foochow, and Amoy ports began trading, while faster, larger tea clippers allowed for increased exports of tea and silk. It appears, then, that attempts to control culture contacts were both social and economic, and fed by self-preservation, fear, policy, and the intent to control outcomes.

Restrictions on culture contact were found not only in China and Japan; the limits imposed on foreign contacts existed elsewhere as well. In the Philippines, for example, Chinese merchants were present long before the Spanish arrived. Specified trading beaches were designated locations for Chinese traders to leave goods, and for the settling of accounts with native traders. The reasons were similar to those described for Canton: by restricting general access to traders, rulers could also keep the commercial activities in the hands of the few. This was also seen on the Malay Peninsula, where the kingdoms that arose around trade were run by elites who restricted access to the profits of trade. However, beyond economics, concern about the cultural results of contact also fueled the restricted model for trade. For example, when the Japanese removed the Portuguese, they also expelled all Japanese converts to Christianity who would not renounce their religion. In this sense, restraint of foreign influences was akin to modern approaches to the control of contagious disease, incorporating containment and removal of affected parts.

SOUTHEAST ASIA

Southeast Asia has attracted attention from Asian, Arabic, and European interests increasingly over the last two millennia. It has many natural resources, some exotic and at various times very valuable. Chinese and Indian merchants were attracted to these resources, including spices, and to commodities like gold, rhinoceros horn, ivory, tortoise shell, pearls, feathers, birds, bêche-de-mer, and exotic woods.

From a maritime perspective, Southeast Asia hangs between India and China, which is how early Arab geographers perceived it: an interface between these two worlds. The international trade routes through Southeast Asia connected China to West Asia, via the Malay Peninsula, the Bay of Bengal and Sri Lanka, India, the Red Sea, and the Persian Gulf. For centuries, goods were transshipped across the

Malay Peninsula, but after the fifth century, shipping had improved to allow passage across the China Sea and through the Straits of Malacca. As a result, many distinct cross-cultural influences are evident in the first and second millennia in Southeast Asia: Indian, Chinese, Islamic, and, from the sixteenth century, European. Thus, archaeological studies of Southeast Asia require taking a longer-term perspective, one that includes local interests as well as the influences of external polities, religions, and broader trade systems.

Contact with Asians

Let us briefly consider the pre-European influences, first, of Indian cultural elements, a process sometimes described as "Indianization" or "Hinduization." This encompasses the evidence for various elements of Indian influence, possibly including Buddhism and Hinduism, ceremonial languages (Sanskrit, Pali), concepts of social and political organization, and elements of design, art, and architecture. These influences were adopted among certain elites and in certain landscapes where visitors had easy access; that is, they were not adopted across the board. In this sense, the impact of foreign influence mirrors many other examples cited in this book where differentials in degrees of interrelationships and change characterize culture contact. In some regions, external influences may have led to the development of kingdoms with many "Indian" elements, including construction of massive religious sanctuaries and other public works such as roads and canals. Early states with Indian elements in modern Thailand, Burma, Cambodia, and Malaysia became dominant polities, as did kingdoms in island Sumatra, Java, western Borneo, and Bali.

There is debate about how "Indian" these attributes were. In a study of archaeological sites in the region near Kedah—a key port on the Malay Peninsula with access to transshipped Chinese goods, locally produced ceramics, and local cardamom, cinnamon, gharuwood, ivory, sandalwood, and tin—Jane Allen found that "Indian" sites, starting after AD 200, were mainly shrines either in harbor settlements or along the inland waterways used by hinterland Malay people to move goods to the coast. She suggests these may have been erected by traders, and that no major "Indianization" occurred among Kedah Malays such as described elsewhere, and that the local Malay state did not shift dramatically toward Indian culture.[14]

Allen's study also indicates that in the last thousand years, the landscape changed dramatically—possibly, increased farming around 1200–1300 resulted in massive erosion—with the development of a greater coastal plain, enlarging at a rate of a kilometer every century. This means that port infrastructure—docks, beacons, and warehouses—are not found on the modern coast, but inland. Archaeological excavations in these towns reveal long histories of trade: for example, Kedah had

Chinese tradewares from AD 100 until the mid-fourteenth century. Allen argues that states arose due to the local elite's role in administering trade.

To understand these processes in the absence of comprehensive archaeological studies of many key historical ports in Southeast Asia, we are reliant on the mix of historical accounts by Arab, Indian, Malay, Chinese, and eventually European visitors to ports like Malacca, Kedah, Aceh, and Banten. These sources suggest that foreigners were welcomed but that local officials supervised storage, overland transport, customs, and gifts for rulers, and restricted visitors to residences in enclaves separated from the wider populace.

Chinese influences in the region are also ancient. After the sixth century, Chinese ceramics start to occur regularly in archaeological sites across island Southeast Asia, reflecting greater participation in economic arenas. This trend escalated from the tenth century.

Under Mongol reigns in China, campaigns were mounted into Southeast Asia in the late thirteenth century. However, this was largely uncharacteristic of Chinese interests, which were often directed toward economic activities. Especially compared with Indian influences, Chinese elements held little sway in Southeast Asia (other than in Vietnam, where Chinese control was significant). That said, there were overseas settlements of Chinese communities, and these people intermarried with locals. As late as the 1830s, George Earl, one of the first British visitors to Chinese gold and diamond mines in northern Borneo, described how the Chinese maintained their own cultural practices but intermarried with local Dyaks: "The Chinese suppose the Dyaks to be descended from a large body of their country men left by accident upon the island, but this opinion is entertained solely on the faith of a Chinese legend [which involved] a monstrous serpent . . . which possessed a talisman of inestimable value . . . a large fleet, with an immense body of men, [were dispatched] to steal it. . . ." The serpent awoke, blew off the fleet of junks, and the Chinese sailors were left behind.[15]

With the growth of Islam came new religious, political, and cultural influences in Southeast Asia. Small communities of Muslim merchants involved in the international maritime trade had been present for centuries.[16] Their presence dated from the seventh century in China, the ninth century along the East African coast, and the eleventh century in India and the Malay Straits. By the thirteenth century, a number of communities converted to Islam. In India, most key trading ports were Muslim, as were those in the Straits of Malacca. Some areas more distant from trade centers remained unchanged, such as Hindu Bali.

Islam was a religion for elites as well as the wider society and was particularly significant in island Southeast Asia; today Indonesia has the largest Muslim population in the world. Mainland Asia saw fewer conversions, finding less support among the large Buddhist population. The process of Islamic conversion was gradual and took root among sectors or enclaves on islands first (see the case study below of the Banda Islands). By 1600, much of the Malay-Indonesian world had adopted Islam, except for Bali, eastern Java, interior Borneo and Sulawesi, northern Philippines, some parts of Sumatra, and certain small islands.

Thus, when the Portuguese arrived in Southeast Asia, most communities were involved in vast regional changes with ancient roots, and increasingly the region was dominated by largely maritime Islamic trade networks, although the coasts and ports also included Indian, Malay, Persian, and other ethnicities.

Contact with Europeans

Let us briefly flesh out the main European presence in the region, which brought in the volatile mix of ships, merchants, soldiers, administrators, missionaries, and adventurers. There is little archaeological work to describe, but I will cover archaeological work in the Banda Islands as a small case study of archaeological evidence for culture contact over the long term.

Given the importance of Islam, it is impossible to separate trade from religion when we consider the Portuguese entry into the Indian Ocean. The Portuguese certainly could not separate them either and focused on ending the hegemony of Islamic trade—indeed, King Manoel adopted the title of "Lord of the conquest, navigation and commerce of Ethiopia, Persia and India."[17] The Portuguese center in the Indian Ocean was Goa[18] (conquered 1510), with the fortified centers of Ormuz (Persian Gulf, captured 1515) and Malacca (Southeast Asia, captured 1519) used as bases to operate against Moslems, whose trade systems they were disrupting.

The Portuguese model was of fortified bases for the prosecution of trade. In addition, new forts acting as trading posts were built in East Africa, India, and Southeast Asia. They had some settlements in places they did not control, such as Macao, which was a Portuguese port and city but with sovereignty becoming shared with China; mutually profitable trade saw Macao survive and thrive. Macao was "handed back" to China in 1999, making it the earliest and most long-lived European colony in Asia: a 422-year intercultural engagement based on international trade. The influences of both the Chinese and Portuguese cultures are evident in the World Heritage–listed city at the heart of Macao.

Some historical sites have been subject to archaeological description, although studies of indigenous reactions to the presence of traders and colonists with their various economic and religious agendas that we have described for Africa and the Americas are less common in Asia. Partly this reflects the presence of historical sources, while it may also be due to the significance of these types of heritage sites in contemporary Asian countries.

Philippines

Portuguese power declined despite the influences of a united Spanish and Portuguese royal dynasty in the late sixteenth century. The Spanish attempted to access the spice trade through their presence in the Philippines, their primary area of influence in Asia. Culture contact in the Philippines after the Spanish arrival was very different from that in other Asian contexts, where mammon was superior to god. Not so in the Philippines, where Catholic orders were instrumental in interactions with indigenous people. The Philippines was essentially closed to other European traders, and even the Spanish trade was restricted to the annual Manila Galleon (between 1571 and 1811) that sailed the Mexico–Manila route. Manila, however, was keyed into Asian trade, being linked to China and with a large community of resident Chinese merchants. Despite bans, some trade was also conducted with Japan. Spanish colonialism in the Philippines lasted for centuries, until the American navy destroyed the Pacific Spanish fleet in Manila harbor in 1898.

Research by archaeologist Laura Lee Junker in the Philippines[19] provides some insight into the Philippines prior to and following the Spanish, who were preceded by a thousand years of texts produced by Arab, Chinese, and Southeast Asian traders. Once again, then, an array of intense contacts preceded the arrival of Europeans. Other information comes from archaeological evidence from excavations of settlements, regional surveys, mortuary analyses, and analyses of various foreign and local artifacts in sites. Evidence also comes from ethnographic literature about the various remote communities in the Philippines that remained largely beyond the reach of culture contacts with the Spanish. Junker raises some important points, although her focus is the pre-Hispanic period.

Thinking about culture contact, the importance of Junker's research is that by looking at non-European and early Spanish colonial accounts, as well as the archaeology, the limits and errors in colonial historical accounts become clearer. The changes in Philippine communities leading up to Spanish colonization included greater access to trade of prestige items, access to exotics for the elite, agricultural intensification, greater competitive feasting, greater specialized craft production, greater militarism and capture of slaves, and attempts to control trade. Many of these trends are seen in the archaeological record but are not found in Spanish historical accounts. For example, Spanish accounts emphasized that there was little regional organization in the Philippines, whereas non-Spanish sources describe powerful chiefs visiting China, and the archaeology reveals within some regions settlements of great complexity and hierarchical organization. Future work will probably measure the impact of the Spanish on the Philippines in greater detail, beyond the limits of Spanish accounts.

The Dutch

The Portuguese and the Spanish (outside Philippines) were usurped in the seventeenth century with the rise of British and Dutch interests in Asia.

The Dutch in Asia were represented by the VOC, chartered in 1602 to access the profitable Asian trade. The VOC attempted to take the Portuguese fort of Malacca, unsuccessfully initially, and other Portuguese bases. Soon the Portuguese were largely restricted to Goa and Canton. This came at a bad time, as Turkish control of the Persian Gulf also hampered the Portuguese. The Dutch muscled into Asia, taking over the Javanese port of Jakarta to create the VOC capital of Batavia, despite retaliation from the Javanese Mataram Kingdom. Once there, the VOC refined the "spoke and wheel" model in which small or older vessels moved goods to the main ports of Batavia and Galle, from which they were transshipped to Holland via their VOC base at the Cape of Good Hope (chapter 5).

The Dutch colonies were composed of Dutch employees of the VOC and other European nationals, and were supported by diverse communities. The army in Batavia, for example, comprised a minority of Dutch and included variously Indians, Portuguese-Indians, Balinese, Bugese, Malays, and Macassarese troops.

As few Dutch women came to Asia, cross-cultural marriages were common. A painting of Pieter Cnoll and his family (Figure 8.4) provides a singular perspective of the cultural complexity of this world.[20] The painting depicts Cnoll, his wife, and daughters; as Cnoll was a senior merchant in the VOC, the boats of the VOC sit in the harbor and Chinese trade ceramics rest on the floor. The artist, Jacob Jansz. Coeman, produced images for the VOC, documenting their ships, forts, and towns and showing life in Batavia and other Southeast Asian ports. These document bustling streets in diverse communities of Muslims, Chinese, Malay, European, and peoples of the Asian archipelago.

The VOC depended on slaves, who constituted the majority of their Asian workers; this remained the case until they abolished slavery in 1819. VOC practice encouraged Dutch men's temporary relationships with slaves, who could be purchased in Batavia, and also encouraged marriage with Asian women. The mixed-descent children found work in the Dutch world, or married into it: some ended up being sent to Holland for education. In the painting, Cnoll's wife Cornelia was of Dutch-Japanese descent; she outlived her first husband (she would remarry another

Figure 8.4. Painting "Pieter Cnoll, senior merchant of Batavia, his wife and their daughters," 1665, by Jacob Jansz. Coeman. (*Rijksmuseum, Amsterdam, object no. SK-A-4062.*)

Dutchman) and their nine children, only one of whom lived to a brief adulthood. Such mixed families were recognized and protected in Dutch law, and characterized their colonial Asian settlements.

The painter suggests the male servant was named Surapati, the name of a prince and charismatic resistance fighter of the second half of the sixteenth century. There is some defiance in his pose, and perhaps support from the unnamed female servant.

The Dutch maintained their colonial presence in Southeast Asia into the mid-twentieth century.

The British

The British accompanied the Dutch into Asia, their interests represented by the English East India Company. In the seventeenth century, the English were less successful in East Asia, except in Canton. Their efforts were particularly directed toward India, where key ports were Madras (1639), Bombay (1665), and Calcutta (1690). Their dealings were with the Mughals, who restricted the British except along the Coromandel coast, then part of the Hindu Kingdom of Vijayanagar.

Calcutta was initially a small port but grew to be very significant to British interests, especially as Mughal power waned. In the eighteenth century, the British activities in Bengal shifted from mercantilism to a colonial program with a heavy military aspect. From here the British colonial presence took root and was rolled out in other Asian settings, in Burma, Ceylon, Malaya, and Borneo.

There have been some archaeological investigations of colonial sites in the key British settlements in East Asia, in Singapore and Hong Kong. Singapore was established at what had once been a Malay port. Archaeological excavations reveal something of this royal settlement abandoned by 1400, which would again gain regional prominence in the colonial era (the British arrived in 1819). Interestingly, the decision to locate the British in Singapore was in part due to observations of ancient archaeological remains of earth ramparts, moat, and brick structures. There have been, however, very few studies of the cross-cultural aspects of these colonial settlements.

The Spice Islands

The potential of archaeological work on culture contact in East Asia is demonstrated in the Maluku Islands (also Moluccas), in an eastern province of Indonesia. The Maluku Islands were historically equated with the Spice Islands, although the latter name sometimes referred specifically to the Banda Islands only. This archipelago includes the islands of Ambon, Halmahera, Banda, and Aru. As the source of mace, nutmeg, and cloves, these islands had been part of the international trade of spices since antiquity; the Roman writer Pliny the Elder refers to cloves in the first century AD.

To meet the demand for these spices, coastal communities dedicated greater amount of land to spice trees, presumably with repercussions for foragers and swidden farmers across the islands. Over time, the control of trade was consolidated in centers on Tidore, Ambon, and Ternate, which became managed by sultanates coming under the influence of Islam.

Archaeological analyses highlight the differentials that existed between groups tied closely to the main nodes of trade and governance and the remainder of the population, often farmers in rural and small village settings. For example, archaeological research into hinterland sites occupied by Batususu people on Ambon suggests that very little changed in a material and subsistence sense between 1100 and the seventeenth century, five centuries of time that saw a shift across the Maluku Islands toward Islam, the alignment of Ambon with the sultanate at Ternate, and finally the arrival of Portuguese and other European interests. Ambon was influenced by Christian missionaries, resulting in a greater indigenous Christian population than on other islands in Southeast Asia. In the hinterland of Ambon, however, the changes were not as dramatic as this historical overview may suggest, and it is likely that more dramatic shifts were reserved for coastal communities.

For the Europeans, the importance of the Spice Islands was clear. To access the spices, the Portuguese and Spanish struck deals with the sultanates, particularly in Ternate and Tidore. For example, in 1512 the Portuguese allied themselves with the Sultan at Ternate, building a fortress there. Later, in the seventeenth century, the Dutch and British dominated trade in these islands. To give a sense of how important these islands were, the British gave up the tiny island of Run in exchange for the Dutch claim to Manhattan.

The tiny Banda Islands were once the world's sole source of nutmeg and mace. From the sixteenth century, these eleven islands would see some of the fiercest conflicts in Asia. The first Europeans to glimpse the steep volcanic peaks rising from the tropical waters of the Banda Sea were on board a Portuguese trading boat in 1512. A century later, a Dutch crew saw the same peaks rise over the horizon, yet the people they met had changed over the preceding century and were probably hardened for the conflict ahead.

The Dutch desire for these islands was great. In 1621, VOC soldiers backed by Japanese mercenaries conquered the islands. The VOC would defeat Bandanese forces on the island of Pulau Ay supported by the British; when they took the British fort, they renamed it "Fort Revenge." The VOC seized valuable farmland at great cost to the Bandanese, who were subject to something we may now call "ethnic cleansing." Since 90 percent of the local population was killed, banished, or enslaved, the VOC needed plantation workers. Dutch farmers with Asian slaves filled the void.

This dramatic shift in the social landscape, with the abandonment of many earlier settlements and at least one fort and the larger settlement of *Labbetacca*, is indicated in the handful of maps from the sixteenth and seventeenth centuries (Figure 8.5). The post-1621 maps picture the islands divided into plantations, each with a number of souls (*zielen*) to work the nutmeg crop. Eventually, Dutch colonialism would extend throughout much of what is now Indonesia.

This version of history focuses on events after the arrival of Europeans. Using archaeological evidence and a range of historical sources, archaeologist Peter Lape from the University of Washington has been interpreting Islamization, trade, and European colonialism in eastern Indonesia, working on the Banda Islands since 1997. Lape has been particularly interested in the tenth to the seventeenth centuries. He has recorded sites across the Banda Islands to understand the archaeological evidence of past communities from both precolonial and colonial periods.

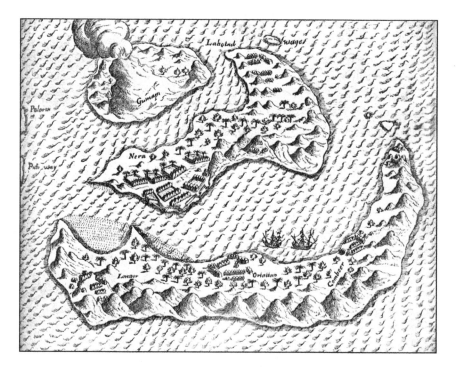

Figure 8.5. Map from 1601 showing the Banda Islands. Some islands have settlements, and some settlements are named. The settlement of Nera is fortified. The focus is very much on coastal ports; there is little information of inland settlements. (*Johann Theodor de Bry, 1601. Bandae insulae designatio. Francofurti: M. Becker. British Library.*)

What becomes clear is that these tiny islands were involved in intensive contacts and transformations prior to 1512. Previous histories had painted a picture of an unchanging homogeneous society until the sixteenth century, when the Portuguese arrived and the population was presumed to have converted to Islam. For example, in 1512 the Portuguese chronicler Tomé Pires stated of the Banda Islands:

> These have no villages; they have no king; they are ruled by *cabilas* and by elders. Those along the sea coast are Moorish merchants. It is thirty years since they began to be Moors in the Banda Islands. There are a few "heathen inside the country."[21]

This suggests conversion to Islam began in the 1480s, that Islamic merchants lived in coastal ports, and that some of the population had not converted. The archaeology makes for a more complicated story, however.

While Arab traders were present from the ninth century, there are no histori-cal accounts of their coming to Banda—yet long-distance traders must have come this far east to get mace and nutmeg. Historical sources suggest regular contacts occurred from the mid-thirteenth century; the earliest historical reference to the islands is from a Chinese text from 1304. The archaeology suggests even earlier ac-cess to Chinese trade goods such as ceramics and coins, possibly as early as the eighth century, certainly by the Song Dynasty (960–1279), and increasingly after the twelfth century. The archaeological record of two coastal settlements (sites BN1 and BN4) suggests each grew in size around this time, until the fifteenth cen-tury. Excavator Peter Lape identified site BN1 as the historic village of *Labbetacca* (referred to above as abandoned around the time of the early Dutch colonial pe-riod) and site BN4 as the village of *Nera*.[22]

The archaeology indicates that all villages tended to use similar earthenware pottery, some with a red slip, some fragments sculpted into animal shapes such as bird's heads. These similarities in pottery occur across the Banda Islands and other Maluku islands. Other archaeological evidence allowed Lape to explore the timing of the introduction of Islam to the islands. His evidence for the *absence* of Muslims relies on the fact that Islamic law bans eating pork and requires inhumation; thus, pig remains and cremated human remains—this being the preferred means of dis-posing of the dead traditionally—were assumed to be signatures for non-Muslim occupation.

One key site (BN1) had pig bones and human cremation from initial occupa-tion around 500 until the sixteenth century. This is consistent with the historical accounts for late conversion to Islam. This town (BN1) was greatly reduced in size around the time of the Dutch conquest. Other sites (BN2, BN4, and PA2), how-ever, reveal *no* evidence for pig from their initial occupation: these settlements were on the best ports in the islands (unlike BN1, located on an exposed coast with no anchorage). Lape interprets these sites as ports engaged in long-distance trade, and at least partly occupied by Muslims. This suggests an earlier presence of Mus-lims than indicated by Chinese and European sources: these may have begun as small enclaves. This evidence supports accounts that describe tensions between Muslim coastal populations and non-Muslim populations in the islands. There may also have been environmental usefulness in ideological diversity, as non-Mus-lims would have kept the population of pig low—and pigs on small islands repre-sent a significant threat to crops.

The islands were clearly increasingly involved in the wider region: by 1609 the Dutch described a multicultural community of "Turks, Persians, Bengalese, Gujeratis, Chinese, Japanese, Malays, Javanese, Macassarese and people from . . . Seram, Ambon, Kei, Ternate, Tidore and Aru."[23] As Lape puts it, maybe it is time to think of places such as this as the crossroads, not as some isolated places on the way to somewhere else.

The long-term result of the arrival of the Portuguese may have been to increasingly polarize the region and encourage resistance: the Banda islanders resisted Portuguese interference in trade and religious affairs. At two settlements (BN1 and BN2), stone walls were built at some stage to protect the towns; these are depicted in Dutch maps and so must predate the seventeenth century. With the shift of power to Muslims to meet the threat posed by the Portuguese, non-Muslim settlements such as BN1 may have been less useful and largely abandoned.

As such, this evidence suggests how regional issues of power and ideology played out in the Banda Islands, and the growing importance of trade. Not surprisingly, the colonial period after the sixteenth century is characterized by other shifts visible in the archaeological record: certain settlements become colonial centers, with the site of the Dutch administrators being the focus for the greatest amount of imported material culture.

OCEANIA

If during the early part of the millennium Asia hung on the margins of European knowledge and imagination as if a dream, the island worlds of Oceania lay far beyond any dreaming. The idea that a large southern landmass (or several) with millions of people developed in the minds of geographers, yet the world of Oceania was not known of at all until the arrival of early explorers in the sixteenth century.

Oceania is a massive region including Australia (see next chapter), the large islands of New Zealand and New Guinea, and the many islands of the Pacific, often divided into Micronesia, Melanesia, and Polynesia (Figure 8.6). I focus on Polynesia here, as there has been more archaeological research into historical contexts. Although archaeological research in Melanesia (Papua New Guinea, Solomon Islands, Vanuatu, and New Caledonia) has increased dramatically in the last two decades, most has dealt with precontact contexts.

The Oceanic world had long been in culture contact. The colonization of the western Pacific by Lapita peoples in the fourth millennium BC had seen the largest trade network on the planet develop, with pots and obsidian tools indicating links from Fiji back into island Southeast Asia. From Lapita-descent communities, the final pulse of human colonization saw the Polynesian population spread from Hawaii in the north, Easter Island in the east, and New Zealand in the west. These places were all occupied by one thousand years ago, with the possible exception of New Zealand. It is certainly an understatement that these Pacific peoples were great travelers, explorers, and colonizers.

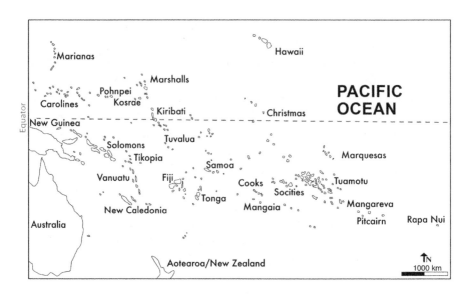

Figure 8.6. Map of Oceania.

Early Contacts

In terms of culture contact between Pacific Islanders and Europeans, we can differentiate contact between explorers, seasonal or occasional visitors (such as whalers), and more sustained contact with European colonists. The earliest voyages were of the Spanish in the early sixteenth century. Magellan's fleet traveled westward from Cape Horn for three months without encountering populated lands, eventually arriving in Guam, in eastern Micronesia.

There were Spanish attempts at colonization of the Solomon Islands in the 1590s—which they named after King Solomon—yet these were short-lived, and failed due to disease, mutiny, and eventual warfare between the Spanish and local Solomon Islanders. After this time, the Spanish rarely visited Pacific islands; instead, their galleons sailed annually from the Philippines across the northern Pacific to New Spain (Mexico), rarely encountering land.

Enlightenment-Era Contacts

Thus, first contact between Pacific Islanders and Europeans remained rare until the late eighteenth century, with the exception of a handful of earlier exploratory voyages such as by Tasman, Schouten, and Le Maire. One of the great European Pacific explorers was Captain James Cook, whose epic voyages brought the British

218

Empire to the Pacific, although voyages of others, such as Vancouver, Bougainville, Bligh, La Pérouse, and d'Entrecasteaux, were equally significant.[24]

Across the vast expanse of Polynesia, some of the most famous historical examples of "first contact" emerged in the eighteenth century, particularly in the voyages of Captain Cook. The "discovery" of Polynesia fed into the Enlightenment thinking of London and Paris, and Polynesians, like earlier non-Europeans brought into the Western sphere of knowledge, required categorization.

There have been many insightful books written on Cook's voyages, and more broadly on European perceptions of the Pacific and Pacific peoples. But archaeology, too, has had an important role, allowing us to understand how various islanders dealt with the Europeans. These cross-cultural encounters were necessarily played out on beaches, in bays, and on the decks of boats. The social experiments that followed early contacts resound through the historical and anthropological literature, and cross-cultural meetings are carefully reconstructed.

For example, the arrival of the crew of the British *HMS Dolphin* in Tahiti (1767) invoked an attack by a flotilla of Tahitians (Figure 8.7), whom the English repelled with cannon and small arms. A more pragmatic set of encounters ensued, wherein the English were drawn into alliances with certain Tahitian elite, attempts were made to obtain objects (particularly metal) from the British boats, and a trade in sex saw the introduction of venereal diseases to Tahiti. Tahiti came to occupy an almost mythical place in the minds of European sailors and those members of the public back in London who cared to think of places as remote as the South Seas.

There was no one dominant foreign society in the region, so Pacific Islanders came into contact with Spanish, Portuguese, British, French, Dutch, German, Russian, American, Chinese, Japanese, and Filipino outsiders. This diversity, coupled with the diversity in Pacific peoples, has encouraged a much less simplistic perception of culture contact in this region than is perhaps seen elsewhere. The understanding that contact was a two-way process driven equally by indigenous people, and understood in cross-cultural rather than Eurocentric terms, seems to characterize much work in this region.

As experienced elsewhere, contact brought many immediate and long-term detrimental effects. For Pacific people, these included the impact of new diseases, loss of land, environmental devastation, and warfare. Many Pacific people maintained strong links to their precontact societies, as demonstrated by cultural survival and, certainly in many regions, the retention of customs, languages, and culture.

We do have some detailed archaeological studies of how islands were used over time, including, in some cases, both precontact and postcontact periods. In many

Figure 8.7. The natives of Otaheite [Tahiti] attacking Captain Wallis, the first European discoverer of that island, 1767 (*nla.pic-an3099865, National Library of Australia*).

instances, contact involved the arrival of a ship or ships, potentially some form of cross-cultural encounter and exchange, and then, with the departure of the vessel, a hiatus. To take one example, in Rapa Nui (Easter Island), first contact was with the Dutch in 1722; the next arrival was Cook in 1774, then La Pérouse in 1786. Each visit reveals how the society of Rapa Nui was changing—with implications for our interpretation of the famous Easter Island archaeology, as discussed below.

Across Polynesia, most societies were not exposed to large numbers of foreigners, except in Hawaii and Aotearoa/New Zealand. Elsewhere, the sheer problems of being outnumbered by invaders were not apparent and, as a result, traditional society and its spatial extent were less hindered. That said, contact was still occasionally disastrous, as seen on Rapa Nui.

CONTACT IN POLYNESIA

Let us consider some archaeological insights into contact from Aotearoa/New Zealand and Hawaii first, and then Rapa Nui.

220

Hawaii

The Hawaiian Islands were the northernmost Polynesian society, and also the most socially complex at contact, having a hierarchical society maintained by large economic production based on farming, aquaculture, tree farming, fishing, and raising of animals—the Polynesian "trinity" of pig, chicken, and dog.

Hawaiian society has been described as both chiefdom and state, meaning that researchers feel it falls somewhere between these two anthropological characterizations of societies. Certainly, high chiefs and administrators ruled over commoners with distinct territories and, with contact, an overarching king arose to rule over the island chain.

British contact with the Hawaiians first occurred in 1778 with the arrival of Captain Cook, who was killed on his second visit in 1779; this misadventure is a classic study in cross-cultural communication. There is much speculation about what led to the murder of Cook, although most interpretations factor Hawaiian cosmology into the equation, whereby a destabilizing situation existed in which Cook was equated with or linked to the deity Lono, whereas the local Hawaiian king Kalani'opu'u identified with the deity Ku. Other factors, such as killings and the exchange of gunfire, probably also played a role in Cook's demise.

After this, others followed—explorers, traders, whalers, loggers, and missionaries keen to capitalize on Hawaii's prominent location in the Pacific at the crossroads of transport routes and resources (such as whale and sandalwood, and then plantation products). The broad elements of contact can be sketched out: population decline through exposure to new diseases; a shift toward kingship under a single ruler, first being King Kamehameha I in 1812, who capitalized on existing struggles between powerful chiefs to control the archipelago; extensive conversion to Christianity in the early nineteenth century; increased migration of ethnically diverse non-Hawaiian settlers (including British, Chinese, Japanese, Filipino, and Portuguese) as farm and plantation workers; land reform (*Mahele*) in the mid-nineteenth century that moved land from traditional owners to historical migrants; and affiliation to the United States leading up annexation in 1900. For Hawaiians, then, the nineteenth century saw a decline in population, poor health, political consolidation and loss of power, technological and material changes, and ideological changes.

Archaeological research in Hawaii has allowed for a reasonable understanding of precontact developments and the results of contact. To take a regional example, at Anahulu Valley on northwestern Oahu, two key Pacific researchers collaborated in a synthetic study that aimed to bring together the archaeological evidence (Patrick Kirch) and ethnohistorical evidence (Marshall Sahlins). As a result, the ways that Hawaiians used Anahulu Valley over a long period of time becomes clear. The archaeological record provides evidence concerning the economy and production, the population and organization of settlements, and social interrelationships. In the early contact period, King Kamehameha used the valley as an important center, and it became enmeshed in the shift toward Christianity and the wider world systems of commerce in which Hawaii became involved in the historical period.

More broadly, across the Hawaiian Islands, analyses of technological and material changes at contact have been conducted, revealing differentials in changes to various material forms, such as housing, adzes, and clothing.[25] This research indicates, for example, that clothing was quick to undergo change, with the traditional *kapa* (bark cloth) garments replaced with Western garments within forty years, especially among women. The shift was embraced by the elite who employed missionaries as seamstresses, as well as by commoners. Missionaries advocated the change on moral grounds, although from the perspective of Hawaiians, it would have held other meanings, perhaps sending a message of connections to non-Hawaiians.

Stone adzes were a key part of the traditional tool kit, and their replacement by iron adzes after contact is often emphasized. However, archaeological deposits indicate that for a century *after* contact, stone adzes were still being used. There may be both functional and symbolic aspects to the retention of this stone technology.

Finally, the traditional post-and-thatch building (*hale*) was slow to change, with some *hale* still being found in the early twentieth century some 140 years after contact. Yet a closer look reveals that the buildings did change. We need to consider the traditional role of *hale*. First, these buildings were used to hide people wanting to avoid transgressions of taboo (*kapu*) between commoners and the chiefly elite, yet after the termination of local religion in 1819 by the Hawaiian elite, *hale* began to be built with windows and larger doors. Second, the precontact practice of having separate, single-room *hale* together in compounds (*kuahale*) to differentiate *hale* for men, sleeping, women during menstruation, equipment storage, and cooking (separated for men and women) shifted to multi-room structures combined of several *hale*.

These material changes reflect shifts in traditional life, societal organization, and belief. This does not mean that change was a new thing in Hawaii: it is important to note that there was much changing in Hawaiian life leading up to contact, and that, as Chris Gosden argues, "Transformation is the key to much of Hawaiian life and thought."[26] The examples he relies on to demonstrate this point exist on both sides of contact: the abandonment of core aspects of ideology like *kapu* (seen in the changes to *kuahale* settlements) as well as the many developments in farming that allowed more intensive production of crops and fish stocks in the centuries prior to 1778. These innovations in food production led to additional food that allowed for the increasingly stratified and specialized society encountered by Cook and his crews in 1779.

Aotearoa/New Zealand

As an Australian, thinking of the Maori in Aotearoa/New Zealand, I am struck by how one of our closest neighbors has such a different sense of its cross-cultural heritage. As a rugby fan, the use of the *haka*—a ceremonial war dance—by the New Zealand All Blacks national rugby team at the start of the international rugby games clearly links Maori culture to the present and perhaps tells us something of the fusing of Maori and *pakeha*—a term initially used for British settlers, now taking on the meaning of all non-Maori. Like Australia, New Zealand is a settler society, dominated by the descendants of British settlers. "Maori" refers to the people who were there when the outsiders arrived. "Maori" means ordinary, as opposed to those who were not ordinary.

The archaeology of the Maori details when Polynesians arrived (there is some debate about timing) and how they went about adapting their tropical domesticates to the colder islands of New Zealand, where the Polynesian staple of taro grew poorly, the only domesticated animal to be successfully introduced was dog (so, no pig or chicken), and where kumara (sweet potato) became an important food. In some regions, particularly on the South Island, people shifted away from farming to a lifeway based on hunting. Initially it was possible to shift toward intensive hunting, given the food potential of moa, a large flightless bird that filled the ecological niche elsewhere filled by small to medium-sized mammals.

The earliest non-Polynesian explorer was Dutchman Abel Tasman who arrived in 1642 (the Maori killed four of his crew at what became Murderers Bay), followed by Cook in 1769. The British and American outsiders from the early nineteenth century were often whalers and sealers. Missionaries soon followed, yet this remained an unofficial colony. The outsiders exacerbated existing intertribal tensions, particularly through trading guns to select Maori tribes, who, with greater access to guns, waged more effective war on their enemies. Decades of instability led up to the annexation by Britain and the 1840 Treaty of Waitangi between various Maori leaders (a majority, but not all) and the British government.

As it has elsewhere, archaeology has tended to focus on the indigenous people prior to contact, and also on the historical-period colonizers. Still, archaeological research into the contact era has somewhat filled the void left by largely European-produced historical sources. Aspects of change in Maori life and of the lives of the early settlers have been discovered in archaeological studies, of early sealing sites (these were mainly in the South Island and offshore islands) where Maori were sometimes co-residents with sealers, of the New Zealand wars between Maori and British, particularly between 1843 and 1872, and of shifts in material culture, and of missions.

Let us explore a region treated to fine-grained archaeological studies of the contact period. In the Waihou Valley of the Hauraki Plains, archaeologists have learned about centuries of Maori life, revealing changes in settlement patterns and subsistence over time, access to traded goods, and the consequences of changes arising from the arrival of British settlers. Studies have encompassed archaeological surveys and excavations, geographical information, European observations, and Maori oral testimony from Land Court Records used to map out affiliations to land.

The main archaeological sites are *pa* (fortified settlements); other sites are *kainga* (undefended settlements), food storage pits, defensive ditches and banks, living terraces, and raised shell middens. The archaeology demonstrates how "traditional" Maori life continued well into the nineteenth century despite the arrival of outsiders: archaeologist Stuart Bedford described this as "the tenacity of the traditional."[27]

Few European objects made their way into Maori sites, at least before 1820, except some glass beads, metal adzes, gunflints, and modified glass—and pigs too. The pattern of settlement remained unchanged, initially. Traditional life changed slowly here; overall for the nineteenth century, there is much that remained undisturbed, although differences existed. For example, at the site of Opitua, in the 1830s a greater amount of European material was uncovered, possibly indicating the movement of goods from missionaries. Objects such as writing slates found at the site were certainly part of the missionary "tool kit." Most of the new objects were applied to functions that already existed among Maori: blankets, decorative beads, and adzes, for example. Others related to new functions, such as clay smoking pipes.

Dramatic change came with the discovery of gold in the mid-nineteenth century. The local people, already worried about an influx of settlers, soon found that land had become a commodity. Special courts were established to determine who owned land and which parcels could be subject to alienation and sale. The Maori Land Court Records were collected from hearings held after 1866, the majority in the 1880s. In the court, claimants used ancestry and land use to argue for landownership, and witnesses were called to corroborate the testimony. The resulting accounts detail ancestry; actions of ancestors; tribal, *hapu* (subtribe), and *whanau* (extended family) alliances; warfare; historical events; movements of people; and societal customs. These records describe the physical landscape, the location of resources, changes in agricultural practice, uses of European materials by Maoris, the organization of trade and exchange, different types of settlement and their durations of use, estimates of population, and the impact of new diseases. It is in this period that many sites were abandoned, the spatial extent of Maori communities became more confined, and depopulation resulted from war and disease.

This work defines stages of Maori–European interaction: first, an initial period of sporadic contact characterized by the introduction of new plants and animals (1769–1821); a second phase marked by increased warfare using muskets, resulting in Maori abandonment of the Hauraki Plain (1821–1830); a third phase of resettlement and increased trade between the permanent European settlements in the region (1830–1850); followed by the movement of land away from Maoris.

Rapa Nui/Easter Island

We finish this chapter on the shores of Rapa Nui (Easter Island), perhaps one of the world's most famous island societies and home to the enthralling carved *moai* statues.

To get to Easter Island today takes hours of flight from South America westward into the expanse of the Pacific. For Polynesians, a vast ocean journey was required for the early colonists. Easter Island society was radically changed in the last few centuries to a much greater extent than other places in the Pacific. The island has become a hot spot for debate among archaeologists. Culture contact is a key part of puzzle, as we'll see.

For centuries, Easter Islanders maintained a society that dedicated much attention to the ancestor cult focused on *ahu* (stone platforms) and the stone *moai*. At some stage, the statues were thrown down, obsidian weapons became numerous, social disturbance occurred with warfare and possibly cannibalism, and there was a shift toward the competitive Orongo birdman cult. There was also contact with outsiders: following a series of encounters with the crews of European ships, the vast majority of the population were enslaved in 1862 and sent to Chile. Those who returned suffered from smallpox, and only a small population remained.

One school of thought focuses on the human impact on the environment.[28] These explanations tend to stress the removal of forests, increased soil erosion, and reduced food production, all or some of which led to the social decay suggested by the destruction of the *moai* statues and the rise of the Orongo birdman cult.

Another school argues that after centuries of successful life on this island, the arrival of Europeans brought about dramatic changes, which included disease, competition between islanders for European material culture, environmental destruction from introduced grazing animals, and finally, the enslavement of much of the population.

Which explanation is correct? It appears that oral history provides few answers, so the answer is still to be determined. What is clear is that understanding culture contact is part of finding the solution to the puzzle. It is also clear that many "classic" features of culture contact are present in this case: a jumbled set of historical observations by various Europeans, the difficulty of assessing the impact of disease, presumptions by researchers about societal "demise" in relation to the destruction of the *moai* heads (why is this always perceived as a bad thing?), a focus on the pre-contact period as the "real" Rapa Nui, and less emphasis on contact-period agency.

There is evidence of culture contact, for example, in the various images of boats depicted in rock art. It is interesting to reflect on how Rapa Nui society perceived these encounters with outsiders and their different material culture.

One issue that may still need to be resolved is how some of these events fit into the timeline of contact. It appears that in 1772, the statue cult still functioned, but fifty years later it was gone. If this is true, what happened to bring about this change? Archaeological evidence of introduced material culture suggests that an increased use of caves as retreats also postdated contact: what role did the changes around contact have in the broader story of change on Rapa Nui?

As we can see, understanding the changes at contact on Easter Island will be essential. Perhaps by understanding better what happened after contact, we can possibly understand better what happened before contact and thus better assess the environmental disaster model.

USEFUL SOURCES

Museums and online resources: Bishop Museum (Honolulu), Museum of New Zealand Te Papa Tongarewa, National Maritime Museum (Greenwich, London), National Museum of the Philippines, National Museum of Indonesia, The National Maritime Museum (Galle), Tokyo National Museum, National Museum of China, The Museum of Macao, National Museum of Singapore.

References: A. Salmond, *The Trial of the Cannibal Dog; Captain Cook in the South Seas* (Auckland: Penguin, 2004); Nicholas Thomas, *Cook: The Extraordinary Voyages of Captain James Cook* (New York: Walker & Company, 2003). Very useful sources are the chapters in Robin Torrence and Anne Clarke, *The Archaeology of Difference: Negotiating Cross-Cultural Engagements in Oceania* (London: Routledge, 2000); Nicholas Thomas, *Entangled Objects: Exchange, Material Culture, and Colonialism in the Pacific* (Cambridge, MA: Harvard University Press, 1991); Patrick V. Kirch and Marshall D. Sahlins, *Anahulu: The Anthropology of History in the Kingdom of Hawaii* (Chicago: University of Chicago Press, 1992).

Key journals: *Asian Perspectives, Before Farming, Archaeology in Oceania, Bulletin of the Indo-Pacific Prehistory Association, International Journal of Historical Archaeology, Journal of the Polynesian Society, Cakalele, Journal of South East Asian Studies, Journal of Coastal and Island Archaeology, Journal of Pacific History, New Zealand Journal of Archaeology* (now *Pacific Archaeology*). Other journals with occasional archaeology references include *Modern Asian Studies, The Journal of Asian Studies, The International Journal of Asian Studies, Bulletin of the School of Oriental and African Studies,* and *Journal of the Royal Asiatic Society.*

CHAPTER 9

AUSTRALIA

And before we judge of them too harshly we must remember what ruthless and utter destruction our own species has wrought, not only upon animals, such as the vanished bison and the dodo, but upon its inferior races. The Tasmanians, in spite of their human likeness, were entirely swept out of existence in a war of extermination waged by European immigrants, in a space of fifty years. Are we such apostles of mercy as to complain if the Martians warred in the same spirit?

– *War of the Worlds*, H. G. Wells (1898)

The first Tasmanians were not utterly wiped out, as detailed in Wells's introduction to *War of the Worlds*, a passage that reminds us of the racially driven prejudices of Victorian times. Today there are joint descendants of Tasmanians and Europeans. When Europeans first arrived in Tasmania, two grand arcs of humanity met on the beaches of the its southeastern shores, where achingly clear cold seas push up against the islands and convoluted coastline. People had been present in Tasmania for at least 35,000 years, as the southernmost humans on the planet during the Pleistocene, and had been isolated on Tasmania for the Holocene after the island was formed by rising seas.

The other human arc comprised Western Europeans: French and English explorers and, soon after, American whalers and sealers and British settlers (from 1803). These encounters encapsulate much of the story of this book: how people separated by great distances of time and space and utterly foreign to each other came into contact. For the Tasmanians, the results were horrific: they lost most of their population and their land within two generations. It is this that allows H.G. Wells to invite the reader to sympathize with invading Martians when we consider humanity.

In this final substantial chapter, I want to explore culture contact in Australia. I focus on pre-European contacts and then consider those of the colonial era. The time period is later than much of the discussion so far in this book, given that contact occurred later there than elsewhere. I focus more on Aboriginal involvement in European colonial institutions than I have elsewhere. This reflects the type of archaeological work in Australia that I am familiar with, including my own, which I cite here.

Only in the seventeenth century did the great southern landmass and Aboriginal Australians become known to Europeans. A 1606 Dutch expedition found little of economic potential for the VOC. In 1642, Abel Tasman was directed on a voyage of exploration in which he would visit Tasmania, New Zealand, and Fiji. His instructions delineate the cautious approach of the world's first multinational company regarding contact with indigenous peoples. Culture contact was endorsed, yet both eyes were firmly on profit:

> In landing with small craft extreme caution will everywhere have to be used, seeing that it is well-known that the southern regions are peopled by fierce savages, for which reason you will always have to be well armed and to use every prudent precaution, since experience has taught in all parts of the world that barbarian men are nowise to be trusted, because they commonly think that the foreigners who so unexpectedly appear before them, have come only to seize their land, which (owing to heedlessness and over-confidence) in the discovery of America occasioned many instances of treacherous slaughter. On which account, you will treat with amity and kindness such barbarian men as you shall meet and come to parley with, and connive at small affronts, thefts and the like which they should put upon or commit against our men, lest punishments inflicted should give them a grudge against us; and by shows of kindness gain them over to us, that you may the more readily from them obtain information touching themselves, their country, and their circumstances, thus learning whether there is anything profitable to be got or effected. (Instruction to Dutch Captain Abel Tasman, prior to 1642 voyage to Tasmania and New Zealand).[1]

The Dutch never settled in Australia, but they did fill the void on the world map with the edges of "New Holland." The British explorer Captain James Cook in 1770 mapped the eastern seaboard, and following his discoveries at Botany Bay, a British penal colony was established in 1788 at Port Jackson (Sydney).

From the First Fleet of prisoners and their guards, Sydney grew. This was the traditional country of the Eora people, the first of the many indigenous Australian societies in contact with British settlers.[2]

Australia commemorates January 26 as the arrival of the First Fleet. Australia Day is also called Invasion Day, a day of mourning for the impacts on indigenous Australians of the last two and a half centuries. For Europeans, Captain Cook has the status of a key ancestor, Australia's Columbus perhaps. He naturally came to represent British exploration but also, in some indigenous minds, European colonization and colonialism.

The Aboriginal man Paddy Ford Wainburranga imagined an indigenous version of Captain Cook, a mythical character who introduced to Aboriginal Australians some good things like metal and cloth, yet also heralded negative things.

> Too many Captain Cooks . . . have been stealing all the women and killing people. They have made war. War makers, these new Captain Cooks. . . . All the Captain Cooks come and call themselves "welfare mob." They were new people now. They wanted to take all of Australia [Paddy Ford Wainburranga].[3]

This brief quote provides a fascinating insight into how different cultural perceptions can exist of the same historical events and individuals. This is not the British Captain Cook, subject of many books and statues, but rather a device to communicate Aboriginal concerns about colonialism. However, our story begins well before 1770 and Captain Cook.

Djulirri, Arnhem Land

Under a protective roof of stone there exists a document whose many pages were written over millennia. The rock shelter of Djulirri in eastern Arnhem Land is extraordinary, for few sites on earth reveal human perceptions of the world around them in one location for this expanse of time.[4]

One enters the shelter and immediately the layers of pigment are visible, some bright and seemingly recent, while other images are more dim or obscured by overlying later images (Figure 9.1). In some places, the layers of pigment are as thick as your finger, something like the layers of whitewash on the walls of a medieval house. One's immediate attention is drawn to a panel with white outline figures of people fighting, dancing, and conducting ceremonies. Alongside these white images are striking depictions of twentieth-century boats—a naval destroyer, an ocean liner, a pearling lugger—as well as a biplane and a bicycle.

As the arrival of outsiders in Arnhem Land occurred only as recently as the late nineteenth century, images depicting relatively late phases of cultural contacts should not be surprising. Clearly, these "historical" images give us a view into how these recent disruptive times were understood and depicted by indigenous people, similar to that already described in detail for Plains Indians whose contact images have also survived in archaeological sites (chapter 7).

Earlier visitors to northern Australia are depicted at Djulirri. Briefly, in the early 1800s, British military forts were established on the nearby Cobourg Peninsula, in western Arnhem Land.[5] At that time, the geopolitical center of the region was Southeast Asia, and the British were keen to maintain a military presence in the area to remind others of their territorial ambitions. It was not unreasonable; British Singapore was closer than Sydney. These were, however, challenging outposts dur-

Figure 9.1. Djulirri rock art site: kangaroo and airplane,
Wellington Range, Eastern Arnhem Land.

ing their short lives, characterized by high mortality rates. The forts were coastal toeholds with no ambitions for inland settlement, and culture contact between the residents and Aboriginal people was apparently limited—until one looks at the rock art at places like Djulirri, where masted sailing vessels that visited the forts are depicted. Some images show the ships lying exposed on the tidal mud flats, as well as depicting their cargoes, their crews, and technical aspects of each ship's stowage, construction, and rigging. Clearly, Aboriginal people in the region traveled to these isolated British forts and were familiar with their vessels. Few other aspects of the forts are depicted in the rock art.

Asians and Europeans in Their Boats

Rock art takes us further back in time to pre-British culture contacts. The British were not the first outsiders to come into contact with the Djulirri artists: underlying the images of Europeans are images of Macassan visitors, Southeast Asian fishermen and traders whose visits to the region since the sixteenth century are reflected in images of their boats, huts, and material culture, such as metal knives.

The Asian visitors were harvesters of trepang (bêche-de-mer) from Macassar in Sulawesi, with crews from Madura, Flores, Timor, and Roti. This trade linked northern Australia to Asian trade and exchange networks. Archaeological remains of Asian settlements have been found on the coast and on offshore islands in the Gulf of Carpentaria, Arnhem Land, and the Kimberley (Figure 9.2).[6]

As European accounts of trepang voyages and seasonal settlements date back only to Matthew Flinders in 1801, we need archaeology to date the earlier visits. Flinders spoke to the captain of a Macassan fleet who suggested that the voyages to Australia began in the eighteenth century. However, the dating of a Djulirri rock painting of a Macassan prau boat to earlier than 1664 indicates older culture contact.[7]

1. Cape Keerweer
2. Sydney & Botany Bay
3. Hobart
4. Melbourne
5. Adelaide
6. Perth
7. Brisbane
8. Wybalenna
9. Inthanoona
10. Strangways
11. Killalpaninna
12. Framlingham & Coranderrk
13. Ebenezer
14. Lake Condah
15. Ramahyuck
16. Burghley
17. Groote Eylandt
18. Barrow Creek
19. Corindi Beach
20. Djulirri

Australian places referred to in text
●●●●●●● Macassan contact zones

Figure 9.2. Map of Australia.

231

We should think of these contacts as "historical" even if no texts were created by those involved, as they linked northern Australia into places where historical records were kept, such as Dutch colonies in Asia. To illustrate this point, today white visitors to Arnhem Land may be called "Balanda" by locals. This word came out of Asian–Aboriginal contacts and was explained in 1845 by Ludwig Leichhardt, the first European explorer in Arnhem Land: "They knew the white people of Victoria [a British military fort], and called them Balanda, which is nothing more than "Hollanders'; a name used by the Malays, from whom they received it." By the seventeenth century, the word was brought to Australia, and today refers to non-indigenous Australians in Arnhem Land.[8]

Although contact with Macassans must have electrified indigenous society in the areas of immediate contact, we must think of the long time frame, as seasonal visits would have been familiar. Presumably, relationships existed between the different societies. There are accounts that some Aboriginal people returned to Macassar with the fleet at the end of the season. Macassans introduced new things to some Aboriginal people, such as metal tools, fishing equipment, new food, customs, and language. It has been suggested that Macassans also introduced dugout canoes. If so, hunters could have hunted better—as seemingly indicated by the food remains in coastal middens.

In Arnhem Land, rock art sometimes depicts local differences in indigenous experiences of culture contact. On Groote Eylandt, located only 400 kilometers east of Djulirri off eastern Arnhem Land, there are clear differences in the Aboriginal depictions of Macassan boats and crew compared with their depictions of European vessels. The artists show the Macassan boats loaded with crew (often waving from the deck), and they demonstrate clear knowledge of the interior of the vessels, their rigging and equipment. These images of Macassans vessels were produced in inland rock shelters away from the coastal setting of direct contact. Presumably, Macassans and their vessels were part of indigenous expectations of the world. By contrast, the European boats depicted at Groote Eylandt are not socialized: they are shown at sail, and no crews are depicted.[9] Perhaps this suggests different types of contact on Groote Eylandt.

In western Arnhem Land, near the Cobourg Peninsula, a different pattern occurs. The art depicting Macassans extends beyond their boats to include material culture like metal knives, and possibly their huts. One depiction appears to shows a vessel being careened or repaired. Unlike at Groote Eylandt, the European vessels depicted suggest close contact with Aboriginal observers. Here it is the later British ships that have the greatest number of people depicted on board, and these include details of clothing and behavior, such as stance. The cargo aboard boats is clearly of great interest to the artists, shown as strapped to decks and stowed in hulls (Figure 9.3).

Figure 9.3. Indigenous images of Macassan and European vessels in Arnhem Land.

In all instances, the knowledge of rigging and masts, and later steam engines, is demonstrated. Clearly, the rock art illustrates local variations and complexities in cross-cultural engagements, extending over centuries in northern Australia.

Rock Documents

Where contact rock art exists, we potentially have insight into indigenous reactions to contact. In some areas, rock art and its production seem linked to resistance. In central Australia, rock art documents the ways that access to traditional lands became restricted when pastoralists and others curtailed indigenous access to country. As a response, art production became focused at a reduced number of places.

For example, in the Keep River region of Northern Territory, following the arrival of white settlers in the late 1800s, indigenous people were able to return to traditional country during the wet season, when their labor was not required by pastoralists. Here, the use of rock shelters was maintained, as indicated by excavations where upper units contain historical material culture, demonstrating that stone tools and rock art were still made in historical times.[10]

On the early colonial frontier in the Pilbara, Western Australia, from the 1860s onward, rock engravings indicate local Aboriginal peoples' interest in specific aspects of the pastoral world: horses, smoking, guns, and clothing. Men are depicted with hands on hips, and shooting and riding. Animals such as sheep and cattle, however, were seldom depicted. Nor was new material culture portrayed, such as the food equipment utilized in Aboriginal campsites.

Here ships are represented at inland sites. Thus, the ship is a key motif of contact—possibly meaning many things: recording arrivals, exchanges, material items, alien societies, and, in the Pilbara specifically, forced labor, as the pastoral luggers forced Aboriginal men and women to be pearl-shell collectors.

Whether ships were viewed positively or negatively, they represent realities that needed to be dealt with, somehow. These are not merely depictions of foreign things—in portrayals of the Macassans, they indicate aspects of contact that were long part of some Aboriginal societies, and thus these images need to be understood not just as superficial representations of the new, but of local attempts to deal with the limits and opportunities in cross-cultural engagements.

The great disruption of the colonial period appears to have resulted in the cessation of rock art production in most places. Where it did continue, as in the places described here, it reveals continued practice as well as the role of graphic systems in internal and external communications, and demonstrates the affiliation of artists to distinct places when traditional country was being usurped.

Aboriginal Australians

This brief summary of the evidence from rock art suggests that indigenous life across the continent was not static following contact, nor before contact, an observation made for most of the regions considered in this book. Similarly, we should not fall into the trap of thinking of contact only between British and Aboriginal people—it is more complicated than that. In modern Australia, we often tend to think of Aboriginal people as "one" people: but they comprise many societies. In fact, over two hundred Aboriginal languages existed in 1788.

As a result of British colonization, many languages and cultures are gone, and many that survive are threatened. Regional names illustrate cultural differences across Australia: for example, in the southwest a large group are the Noongar; in other western regions are Wongatha, Yamatji, and Anangu; in the islands between Cape York and Papua New Guinea are Torres Strait Islanders; in the southeast are Murri and Koori/Koorie people; in Tasmania are Palawah people; while in Arnhem Land there are the Yolngu people. There are also distinct tribal groups within regions.

As detailed for the Americas and Africa, factors external to the specifics of contact are significant: environment, resources, demography, disease vectors, and social organization.[11] The environment of Australia varies greatly, with arid and semiarid regions in much of inland Australia, tropical regions in the north (Kimberly, Top End, Cape York), and temperate regions in the southeast and southwest. Aboriginal economies developed for the various opportunities of coasts and waterways, deserts and tropics, swamps, grasslands, forests, and woodlands. The arid desert regions posed great challenges, and population densities ranged between 80 and 200 square kilometers per person. In well-watered regions such as along the eastern seaboard, population density was up to one hundred times greater.

Despite these differences, indigenous societies shared many similarities, particularly in the organization of production and distribution of goods. Kinship and marriage varied slightly, with a greater degree of polygamy in areas that supported higher populations. Variances in the strength of power structures, too, may have resulted in different degrees of effective resistance to Europeans. Overall, similarities across the continent characterize Aboriginal Australia. Exchange networks between some groups were very important, moving items and people, allowing stories to be circulated, allowing marriage outside of one's clan. In some instances, items were exchanged over vast distances. These networks would be eventually disrupted by European colonization and by the impact of introduced diseases such as smallpox, epidemics of which would have occurred well in advance of European observers.

Similar to that detailed for North America and elsewhere, the politics of the present are increasingly important to contemporary practice. In Australia, understanding culture contact in the past may historicize processes that underlie contemporary communities.

Herein lies some of the contemporary significance of culture contact studies and related cultural heritage. Indigenous Australians have become more involved in the management of their own cultural heritage, including in archaeology, which is being driven by indigenous concerns and interests now more so than previously.[12]

Our understanding of recent centuries acts to place the situations of recent Australians in a longer perspective, which, of course, in Australia extends back into the Holocene and Pleistocene through archaeology. The idea of historical communities having roots in earlier eras is potentially problematic, capturing modern peoples in some form of chronological amber reserved for indigenous people.

To flip the coin, let us consider the British of two centuries ago: to what extent do modern Anglo-Australians reflect this cultural heritage? In some ways, Australians did remain very "British" and still do (language and political structure are two clear examples).[13] Similarly, Aboriginal people carry with them a cultural legacy as well as the repercussions of recent centuries, often marked by intensive cultural change.

Recognizing Aboriginal History

Today, several disciplines, and indeed Aboriginal and non-Aboriginal Australians more broadly, are interested in what happened to Aboriginal people in Australia following British settlement. While there have been several powerful explanations over time, for much of Australian history, this was not a terribly important question. For a long time, among those interested in the idea of a fatal impact (to use Alan Moorehead's term; chapter 1), the perception that Aboriginal people would inevitably die out was particularly strong.

I probably began as an archaeologist because I grew up in Tasmania, where until recent times, a prevailing idea was that Tasmanians had "died out," as per H. G. Wells's passage at the start of this chapter. (The term appears to imply that Tasmanian population decline was not the fault of the British—when it actually was). I was interested in why people did not widely know the details of Tasmanian survival.

The stories of survival were sometimes lost in the heady mix of personal tragedy, loss, policy, fear, and shame. Many nineteenth-century Tasmanians survived in communities of sealers, where indigenous women came to live (some unwillingly) with these men, many located beyond the gaze of colonial authorities. These stories were not often subject to mainstream dominant histories, and were overlooked until recently.

The last fifty years have seen key developments: the recognition of Aboriginal people as citizens (in the late 1960s), increased scholarship on Aboriginal society, protection of Aboriginal cultural and heritage sites, the acknowledgment of Native Title, the creation of various representative bodies, and elected members of state and federal parliaments. Today, indigenous culture is widely recognized and increasingly dominant, as demonstrated by the increased practice of acknowledging Aboriginal country at the start of public events.

Across Australia, official colonial policies toward indigenous peoples have stood in law, although the existence of laws does not necessarily dictate behavior in remote regions far from officialdom. Over time, the track of government policies toward Aboriginal people reflects largely white people's ideas about indigenous people, shifting from attempts to isolate populations (such as on reserves), to conversion (such as on Christianizing missions), to assimilation policies. Today's challenge seems to be one of recognizing indigenous needs and culture within the setting of a democratic nation-state that has inherited the legacy of past governments. In 2008, the Federal Parliament formally apologized to Australians of the Stolen Generations.[14]

Survival and loss are core aspects of Australian culture contact, as they are elsewhere. The ways that Aboriginal people negotiated contact are also significant. There is evidence for resistance in many ways, from that on frontiers to more subtle resistance with colonial institutions. Similarly, the decisions made by Aboriginal people about what was of use or desirable to them, in forms of material culture or practice, are important. The processes of dominance are likewise significant, as are the ways that colonial authorities tried to manage and control indigenous people. Over time, in Australian studies we have seen shifting interpretive perspectives about culture contact, including acculturation, resistance, creolization, accommodation, and agency, to name some. Each approach brings a new perspective to our understanding of these complex pasts.

FORMS OF EVIDENCE

The presence of "new" or "introduced" material culture—glass, metal, or ceramics—has long been an identifier of the contact period in Australian archaeological sites. Our understanding of these objects' role now extends beyond their mere presence (which admittedly is useful for chronological determinations) to how they were used. In a now-classic early study, for example, Lauriston Sharp considered how local power relations in Cape York were altered when young men and some women began to use new metal axes, as until then, older men held power over others in part through their privileged access to stone axes. In this scenario, the availability of new materials threatened traditional structures in indigenous society.[15]

In other interpretations, the new materials offered possibilities for change. One example is the availability of new foods as indicated in archaeological sites; for example, rations of flour were distributed to workers and other Aboriginal people in various colonial settings, which seems to have reduced or eliminated the need for stone-tool grinding equipment.

In another example, access to metal tools such as axes and fishing hooks, as well as dugout canoe technology, seems to have changed local subsistence in Arnhem Land. The canoes were more stable than rafts, and with improved fishing and hunting equipment, Aboriginal people had access to a greater range of marine foods. This in turn allowed for sizable gatherings of Aboriginal people close to the coast at different seasons than in the past. This is indicated in the location and extent of archaeological sites.[16]

A great range of newly introduced material culture occurs in archaeological sites. Some derive from new options within existing technologies. For example, glass bottles were often obtained by Aboriginal people to be used to produce glass flakes similar to those made from stone (Figure 9.4).[17] Bottle garbage dumps in certain regions were quarried for the most desirable glass (often the thick bases of eighteenth- and nineteenth-century bottles), which was in turn flaked, and finally the flakes used; these different phases form a reduction sequence directly comparable to stone tools. While artifacts may have had very functional uses, they also existed in cross-cultural settings. So discarded glass bottles became a desirable resource, as did many other items used innovatively by Aboriginal people.

Objects take on specific meaning in cross-cultural cultural exchanges. One well-cited example is the production of distinctive bifacially flaked points known as Kimberly Points, as they were found in the Kimberley region of Northwestern Australia. This region was settled by Europeans only in the late 1800s. Europeans were particularly attracted to these artifacts, and collected them. Today many museums around the world exhibit Kimberley Points made from stone and, following contact, from ceramic telegraph insulators and glass bottles. Presumably, these points were used traditionally in trading between groups and possibly as spear heads. Following contact, the production of these objects shifted to meet European desires.

The work around these objects provides an image of Aboriginal people as active participants in the production of machinations of cross-cultural exchanges, and also projects some form of agency relative to the objects themselves, which presumably had very specific meanings in both Aboriginal and European cultural settings.[18] This is comparable to the discussion of beads in North America (chapters 6 and 7).

Figure 9.4. Flaked glass bottle base from Old Woodbrook Station. *Photo by the author.*

The potentials and pitfalls for material culture to be interpreted within the complexity of the contact period are becoming increasingly clear. As objects move between different societies and gain different meanings, to understand the ways that this happens requires a contextualized approach in which the history and cultural setting are considered.[19]

While the presence of new material culture is usually a marker of contact, there are limitations to this approach. For instance, many sites used in the historical era may have no clear evidence for new materials and thus remain indistinguishable from older sites. In such cases, we have to look for evidence of broader changes in behavior following contact, perhaps akin to work by Ann Stahl in Ghana (chapter 5).

One possible avenue for this type of investigation is to examine continuities and changes in the way the landscape and resources were used following contact. In this vein, in their study of the Keep River in the Northern Territory, Lesley Head and Richard Fullagar look across a range of evidence, including rock art, the use of rock shelters, settlement location, tool kits, diet, and the use of plants, to understand landscape use over time.[20]

Land is key to understanding indigenous Australians, yet it is difficult for outsiders to conceptualize how Aboriginal attachments to land function. Aboriginal knowledge is structured by land; land reflects ancestral beings whose actions marked and created the landscape. This relationship is described by G. Yunupingu:

> The land is my backbone; I only stand straight, happy, proud and not ashamed about my color because I still have my land. The land is the art. I can paint, dance, create and sing as my ancestors did before me. My people recorded these things about our land this way, so that I and others like me may do the same. . . . I think of land as the history of my nation. It tells us how we came into being and in what system we must live.[21]

239

Given the importance of country from an indigenous perspective, the attempt to match concepts of landscape to archaeological evidence for spatial patterns is important.[22] This entails looking at environmental parameters, which remain of concern to Aboriginal people today. For example, the sites of important resources retain significant value for many Aboriginal people, as described in a recent study of the cultural values Gumbaingirr people ascribe to Corindi Beach, New South Wales:

> The cultural values that Aboriginal people ascribe to the environment are many and complex. The active utilization of wild foods and medicines is but one value, but it is linked to many aspects of contemporary culture and identity. Fishing, plant food collecting and hunting continue to play an important role in people's lives. Such activities may be viewed as embodying a continuation of cultural practice and as a primary means of passing on ecological knowledge, looking after and observing country, and maintaining links with valued places.[23]

EXCHANGE AND COMMUNICATIONS

Attempts were made to communicate from the earliest instances of contact.[24] In 1770 at Botany Bay, Captain Cook, in a scene presumably very familiar to him and his crew across Oceania, arrived at the shore in a small boat to participate in first contact. Cross-cultural communication was obviously an immediate challenge. At Botany Bay, communication was presumably initiated by Tupaiai, the Tahitian who had joined Cook and acted as a translator when meeting Polynesians. However, they were now well beyond Polynesia, and as such, neither group understood the other, as Polynesian was just as meaningless as English to the Aborigines.

The Aboriginal men on the shore brandished long spears, and Cook fired upon one man, and dispersed the group. After Cook was gone, it seems likely that images in rock art of the ships were used to communicate about these events among the local Eora people, as it appears that rock art functioned as an important network of information exchange in the Sydney region.[25]

Eighteen years later, the British returned and, for a brief period, again rock art depicted the new—a convict in chains, escaped bulls, the British costumes—but the information network closed down almost immediately, presumably from the great impact on the native population, possibly halved through smallpox within the first year of settlement.

> An extraordinary calamity was now observed among the natives. Repeated accounts brought by our boats, of finding bodies of the Indians in all of the coves and inlets of the harbor . . . it appeared that all the parties had died a natural

death. Pustules similar to those occasioned by the smallpox, were thickly spread on the bodies; but how a disease to which our former observations had led us to suppose them strangers could at once have introduced itself, and have spread so widely, is inexplicable.[26]

Meetings were initially diplomatic attempts to negotiate the cross-cultural landscape, involving gift giving and exchange. Exchange sometimes occurred, and key individuals rose to lead the communication. The best known may be Bennelong, who was in direct communication with Port Jackson's governor, Arthur Phillip.[27] Aboriginal life continued in and around the settlement, and early observers witnessed ceremonies and group activities, yet British colonization was very disruptive, and many Eora survivors ended up on the peripheries of the settlement, where eventually dependencies would develop.

The early British colonists were prepared for trade, having left London with tools, knives, and beads for that purpose. Exchange was directed by the colonial elite, but presumably occurred illicitly too. Metal objects were very desirable for Aboriginal Australians and could be used to improve existing technology.

Not all desired things were tools, however: hats were objects of intrigue. Aboriginal objects were collected by the British, such as spears and spear throwers. A cat-of-nine-tails whip from Sydney was manufactured from an Aboriginal wooden artifact, perhaps one of the most symbolic items in existence from the early colony, merging themes of indigenous–British culture contact with the events of the penal colony at the birth of the nation. These were not mere curios, for the British had a strong sense of what a fair trade was, as did Aboriginals. Back in London, such collections provided status within the Enlightenment community.[28]

Exchange was sometimes fraught. Some convicts took to raiding Aboriginal camps, leading to repercussions, and at least one convict was killed in retaliation. Governor Phillip himself was speared during a meeting in 1780 involving exchange. Bennelong was a central diplomat in dealing with the governor (Figure 9.5). Eventually Bennelong would come to live in Government House (as did other Aboriginal people), travel to England and return in 1795, seven years after the establishment of the colony, by which time he was probably more aware than most Aboriginal people of the British colonial intentions. His alliance with the governor had the effect of increasing his own power and prestige, a process seen elsewhere in Australia when key individuals or groups monopolized access to colonizing whites, sometimes to the detriment of other indigenous people. This would be dramatically demonstrated with the use of Native Police in incidents of frontier violence in later years.[29]

As the British settlement grew, so did indigenous dispossession. Attempts to manage a problem, as perceived by the British, led to the first institutions for

Figure 9.5. Bennelong engraving:
"Bennelong, a native of New Holland, 1795," by Samuel John Neele
(*nla.pic-an9353133. National Library of Australia*).

indigenous people, Native Schools for children, to name one.[30] Over time, land was set aside for Aboriginal people, in reserves. In some instances, reform was seen as part of the solution. For example, people were encouraged to settle on plots of farming land or engage in commercial food production.

The number of dwellers on the fringes of colonial society grew, along with poverty and alcohol and tobacco addiction. Colonial government solutions to these problems continued in fits and starts and can be tracked from these early days to the present.

MISSIONS AND OTHER INSTITUTIONS

Ebenezer itself as a building is neither here nor there for me but Ebenezer in
my story lines is like my left or right arm, it's quintessential to my whole being
. . . it's just part of our story.

—Mark Dugay-Grist, 2008[31]

Official institutions designed by whites for Aborigines became popular in the
nineteenth and twentieth centuries, and included missions, reserves, children's
homes, places for mixed-descent or half-caste children, leprosariums, and hospitals. Christianizing missions have proven to be important locations in our understanding of early cross-cultural interactions.

There are several reasons for this. They are, first and foremost, places where
culture contact necessarily occurs. The locations of sites are known, either from
documents or from descendants of indigenous participants and mission staff. In
terms of studying culture contact, they are appealing—to explain what happened
at missions, given the attempts to convert Aborigines ideologically and spiritually
and toward more "European" lifeways and economic practice. And, they can be
compared with institutions in other parts of the world.

Here I consider mission settlements archaeologists have worked at:
Wybalenna in Tasmania, Killalpaninna in Central Australia, and missions in the
southern state of Victoria.

Wybalenna, Tasmania

Wybalenna was a settlement created for Tasmanian Aborigines by the British on
the remote Flinders Island. It is well known as one of the earliest Australian sites
of culture contact to be studied archaeologically. Indigenous Tasmanians faced a
great threat from the British invaders, who arrived around 1804 to establish a
penal settlement for convicts. Within a short time, the island comprised an increasingly dense population of convicts, soldiers, freemen, and sheep farmers who
met guerilla warfare from Tasmanians. Attempts to negotiate a shared peace failed,
and hostilities occurred.

A few material traces are left from Aboriginal people in the niches of a colonial
world. For example, at a small shepherd's hut at Burleigh in the northwest of the island, some Aboriginal people reoccupied the structure following European abandonment, as suggested by the tools in their hut. However, such evidence is rare.[32]

A decision to remove the Tasmanians who survived the first generation of
British colonization and the period that came to be known as the Black War saw

the establishment of the so-called Friendly Mission, led by George Augustus Robinson and some surviving Tasmanians. Robinson convinced some survivors to relocate to Wybalenna to create a settlement designed in part to convert and change the Tasmanians, making them more like the British, equipping them with new behaviors and practices. The main island was left to the British. The Wybalenna settlement lasted a few years (1834–1847) before the survivors were removed to Hobart.

In the early 1970s, a local heritage group invited Sydney University archaeologist Judy Birmingham to direct their amateur excavations. The area chosen to excavate encompassed the small cottages where the Tasmanians had once lived. From their detritus, it was possible to determine how they had responded to the British attempts to transform them.

The archaeology delineated how different Aboriginal households responded—some maintaining hunting of wallaby and other foods used traditionally, despite the European prohibitions on hunting. Some households were well maintained, as per the overseers' prescription, while others clearly did not keep ordered houses, with rubbish discarded within and outside the huts. Some gambled, smoked, and drank alcohol; others, encouraged by the British, took up work such as sewing in and around the cottages. Birmingham described this selectivity as "cultural accommodation."[33]

Killalpaninna, Central Australia

In a vastly different environment—the arid desert of Central Australia—the archaeological sites in and around Killalpaninna mission (also called Bethesda) indicate how Aboriginal people here responded to the mission. This is the traditional country of people of the eastern Lake Eyre and the Simpson Desert.

Here various groups, particularly the Deiri, encountered black-garbed Lutheran missionaries from the 1860s. Moravians and Lutherans had arrived in South Australia as religious refugees and were keen to promote their faith to Aborigines. In the inhospitable desert country, they encountered people whose lifeways were finely tuned to hunting and foraging in these relatively extreme conditions. Aboriginal people in Central Australia were about to become enfolded into colonial Australia.

The archaeology in around the mission reflects how Aboriginal people used the mission. The settlements of those closest to the mission show their access to European goods, such as clothing and ceramics, glass and metal objects. Goods moved out from the mission station into the camps of people in contact with those "within" the mission world. These camps are still close to Bethesda, within a few kilometers, but reveal how, at least in the early years, some Aboriginal people used the mission as a source of objects and possible food, but as only one resource location in a landscape of resources. The new opportunities of the mission were added onto traditional economic practices.

For some within the mission, their lives were markedly changing. They were learning new languages and customs, wearing clothes (at least for some photographs), and tending animals on the mission grounds. These differentials within mission communities derive from individual opportunities and decisions.[34]

Killalpaninna was one of several missions in colonial South Australia, and represents a place that held little interest for colonizing whites, given the arid environment in which it was located. Elsewhere in Australia, missions and reserves responded to a need to deal with people being driven off their traditional land.

Victorian Missions and Reserves

In the colony of Victoria, missions were an important aspect of nineteenth-century colonization, land invasion, and cross-cultural interactions. From 1859, a central board was established to manage six reserves that would address a problem: what to do with increasingly disenfranchised indigenous people in the colony of Victoria.[35] European perceptions of traditional Aboriginal society being debased and in need of improvement justified the colonization program and the right to assume Aboriginal land. Some Europeans were concerned about sexual relationships between these groups, and saw institutions as part of the answer as well as a means to deliver a humanitarian program involving teaching in Christianity, cultivation, domesticity, and orderly behavior. The termination of access to traditional country was answered in part by rations distribution.

A significant percentage of the indigenous population of Victoria ended up in Ramahyuck, Coranderrk, Framlingham, Lake Tyers, Lake Condah, and Ebenezer. The reserves were meant to be islands of Aboriginals separated from whites. The settlements were planned as morphing machines, intended to alter Aboriginal behavior, thinking, and appearance. Success could be measured by the extent that indigenous people acted like—or *appeared* to act like—bourgeois Christians.

Some have argued that within missions, Aboriginal resistance to these efforts strengthened rather than diminished traditions. This bimodal view of moving from an indigenous to a European way of living avoids the complexity of cultural change, the formation of new and composite societies.

Photographs and other images of Victorian missions provide interesting evidence about these places, as studied by Monash University–based archaeologist Jane Lydon. Aboriginal people were often depicted in some "traditional" setting or as victims of colonialism in some depraved or unenlightened manner at the edges

Malcolm's Residence.

Figure 9.6. Photograph of residents at Victorian Mission. Malcolm, or Gindarmin, and wife Gilpoormanning flanked by their daughter Caroline and her husband, or Mr. and Mrs. Ferguson. (*Acc. no. H13881/8. Photographs by Charles Walter. La Trobe Picture Collection, State Library of Victoria, Melbourne.*)

of the colonial world. For example, Charles Walter photographed the early years of the Victorian reserves for his album *Australian Aborigines under Civilization* (Figure 9.6). The images indicate an emphasis on families and family residences, with each household identified by the male head. This reflects the colonial ambition to create within missions appropriate (i.e., European, Christian) gender roles, and a spatial regime that distinguished between public and private spheres. In these images, the individual family homes are the site of demonstrated domesticity, individuality, and correct behavior. However, houses were not private; they were inspected by missionaries to monitor domestic life. They observed how Aboriginal people used space and objects as a measure of desired behavior. This attitude toward Aboriginal privacy reinforced ideas of paternalism and racial difference. However, beyond these photographs and beyond the mission landscape, there were Aboriginal domains less easy to inspect, where collective behavior and cross-cutting social regimes could come into play.

Missions and reserves were important in some places, but many Aboriginal people lived in less formal settings—for example, at the fringes of European settlements or as part of other domains, such as the pastoral domain (below).

CONTACT IN PASTORAL AUSTRALIA

A popular image of Australia in the twentieth century was of the white pastoral worker. Sheep and cattle were a significant part of the economy. It was said Australia "rode on the sheep's back." Sheep and cattle properties extended across much of Australia, from Tasmania to the tropical north. In well-watered regions in eastern and southern Australia, vast numbers of sheep and cattle were successfully raised. In other places, more semiarid environments, pastoralism was the *only* viable economic pursuit for white settlers. In these more remote regions, pastoral properties tended to be lightly stocked, and stations were often vast. Consequently, in terms of area, pastoral domains were the setting for a great number of instances of contact between various Aboriginal societies and outsiders.

Several phases of contact occurred from initial contact through to the eventual success or failure of pastoral ventures. The greatest change was the seismic shift from a landscape occupied by indigenous hunter-foragers to settler pastoralists. Introduced animals and plants caused extinctions and the reorganization of ecologies. Water use and manipulation further changed the environment and the organization of its use by humans and animals. Landscape degradation through erosion, earth movement, stock, and salination has also been dramatic. Other changes were political and social, such as granting citizenship to Aboriginal people and wage equity only as late as the 1960s. The recent recognition of Native Title has seen land management and ownership shift back toward some indigenous people. These changes occurred alongside government policies regarding indigenous people which haven been variously paternal, controlling, harsh, and neglectful.

Archaeological studies of pastoral domains have been instructive, filling some gaps in the historical record. Since history is written by "the winners," in colonial contexts there remain many "hidden histories," of those absent from known histories, those ignored, forgotten, overlooked, or obscured.[36] There have been many studies on this topic; here I consider two sheep stations I have worked at: Strangways Springs in South Australia and Inthanoona in Western Australia.

Strangways Springs, Central AuFstralia

Contact places are often invested with multiple cultural meanings. Strangways Springs was, and is, known to Arabana people as Pangki Warruna. It is a complex of low artesian springs that rise up into the arid landscape.[37] For thousands of years, indigenous people have used reliable artesian springs at such places as Pangki Warruna in combination with more ephemeral water sources.

In the 1860s, the arrival of pastoralists, also attracted to these artesian waters, brought a radical transformation. The role of violence along this colonial frontier is unclear, although elsewhere it was often brutal, sometimes benign.

Sheep stations meant one thing for local Arabana people—their country was now claimed by outsiders, having been invaded by sheep and a handful of Europeans who viewed this country as their entitlement. The station manager at Strangways Springs during these early years describes it thus: "To break these wild tribes into something like obedience and to teach them the law of ownership and property, and that their laws must give way to white mans' law, were the most difficult tasks."[38]

Aboriginal people in these regions were, at least initially, an asset for the whites. They knew the environment and held significant information, such as where water could be found. They were potential translators and mediators. Their brains, eyes, and ears were useful tools for the small number of Europeans who comprised the front of the pastoral wave. Aboriginal people were also available labor in a labor shortage. At Strangways Springs, children were indoctrinated as pastoral trainees, as recalled by John Oastler:

> My boy Kalli Kalli, whom I found starving, without parents, at eight years of age, equipped with a small boomerang and yam stick in search for lizards, mice and rats for food with the proviso that should he kill anything extra good it must be taken into the camp for the old men, the inferior articles only being allowed to the youngsters. This being part of their religion it was strictly adhered to, but being in contact with civilization the aboriginal mind does not carry out this order to the present day. So I gave poor Kalli Kalli a share of my dinner that I happened to have with me, and I adopted him of the spot, and kept him as my henchman for many years . . . and I am happy to say he has proved useful in many ways, being even able to take a contract on his own account.[39]

The pastoral system was, for many years, essentially medieval in character—animals were kept on a free range and then herded into protective yards. This required lots of shepherding and was very labor intensive. Male and female workers, mainly Arabana, became the mainstay of the pastoral station. Their campsites indicate how the ancient camping site at Pangki Warruna became important as a place close to the station for workers and their kin and their kin's kin. Most were within two miles of the station, close but out of immediate sight and earshot. Many other campsites were located over the vast station, some related to pastoral outstations, others probably reflecting how some Arabana continued to access their traditional country in a time of great change.

Not all indigenous people were allowed into the station. The white pastoralists describe their attempts to deter "strangers" or "outsiders" who came onto the station. Long-range travel, such as for ceremonies and social gatherings and to access traded goods, as well as *pinyaroo* (missions for revenge), were greatly reduced or stopped as the landscape became controlled by colonial and pastoral interests.

Eventually the whites changed the pastoral landscape with the use of dams and artesian bores, dividing up the land with fences, and improving transport infrastructure.

The camps of the Arabana reveal that across the station they had access to a wide range of new materials, although often in very small quantities. These goods included clothing, new foods such as flour, pipes, food preparation and consumption equipment, and new raw materials suitable for making implements. They delineate new practices as well as changes to existing ones. Materials and food would have been accessed by workers and their kin, while over time rations provided by the pastoralists and the colonial bureaucracy were also available, in a limited way, to Aboriginal people, in part for humanitarian reasons, but also with the result of spatially controlling the location of Aboriginal people. Hunting and traditional food collection continued as well.

During these early years of contact, pastoralists learned to use rationing as a cross-cultural practice: at one level there was comprehension—the exchange required some agreement—although the practice of rationing would have its own cultural meaning as well. In some ways, rationed camps provided opportunities that large gatherings had always offered—they were a type of "super waterhole." They also represent the diminishing prospects for access to traditional country.

Over time, pastoralists' dependence on Aboriginal people shifted as they gained their own knowledge of the environments and resources. Yet reliance on workers remained, especially at times when few other workers could be cajoled into working in these places. The gold rushes, in particular, created a greater demand for workers. Aboriginal people filled that need, and across parts of New South Wales, Queensland, the Northern Territory, and Western Australia, stations were cross-cultural settings for over a century.

In the late 1960s, demands for equal wages for Aboriginal people were largely agreed to, and in a national referendum Aboriginal Australians were recognized as citizens in their own land. The results of these events were not all positive, however, for many pastoralists who had been happy with a cheap local labor force were unwilling to support Aboriginal residents, many of whom ended up relocating to the fringes of small towns or reserves.

Pilbara, Western Australia

In the western Pilbara region of Western Australia, we see similar events in Ngarluma country as described for Strangways Springs: the arrival of white settlers with a mind-set of rightful colonization. They viewed Aboriginal people as, among other things, cheap labor.

Studies of their early nineteenth-century settlements reveal the successes and failures of colonization of unfamiliar landscapes. They show, too, the imported and adapted ways of doing things, the places where Aboriginal people became enmeshed with the settlers, who in turn developed special laws to guarantee access to cheap labor.

There were no convicts or African slaves in this remote frontier, but the colony's Master and Servant Act restricted Aboriginal workers, who were often trapped in agreements that they did not initially comprehend.

The Northwest, as the region was known, was remote from the tiny colony on the Swan River (Perth) far to the south. Its remoteness meant that no convicts were allowed, as controlling a prison population was difficult. (Although, in some ways, the Australian continent was a prison from which few British convicts ever escaped.) In the Pilbara, settlers arrived in 1861 and quickly established industries based on pastoralism and collecting pearl shell.

At one early colonial settlement, Inthanoona, we can see in rock art how Ngarluma people made their own account of these events. These engravings are "rock documents" in a historical period when accounts of Aboriginal people and their reaction to the pastoral invaders are rare. Inthanoona is a small head-station of a sheep station, comprised of buildings for the elite manager and the white workers, and camps for Aboriginal people, some of whom would have been workers.[40]

Overlooking the head station, a stony hill is covered with engravings, many of which show the nineteenth-century cross-cultural world. Of more than 250 rock engravings, one-fifth are identifiable contact-period motifs. These include images of clothed men and women, guns, horses, sheep, wheeled vehicles, houses and ships (Figure 9.7). Images of men with European clothing abound, showing smoking, shooting, riding, and posing. Horses are popular, some ridden, some alone. Guns are popular, too. Some are held; many are being discharged.

Spatial analysis of the structures, artifacts, and engravings on the site supports the conclusion that the contact motifs demonstrate continuity in indigenous

Figure 9.7. Contact rock engravings at Inthanoona: (*a*) figure shooting, (*b*) wheeled vehicle and quadruped, (*c*) men, woman, and horse, (*d*) ship, and (*e*) hut with chimney.

modes of representation and innovation in subjects. They provide direct evidence of Aboriginal participation in, and perceptions of, the pastoral and pearl-shell industries of the Pilbara.

Some clear trends are present. First, rock art continues to be made after contact. Second, all the art was produced in sight of the station, so while rock art was often conducted in socially restricted settings, here it seems to be public and open (Figure 9.8). Everyone at the settlement could see and hear the art being pounded

251

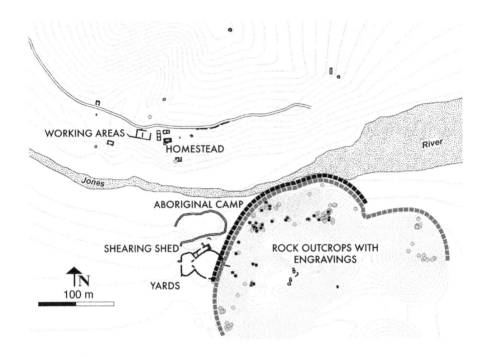

Figure 9.8. Plan of Inthanoona site showing the remains of the homestead complex north of Jones River and the yards and shearing shed to the south, and the distribution of engraved motifs. Traditional motifs and the frontage line are in gray. Contact motifs and the frontage line are in black. Contour interval = 1 m. (*Courtesy Andrew Wilson.*)

out—it was not hidden. Third, certain motifs are popular—in a landscape numerically dominated by sheep, it is largely men and their horses that are represented.

What does this tell us of indigenous interests and concerns? Women are present in the full British costume that would have been stifling in the Pilbara heat. The only element that was not local is ships—of which seven are shown, most depicting the detailed knowledge of their rigging and below-waterline form. These probably result from Aboriginal divers—the pastoralists were all pearlers and seem to have used pastoral stations as a means to access a permanent diving force for the pearling season. This was dangerous and often forced labor, so the images may have served as narratives of this indentured work.

THE PRESENT

There is much more to be learned of cross-cultural aspects of Australian history and, indeed, from very active debates. A core debate in the early twenty-first century has developed over how to regard Australian history following 1788. Did the British invade or colonize? How deliberate were attempts to remove Aboriginal people from their country? What was the role of frontier violence in different colonies?

Of particular interest to this debate is the issue of Tasmania, where historical studies have revealed both how Tasmanians resisted British settlement and how various British colonials responded to these efforts, as at Wybalenna settlement. How should resistance be understood? Was this a guerilla war? Do agreements between surviving Tasmanians in the early eighteenth century and the colonial administration mean a treaty existed between the two societies, and if so, what are the contemporary social and legal ramifications?

Some key debates about culture contact and cross-cultural violence have occurred in the so-called History Wars, characterized by an argument regarding historiography and historical accuracy. Particular attention has revolved around the evidence for killings, with one school of thought demanding that only those killings and violent events specifically detailed in historical sources can be considered, while others believe that historical sources tell only part of the picture of frontier violence.[41]

Beyond this debate, there are also opportunities through studies of culture contact to better understand Aboriginal survival and the contribution of Aboriginal people to phases of Australian history where they once were often absent.

USEFUL SOURCES

Museums and online resources: National Museum of Australia, Australian Institute of Aboriginal and Torres Strait Islander Studies, Australian Museum (Sydney), various state museums.

References: For overviews of culture contact relevant to Australia, see *Archaeology in Oceania* 38, no. 2 (2003); Tim Murray, ed., *The Archaeology of Contact in Settler Societies* (Cambridge University Press, 2004); Robin Torrence and Anne Clarke, eds., *The Archaeology of Difference: Negotiating Cross-Cultural Engagements in Oceania* (London: Routledge, 2000); Ian Lilley, ed., *Native Title and the Transformation of Archaeology in the Postcolonial World* (Oceania Monograph 50, University of Sydney, 2000); Rodney Harrison and Christine Williamson, eds., *After Captain Cook: The Archaeology of the Recent Indigenous Past in Australia* (Walnut Creek, CA: AltaMira, 2004); Lynette Russell, ed., *Colonial*

Frontiers: Indigenous-European Encounters in Settler Societies (Manchester University Press, 2001); Peter Veth, Peter Sutton, and Margaret Neale, eds., *Strangers on the Shore: Early Coastal Contact in Australia* (Canberra: National Museum of Australia Press, 2008).

General sources on Aboriginal Australia: Bill Arthur and Frances Morphy, eds., *Macquarie Atlas of Indigenous Australia: Culture and Society through Space and Time* (North Ryde: Macquarie Library, 2005); David Horton, ed., *The Encyclopedia of Aboriginal Australia: Aboriginal and Torres Strait Islander History, Society and Culture* (Canberra: Aboriginal Studies Press for the Australian Institute of Aboriginal and Torres Strait Islander Studies, 1994); D. J. Mulvaney and J. Peter White, *Australians to 1788* (Broadway: Fairfax Syme & Weldon Associates, 1987).

Key journals: *Australian Archaeology, Australasian Historical Archaeology, Archaeology in Oceania, Rock Art Research, Historic Environment.*

CHAPTER 10

MILLENNIUM

I have but one lamp by which my feet are guided, and that is the lamp of experience. I know no way of judging of the future but by the past.

–Patrick Henry

The end of the millennium of culture contact did not mark the end of relevance of these events. What can we learn, in the new millennium, of the last? The events described here are in some regions part of very significant contemporary issues: of identity, of history, of rights to land and other forms of cultural property, or recognition of rights, of a future where the events of the past are given appropriate weight.

Hopefully, by focusing on the presence of Europeans, this book has not suggested a teleological progression toward a world where superior Europeans eventually were victorious in their various colonization episodes and invasions. That said, the fate of many indigenous people and their descendants has often been negative. This is sometimes reflected in the lives of today's descent communities.

The withdrawal of colonial powers has resulted in various situations that are not explored here, where the focus has largely been on the early phases of cultural contact. My choice of topic was selected for its suitability to archaeological approaches, and I have drawn on examples where archaeology has something important to bring to the present.

I want to broadly consider the processes considered here in a comparative manner, remembering the aim has not been to find universals, but to provide a map of some key archaeological work into contacts between aboriginal Europeans and non-Europeans in the last millennium.

I started this book with an interest in how individuals in the past were visible in various investigations, particularly when thinking of the archaeological record. After all, as individuals ourselves, we perhaps best understand the lessons of the past at this level—of a person, his or her agency, actions, and life. Archaeological records are essentially the outcomes of the actions of many individuals, from a worn hearth to the Great Wall of China. Sometimes individuals do become visible to us, either from individual artifacts or structures, or through historical sources. In other cases, we can really discern the broader activities in which individuals were a part. It is this tension between levels of evidence that characterizes the archaeology of culture contact. In this conclusion, I briefly explore some aspects of the archaeology of culture contact that I observed in the process of writing this review.

THE IMPORTANCE OF THE PAST

The past is important. We say this a lot as archaeologists and historians, often in the context of applying for research funds. Nonetheless, it is often true. There are immediate, in-your-face contemporary issues that may be advanced, in part, by knowing history. To take one example from my own experience, in Australia the indigenous population suffers from violence, disease, poverty, and poor services at a higher rate than the remainder of the population. Many indigenous people live in remote parts of Australia, which were not subject to intensive colonization by white settlers; however, many Australian Aboriginal people in cities also struggle. Understanding those different histories can possibly lead us to resolve these problems in more targeted ways.

I am not attempting to provide answers here, but to observe that the understanding of how events lead from precontact times to the present is a useful tool for both indigenous people and for the wider community. There are many examples of this I could draw upon from around the world: in California, for instance, Kent Lightfoot has conducted an overview of the contact legacy in *Indians, Missionaries, and Merchants: The Legacy of Colonial Encounters on the Californian Frontiers* (2005). This type of work takes substantial archaeological research to be able to explore the trajectories of various indigenous groups into the present.

In some regions, contact histories are not very well known and remain to be rediscovered. In other regions, the past is probably better known: to take an example, the relationships between various Asian nations today and Europeans are recorded in Asian and European historical sources.

A significant shift in many countries and in subdisciplines in archaeology and anthropology has been toward collaboration between investigators and stakeholder communities, often indigenous communities. While this varies across the globe, I want to consider it here as ultimately one of the most important aspects of culture-contact studies. By becoming involved with stakeholder communities, archaeologists themselves are involved in forms of culture contact. I generalize, as there are increasingly indigenous archaeologists too, and these old distinctions are being blurred.

With the rise of the heritage sector and consultancy archaeology, most archaeologists in places like Australia and North America work with indigenous communities in collaborative ways that illustrate very different power structures than existed even two decades ago. While this is a general shift, collaboration tends to relate to legislation in individual countries. By the same token, increased collaboration has sometimes led to changed research designs, as the questions asked by archaeologists are often very different from the questions being asked by indigenous descendants.

Another aspect concerns interpretation, for stakeholders may interpret the meaning of archaeological evidence differently than archaeologists. For example, archaeologists often ask, "how much can I rely on this information?" when using ethnographic and historical information to interpret archaeological findings. It is not that the ethnographic information may be wrong or untrustworthy, but it is sometimes unclear whether there exist great discontinuities in the past that make problematic the use of data collected *after* the discontinuity to interpret archaeological material deposited *before* the discontinuity. In some cases, researchers may feel that the match of evidence is good, as seen where a "direct historical approach" is applied, as this assumes continuity between archaeological cultures and those observed by historical reporters. From cases in this book, however, it is clear that we need to understand what happens when cultures come into contact so we can understand how applicable the use of such analogies are—that is, whether the data is "good" or not.

Let us consider one example to highlight the issue. In this case, the "transformation" in practice through contact with indigenous communities occurred on behalf of the archaeologist, Canadian archaeologist Max Friesen, working in the Arctic, where the archaeology relevant to this discussion relates to two groups:

1. Thule (Neo-Eskimo) who colonized much of the Arctic around 1,000 years ago and are viewed as ancestors of Inuit cultures, and

2. earlier Dorset people (Palaeo-Eskimo) and even more ancient archaeological cultures (see chapter 3).

The problem faced by Arctic archaeologists is: how much should ethnography of Inuit people (and this is sometimes very comprehensive) be used to interpret both Neo- and Palaeo-Eskimo archaeological remains? For Friesen, the transformation was from an initial position of not using information about the Inuit to interpret Dorset sites, to one of embracing the ethnography to generate analogues in a critical research framework. (Like many archaeologists, Friesen cites the writing of Alison Wylie, who mapped out the problems and potentials of the use of analogies in archaeological interpretation.)[1]

Friesen, working near Iqaluktuuq on Victoria Island in the Arctic, puts the shift down to two causes. First,

> The Iqaluktuuq Project exists *because of* the enthusiastic efforts of a group of elders, who want to be involved in the research process. Therefore, I feel an obligation to reflect their efforts, ideas and intellectual authority as much as possible. This is most effectively done by directly linking their traditional knowledge to the interpretation of the archaeological record.

His second reason

> is what might be described as a subjective "gut feeling" that the interests of academic archaeology are *not* well served by ignoring the incomparably rich data set afforded by recent Inuit lifeways.[2]

This type of approach does not require a less critical approach, but does demand a careful awareness of the various aspects and outcomes of archaeological research, where positive indigenous outcomes are not necessarily the same as the ambitions of archaeologists. Importantly, it need not mean abandoning the important principles of scientific inquiry.

STUDYING CONTACT

In writing this book, I have been drawn toward archaeological studies that take into account a sufficiently long-term approach to "bridge" culture contact. This does not necessarily mean a very long-term approach, particularly given the time scales at which some archaeologists operate. It does mean coming to the topic with an awareness of the history of past investigations because, as a generalization, the frameworks of investigation may actually hinder an understanding of intercultural contacts.

To put it simply, historical archaeologists may have tended to pursue questions about colonists and not the aboriginal people with whom they were in contact (or not), while "prehistorians" may have been less interested in what happened after contact. There are many exceptions to this generalization, of course, but there are also many studies that have failed to deal with the gap between these two archaeological traditions—where the gap existed.

Many of the studies cited in this book reveal that there is much work that takes into account the longer time period that bridges contact periods. Such studies often constitute difficult work, requiring familiarity with indigenous archaeological material as well as historical archaeological records, the use of historical and/or oral sources, and perhaps even requiring regional rather than site-based fieldwork. There are, however, some important studies in this regard. Some are interested in the *longue durée* as a setting for historical events; others see historical events as part of longer culture history.

I have found several projects useful, such as the work in Greenland (chapter 3), much of which situates the contact that occurred with Norsemen and later whalers into a regional framework of contacts between various groups, best resolved through archaeology. In North America, I have particularly relied on Kent Lightfoot's work at Fort Ross (described in chapter 7). In the Pacific, this type of approach is seemingly more common (see, for example, Patrick Kirch and Marshall Sahlin's study of the Anahulu Valley and the research into the Waihou Valley in New Zealand/Aotearoa discussed in chapter 8). The work on St. Catherines Island by David Hurst Thomas and colleagues is a very clear example of a project that treats all archaeological time periods equally (chapter 7). Similarly, the work in West Africa by Ann Stahl and others begins the task of mapping out changes in African societies away from the "front line" of contact with Europeans, but still very much involved in momentous times (chapter 5). Part of this means moving away from European colonial sites to broader indigenous landscapes: Peter Lape, looking at culture contact in island Southeast Asia (chapter 8) in a time scale extending from the Neolithic to the arrival of Europeans proposed an approach that envelops local culture contacts with regional studies, encouraging

> [contact studies that] document local developments in the context of large regional scale interactions and influences. This type of approach, which represents a shift away from simplistic explanations of change attributed to external civilizations to more sophisticated ones that consider both internal forces and localized accommodations of foreigners is mirrored in shifts away from acculturation in general culture contact theory. Features of this shift include a focus on the two-way transfer of ideas, influences and technologies in contact situations, an increased concern with the specific mechanisms of information transfer and a related focus on local uses and meanings of foreign ideas and material objects.[3]

The idea of two cultures in contact, between aboriginals and Europeans or others native to somewhere else, has dominated this book. As stated in the last quote, we envisage a "two-way process." This may be appropriate, yet it requires that we be attuned to the much messier, complex nature of these types of intercultural contacts.

When British ships came into contact with Tahitians, the encounter involved the British ship hierarchy as much as the various strata and roles of Polynesian society. The research into contacts across North America involving fur trading have begun mapping out this complexity, with varying degrees of direct contact, key roles for certain individuals such as Indian middlemen, the creation of mixed-descent individuals and communities like the Métis, and differing forms of culture-contact policy and procedure depending on nationality and corporation. To cite Lightfoot once more, at Fort Ross contact is made up of many two-way transactions; it is "pluralistic," enfolding

Russians, aboriginal Alaskans, and native Californians. The archaeology potentially reflects these complexities.

The simple idea of two-way contacts leads us to another simplification, and perhaps falsehood: the sometimes myth of contact that indigenous societies were isolated and not in contact with outsiders until the arrival of Europeans. I hope this books helps dispel any lingering sense of this, and that examples of Europeans meeting people engaged in existing regional, continental, and intercontinental relationships—both directly and indirectly mediated by the movement of resources, pathogens, artifacts, and ideas—help debunk that fiction. Of course, some societies had more exposure to different societies than others. As a rule, Europeans tended to be most prepared for culture contacts, as they were moving into regions anticipating these events.

Materially this is reflected in the items they brought with them, with cargoes including not only the stuff needed for survival, but also for intercultural dealings: armaments and trade goods. In each case there was probably a policy toward culture contact in place, and we see differences over time and cultures in this regard.

Different indigenous cultures came to contact with different experiences of outsiders. For many, outsiders initially had to be categorized as non-human, creating the need for new categories. Thus, the Maoris became *Maori,* as distinct from *pakeha*. Familiarity over time would have fed into these perceptions, as British in Australia shifted in various Australian Aboriginal people's minds from non-earthly spirits to a form of human.

In some cases, contact was already deeply ingrained, as it was in the various communities of coastal Southeast Asia, whose populace added Europeans to a set of people from "above the wind" which included parts of the world where Hinduism, Buddhism, and Islam originated. Southeast Asians saw themselves as "below the winds" in relation to India and all points west. This is a geographical and meteorological reference, but even the Spanish who traveled from the east across the Pacific Ocean—unlike the other European merchants—were part of this set. In any case, the Southeast Asians' familiarity reflects the fact that the maritime cultures of the region had long been in contact with external powers and influences. For them, contact with Europeans required no major shift in their perception—of either themselves or the world.

MATERIAL ASPECTS OF CULTURE CONTACTS

Archaeology is primarily about the material evidence, although sometimes it requires also taking into account a wider range of sources, from historical accounts, oral histories, and pictorial evidence, to evidence of changes in the environment.

260

The focus on the material aspects of cultural entanglements poses serious challenges and potential insights.

On the upside is the fact that we are often aware of the subtleties of material culture. The once taken-for-granted assumption that people = things—that is, that objects and the style in which they were made were absolutely linked to social identity—is today less convincing. The ways that objects shift in meaning as they pass through hands bring us insight, cautioning us against simplistic interpretation. The work of people like anthropologist Nicholas Thomas has been particularly influential for his commentary on historical cross-cultural contact.[4] He underscores that while that European objects have tended to be understood as linkages to European concepts, such as colonialism, the objects themselves were in the process of being rejected, embraced, and manipulated, among other options, by indigenous agents. Given this, we need to be concerned about loading too much meaning onto objects in situations where societies are not merely in contact, but are perhaps engaged in various forms of conflict and cross-cultural interpretation and manipulation.

Material objects also convey value. Exchange tends to involve those things that are considered valuable—thus demonstrating what past societies found important. Obviously, since objects or commodities—what archaeologists term "material culture"—shift meaning in different cultural contexts, the analysis of archaeological material needs to take this into account. And, this is only part of the process of exchange, since not only are goods exchanged or traded, but so too are services, which may include labor, knowledge, or companionship.

In many examples cited in this book, historical sources add depth to the archaeology, allowing us, for example, to consider the archaeological evidence at settlements of American Indians involved in the fur trade alongside an understanding of the goods that moved into these societies in exchange for furs and hides, animal parts now dust in Europe.

From an archaeological perspective, then, we need to move from "artifact" to an understanding of its value in cross-cultural exchanges, and then we can start to think of goods, commodities, and value. Obviously, this depends very much on the context and on the data available to us in the present. However, there may be general patterns we can start to use to explore the ways that material evidence tells us about cultural entanglements.

One aspect of contact studies is the use of acculturation as an interpretive tool. Of course, this needs to be used in a thoughtful way and not as the sole barometer. In the past, as discussed earlier, the problem with acculturation was that it was used as an index of cultural change, based on the common assumption that we could accurately measure a shift from aboriginal to European. Not surprisingly, this idea fell from favor, although sincere efforts have been made to refine its use. I think this is important, as we continue to look for the presence of "introduced" items in archaeological deposits and need to use them in our analyses. The amount of introduced material is meaningful, true, but it may not reflect cultural change as much as engagement with European systems of trade, ideology, or administration.

In this review I have noted four variables that we can place in an interpretive grid. The quadrants of the grid are (1) old things, (2) old ways, (3) new things, and (4) new ways. These four elements are often seen in the material record, especially when the archaeology is sufficiently comprehensive to reconstruct a wide range of economic and social activities across time and space. The grid allows for conservatism, experimentation, and change, as well as ethnogenesis as reflected in new or revised materialities. This grid need not be restricted to material culture but could also incorporate practice—that is, the way people do things.

Let us explore some examples from this book. One shift across Asia, Europe, and Africa in the second millennium was conversion to Islam, which may be seen in *new things* (places of worship, architectural styles, texts) but perhaps, more subtly, in a shift in diet. The absence of pig remains would not easily fit into an acculturation index, but in the grid would be a form of evidence for *new ways*.

A more classic example that fits with acculturation indexes is the introduction of iron where it was not common before. Rather than indicating just the material presence of a *new thing*, it could also reflect *old ways*—say, hunting or cooking—as well as *new ways* of thinking of hunting—that is, not just for immediate returns but as a way to meet external demands for hides and fur as individuals become engaged in becoming client hunters.

The idea of these crosscutting categories, then, extends our thinking of contact, inviting a landscape approach that comprises the location of activities in the landscape, the use of elements of the environment, and the ways that people's actions restrict and encourage certain actions and their location.

The grid's categories, employed in qualitative and non-empirical analyses, also accommodate the creation of new practices and societies.

Ideally, the grid needs to be read in every direction, not just focused on indigenous people. The reasons why are clear. Yes, the European settlers have their history and so there is less need for archaeology. I get that, and it is sometimes the case. That said, it is important to get a sense of what happens across the spectrum of societies in culture contact. If we return to Coeman's 1665 painting (chapter 8), we see an image of Indonesian servants, a Japanese woman and her Dutch merchant husband, and their daughters: all are clearly entangled together and it would weaken any study to pick only one individual out and leave the rest.

Looking across this millennium, we see from the fulcrum of cultural entanglements the formation of identities, some new like Métis or American, some that refer to older societies like British or Inuit. All also have material aspects that derive from the full spectrum of identity and action as it occurred in the past. While we fall back on categories like "English," "Bandanese," "Inuit," and "Cree," the best studies focus in on these categories and treat them as problems that require very careful investigation: What does it mean to be "French Canadian" in Montreal in 1710, "British" in Tasmania in 1870, "Swahili" in Zanzibar in 1500, or "Norse" in Greenland in 1340? These questions need tackling. Although illuminating the path (or possible paths) to the answer may be the aim, it is the journey, not the destination, that enlightens us.

In each case, the answer would depend on the perspective of the observer and the context. However the Eora people explained the visit of Captain Cook in 1770 to one another, by 1790 their explanation of the British hunkering down on the Tank Stream would have changed to envelop more pragmatic familiarity with the mortal outsiders, and perhaps the beginning of the realization that the world was changing fast, and forever.

NOTES

PREFACE

[1] There is some important archaeological work on colonialism, e.g., Chris Gosden, *Archaeology and Colonialism: Cultural Contact from 5000 B.C. to the Present* (Cambridge: Cambridge University Press, 2004). Several other books explore colonialism across ancient and more recent contexts, e.g., Claire Lyons and John Papadopoulos, eds., *The Archaeology of Colonialism* (Los Angeles: Getty Research Institute, 2002). See also Stephen Silliman, "Culture Contact or Colonialism? Challenges in the Archaeology of Native North America," *American Antiquity* 70, no. 1 (2005): 55–74.

[2] Historical archaeologists debate what defines their discipline. Some highlight the need for historical archaeologists to use both archaeological and historical evidence to interpret historical archaeological events, processes, and sites. Others focus on the study of the world after 1492 and explore how the modern world came about. Archaeologist James Deetz described historical archaeology initially as "the archaeology of the spread of European cultures throughout the world since the fifteenth century"; then, as his own interest and that of other archaeologists in cross-cultural encounters grew, he added ". . . and their impact on and interaction with the cultures of indigenous peoples" (James Deetz, *In Small Things Forgotten: The Archaeology of Early American Life*. (Garden City: Anchor Press/Doubleday, 1977), 5.

[3] Charles E. Orser,"Historical Archaeology as Modern-World Archaeology in Argentina," *International Journal of Historical Archaeology* 13, no. 3 (2008): 181–194. Orser has been a leading advocate of the argument to develop a global focus to historical archaeology.

[4] The influence of Immanuel Wallerstein on this topic is immense. Key to his contribution is the development of the idea of core/center and periphery, terms that had been in use since the 1960s. Wallerstein's three volumes, *The Modern World-System* (New York: Academic Press, 1974–1989), refined the idea to situate the development of cores and peripheries in the early modern era in a broader world perspective. The core-periphery idea has been employed and critiqued, with some finding the concept too general to be useful to explain what happened in places such as Latin America and elsewhere. The concept added some refinement to other dominant models, such as frontier theory typified by Frederick Jackson Turner. The influence of Fernand Braudel and Karl Marx on Wallerstein is of particular note. Another key work is Eric R. Wolf's, *Europe and the People Without History* (Berkeley: University of California Press, 1982), which focused in on the histories of those beyond the standard narratives of literate "winners." Others have also adopted a global scope to demonstrate the biological component that accompanies the movement of humans, e.g., Alfred Crosby, *The Columbian Exchange: Biological and Cultural Consequences of 1492* (London: Praeger, 2003).

[5] Kent Lightfoot, *Indians, Missionaries, and Merchants: The Legacy of Colonial Encounters on the Californian Frontiers* (Berkeley: University of California Press, 2005).

CHAPTER 1

[1] The idea of the world as it was in AD1000 relies on several sources cited throughout this book. General accounts of world history range from Gordon Childe's *What Happened in History* (Harmondsworth: Penguin Books, 1943)—with a Europe/West Asia bias admittedly—to Wolf's *Europe and the People without History*. The former ends with the fall of the Mediterranean classical civilizations; the second fills that gap in a monumental attempt to look at the global nature of the world after 1400. Wolf's study takes a political and economic perspective and is blessed with very substantial reading lists for further research.

[2] Crosby, *The Columbian Exchange*.

[3] Atholl Anderson and Gerard O'Regan, "To the Final Shore: Prehistoric Colonisation of the Subantarctic Islands in South Polynesia," in *Australian Archaeologist: Collected Papers in Honour of Jim Allen*, ed. Atholl Anderson and Tim Murray (Canberra: Coombs Academic Publishing, The Australian National University, 2000), 440–454, summarize the three models for the colonization of southern Polynesia as the long prehistory model with initial colonization after 2000BP, an orthodox model of AD1000–1200, and a shorter prehistory beginning after 800 BP.

[4] Damien Evans et al., "A Comprehensive Archaeological Map of the World's Largest Preindustrial Settlement Complex at Angkor, Cambodia," *Proceedings of the Natural Academy of Sciences* 104 (2007): 14277–14282.

[5] There are other factors to consider. There were different calendars in use, and with the widespread European adoption of the *Anno Domini* calendar centuries ahead, the year 1000 would have been recognized only by people using the modern calendar rather than those based on Roman events or Creation. The start of the year varied greatly, and few placed it on January 1, but overall there would have been heightened anxiety regarding the end of the tenth century by many Christians, whenever they marked it.

[6] John Schofield and Heiko Steuer, "Urban Settlement," in *The Archaeology of Medieval Europe*, ed. J. Graham-Campbell and M. Valor (Aarhus: Aarhus University Press, 2007), 111–154.

CHAPTER 2

[1] The film was based on the book *Contact* by Carl Sagan (New York: Simon and Schuster, 1985). One could also consider the Star Trek film *First Contact* (Paramount Pictures, 1996), as it depicts an attempt (by the Borg) to stop humans from coming into contact with aliens.

[2] Carmel Schrire, "Wild Surmises on Savage Thoughts," in *Past and Present in Hunter-Gatherer Studies*, ed. C. Schrire (London: Academic Press, 1984), 1–25.

[3] Silliman, "Culture Contact or Colonialism."

[4] Kent Lightfoot, "Culture Contact Studies: Redefining the Relationship between Prehistoric and Historical Archaeology," *American Antiquity* 60, no. 2 (1995): 199–217.

[5] Lightfoot, "Culture Contact Studies."

[6] Lightfoot, "Culture Contact Studies"; and Sarah Colley and Annie Bickford, "'Real' Aborigines and 'Real' Archaeology: Aboriginal Places and Australian Historical Archaeology," *World Archaeological Bulletin* 7 (1996): 5–21. See also Kathleen Deagan, "Neither History nor Prehistory: The Questions That Count in Historical Archaeology," *Historical Archaeology* 22 (1988): 7–12.

[7] Such long-term approaches are particularly favored by those influenced by the Annales School of historical research developed in the twentieth century by French scholars such as Marc Bloch and Fernand Braudel, among others. Its emphasis on social and cultural aspects of history, as well as on long-term processes and short-term events, attracted geographers and archaeologists.

[8] The impact of diseases in culture contact has become an increasingly significant area of research. Several things are worth noting. First, disease sometimes caused major loss of life. Second, diseases impacted differently across different peoples, depending on population size, previous exposure to diseases, and knowledge of treatments. Third, there are many things we do not yet know about the size of some populations prior to contact and the degree of impact of diseases. Fourth, the impact of disease was often not observed or commented upon, occurring beyond the particular instances of early culture contact. Explorers and settlers arrived in regions where major and minor epidemics had already occurred.

[9] This is raised in Patrick V. Kirch and Jean-Louis Rallu, *The Growth and Collapse of Pacific Island Communities: Archaeological and Demographic Perspectives* (Honolulu: University of Hawai'i Press, 2007), 5, and chap. 9.

[10] Described in Sturt's account, *Two Expeditions into the Interior of Southern Australia during the Years 1828, 1829, 1830, 1831: With Observations on the Soil, Climate, and General Resources of the Colony of New South Wales* (Canberra: Petherick Reading Room, National Library of Australia).

[11] Ann Ramenofsky, "Historical Science and Contact Period Studies," in *Columbian Consequences. Vol.3: The Spanish Borderlands in Pan-American Perspective*, ed. D. H. Thomas (Washington, DC: Smithsonian Institution Press, 1991), 446.

[12] A good example being Nicholas Thomas, *Entangled Objects: Exchange, Material Culture, and Colonialism in the Pacific* (Cambridge, MA: Harvard University Press, 1991).

[13] This was cited by Floyd W. Rudmin in his review of acculturation across many disciplines: "Catalogue of Acculturation Constructs: Descriptions of 126 Taxonomies, 1918–2003," in *Online Readings in Psychology and Culture,* eds. W. V. Lonner, D. L. Dinnel, S. A. Hayes, and D. N. Sattler (Bellingham, Washington: Center for Cross-Cultural Research, Western Washington University, 2003), *http://www.wwu.edu/ culture* (accessed 1 January 2009). His review of the concept begins with Plato:

> The intercourse of cities with one another is apt to create a confusion of manners; strangers are always suggesting novelties to strangers. When states are well governed by good laws, the mixture causes the greatest possible injury; but seeing that most cities are the reverse of well-ordered, the confusion which arises in them from the reception of strangers, and from the citizens themselves rushing off into other cities, when any one either young or old desires to travel anywhere abroad at whatever time, is of no consequence. On the other hand, the refusal of states to receive others, and for their own citizens never to go to other places, is an utter impossibility, and to the rest of the world is likely to appear ruthless and uncivilized; it is a practice adopted by people who use harsh words, such as xenelasia or banishment of strangers, and who have harsh and morose ways. Plato, *Laws* (Oxford: Oxford University Press, 1892 [original 348 BC), 338–339.

[14] Quote from Alan Moorehead, *The Fatal Impact: An Account of the Invasion of the South Pacific, 1767–1840* (London: Hamish Hamilton, 1966), xx.

[15] Charles Darwin, *The Voyage of the Beagle* (London: Dent, 1959), 418.

[16] J. W. Powell, *Introduction to the Study of Indian Languages* (Washington, DC: U.S. Government Printing Office, 1880), and "Human Evolution: Annual Address of the President, J. W. Powell, Delivered November 6, 1883," *Transactions of the Anthropological Society of Washington* 2 (1883): 176–208.

[17] W. J. McGee and Bernard L. Fontana, *Trails to Tiburón: The 1894 and 1895 Field Diaries of W J McGee* (Tucson: University of Arizona Press, 2000).

[18] Robert Redfield, Ralph Linton, and Melville J. Herskovits, "Memorandum for the Study of Acculturation," *American Anthropologist* 38 (1936): 149–152.

[19] E. H. Spicer, *Perspectives in American Indian Culture Change* (Chicago: University of Chicago Press, 1961).

[20] Bronislaw Malinowski, *The Dynamics of Culture Change: An Inquiry into Race Relations in Africa* (New Haven: Yale University Press, 1945), 17–18.

[21] Malinowski, *The Dynamics of Culture Change*, 17–18.

[22] J. Daniel Rogers and Samuel M. Wilson, eds., *Ethnohistory and Archaeology: Approaches to Postcontact Change in the Americas* (New York: Plenum Press, 1993).

[23] The example of the Pueblo Revolt is from Matthew Liebmann, "The Innovative Materiality of Revitalization Movements: Lessons from the Pueblo Revolt of 1680," *American Anthropologist* 110, no. 3 (2008): 360–372. Leibmann's study is considered in chapter 7. For studies of material culture, start with Nicholas Thomas, *Entangled Objects: Exchange, Material Culture, and Colonialism in the Pacific* (Cambridge, MA: Harvard University Press, 1991), as this work is often cited by archaeologists and anthropologists. Most studies with an interest in materialities derive their ideas from Pierre Bourdieu, *Outline of a Theory of Practice* (Cambridge: Cambridge University Press, 1977). Recent volumes include Lynn Meskell, *Archaeologies of Materiality* (London: Blackwell, 2005) and Daniel Miller, *Materiality* (Durham, NC: Duke University Press, 2005).

[24] Philip D. Curtin, *Cross-Cultural Trade in World History* (New York: Cambridge University Press, 1984).

CHAPTER 3

[1] A. E. Christensen, "Viking. A Gokstad Ship Replica from 1893," in *Sailing into the Past: Proceedings of the International Seminar on Replicas of Ancient and Medieval Vessels, Roskilde, 1984*, ed. O. Crumlin-Pedersen and M. Vinner (Roskilde: Viking Ship Museum, 1986).

[2] James H. Barrett, *Contact, Continuity, and Collapse: The Norse Colonization of the North Atlantic, Studies in the Early Middle Ages* (Turnhout: Brepols, 2003).

[3] In terms of culture contact between the Vikings and the Irish, Mytum concludes that the Norse "became integrated within some aspects of cultural, political, and economic life in Ireland" rather than involved in the raiding that—unsurprisingly—characterized early reports of Vikings. Norse influence became stronger with the establishment of permanent trading centers, such as Dublin. Harold Mytum, "The Vikings and Ireland: Ethnicity, Identity, and Culture Change," in Barrett, *Contact, Continuity, and Collapse*, 131.

[4] Contact involved the introduction to Scotland in the ninth century of Norse burial traditions, architecture, material culture, and economic patterns. Language shifts are demonstrated by the prevalence of Norse place-names, and the demise of Pictish. Coupled with genetic evidence, these data suggest a substantial migration to Scotland, while material culture suggests the coexistence of migrant and indigenous groups, with the adoption of each other's behavior (Barrett, *Contact, Continuity, and Collapse*, 99).

[5] Steffan Stumman Hansen, "The Early Settlement of the Faroe Islands: The Creation of Cultural Identity," in Barrett, *Contact, Continuity, and Collapse*, 33–71, summarizes the debate around a pre-Norse settlement by either Irish or other monks on the Faroe Islands possibly during the eighth century prior to Norse settlement in the ninth century, and he concludes there is little archaeological evidence to support the claims found in historical texts.

[6] Tinna Møbjerg, "The Saqqaq Culture in the Sisimiut Municipality Elucidated by the Two Sites Nipisat and Asummiut," in *Man, Culture and Environment in Ancient Greenland: Report on a Research Program*, ed. J. Arneborg and H. C. Gulløv (Copenhagen: The Danish National Museum and Danish Polar Center, 1998), 98–118.

[7] See Martin Appelt and Hans Christian Grønnow, *Late Dorset in High Arctic Greenland: Final Report on the Gateway to Greenland Project* (Copenhagen: Danish National Museum and Danish Polar Center, 1999); and idem, "Tunit, Norsemen, and Inuit in Thirteenth-Century Northwest Greenland-Dorset Between the Devil and the Deep Sea," in *The Northern World, AD 900–1400*, ed. H. Maschner, O. Mason and R. McGhee (Salt Lake City: University of Utah Press, 2009), where they describe these structures found in the far northwest of Arctic Greenland. These authors consider the megalithic structures to have a ritual and non-utilitarian purpose that may relate to shamanism. The sites suggest a Late Dorset settlement of the Thule District from 800 to 1300. The final date is controversial, as most previous work has suggested that the Dorset culture was no longer present in Greenland this late. The overall picture is of greater complexity than perhaps previously accepted, with interactions between Thule and Late Dorset as well as with the Norse, and with diversity within the Thule traditions also.

[8] This is described in the fieldwork reports in Martin Appelt, Hans Christian Gulløv, and Hans Kapel, "The Gateway to Greenland. Report on the Field Season 1996," in *Man, Culture and Environment in Ancient Greenland: Report on a Research Program*, ed. J. Arneborg and H. C. Gulløv (Copenhagen: The Danish National Museum and Danish Polar Center, 1998), 136–196; and Appelt and Gulløv, *Late Dorset in High Arctic Greenland*, 1999. The evidence of Late Dorset includes a dwelling with a Norse bronze pot. Evidence of ongoing contact between Dorset in the Canadian Arctic and the Late Dorset is indicated by the presence of points made from Canadian natural copper in Late Dorset huts. Going the other direction, iron from the meteorite location at Cape York was traded farther west.

[9] Jette Arneborg, "Norse Greenland: Reflections on Settlement and Depopulation," in Barrett, *Contact, Continuity, and Collapse*, 173.

[10] Jared M. Diamond, *Collapse: How Societies Choose to Fail or Survive* (London: Allen Lane, 2005), 257.

[11] Reported in Appelt et al., "Gateway to Greenland," 151.

[12] The main sources are *Íslendingabók* from 1122–1132 by the Icelandic scholar Ari fróði Þorgilsson, whose uncle was told about the voyages by one of the participants, and the *Greenland Description* written after 1342 by Ívarr Bárðarson, of which only seventeenth-century translations survive (Arneborg, "Norse Greenland"; Else Roesdahl, *The Vikings* [London: Allen Lane, 1991], 271). Bárðarson describes Greenland as being abandoned by the mid-fourteenth century. There are also two sagas, which largely relate to the voyages to Vinland. There are some finds of writing in Greenland, some dating to the time of initial Norse settlement. These rare finds are largely a form of Greenland runic and Latin and often relate to religion and magic. The writing is on a range of media, including utensils, sticks, bone, baleen, and soapstone; see Marie Stoklund, "Greenland Runes: Isolation or Culture Change," in *The Viking Age in Caithness, Orkney and the North Atlantic*, ed. C. E. Batey, J. Jesch and C. D. B. A. Morris (Edinburgh: Edinburgh University Press, 1993), 528–543.

[13] Arneborg, "Norse Greenland," 166. For a description of the Norse farms, written in Icelandic and Danish, see Kund J. Krogh, *Qallunaatsiaaqarfik Grønland* (Copenhagen: Nationalmuseets Forlag, 1982).

[14] See Krogh, *Qallunaatsiaaqarfik Grønland*, 102, for a distribution map showing the location of farms and summer camps.

[15] Arneborg et al. (Jette Arneborg, J. Heineneier, N. Lynnerup, H. L. Nielsen, N. Rud, and Á. E. Sveinbjörnsdóttir, "Change of Diet of the Greenland Vikings Determined from Stable Isotope Analysis and 14C Dating of Their Bones," *Radiocarbon* 41, 2 [1999]: 157–168) suggest that marine protein rose from 24–40 percent of the diet to 80 percent over time. However, the same trends could result from the early graves being from the interior while later graves were closer to the sea. .

[16] Arneborg, "Norse Greenland," 170.

[17] Martin Appelt (pers. comm., 4 March 2009, National Museum, Copenhagen) observed that many of the walrus tusks thought to have come from Novgorod may not have originated from the White Sea region as popularly believed, but came from Greenland via the Norse. Much of this material ended up in the Middle East, where walrus ivory was considered to be of greater value than elephant ivory. The demand in walrus from Greenland may reflect the difficulty in getting African ivory during the period of the Crusades.

[18] Arneborg, "Norse Greenland," 171; and P. Schledermann, "A.D. 1000: East Meets West," in *Vikings: The North Atlantic Saga*, ed. W. R. Fitzgerald and E. I. Ward (Washington, DC: Smithsonian Institution Press, 2000), 189–192.

[19] Thomas H. McGovern, "The Arctic Frontier of Norse Greenland," in *The Archaeology of Frontiers and Boundaries*, ed. S. W. Green and S. M. Perlman (Orlando: Academic Press, 1985), 283.

[20] Arneborg, "Norse Greenland," 172.

[21] This information is summarized in Jared Diamond's overview of the Norse in *Collapse*, where he argues that environmental change in a marginal environment for farming lay behind the end of Greenland Norse.

[22] This is proposed as a possibility in several locations; see Robert McGhee, "Epilogue: Was There Continuity from Norse to Post-Medieval Explorations of the New World?" in Barrett, *Contact, Continuity, and Collapse*, 239–248. He is citing the argument based on population estimates derived from an analysis of burials in Greenland: N. Lynnerup, "Palaeodemography of the Greenland Norse," *Arctic Anthropology* 33, no. 2 (1996): 122–136.

[23] See Debra Kunin, trans., and Carl Phelpstead, ed., *A History of Norway and the Passion and Miracles of the Blessed Óláfr* (London: Viking Society for Northern Research, University College London, 2001), 78–79, for translation as "wretches." The terms *Skrælingar, krælingar,* and *skrælings* are all used in various sources. For references related to Greenland, see Robert McGhee, "Contact between Native North Americans and The Medieval Norse: A Review of Evidence," *American Antiquity* 49, no. 1 (1984): 4–26.

[24] The saga is available at *http://www.sagadb.org/eiriks_saga_rauda.en.*

[25] In 1892, Fiske summarized much of the evidence from the Norse sagas and felt convinced that the Norse had traveled to the eastern seaboard, although he believed that Vinland lay farther south in Massachusetts, between Cape Cod and Cape Ann. A more recent review is provided by Sigurðsson, who takes into account the archaeological evidence: Gísli Sigurðsson, "The Quest for Vinland in Saga Scholarship," in *Vikings: The North Atlantic Saga*, ed. W. R. Fitzgerald and E. I. Ward (Washington, DC: Smithsonian Institution Press, 2000), 232–237;

and idem, "An Introduction to the Vinland Sagas," in *Vikings: The North Atlantic Saga*, ed. W. R. Fitzgerald and E. I. Ward (Washington, DC: Smithsonian Institution Press, 2000), 218–224.

[26] The association between places in the sagas and modern geography is in several texts, such as Schledermann, "A.D. 1000," and Diamond, *Collapse*.

[27] Birgitta Linderoth Wallace, "An Archaeologist's Interpretation of the Vinland Sagas," in *Vikings: The North Atlantic Saga*, ed. W. R. Fitzgerald and E. I. Ward (Washington, DC: Smithsonian Institution Press, 2000), 225–231.

[28] The earliest reference to Vinland is in 1075 by a Hamburg bishop referring to the Danish king's knowledge of islands with grapes being discovered (Sigurðsson, "The Quest for Vinland").

[29] There is not much archaeological evidence for Norse settlement south of Newfoundland other than the walnuts at L'Anse aux Meadows; the only contemporary artifact is the Norwegian coin. However, the evidence from sagas is convincing regarding an exploration zone to the south (Sigurðsson, "An Introduction to the Vinland Sagas"; Birgitta Linderoth Wallace, "The Viking Settlement at L'Anse Aux Meadows," in *Vikings: The North Atlantic Saga*, ed. W. R. Fitzgerald and E. I. Ward (Washington, DC: Smithsonian Institution Press, 2000), 208–216. Some feel that the settlement of Hóp could be located as far south as New York (Sigurðsson, "The Quest for Vinland," 237).

[30] Wallace, "An Archaeologist's Interpretation," describes the discovery of the site.

[31] The diverse communities of the Atlantic coast are described in Daniel Odess, Stephen Loring, and William W. Fitzhugh, "*Skraeling*: First People of Helliland, Markland, and Vinland," in *Vikings: The North Atlantic Saga*, ed. W. W. Fitzhugh and E. I. Ward (Washington, DC: Smithsonian Institution Press, 2000), 193–205.

[32] South of the Gulf of St. Lawrence were Algonquian-speaking people. Odess et al., *Skraeling*, also refer to ancestors of the Maliseet and Abenaki as being potentially present on the coast.

[33] The island had been used in more ancient times by Dorset people, and well after the Viking settlement by Native Americans (Wallace, "An Archaeologist's Interpretation").

[34] Wallace, "An Archaeologist's Interpretation."

[35] Wallace, "An Archaeologist's Interpretation," 230.

[36] Patricia Sutherland, "The Norse and Native Americans," in *Vikings: The North Atlantic Saga*, ed. W. R. Fitzgerald and E. I. Ward (Washington, DC: Smithsonian Institution Press, 2000), 239.

[37] Sutherland, "The Norse and Native Americans," 240, describes the voyage of 1347.

[38] The Norse coin is described in Stephen Cox, "A Norse Penny from Maine," in *Vikings: The North Atlantic Saga*, ed. W. R. Fitzgerald and E. I. Ward (Washington, DC: Smithsonian Institution Press, 2000), 206–207. The traded items in the Goddard site included Ramah chert from Labrador which was popularly traded by coastal groups north of Newfoundland. A stone artifact was a Dorset-like burin, again typical of areas north of Newfoundland. The Norse coin has been described as perforated, presumably to allow for its ornamental use, and was minted between 1066 and 1080 (McGhee, "Contact"; Roesdahl, *The Vikings,* 275). However, others do not think it was perforated and that it should be considered as a potential prank planted in the site: see Edmund Carpenter, *Norse Penny* (New York: The Rock Foundation, 2003).

[39] Sutherland, "The Norse and Native Americans," 241; idem, "Strands of Culture Contact: Dorset-Norse Interactions in the Canadian Eastern Arctic," in *Identities and Cultural Contacts in the Arctic: Proceedings from a Conference at the Danish National Museum, Copenhagen November 30 to December 2, 1999*, ed. M. Appelt, J. Berglund, and H. C. Gulløv (Copenhagen: The Danish National Museum and Danish Polar Center, 2000), 159–169.

[40] Sutherland, "The Norse and Native Americans."

[41] P. W. Rogers, "The Raw Materials of Textiles from GUS—With a Note on Fragments of Fleece and Animal Pelts from the Same Site," in *Man, Culture and Environment in Ancient Greenland: Report on a Research Programme*, ed. J. Arneborg and H. C. Gulløv (Copenhagen: The Danish National Museum and The Danish Polar Center, 1998), 66–73; and K. Secher, "Stone Finds from the Hall (XVII) and Their Functions—Geological Commentary," ibid., 45–47, cited in Arneborg, "Norse Greenland." At the site of the Farm Beneath the Sands, the animal remains included northern species, such as musk ox, as well as wolf, caribou, Arctic hare, and fox. The brown and black bear fibers could have originated from either Scandinavia or North America. Bison fibers could only have originated from North America (Rogers, "The Raw Materials.")

[42] McGovern, "The Arctic Frontier."

[43] McGovern, "The Arctic Frontier," 290.

[44] McGovern, "The Arctic Frontier," 295.

[45] Sutherland, "The Norse and Native Americans,"247.

[46] *Historia Norvegiae: A History of Norway and the Passion and Miracles of the Blessed Óláfr*, trans. D. Kunin, ed. C. Phelpshead (London: Viking Society for Northern Research, University College London, 2001). For other potential references to Dorset and Greenland, see McGhee, "Contact.".

[47] McGhee, "Contact."

[48] Schledermann describes these finds in detail: see Schledermann, "A.D. 1000."

[49] These include a Dorset soapstone-style lamp found in the L'Anse aux Meadows smithy (Odess, *Vikings: The North Atlantic Saga,* 197), suggesting either contact or Norse scavenging of Dorset sites on Baffin Island or Labrador while voyaging to Vinland.

[50] The figure known as the Baffin Island Bishop seems to show a person wearing a long gown, possibly decorated, and a cross. One proposal that this is a knight is based on the fact that Teutonic knights were active with the Hanseatic League, with a base in Bergen after 1344 (Sutherland, "The Norse and Native Americans," 245).

[51] See Hans Christian Gulløv, "The Eskimo's View of the European: The So-Called Norse Dolls and Other Questionable Carvings," *Arctic Anthropology* 20, no. 2 (1982): 121–129.

[52] Svend E. Albrethsen and Jette Arneborg, *Norse Ruins of the Southern Paamiut and Ivittuut Region* (Copenhagen: SILA—The Greenland Research Centre at the Danish National Museum: Danish Polar Center, 2004), 66–67, 86–87. Their description of the Middle Settlement, which is considered part of the Eastern Settlement, describes how early observers at the site of Tissaluk, for example, observed that "Eskimos" (Inuit) had settled in Norse buildings and modified their organization. The timing of this use is not stated. In other locations, Inuit settlements lay in and around abandoned Norse features, such as small huts and animals pens. In some cases, it is not clear whether simple stone features were Norse or Inuit. The 1712 expedition is detailed in Roesdahl, *The Vikings,* 276. Gulløv's study of Thule culture provides some insight into the complexity of Thule populations, invoking the "parallel traditions" of Thule, which extend into the Norse and then later historical periods, with particular relevance to southwest Greenland, where the different qualities of Thule groups who moved down the west and east coasts of the country are evident: Hans Christian Gulløv, *From Middle Ages to Colonial Times: Archaeological and Ethnohistorical Studies of the Thule Culture in South West Greenland 1300–1800 A.D.* (Copenhagen: The Commission for Scientific Research in Greenland, 1997).

[53] For a review of metal in Greenland from meteors and Norse sources, see Vagn Fabritius Buchwald and Gert Mosdal, *Meteoritic Iron, Telluric Iron and Wrought Iron in Greenland* (Copenhagen: Museum Tusculanum Press, 1985).

[54] In 1497, the Venetian captain John Cabot arrived on the Newfoundland coast, while in 1499 grants to Azorean captains from the Portuguese king suggest voyages of exploration: Bruce G. Trigger, *Natives and Newcomers: Canada's "Heroic Age" Reconsidered* (Kingston: McGill-Queen's University Press, 1985), 122. Robert McGhee ("Contact") reviews the evidence for contact between Europeans and Inuit in the fifteenth century, and finds none supported in any convincing way. It does appear that there was some knowledge in fifteenth-century Europe regarding America landfalls prior to the voyages of Cabot and later voyages, perhaps accumulated from the experiences of fishing voyages from Iceland: D. Quinn, ed., *New American World: A Documentary History of North America to 1612* (New York: Arno Press, 1979). The occasional accidental or deliberate voyage west beyond Greenland does seem probable, although there is no strong evidence to support this.

[55] For descriptions of later periods, see Møbjerg, "The Saqqaq Culture," 98–118; and William W. Fitzhugh, ed., *Cultures in Contact: The Impact of European Contacts on Native American Cultural Institutions A.D. 1000–1800* (Washington, DC: Smithsonian Institution Press, 1985).

[56] Buchwald and Mosdal, *Meteoritic Iron*, 43.

[57] Hans Christian Gulløv (National Museum of Denmark) advises me that the quotation is from the so-called "Pook-book" published by the Greenland printer Lars Møller in 1857 in Nuuk after the oral tradition taken down from local Greenlanders, who had retold the experiences of Pooq's 1724–25 Denmark visit through generations. The original title is:

> Pok. Kalalek avalangnek, nunalikame nunakatiminut okaluktuartok.
> Angakordlo palasimik napitsivdlune agssortuissok.
> Agdlagkat pisorkat navssarissat nongmiut ilanit.
> Akêt missigssuissut avguasavait uvigdlarnernut kainakut pisut kinguainut.
> (Nongme [Gothaab, Greenland]: R. Bertelsen and L. Möller, Peles Sön, i Inspecteurens Bogtrykkeri, 1857).

[58] The smallpox epidemic of 1733 is described in Hans Christian Gulløv, "Whales, Whalers, and Eskimos: The Impact of European Whaling on the Demography and Economy of Eskimo Society in West Greenland," in *Culture in Contact: The European Impact on Native Cultural Institutions in Eastern North America, A.D. 1000–1800*, ed. W. W. Fitzhugh (Washington, DC: Smithsonian Institution Press, 1985), 91.

[59] James M. Woollet, "Living in the Narrows: Subsistence Economy and Culture Change in Labrador Inuit Society during the Contact Period," *World Archaeology* 30, no. 3 (1999): 370–387; and Susan A. Kaplan, "European Goods and Socio-Economic Change in Early Labrador Inuit Society," in *Culture in Contact: The European Impact on Native Cultural Institutions in Eastern North America, A.D. 1000–1800*, ed. W. W. Fitzhugh. (Washington, DC: Smithsonian Institution Press, 1985), 45–69.

[60] Described in Hans Christian Gulløv, "Aasiviit as Focal Places in Historical Greenland," in *Dynamics of Northern Societies: Proceedings of the SILA/NABO Conference on Arctic and North Atlantic Archaeology, Copenhagen, May 10th–14th, 2004*, ed. J. Arneborg and B. Grønnow (Copenhagen: Publications from the National Museum Studies in Archaeology and History, 2006), 209–214.

[61] Einar Lund Jensen, "Uiarnerit—Migrations from Southeast to Southwest Greenland in the 19th Century," in *Dynamics of Northern Societies: Proceedings of the SILA/NABO Conference on*

Arctic and North Atlantic Archaeology, Copenhagen, May 10th–14th, 2004, ed. J. Arneborg and B. Grønnow (Copenhagen: Publications from the National Museum Studies in Archaeology and History, 2006), 225–234.

[62] Bjarne Grønnow, M. Meldgaard, and J. B. Nielsen, *The Great Summer Camp. Archaeological, Ethnographical and Zoo-Archaeological Studies of a Caribou-Hunting Site in West Greenland* (Copenhagen: National Museum of Denmark, 1983).

CHAPTER 4

[1] In French: "Chacun appelle barbarie ce qui n'est pas de son usage." Montaigne, *Essais*, I, 31.

[2] Usamah Ibn Munqidh was a twelfth-century Muslim warrior who fought with Saladin, who met Europeans in Palestine. Available at the Medieval Sourcebook, online at *http://www.fordham.edu/halsall/source/usamah2.html*.

[3] The Kingdom of Cyprus was founded during Crusader actions, as were polities in parts of the Balkans and the Baltic.

[4] That said, when we consider a single region such as Denmark, even these seemingly sensible developments did not necessarily find popular success. The earliest bridge in Scandinavia built at Ravning Enge by Harald Bluetooth was never cared for and fell into disrepair—so, a minor Danish bridge-boom around 1000 was not to be repeated for a century. Jan Bill and Else Roesdahl, "Travel and Transport," in *The Archaeology of Medieval Europe*, ed. J. Graham-Campbell and M. Valor (Aarhus: Aarhus University Press, 2007), 261–315.

[5] Else Roesdahl and Barbara Scholkmann, "Housing Culture," in *The Archaeology of Medieval Europe*, ed. J. Graham-Campbell and M. Valor (Aarhus: Aarhus University Press, 2007), 154–180.

[6] "Geoffrey de Vinsauf's Itinerary of Richard I and Others, to the Holy Land," translated in H. G. Bohn's (1848) *Chronicle's of the Crusades*. Cited in Margaret King, ed., *Western Civilisation: A Social and Cultural History* (Upper Saddle River, NJ: Prentice Hall, 2003), 315.

[7] There are various positions on the origins and uses of spices. One debate concerns whether spices were required primarily to preserve meat (see Wolf, *Europe and People without History*, 236) or not. Paul Freedman (*Out of the East: Spices and the Medieval Imagination* (New Haven: Yale University Press, 2008), 6, rejects this as being like using expensive truffles on a cheeseburger. Another debate is whether the use of spices in Europe reflects the influences of Asian and Muslim cooking (Wolf, *Europe and People without History*, 236) or is not so much "Asian" but a shared tradition of spicy food occurring in both Europe and Asia, dating to the Romans at least. In the latter case, the question is why Europeans *stop* using so many spices.

[8] Cited in Freedman, *Out of the East*, 23. This is a very readable historical review of the spice trade and the medieval world.

[9] Francesco Balducci Pegolotti, *La pratica della mercatura*, ed. A. Evans (Cambridge, MA: Mediaeval Academy of America, 1936).

[10] See Freedman, *Out of the East*, 64. The doctors of the French royal family recommended that they carry lumps of ambergris with them at all times. Others were protected by burning incense, including "aloe wood, . . . myrrh, frankincense, storax, dried rose petals, and sandalwood."

[11] This discussion draws from Freedman, *Out of the East*, chap. 3.

[12] Freedman, *Out of the East*, 99.

[13] See Apian's map (Apian, Petrus 1550, *Cosmographie*) replicated in Rachel Doggett, Monique Hulvey, and Julie Ainsworth, eds. *New World of Wonders: European Images of the Americas 1492–1700* (Seattle: University of Washington Press, 1992), 45.

[14] For Cook's encounters with cannibalism among Maoris, see Anne Salmond, *The Trial of the Cannibal Dog: Captain Cook in the South Seas* (Auckland: Penguin, 2004).

[15] Freedman, *Out of the East,* 102.

[16] Freedman, *Out of the East,* 129.

[17] Janet Abu-Lughod, *Before European Hegemony: The World System A.D. 1250–1350* (Oxford University Press, 1989), 137–149.

[18] Bill and Roesdahl, "Travel and Transport."

[19] Abu-Lughod, *Before European Hegemony,* 275–276.

[20] Lech Leciejewicz and Magdalena Valor, "Peoples and Environments," in *The Archaeology of Medieval Europe,* ed. J. Graham-Campbell and M. Valor (Aarhus: Aarhus University Press, 2007), 46–75.

[21] See brief review by Johnny de Meulemeester, "Islamic Archaeology in the Iberian Peninsula and Morocco," *Antiquity* 79, no. 306 (2005): 837–843.

[22] Hugh Kennedy, *Crusader Castles* (Cambridge: Cambridge University Press, 1994), 19. One example is the castle of Uxo near Valencia.

[23] Thomas Glick, *From Muslim Fortress to Christian Castle: Social and Cultural Change in Medieval Spain* (Manchester/New York: Manchester University Press, 1995). This study provides a comprehensive analysis across Muslim and Christian eras and contexts, as well as across various parts of medieval society and the landscape of al-Andalus.

[24] Leciejewicz and Valor, "Peoples and Environments," 66.

[25] Leszek Slupecki and Magdalena Valor, "Religions," in *The Archaeology of Medieval Europe,* ed. J. Graham-Campbell and M. Valor (Aarhus: AarhusUniversity Press, 2007), 366–397.

[26] This discussion of food is drawn from Sabine Karg and Pilar Lafuente, "Food," in *The Archaeology of Medieval Europe,* ed. J. Graham-Campbell and M. Valor (Aarhus: Aarhus University Press, 2007), 181–207; and from the discussion of a Muslim house in Roesdahl and Scholkmann, "Housing Culture."

[27] C. N. Johns and Denys Pringle, *Pilgrims' Castle ('Atlit), David's Tower (Jerusalem), and Qal'a tar-Rabad ('Ajlun): Three Middle Eastern Castles from the Time of the Crusades* (Aldershot: Ashgate, 1997), 288. See also Hugh Kennedy, *The Prophet and the Age of the Caliphates: The Islamic Near East from the Sixth to the Eleventh Century* (London: Longman, 1986).

[28] Johns and Pringle, *Pilgrims' Castle,* 290.

[29] Usamah Ibn Munqidh, cited above (chapter 4, n. 2).

[30] Kennedy, *Crusader Castles,* Prologue.

[31] See Kennedy, *Crusader Castles,* for a thorough overview of studies of Crusader-era fortifications in the eastern Mediterranean. Key castles in the Palestine were surveyed by C. N. Johns prior to the Second World War, making his a useful text.

[32] For example, see the study of Red Tower in Caesarea described by Pringle, cited in Kennedy, *Crusader Castles.*

[33] See Kennedy, *Crusader Castles,* 19–20, who cites Muslim defenses at Cafarlet, north of Caesarea, a fort south of Ashdod that may be a Fatimid fortification, and the defenses of Cairo, built in the immediate pre-Crusader period.

[34] Kennedy, *Crusader Castles,* 9.

[35] Acre, Castle Chepstow, York, Carisbrooke, Hen Domen: Kennedy, *Crusader Castles,* 12.

[36] Johns and Pringle, *Pilgrims' Castle,* 291.

[37] See Kennedy, *Crusader Castles,* 17–18. The discussion of Armenian forts cites Anavarza on the Cilician Plain.

[38] Kennedy, *Crusader Castles,* 43–45

[39] Kennedy, *Crusader Castles,* chap. 8.

[40] Johns and Pringle, *Pilgrims' Castle,* 293.

[41] Adrian Boas, *Archaeology of the Military Orders: A Survey of the Urban Centres, Rural Settlement and Castles of the Military Orders in the Latin East (c. 1120–1291)* (London: Routledge, 2006), has a comprehensive reference list on the topic. Military orders were also active in Italy, France, and the Iberian Peninsula.

[42] See Herbert S. Klein, *The Atlantic Slave Trade* (Cambridge: Cambridge University Press, 1999), chap. 1, "Slavery in Western Development."

[43] This discussion is based on Philip D. Curtin, *The Rise and Fall of the Plantation Complex* (Cambridge: Cambridge University Press, 1999).

[44] Boas, *Archaeology of the Military Orders,* "Sugar-Cane Cultivation and the Sugar Industry".

[45] M.-L. von Wartburg, "Production du sucre de canne a Chypre: Un chapitre de technologie medievale," in *Coliniser au Moyen Age,* ed. M. Balard and A. Ducellier (Paris: A. Colin, 1995), 126–131.

[46] Marina Solomidou-Ieronymidou, "The Crusaders, Sugar Mills and Sugar Production in Medieval Cyprus," in *Archaeology and the Crusades,* ed. P. Edbury and S. Kalopissi-Verti (Athens: Pierides Foundation, 2007), 63–81, details how sugarcane, originally from East Asia, arrives in Cyprus around the tenth century and increases in production at the end of the twelfth century.

[47] For a review of what he terms the "plantation complex," see Curtin, *The Rise and Fall.* In addition to sugar, Asian tropical crops introduced into the Mediterranean basin after the rise of Islam included rice, taro, coconuts, sorrel, certain citrus fruits, plantains, bananas, and mangoes. In fact, the arc of the commercial production of this tropical crops tracks back to the Levant, where the disruption of the Crusades saw these industries move into the Mediterranean, then into the Atlantic, and then into the Americas. By the twentieth century, plantations were found as far spread as Hawaii, Fiji, Queensland, Peru, Zanzibar, and Natal.

[48] A. W. Crosby, *Ecological Imperialism: The Biological Expansion of Europe, 900–1900* (Cambridge: Cambridge University Press, 1986), chap. 4, "The Fortunate Isles," details the admittedly small amount of attention to the history of the indigenous Guanches.

[49] Crosby, *Ecological Imperialism,* 84.

[50] Crosby, *Ecological Imperialism,* 75.

[51] Crosby, *Ecological Imperialism,* 78–79.

[52] Crosby, *Ecological Imperialism,* 79.

CHAPTER 5

[1] Basil Davidson, *Old Africa Rediscovered* (London: Victor Gollancz, 1961), 164.

[2] I follow Paul Lane's themes in "Whither Historical Archaeology in Africa?" *Review of Archaeology* 28, no. 2 (2007): 1–24; the dominant themes of past research are (1) in West Africa and the Atlantic slave trade, (2) in southern Africa, culture contacts and European colonization, and (3) in coastal East Africa, the Indian Ocean trade from early Swahili origins through European colonization.

[3] Timothy Insoll, *The Archaeology of Islam in Sub-Saharan Africa* (Cambridge: Cambridge University Press, 2003), 397. This book provides a thorough overview of the topic. For architecture on the east coast, see P. S. Garlake, *The Early Islamic Architecture of the East African*

Coast (Nairobi/London: Oxford University Press, 1966). For Northern African archaeology, see also papers in James Boone and Nancy Benco, "Islamic Settlement in North Africa and the Iberian Peninsula," *Annual Review of Anthropology* 28 (1999): 51–71; and Johnny de Meulemeester, "Islamic Archaeology in the Iberian Peninsula and Morocco," *Antiquity* 79, no. 306 (2005): 837–843. For slavery, see J. Alexander, "Islam, Archaeology and Slavery in Africa," *World Archaeology* 33, no. 1 (2001): 44–60.

[4] Insoll, *The Archaeology of Islam in Sub-Saharan Africa*, 374–376.

[5] East Asia was described as various places: Cathay, the East Indies, and India, among others.

[6] James Kirkman, *Fort Jesus, Mombasa* (Mombasa: Museum Trustees of Kenya, 1981). See also Christopher R. DeCorse, *An Archaeology of Elmina: Africans and Europeans on the Gold Coast, 1400–1900* (Washington, DC: Smithsonian Institution Press, 2001).

[7] Peter Mitchell, *The Archaeology of Southern Africa* (Cambridge: Cambridge University Press, 2002), 384, referring to sites of Vungu Vungu and Xaro.

[8] James Sweet, *Recreating Africa: Culture, Kinship, and Religion in the African-Portuguese World, 1441–1770* (Chapel Hill: University of North Carolina Press, 2003), 15.

[9] Allison Blakely, *Blacks in the Dutch World: The Evolution of Racial Imagery in a Modern Society* (Bloomington: Indiana University Press, 1993).

[10] See Wolf, *Europe and the People without History*, chap. 7: "The Slave Trade," for a detailed description of the situation in Africa. For an account of the origins of slaves, there are many sources; Philip D. Curtin's, *The Atlantic Slave Trade: A Census* (Madison: University of Wisconsin Press, 1969), was a significant study.

[11] See the introduction to Andrew M. Reid and Paul J. Lane, eds., *African Historical Archaeologies* (London: Kluwer Academic/Plenum, 2004), for an insightful review of the role of archaeology in studies of the last millennium in Africa.

[12] Alexander, "Islam, Archaeology and Slavery."

[13] There are many historical overviews of the Atlantic slave trade; for example, see Paul E. Lovejoy, *Transformations in Slavery: A History of Slavery in Africa* (Cambridge: Cambridge University Press, 2000) for an overview. The number of 11 million slaves is provided by Lovejoy. He states that a similar number were probably moved through Islamic slave trades over time. Other accounts suggest 12 million up to 18 million, taking into account high death rates during shipping; see Robin Law, *The Impact of the Atlantic Slave Trade upon Africa* (Lit. Verlag: Vienna, 2008).

[14] See Ann Stahl, "The Slave Trade as Practice and Memory," in *Invisible Citizens: Captives and Their Consequences*, ed. C. M. Cameron (Salt Lake City: University of Utah Press, 2008), 25–56, for an excellent review of these issues. Also see the UNESCO Slave Route Project at *UNESCO.org*.

[15] See *http://www.slavevoyages.org/* for the names of voyages, slaves, and a quantitative assessment of slave transportation to the Americas.

[16] Law, *The Impact of the Atlantic Slave Trade*, 20.

[17] For discussions of Elmina and West Africa, see publications in the References by Christopher DeCorse (1996, 1998, 2001, 2005), and for Hueda and Dahomey in Benin, see Kenneth Kelly (1997, 2002, 2008).

[18] For Banda, see publications by Ann Stahl (1993, 1994, 1999, 2001, 2004).

[19] Stahl, "The Slave Trade as Practice and Memory: What are the Issues for Archaeologists?" in *Invisible Citizens: Captives and Their Consequences*, ed. C. M. Cameron (Salt Lake City: University of Utah Press, 2008), 42.

[20] Merrick Posnansky, "Toward an Archaeology of the Black Diaspora," *Journal of Black Studies* 15, no. 2 (1984): 195–205; and Posnansky and Christopher R. DeCorse, "Historical Archaeology in Sub-Saharan Africa: A Review," *Journal of Historical Archaeology* 20, no. 1 (1986): 1–14.

[21] See summary in Kenneth Kelly, "Indigenous Responses to Colonial Encounters on the West African Coast: Hueda and Dahomey from the Seventeenth through Nineteenth Century," in *The Archaeology of Colonialism*, ed. C. L. Lyons and J. K. Papadopoulos (Los Angeles: Getty Research Institute, 2002), 96–120.

[22] Wolf, *Europe and the People without History*, 210

[23] Graham Connah, *The Archaeology of Benin: Excavations and Other Researches in and around Benin City, Nigeria* (Oxford: Clarendon Press, 1975).

[24] Wolf, *Europe and the People without History*, chap. 7.

[25] Kelly, "Indigenous Responses," 99.

[26] Stahl, "The Slave Trade as Practice and Memory," 35.

[27] See Anne Stahl, "Political Economic Mosaics: Archaeology of the Last Two Millennia in Tropical Sub-Saharan Africa," *Annual Review of Anthropology* 33, no. 1 (2004): 145–172, for a thorough continental review of the idea of changes in the various mosaics over time and space in African political, social, and economic spheres.

[28] Yaw Bredwa-Mensah, "Historical-Archaeological Investigations at the Fredericksgave Plantation, Ghana: A Case Study of Slavery and Plantation Life on a Nineteenth Century Danish Plantation on the Gold Coast," Ph.D. diss. (Legon/Accra: Department of Archaeology, University of Ghana, 2002), 112.

[29] For the archaeology of Fredericksgave, see Theodore W. Awadzi, Yaw Bredwa-Mensah, Henrik Breuning-Madsen, and Enoch Boateng, "A Scientific Evaluation of the Agricultural Experiments at Frederiksgave, The Royal Danish Plantation on the Gold Coast, Ghana," *Danish Journal of Geography* 101 (2001): 33–41; and Henrik Breuning-Madsen, Theodore W. Awadzi, Yaw Bredwa-Mensah, Henry R. Mount, and Berman D. Hudson. "The Danish Plantations on the Gold Coast of Ghana—Why Did They Fail," *Soil Survey Horizon* 43, no. 1 (2002): 1–8.

[30] Bredwa-Mensah, "Historical-Archaeological Investigations," 141.

[31] Bredwa-Mensah, "Historical-Archaeological Investigations," 206, 224.

[32] Bredwa-Mensah, "Historical-Archaeological Investigations," 162.

[33] Akin Ogundiran, "Of Small Things Remembered: Beads, Cowries, and Cultural Translations of the Atlantic Experience in Yorubaland," *International Journal of African Historical Studies* 35 (2002): 427–457; and idem, "Four Millennia of Cultural History in Nigeria (ca. 2000 B.C.–A.D. 1900): Archaeological Perspectives," *Journal of World Prehistory* 19, no. 2 (2005): 133–168.

[34] Martin Hall, "The Archaeology of Colonial Settlement in Southern Africa," *Annual Review of Anthropology* 22 (1993): 177–200.

[35] Citing Schrire, "Wild Surmises on Savage Thoughts," in *Past and Present in Hunter-Gatherer Studies*, ed. C. Schrire (Orlando: Academic Press, 1984), 67.

[36] See, for example, John E. Parkington, "Soaqua and Bushmen: Hunters and Robbers," in *Past and Present in Hunter Gatherer Studies*, ed. C. Schrire (Orlando: Academic Press, 1984), 151–174. The discussion of Sonqua and Khoikhoi draws on Andrew Smith, "Keeping People on the Periphery: The Ideology of Social Hierarchies between Hunters and Herders," *Journal of Anthropological Archaeology* 17, no. 2 (1998): 201–215. There is an argument that there is no difference between the two groups, that Sonqua are lowly members of one hierarchical society (see P. Mitchell, *The Archaeology of Southern Africa*, chap. 9.)

[37] This argument is put forward in P. Mitchell, *The Archaeology of Southern Africa*, with reference to J. Kinahan.

[38] Stacey Jordan and Carmel Schrire, "Material Culture and the Roots of Colonial Society at the South African Cape of Good Hope," in *The Archaeology of Colonialism*, ed. C. L. Lyons and J. K. Papadopoulos (Los Angeles: Getty Research Institute, 2002), 241–272.

[39] For the case study of Oudeposte, see Carmel Schrire (2005)

[40] Mitchell, *The Archaeology of Southern Africa*, chap. 13.

[41] See introduction to Thomas A. Dowson and J. David Lewis-Williams, *Contested Images: Diversity in Southern African Rock Art Research* (Johannesburg: Witwatersrand University Press, 1994), where they state *most* painted art is probably 800 years old or younger, and thus closer to the ethnographic present.

[42] Citing Dowson and Lewis-Williams, *Contested Images*, 332–333.

[43] Citing Sven Ouzman, "Indigenous Images of a Colonial Exotic: Imaginings from Bushman Southern Africa," *Before Farming* 1, no. 6 (2003): 12.

[44] While outside this discussion, the work of Jill Kinahan is particularly useful; see *Cattle for Beads: The Archaeology of Historical Contact and Trade on the Namib Coast, Studies in African Archaeology* (Windhoek/Uppsala: Namibia Archaeological Trust and the Department of Archaeology and Ancient History, University of Uppsala, Sweden, 2000).

[45] The archaeological study of East African sites is summarized in Insoll's *The Archaeology of Islam in Sub-Saharan Africa,* on which this discussion draws heavily. For Kilwa, see Jeff Fleisher, "Beyond the Sultan of Kilwa's 'Rebellious Conduct': Local Perspectives on an International East African Town," in *African Historical Archaeologies*, ed. A. M. Reid and P. J. Lane (New York: Kluwer Academic/Plenum Publishers, 2004). For excavations of Shanga (Lamu archipelago), see Mark Horton, Helen W. Brown, and Nina Mudida, *Shanga: The Archaeology of a Muslim Trading Community on the Coast of East Africa* (London: British Institute in Eastern Africa, 1996). For Zanzibar, see Mark Horton and C. Clark, "Archaeological Survey of Zanzibar," *Azania* 20 (1985): 115–123. See also Mark Horton and J. Middleton, *The Swahili* (Oxford: Blackwell, 2000).

[46] For a survey of Swahili sites in the period up to contact, see Adria LaViolette, "Swahili Cosmopolitanism in Africa and the Indian Ocean World, A.D. 600–1500," *Archaeologies: Journal of the World Archaeological Congress* 4, no. 1 (2008): 24–49.

[47] Reid and Lane, *African Historical Archaeologies.*

CHAPTER 6

[1] Cited in Ronald Wright, *Stolen Continents: The "New World" through Indian Eyes* (New York: Houghton Mifflin, 1992), 165–166.

[2] Kathleen A. Deagan, "Transculturation and Spanish American Ethnogenesis: The Archaeological Legacy of the Quincentenary," in *Studies in Culture Contact: Interaction, Culture Change, and Archaeology*, ed. J. G. Cusick (Carbondale: Southern Illinois University, 1998), 34.

[3] The other Iberian power was Portugal in Brazil, where studies of culture contact are detailed in Pedro Funari's "Archaeology, History, and Historical Archaeology in South America," *International Journal of Historical Archaeology* 1, no. 3 (1997):189–206.

[4] Columbus had been for years in communication with the Italian cartographer Paolo Toscanelli who "perceive[d his] magnificent and great desire to find way to where the spices

grow": Toscanelli, cited in Samuel Wilson, *Hispaniola: Caribbean Chiefdoms in the Age of Columbus* (Tuscaloosa: The University of Alabama Press, 1990), 37.

[5] Cited in Wilson, *Hispaniola*, 49.

[6] Resistance is a core theme in New World archaeology. A useful paper describes resistance and rebellion at Palmares in Brazil: Charles E. Orser and Pedro P. A. Funari "Archaeology and Slave Resistance and Rebellion," *World Archaeology* 33, no. 1 (2001): 61–72.

[7] Research at the colonial city of Cuenca, Ecuador, by Ross W. Jamieson, provides a nice example of how household refuse and architectural remains provide information about daily life, different elements in colonial society, and ideology: see "Colonialism, Social Archaeology and lo Andino: Historical Archaeology in the Andes," *World Archaeology* 37, no. 3 (2005): 352–372.

[8] Cited in Kathleen Deagan and José María Cruxent, *Archaeology at La Isabela: America's First European Town* (New Haven/London: Yale University Press, 2002), 47.

[9] La Isabela: Deagan and Cruxent, *Archaeology at La Isabela;* and in Kathleen Deagan and José María Cruxent, *Columbus's Outpost among the Tainos: Spain and America at La Isabela, 1493–1498* (New Haven/London: Yale University Press, 2002).

[10] Puerto Real: Samuel Wilson, "From Spaniard to Creole: The Archaeology of Cultural Formation at Puerto Real, Haiti," *American Anthropologist* 94, no. 3 (1992): 755–756; and Kathleen Deagan, *Puerto Real: The Archaeology of a Sixteenth-Century Spanish Town in Hispaniola* (Gainesville: University Press of Florida, 1995).

[11] Deagan and Cruxent, *Archaeology at La Isabela*, chaps. 1 and 11.

[12] Deagan and Cruxent, *Archaeology at La Isabela*, 285.

[13] Wright, *Stolen Continents*, 15.

[14] See papers in Charles R. Cobb, *Stone Tool Traditions in the Contact Era* (Tuscaloosa: University of Alabama Press, 2003).

[15] Cited in William R. Fowler et al., "Landscape Archaeology and Remote Sensing of a Spanish-Conquest Town: Ciudad Vieja, El Salvador," in *Remote Sensing in Archaeology*, ed. J. Wiseman and F. El-Baz (New York: Springer, 2007), 395–421.

[16] Clark Spencer Larsen, *The Archaeology of Mission Santa Catalina de Guale: 2. Biocultural Interpretations of a Population in Transition* (New York: American Museum of Natural History, 1990), 18.

[17] Cited Jerald T. Milanich, *Laboring in the Fields of the Lord: Spanish Missions and Southeastern Indians* (Gainesville: University Press of Florida, 2006), 103.

[18] For an overview of archaeological studies of missions, see Milanich, *Laboring in the Fields*. Other overviews of La Florida archaeology are detailed in Charles R. Ewen, "The Archaeology of La Florida," in *International Handbook of Historical Archaeology*, ed. T. Majewski and D. Gaimster (New York: Springer, 2009), 383–398.

[19] This figure is based on previous research cited in Kathleen Deagan, "Spanish-Indian Interaction in Sixteenth-Century Florida and Hispaniola," in *Cultures in Contact: The Impact of European Contacts on Native American Cultural Institutions A.D. 1000–1800*, ed. W. W. Fitzhugh (Washington, DC: Smithsonian Institution Press, 1985), 298–299.

[20] The American Museum of Natural History has published the research from St. Catherines Island for three decades, making it one of the most accessible studies of culture contact anywhere, let alone the Americas.

[21] Cited in Elliot H. Blair et al., *The Beads of St. Catherines Island. The Archaeology of Mission Santa Catalina de Guale* (New York: American Museum of Natural History, 2009), 87.

[22] Kathleen A. Deagan et al., *From Santa Elena to St. Augustine: Indigenous Ceramic Variability (A.D. 1400–1700): Proceedings of the Second Caldwell Conference, St. Catherines Island, Georgia, March 30–April 1, 2007* (New York: American Museum of Natural History, 2009), 209, describing the Altahama/San Marcos tradition.

[23] From Katherine Spielmann et al., "'...being weary, they had rebelled': Pueblo Subsistence and Labor under Spanish Colonialism," *Journal of Anthropological Archaeology* 28 (2009): 102–125.

[24] Barbara Voss states, "At El Presidio de San Francisco, the colonizers were themselves the very product of colonization": "From Casta to Californio: Social Identity and the Archaeology of Culture Contact," *American Anthropologist* 107, no. 3 (2005): 465.

CHAPTER 7

[1] J. Marquette, *The Mississippi Voyage of Jolliet and Marquette, 1673* (AJ-051, Wisconsin Historical Society, 1673).

[2] See Volume 4 of William C. Sturtevant, *The Handbook of North American Indians* (Washington: Smithsonian Institution, 2004) for a summary of landownership and treaties.

[3] Tribe, as defined by the U.S. government, means an Indian or Alaska Native Tribe, band, nation, pueblo, village, or community that the Secretary of the Interior acknowledges to exist as an Indian Tribe under the Federally Recognized Indian Tribe List Act of 1994, 25 U.S.C. 479a.

[4] From Wolf, *Europe and the People Without History*, 409. This chapter reviews the fur trade, as does Bruce Trigger, *Time and Traditions: Essays in Archaeological Interpretation* (Edinburgh: Edinburgh University Press, 1978).

[5] *The Middle Ground: Indians, Empires, and Republics in the Great Lakes Region, 1650–1815* (Cambridge/New York: Cambridge University Press, 1991).

[6] *The Invasion of America: Indians, Colonialism, and the Cant of Conquest* (New York: Norton, 1976).

[7] Silliman, "Social and Physical Landscapes of Contact," 273.

[8] Patricia Rubertone, "The Historical Archaeology of Native Americans," *Annual Review of Anthropology* 29 (2000): 425.

[9] Rubertone, "The Historical Archaeology of Native Americans," 426.

[10] Rubertone, "The Historical Archaeology of Native Americans," 434, citing work by Galloway. See P. K. Galloway, *Practicing Ethnohistory: Mining Archives, Hearing Testimony, Constructing Narrative* (Lincoln: University of Nebraska Press, 2006).

[11] George Irving Quimby and Alexander Spoehr, "Acculturation and Material Culture," *Fieldiana: Anthropology* 36, no. 6 (1951): 107–147.

[12] Janet Spector, *What This Awl Means: Feminist Archaeology at a Wahpeton Dakota Village* (St. Paul: Minnesota Historical Society Press, 1993), 9.

[13] The quote is from Janet Spector, "What This Awl Means: Towards a Feminist Archaeology" in *Engendering Archaeology: Women and Prehistory*, ed. Joan Gero and Meg Conkey (Oxford: Blackwell, 1991) 388–406; however, see Spector's book, *What This Awl Means*.

[14] Rubertone, "The Historical Archaeology of Native Americans," 436.

[15] Giles Milton, *Big Chief Elizabeth: How England's Adventurers Gambled and Won the New World* (London: Hodder and Stoughton, 2000), 64–65, cites Barlowe in observing an important stage in the development of the "noble savage" which would rise to great importance in the Enlightenment era.

[16] David Hurst Thomas, *Exploring Native North America* (Oxford/New York: Oxford University Press, 2000), chap. 16.

[17] Volume 12 of *International Journal of Historical Archaeology* (New York: Plenum Press, 2008) is about the French in the New World.

[18] A summary of efforts to locate these colonies can be found at *firstcolonyfoundation.org/archaeology.*

[19] For a recent edition of this work, see Thomas Harriot and Theodor de Bry, *A Briefe and True Report of the New Found Land of Virginia* (Charlottesville: Library at the Mariners' Museum and the University of Virginia Press, 2007). The various versions of White's and de Bry's images are available online at various sites for comparison.

[20] "Jamestown Rediscovery Archaeology Project" is a project by Preservation Virginia, described at *www.preservationvirginia.org.*

[21] Stuart B. Schwartz, *Implicit Understandings: Observing, Reporting, and Reflecting on the Encounters between Europeans and Other Peoples in the Early Modern Era* (Cambridge: Cambridge University Press, 1994), 495.

[22] This discussion draws on Paul Robinson et al.'s chapter in William W. Fitzhugh, ed., *Cultures in Contact: The Impact of European Contacts on Native American Cultural Institutions A.D. 1000–1800* (Washington, DC: Smithsonian Institution Press, 1985). For a discussion of sources related to New England, see work by Rubertone, "The Historical Archaeology of Native Americans," and John Menta, *The Quinnipiac: Cultural Conflict in Southern New England* (New Haven: Yale Peabody Museum, 2003).

[23] Reference in Laurier Turgeon, "Beads, Bodies and Regimes of Value: From France to North America, c. 1500–c. 1650," in T. Murray, ed., *The Archaeology of Contact in Settler Societies* (Cambridge: Cambridge University Press, 2004), 19–47.

[24] These questions are raised in a review by Silliman, "Change and Continuity, Practice and Memory: Native American Persistence in Colonial New England," *American Antiquity* 74, no. 2 (2009): 211–230.

[25] Several useful overviews are found in Volume 4 of Sturtevant, ed., *The Handbook of North American Indians*: William Eccles, "The Fur Trade in the Colonial Northeast"; Arthur J. Ray, "The Hudson's Bay Company and Native People"; and James R. Gibson, "The Maritime Trade of the North Pacific Coast."

[26] See Scott Hamilton and B. A. Nicholson, "The Middleman Fur Trade and Slot Knives: Selective Integration of European Technology at the Mortlach Twin Fawns Site (DiMe-23)," *Canadian Journal of Archaeology* 31, no. 3 (2007):137–162; and Heinz W. Pyszczyk, "The Use of Fur Trade Goods by the Plains Indians, Central and Southern Alberta, Canada," *Canadian Journal of Archaeology* 21, no. 1 (1997): 45–84.

[27] His account is very similar to what Europeans would observe in Australia, where Aboriginal fire management burned the landscape regularly.

[28] Cited in David Thompson, *David Thompson's Narrative of his Explorations in Western America 1784–1812,* ed. J. B. Tyrrell (Toronto: Champlain Society, 1916). Available at *www.archive.org/stream/davidthompsonsna00thom.*

[29] See Volume 4 of Sturtevant, *Handbook of the North American Indians*: E. S. Lohse, "Trade Goods."

[30] Michael Nassaney, "Identity Formation at a French Colonial Outpost in the North American Interior," *International Journal of Historical Archaeology* 12, no. 4 (2008): 297–318; the

quote is from C. W. Hackett, *Pichardos' Treatise on the Limits of Louisiana and Texas,* Vol. 5 (Austin: University of Texas Press, 1934).

[31] Elsewhere in the Americas, horses transformed indigenous societies; for example, in the pampas of South America, horses would underlie the development of gauchos.

[32] This discussion of rock art draws on the publications listed at the end of the chapter by James Keyser, Michael Klassen, and Mark Mitchell.

[33] Michael Klassen, "Icon and Narrative in Transition: Contact-Period Rock-Art at Writing-On-Stone, Southern Alberta, Canada," in *The Archaeology of Rock-Art,* ed. Christopher Chippindale and Paul S. C. Taçon (Cambridge: Cambridge University Press, 1998), 64.

[34] A dominant theme in Indian–white relationships in North America is the battle scene. The most famous may be Little Bighorn, scene of the 1876 battle between Sioux led by Chief Sitting Bull, their Cheyenne allies, and General Custer. Archaeology has contributed to our understanding of this site.

The battle took place as a response to territorial losses by Native Americans in the face of the settlement of the American West, where conflicts had increasingly characterized cross-cultural encounters on this "frontier." These battles were also between various Indian cultures, as they vied for hunting grounds and regions safe from incursions; this included warfare between the Sioux (led by Sitting Bull) and neighboring cultures (such as the Crow). The Sioux and others were involved in a domino effect, as white settlement of Indian lands pushed groups westward and into conflicts. The gold rush of 1849 brought migrants and settlers to the hunting grounds. The army established forts to control these distant regions; government administrators attempted peace treaties against logical expectations.

The battle between the Indians and the U.S. cavalry was known about from the military burial parties in subsequent years, and from Indian accounts of the battle. The archaeological recording of the site reveals where the cavalry was held down, the scene of the last battles, and the fact that it was a short, intense battle ending in a rout as the cavalry positions were overrun. This record supports the oral histories of these battles.

[35] Rubertone, "The Historical Archaeology of Native Americans," 427.

CHAPTER 8

[1] Marco Polo, translation by Yule and edited by Cordier (1993). The reference to Java as a source of nutmeg and pepper must refer to its role as an intermediate port for these spices. This reference reveals the poor knowledge of the extent of Java, as most travelers would frequent the northern ports. Chamba refers to Indochina.

[2] Tomé Pires, *The Suma Oriental of Tomé Pires: An Account of the East, from the Red Sea to Japan, Written in Malacca and India in 1512–1515,* trans. Armando Cortesão (Nendeln: Kraus Reprint Limited, 1967), 116 [fol. 138].

[3] A useful edited volume on the terrestrial and silk roads from an archaeological perspective is V. Elisseeff, ed., *The Silk Roads: Highways of Culture and Commerce* (New York: Berghahn Books, 2000).

[4] See Miriam Stark for a review of the first millennium when these routes are developed: "Early Mainland Southeast Asian Landscapes in the First Millennium A.D.," *Annual Review of Anthropology* 35, no. 1 (2006): 407–432.

[5] General texts I have used on the arrival of Europeans in the Indian Ocean and the Orient are Wolf, *Europe and the People without History,* and Curtin, *Cross-Cultural Trade in World History.* The amount of archaeological work on culture contact is markedly less than in the Americas.

This may originate from the ways that Europeans were essentially contained, as well as the greater number of historical sources in European and Asian languages.

[6] Some of the elements of this discussion are drawn from Konrad Bekker, "Historical Patterns of Culture Contact in Southern Asia," *Far Eastern Quarterly* 11, no. 1 (1951): 3–15. His argument is that the first few centuries of contact with European trading powers, mainly through company men, "did not carry European culture or institutions to Southeast Asia, and it froze Southeast Asia's acquaintance with foreign civilizations at the level of the 16th century" (p. 13).

[7] Crosby, *Ecological Imperialism*, chap. 2.

[8] K. M. Mathew, *History of the Portuguese Navigation in India, 1497–1600* (Delhi: Mittal Publications, 1988); K. S. Mathew and J. Varkey, *Winds of Spices: Essays on Portuguese Establishments in Medieval India with Special Reference to Cannanore* (Tellicherry: Institute for Research in Social Sciences and Humanities, 2006).

[9] See, for example, Chao Ju-kua's *Chu Fan Chih* (An Account of the Various Barbarians), in F. Hirth and W. Rockhill, trans., *Chau Ju-kua* (St. Petersburg: Imperial Academy of Sciences, 1911).

[10] C. R. Boxer, *Fidalgos in the Far East 1550–1770: Fact and Fancy in the History of Macao* (The Hague: Martinus Nijhoff, 1948).

[11] C. P. Fitzgerald, *China: A Short Cultural History* (Sydney: The Cresset Library, 1986 [first published 1935]).

[12] There also exists a rich archaeological tradition of studies of later Chinese communities in America, Australia, and New Zealand.

[13] C. L. Crossman, *The China Trade: Export Paintings, Furniture, Silver and Other Objects* (Princeton: Pyne Press, 1972).

[14] Jane Allen, "Trade and Site Distribution in Early Historic-Period Kedah: Geoarchaeological, Historic, and Locational Evidence," *Bulletin of the Indo-Pacific Prehistory Association* 10 (1991): 307–319. For another study of an early Malay port, see Pierre-Yves Manguin, "Palembang and Sriwijaya: An Early Malay Harbour-City Rediscovered," *Journal of the Malaysian Branch of the Royal Asiatic Society* 66, no. 1 (1993): 23–46.

[15] G. W. Earl, *The Eastern Seas* (Oxford University Press, 1974 [1837]), 294. It is merely a myth, but one that appeared to sanction intermarriage. There is no account of what the Dyak thought of this account. Earl's narrative is an interesting description of life in the islands in the early nineteenth century. He spent a period in Australia, and his appendix includes an implausible account (yet possibly popularly received in some quarters of "optimistic colonialism") of an inland sea in northwestern Australia.

[16] Research by David Bulbeck and others in Sulawesi provides a rare archaeological regional study of the period of state formation and growing regional trade leading up to Islamic periods: see David Bulbeck, "Economy, Military and Ideology in Pre-Islamic Luwu, South Sulawesi, Indonesia," *Australasian Historical Archaeology* 18 (2000): 3–16; and David Bulbeck and Ian Caldwell, *Land of Iron: The Historical Archaeology of Luwu and the Cenrana Valley: Results of the Origin of Complex Society in South Sulawesi Project (OXIS)* (Hull: Centre for South-East Asian Studies, University of Hull, 2000).

[17] Cited in R. A. Skelton, *Explorer's Maps: Chapters in the Cartographic Record of Geographical Discovery* (London: Spring Books, 1958), 37.

[18] The study of Portuguese archaeological sites is not reviewed here, the main monuments being related to the church.

[19] Laura Lee Junker, "Integrating History and Archaeology in the Study of Contact Period Philippine Chiefdoms," *International Journal of Historical Archaeology* 2, no. 4 (1998): 291–320.

[20] Jean Gelman Taylor, "Meditations on a Portrait from Seventeenth-century Batavia." *Journal of Southeast Asian Studies* 23, no. 1 (2006): 23–31.

[21] Pires, *The Suma Oriental*, 206 [fols. 155–156].

[22] Peter Lape, "Political Dynamics and Religious Change in the late Pre-colonial Banda Islands, Eastern Indonesia," *World Archaeology* 32, no. 1 (2000), 149.

[23] Lape, "Political Dynamics and Religious Change," 149.

[24] Patrick V. Kirch and Jean-Louis Rallu, *The Growth and Collapse of Pacific Island Communities: Archaeological and Demographic Perspectives* (Honolulu: University of Hawai'i Press, 2007). Their book attempts to determine population trends in the Pacific leading up to and following contact.

[25] James Bayman, "Technological Change and the Archaeology of Emergent Colonialism in the Kingdom of Hawai'i," *International Journal of Historical Archaeology* 13 (2009): 127–157.

[26] Chris Gosden, "Transformations: History and Prehistory in Hawaii," *Archaeology in Oceania* 31 (1996): 171.

[27] Stuart Bedford, "Tenacity of the Traditional: The First Hundred Years of Maori-European Settler Contact on the Hauraki Plains, Aotearoa/New Zealand," in T. Murray, ed., *The Archaeology of Contact in Settler Societies* (Cambridge: Cambridge University Press, 2004), 144–154.

[28] See Paul Bahn, *Easter Island, Earth Island* (London: Thames and Hudson, 1992); J. A. Brandner and M. S. Taylor, "The Simple Economics of Easter Island: A Ricardo-Malthus Model of Renewable Resource Use, *American Economic Review* 88 (1998): 119.

CHAPTER 9

[1] From "Instructions for Skipper Commander Abel Jansz Tasman, Pilot-Major Franchoys Jacobsz Visscher, and the Council of the Ship Heemskerck and the Flute de Zeehaen, destined for the discovery and exploration of the unknown and known South-land, of the South-east coast of Nova Guinea, and of the islands circumjacent," in J. E. Heeres, ed., *Abel Janszoon Tasman's Journal of His Discovery of Van Diemens Land and New Zealand in 1642* (Los Angeles: Kovach, 1965).

[2] The colonization was largely by the British, but in the nineteenth century, other migrant populations were important members of the colonial society and came into contact with Aborigines, including the Chinese and other Asian pearl divers and camel handlers (largely from Afghanistan).

[3] This excerpt was used in the introduction to Rodney Harrison and Christine Williamson, eds., *After Captain Cook: The Archaeology of the Recent Indigenous Past in Australia* (Walnut Creek, CA: AltaMira Press, 2004).

[4] The rock art sites in the Wellington Ranges are recorded as part of the "Picturing Change" project (see Acknowledgments).

[5] Jim Allen's "Archaeology and the History of Port Essington" (Ph.D. diss., Australian National University, 1969), a doctoral study of the Port Essington British military settlement, is considered the first thesis in Australian historical archaeology.

[6] A useful review of the topic is found in Anne Clarke, "The 'Moormans Trowsers': Macassan and Aboriginal Interactions and the Changing Fabric of Indigenous Social Life," *Modern Quaternary Research in Southeast Asia* 16 (2000): 315–335. The earliest archaeological excavations of Macassan sites were reported by Charles Macknight in *The Voyage to Marege* (Melbourne: Melbourne University Press, 1976). For an analysis of the effect of new materials in Aboriginal exchange networks, see Scott Mitchell, "Dugongs and Dugouts, Sharp Tacks and Shellbacks: Macassan Contact and Aboriginal Marine Hunting on the Cobourg Peninsula,

Northwestern Arnhem Land," *Bulletin of the Indo-Pacific Prehistory Association* 15, no. 2 (1996): 181–191. For Groote Eylandt, see Anne Clarke, "The Ideal and the Real: Cultural and Personal Transformations of Archaeological Research on Groote Eylandt, Northern Australia," *World Archaeology* 34, no. 2 (2002): 249–264. For the Kimberley coast, see Mike Morwood and D. R. Hobbs, "The Asian Connection: Preliminary Report on Indonesian Trepang Sites on the Kimberley Coast, N.W. Australia," *Archaeology in Oceania* 32, no. 3 (1997): 197–206.

[7] In Matthew Flinders, *A Voyage to Terra Australis* (London: G. W. Nicol, 1814). Macknight, *The Voyage to Marege,* revised the earliest date to 1710. Direct dating of beeswax overlying an image of a boat at Djulirri suggests the image is older than 1664, as detailed in P. S. C. Taçon et al., "A Minimum Age for Early Depictions of Southeast Asian Praus in the Rock Art of Arnhem Land, Northern Territory," *Australian Archaeology* 71 (2010): 1–9. Macknight's excavations produced older radiocarbon dates, but the interpretation of these remains disputed, as detailed in Taçon et al.

[8] The Australian National Dictionary describes it as: balander, also balanda, ballanda. [a. Maccasarese balanda, a. Malay belanda (corruption of Hollander), a Dutchman, a white man.] Leichhardt's description is in Ludwig Leichhardt, *Journal of An Overland Expedition in Australia, from Moreton Bay to Port Essington* (London: T. & W. Boone, 1847).

[9] Anne Clarke and Ursula Frederick, "Closing the Distance: Interpreting Cross-Cultural Engagements through Indigenous Rock Art," in *The Archaeology of Oceania: Australia and the Pacific Islands*, ed. I. Lilley (Oxford: Blackwell, 2004), 116–133.

[10] The production of Kimberley points occurred in stone, glass, and ceramic. For a discussion of the colonial production of these objects, see Rodney Harrison, "An Artefact of Colonial Desire? Kimberley Points and the Technologies of Enchantment," *Current Anthropology* 47, no. 1 (2006): 63–88.

[11] A recent review explores seven Aboriginal groups across Australia as they were at contact, and also provides a useful introduction to key ethnographic sources for these regions: Ian Keen, "Aboriginal Economy and Society at the Threshold of Colonisation: A Comparative Study," *Before Farming* 3, no. 2 (2003): 1–24.

[12] There is some literature regarding the role of indigenous collaborations with archaeologists listed in the references. See, e.g., Ian McNiven and Lynette Russell, *Appropriated Pasts: Indigenous Peoples and the Colonial Culture of Archaeology* (Walnut Creek, CA: AltaMira Press, 2005) and Laurajane Smith et al., "Community-Driven Research in Cultural Heritage Management: The Waanyi Women's History Project," *International Journal of Heritage Studies* 9, no. 1 (2003): 65–80.

[13] This is the subject of recent research, distilled best in Susan Lawrence, ed., *Archaeologies of the British: Explorations of Identity in Great Britain and Its Colonies, 1600–1945* (London/New York: Routledge, 2003).

[14] In 1997, the National Inquiry into the Separation of Aboriginal and Torres Strait Islander Children from Their Families presented their report on the various policies that led to the forced separation of indigenous children from their families: Ronald Wilson, *Bringing Them Home: Report of the National Inquiry into the Separation of Aboriginal and Torres Strait Islander Children from Their Families* (Sydney: Human Rights and Equal Opportunity Commission, 1997).

[15] L. Sharp, "Steel Axes for Stone Age Australians," in *Human Problems in Technological Change: A Casebook*, ed. E. H. Spicer (New York: Russell Sage Foundation, 1952), 69–90.

[16] This evidence needs to be considered in relation to longer debates about the degree that contact with Macassans changed Aboriginal society. There has been an argument that the de-

gree of change was slight. Others have suggested more extensive change, such as in subsistence and the timing of seasonal activities, in part to allow access to Macassans at key times.

[17] These artifacts were recognized early by Henry Balfour, "On the Method Employed by the Natives of N. W. Australia in the Manufacture of Glass Spear Heads," *Man* 3 (1903): 65–66. See also defining terminology in Jim Allen and Rhys Jones, "Oyster Cove: Archaeological Traces of the Last Tasmanians and Notes on the Criteria for the Authentication of Flaked Glass Artefacts," *Papers and Proceedings of the Royal Society of Tasmania* 114 (1980): 225–233; and Rodney Harrison, "'Nowadays with Glass': Regional Variation in Aboriginal Bottle Glass Artefacts from Western Australia," *Archaeology in Oceania* 35, no. 1 (2000): 34–47.

[18] Material culture is described in Rodney Harrison, "Australia's Iron Age: Aboriginal Post-Contact Metal Artefacts from Old Lamboo Station, Southeast Kimberley, Western Australia," *Australasian Historical Archaeology* 20 (2002): 67–76.

[19] Philip Jones, *Ochre and Rust: Artefacts and Encounters on Australian Frontiers* (Kent Town: Wakefield Press, 2007). A significant influence comes from studies like that of Nicholas Thomas, *Entangled Objects: Exchange, Material Culture, and Colonialism in the Pacific* (Cambridge, MA: Harvard University Press, 1991).

[20] "Exploring the Prehistory of Hunter-Gatherer Attachment to Place: An Example from the Keep River Area, Northern Territory, Australia," in *The Archaeology and Anthropology of Landscape*, ed. P. Ucko and R. Layton (London: Routledge, 1999), 322–335; "Hunter-Gatherer Archaeology and Pastoral Contact: Perspectives from the Northwest Northern Territory, Australia," *World Archaeology* 28 (1997): 418–428.

[21] I came upon this quote first in Ursula Frederick's book chapter, "Keeping the Land Alive: Changing Social Contexts of Landscape and Rock Art Production," in *The Archaeology of Difference. Negotiating Cross-Cultural Engagements in Oceania,* ed. R. Torrence and A. Clarke (London: Routledge, 2000), 300–330. She is, in turn, citing it from work by the anthropologist Deborah Bird Rose, *Nourishing Terrains: Australian Aboriginal Views of Landscape and Wilderness* (Canberra: Australian Heritage Commission, 1996).

[22] See, for example, Rodney Harrison, *Shared Landscapes: Archaeologies of Attachment and the Pastoral Industry in New South Wales, Studies in the Cultural Construction of Open Space* (Sydney: UNSW Press, 2004).

[23] Tony English, *The Sea and the Rock Gives Us a Feed. Mapping and Managing Gumbaingirr Wild Resource Use Places* (Sydney: NSW National Parks and Wildlife Service, 2002).

[24] Isabel McBryde, who specialized in the archaeological evidence for indigenous exchange, discusses two examples of exchange, both precontact and postcontact. In central Australia, exchange networks moved a range of commodities over vast distances, while exchange also characterized early communication between Eora and British at Sydney Cove: Isabel McBryde, "Goods from Another Country: Exchange Networks and the People of the Lake Eyre Basin," in *Australians to 1788*, ed. D. J. Mulvaney and J. Peter White (Broadway: Fairfax Syme & Weldon Associates, 1987), 253–274.

[25] Jo McDonald, "Rock Art and Cross-Cultural Interaction in Sydney: How Did Both Sides Perceive the Other?" in *Strangers on the Shore: Early Coastal Contact in Australia*, ed. P. Veth, P. Sutton, and M. Neale (Canberra: National Museum of Australia, 2008), 46–89.

[26] Tench was a keen observer of the early settlement: Watkins Tench, *A Complete Account of the Settlement at Port Jackson* (Pall Mall: G. Nichol, 1793).

[27] Isabel McBryde, "... to establish a commerce of this sort": Cross Cultural Exchange at the Port Jackson Settlement," in *Studies from Terra Australis to Australia*, ed. J. Hardy and A. Frost

(Canberra: Australian Academy of the Humanities, 1989), 169–182; and idem, *Guests of the Governor—Aboriginal Residents of the First Government House* (Sydney: The Friends of the First Government House Site, 1989).

[28] Jones, *Ochre and Rust.*

[29] Native Police in Queensland being involved in the best-known incidents. For more on how Aboriginal people came to be "with the white people," see Henry Reynolds, *With the White People* (Ringwood: Penguin, 1990). Reynolds was one of a handful of historians who revised Australian history by focusing on culture contacts and Aboriginal history.

[30] Jane Lydon, "'Men in Black': The Blacktown Native Institution and the Origins of the 'Stolen Generation,'" in *Object Lessons: Archaeology and Heritage in Australia*, ed. J. Lydon and T. Ireland (Melbourne: Australian Scholarly Publishing, 2005), 201–224.

[31] Cited in chap. 8 of Jane Lydon, *Fantastic Dreaming: The Archaeology of an Australian Aboriginal Mission* (Lanham, MD: AltaMira, 2009).

[32] The work at the hut at Burleigh is described in Tim Murray, "The Childhood of William Lanne: Contact Archaeology and Aboriginality in Tasmania," *Antiquity* 67 (1993): 507–519; and in Christine Williamson, "Finding Meaning in the Patterns: The Analysis of Material Culture from a Contact Site in Tasmania," in *After Captain Cook: The Archaeology of the Recent Indigenous Past in Australia*, ed. R. Harrison and C. Williamson (Sydney: Sydney University Archaeological Methods Series, 2002), 76–101.

[33] For a description of this, see Judy Birmingham, *Wybalenna: The Archaeology of Cultural Accommodation in Nineteenth Century Tasmania* (Sydney: Australian Society for Historical Archaeology, 1992). The European records are detailed in George Augustus Robinson and N. J. B. Plomley, *Friendly Mission: The Tasmanian Journals and Papers of George Augustus Robinson, 1829–1834* (Launceston: Queen Victoria Museum and Art Gallery, 2008); and N. J. B. Plomley, *Weep in Silence: A History of the Flinders Island Aboriginal Settlement* (Netley: Blubber Head Press, 1987).

[34] The Lutherans went on to establish a mission named Hermannsburg in Central Australia where, in the mid-twentieth century, the famous painter Albert Namitjira worked.

[35] The discussion of Victorian missions is focused on the recent research by Jane Lydon.

[36] The term "hidden histories" comes from Deborah Bird Rose, *Hidden Histories: Black Stories from Victoria River Downs, Humbert River and Wave Hill Stations* (Canberra: Aboriginal Studies Press, 1991).

[37] The work at Strangways Springs is summarized in Alistair Paterson, *The Lost Legions: Culture Contact in Colonial Australia* (Lanham, MD: AltaMira Press, 2008).

[38] John Oastler, "The Honorary Magistrate," MS. in Mortlock Library of South Australiana, Adelaide (1908).

[39] Oastler, "The Honorary Magistrate."

[40] A. G. Paterson and A. Wilson, "Indigenous Perceptions of Contact at Inthanoona, Northwest Western Australia," *Archaeology in Oceania* 44 (2009): 98–110.

[41] Key texts related to this polarized debate are listed. Archaeology has made little contribution to these debates, as there is often little archaeological evidence of killing sites. The role of archaeology seems to be to investigate frontier violence, social avoidance, and differentials in cross-cultural engagements.

CHAPTER 10

[1] A. Wylie, "'Simple' Analogy and the Role of Relevance Assumptions: Implications of Archaeological Practice," *International Studies in the Philosophy of Science* 2 (1988): 134-150.

[2] M. T. Friesen, "Analogues at Iqaluktuuq: The Social Context of Archaeological Inference in Nunavut, Arctic Canada, *World Archaeology* 34, no. 2 (2002): 338, 339.

[3] Peter Lape, "A Highway and a Crossroads: Island Southeast Asia and Culture Contact Archaeology," *Archaeology in Oceania* 38 (2003): 103.

[4] Nicholas Thomas, *Entangled Objects: Exchange, Material Culture, and Colonialism in the Pacific* (Cambridge, MA: Harvard University Press, 1991); *Colonialism's Culture: Anthropology, Travel and Government* (Princeton: Princeton University Press, 1994).

REFERENCES

Abu-Lughod, J. L. *Before European Hegemony: The World System A.D. 1250–1350.* Oxford University Press, 1989.

Acheson, S., and J. P. Delgado. "Ships for the Taking: Culture Contact and the Maritime Fur Trade on the Northwest Coast of North America." In *The Archaeology of Contact in Settler Societies*, ed. T. Murray, 48–77. Cambridge: Cambridge University Press, 2004.

Albrethsen, S. E., and J. Arneborg. *Norse Ruins of the Southern Paamiut and Ivittuut Region.* Danish Polar Center Publication, 1398–0300. Copenhagen: SILA—The Greenland Research Centre at the Danish National Museum and Danish Polar Center, 2004.

Alexander, J. "Islam, Archaeology and Slavery in Africa." *World Archaeology* 33, no. 1 (2001): 44–60.

Alexander, R. T. *Yaxcabá and the Caste War of Yucatán: An Archaeological Perspective.* 1st ed. Albuquerque: University of New Mexico Press, 2004.

Allen, Jane. "Trade and Site Distribution in Early Historic-Period Kedah: Geoarchaeological, Historic, and Locational Evidence." *Bulletin of the Indo-Pacific Prehistory Association* 10 (1991): 307–319.

———. "History, Archaeology, and the Question of Foreign Control in Early Historic-Period Peninsular Malaysia." *International Journal of Historical Archaeology* 2, no. 4 (1998): 261–289.

Allen, Jim. "Archaeology and the History of Port Essington." Ph.D. diss., Australian National University, 1969.

———. *Port Essington: The Historical Archaeology of a North Australian Nineteenth Century Military Outpost.* Studies in Australasian Historical Archaeology, no. 1. Sydney: Sydney University Press in association with the Australasian Society for Historical Archaeology, 2008.

Allen, Jim, and R. Jones. "Oyster Cove: Archaeological Traces of the Last Tasmanians and Notes on the Criteria for the Authentication of Flaked Glass Artefacts." *Papers and Proceedings of the Royal Society of Tasmania* 114 (1980): 225–233.

Anderson, A., and G. O'Regan. "To the Final Shore: Prehistoric Colonisation of the Subantarctic Islands in South Polynesia." In *Australian Archaeologist: Collected Papers in Honour of Jim Allen*, ed. A. Anderson and T. Murray, 440–454. Canberra: Coombs Academic Publishing, Australian National University, 2000.

Andreasen, C. "NEWLand: Settlement Patterns, Social Organization and Economic Strategies at a High Artic Polynya." In *Man, Culture and Environment in Ancient Greenland: Report on a Research Program*, ed. J. Arneborg and H. C. Gulløv, 198–212. Copenhagen: Danish National Museum and Danish Polar Center, 1998.

Appelt, M., and H. C. Gulløv. 1999. *Late Dorset in High Arctic Greenland: Final Report on the Gateway to Greenland Project*. Copenhagen: Danish National Museum and Danish Polar Center.

———. "Tunit, Norsemen, and Inuit in Thirteenth-Century Northwest Greenland-Dorset between the Devil and the Deep Sea." In *The Northern World, AD 900–1400*, ed. H. Maschner, O. Mason, and R. McGhee. Salt Lake City: University of Utah Press, 2009.

Appelt, M., J. Berglund, and H. C. Gulløv. *Identities and Cultural Contacts in the Arctic: Proceedings from a Conference at The Danish National Museum, Copenhagen, November 30 to December 2, 1999*. Copenhagen: Danish National Museum and Danish Polar Center, 2000.

Appelt, M., H. C. Gulløv, and H. Kapel. "The Gateway to Greenland. Report on the Field Season 1996." In *Man, Culture and Environment in Ancient Greenland: Report on a Research Program*, ed. J. Arneborg and H. C. Gulløv, 136–196. Copenhagen: The Danish National Museum and Danish Polar Center, 1998.

Arneborg, J. "The Farm Beneath the Sand Summary." In *Man, Culture and Environment in Ancient Greenland: Report on a Research Program*, ed. J. Arneborg and H. C. Gulløv, 80–82. Copenhagen: The Danish National Museum and Danish Polar Center, 1998.

———. "Norse Greenland: Reflections on Settlement and Depopulation." In *Contact, Continuity, and Collapse: The Norse Colonization of the North Atlantic*, ed. J. H. Barrett, 163–181. Turnhout: Brepols, 2003.

Arneborg, J., J. Heineneier, N. Lynnerup, H. L. Nielsen, N. Rud, and Á. E. Sveinbjörnsdóttir. "Change of Diet of the Greenland Vikings Determined from Stable Isotope Analysis and 14C Dating of Their Bones." *Radiocarbon* 41, no. 2 (1999): 157–168.

Arthur, B., and F. Morphy, eds. *Macquarie Atlas of Indigenous Australia: Culture and Society through Space and Time*. North Ryde: Macquarie Library, 2005.

Attwood, B., and S. G. Foster. *Frontier Conflict: The Australian Experience*. Canberra: National Museum of Australia, 2003.

Awadzi, T. W., Y. Bredwa-Mensah, H. Breuning-Madsen, and E. Boateng. "A Scientific Evaluation of the Agricultural Experiments at Frederiksgave, The Royal Danish Plantation on the Gold Coast, Ghana." *Danish Journal of Geography* 101 (2001): 33–41.

Bahn, Paul. 1992. *Easter Island, Earth Island*. London: Thames and Hudson.

Balfour, H. "On the Method Employed by the Natives of N. W. Australia in the Manufacture of Glass Spear Heads." *Man* 3 (1903): 65–66.

Barrett, J. H. *Contact, Continuity, and Collapse: The Norse Colonization of the North Atlantic, Studies in the Early Middle Ages*. Turnhout: Brepols, 2003.

Bayman, J. M. "Technological Change and the Archaeology of Emergent Colonialism in the Kingdom of Hawai'i." *International Journal of Historical Archaeology* 13 (2009): 127–157.

Bedford, S. "Post-contact Maori—The Ignored Component in New Zealand Archaeology." *Journal of Polynesian Society* 105 (1996): 411–439.

———. "Tenacity of the Traditional: The First Hundred Years of Maori-European Settler Contact on the Hauraki Plains, Aotearoa/New Zealand." In *The Archaeology of Contact in Settler Societies*, ed. T. Murray, 144–154. Cambridge: Cambridge University Press, 2004.

Bekker, K. "Historical Patterns of Culture Contact in Southern Asia." *Far Eastern Quarterly* 11, no. 1 (1951): 3–15.

Bense, J. A. *Presidio Santa Maria de Galve: A Struggle for Survival in Colonial Spanish Pensacola*. Ripley P. Bullen Series. Gainesville: University Press of Florida, 2003.

Bense, J. A., N. B. Miller, and M. Lander. *Unearthing Pensacola*. Pensacola: University of West Florida Foundation, 2006.

Bill, J., and E. Roesdahl. "Travel and Transport." In *The Archaeology of Medieval Europe*, ed. J. Graham-Campbell and M. Valor, 261–315. Aarhus: Aarhus University Press, 2007.

Birmingham, J. *Wybalenna: The Archaeology of Cultural Accommodation in Nineteenth Century Tasmania*. Sydney: Australian Society for Historical Archaeology, 1992.

———. "Resistance, Creolization or Optimal Foraging at Killalpaninna Mission, South Australia." In *The Archaeology of Difference. Negotiating Cross-Cultural Engagements in Oceania*, ed. R. Torrence and A. Clarke, 360–405. London: Routledge, 2000.

Blair, E. H., L. S. A. Pendleton, P. J. Francis, E. Powell, and D. H. Thomas. *The Beads of St. Catherines Island. The Archaeology of Mission Santa Catalina de Guale*. Anthropological Papers of the American Museum of Natural History, no. 89. New York: American Museum of Natural History, 2009.

Blakely, A. *Blacks in the Dutch World: The Evolution of Racial Imagery in a Modern Society*. Bloomington: Indiana University Press, 1993.

Blanton, D. B., and J. A. King. *Indian and European Contact in Context: The Mid-Atlantic Region*. Gainesville: University Press of Florida, 2004.

Boas, A. J. *Crusader Archaeology: The Material Culture of the Latin East*. London: Routledge, 1999.

———. *Jerusalem in the Time of the Crusades: Society, Landscape and Art in the Holy City under Frankish Rule*. London: Routledge, 2001.

———. *Archaeology of the Military Orders: A Survey of the Urban Centres, Rural Settlement and Castles of the Military Orders in the Latin East (c. 1120–1291)*. London: Routledge, 2006.

Boone, J. L., and N. L. Benco. "Islamic Settlement in North Africa and the Iberian Peninsula." *Annual Review of Anthropology* 28 (1999): 51–71.

Bourdieu, P. *Outline of a Theory of Practice*. Cambridge: Cambridge University Press, 1977.

Boxer, C. R. *Fidalgos in the Far East 1550–1770: Fact and Fancy in the History of Macao*. The Hague: Martinus Nijhoff, 1948.

Brandner, J. A., and M. S. Taylor. "The Simple Economics of Easter Island: A Ricardo-Malthus Model of Renewable Resource Use." *American Economic Review* 88 (1998): 119.

Bredwa-Mensah, Y. "Historical-Archaeological Investigations at the Fredericksgave Plantation, Ghana: A Case Study of Slavery and Plantation Life on a Nineteenth Century Danish Plantation on the Gold Coast." Ph.D. diss. Department of Archaeology, University of Ghana, Legon/Accra, 2002.

Breuning-Madsen, H., T. W. Awadzi, Y. Bredwa-Mensah, H. R. Mount, and B. D. Hudson. "The Danish Plantations on the Gold Coast of Ghana—Why Did They Fail?" *Soil Survey Horizon* 43, no. 1 (2002): 1–8.

Brown, J. S. H., W. J. Eccles, and D. P. Heldman. *The Fur Trade Revisited: Selected Papers of the Sixth North American Fur Trade Conference, Mackinac Island, Michigan, 1991*. East Lansing: Michigan State University Press, 1994.

Brumfiel, E. M., and G. M. Feinman. *The Aztec World*. New York: Abrams, 2008.

Buchwald, V. F., and G. Mosdal. *Meteoritic Iron, Telluric Iron and Wrought Iron in Greenland*. Meddelelser om Grønland, Man and Society, no. 9. Copenhagen: National Museum of Denmark, 1985.

Bulbeck, D. "Economy, Military and Ideology in Pre-Islamic Luwu, South Sulawesi, Indonesia." *Australasian Historical Archaeology* 18 (2000): 3–16.

Bulbeck, D., and I. Caldwell. *Land of Iron: The Historical Archaeology of Luwu and the Cenrana Valley: Results of the Origin of Complex Society in South Sulawesi Project (OXIS)*. Hull: Centre for South-East Asian Studies, University of Hull, 2000.

Buren, M. "Tasapaya: An Elite Spanish Residence near Colonial Potosi in Comparative Perspective." *International Journal of Historical Archaeology* 33, no. 2 (1999): 101–115.

Burley, D. V., S. Hamilton, and K. Fladmark. *Prophecy of the Swan: The Peace River Fur Trade of 1794–1823*. Vancouver: University of British Columbia Press, 1996.

Burley, D. V., G. Horsfall, and J. Brandon. *Structural Considerations of Métis Ethnicity: An Archaeological, Historical, and Architectural Study*. Pierre/Brunswick: University of South Dakota Press, 1992.

Bushnell, A. T. *Situado and Sabana: Spain's Support System for the Presidio and Mission Provinces of Florida*: Anthropological Papers of the American Museum of Natural History, no. 74. New York: American Museum of Natural History, 1994.

Campbell, I. C. "Culture Contact and Polynesian Identity in the European Age." *Journal of World History* 8, no. 1 (1997): 29–56.

Carlson, C. C. "Indigenous Historic Archaeology of the 19th-Century Secwepemc Village at Thompson's River Post, Kamloops, British Columbia." *Canadian Journal of Archaeology* 30, no. 2 (2006): 193–250.

Carpenter, E. *Norse Penny*. New York: The Rock Foundation, 2003.

Childe, V. G. *What Happened in History*. Harmondsworth, Middlesex: Penguin Books, 1943.

Christensen, A. E. "Viking. A Gokstad Ship Replica from 1893." In *Sailing into the Past: Proceedings of the International Seminar on Replicas of Ancient and Medieval Vessels, Roskilde, 1984*, ed. O. Crumlin-Pedersen and M. Vinner. Roskilde: Viking Ship Museum, 1986.

Christie, N., and S. T. Loseby. *Towns in Transition: Urban Evolution in Late Antiquity and the Early Middle Ages*. Aldershot: Scolar Press, 1996.

Clarke, A. "The 'Moormans Trowsers': Macassan and Aboriginal Interactions and the Changing Fabric of Indigenous Social Life." *Modern Quaternary Research in Southeast Asia* 16 (2000): 315–335.

———. "The Ideal and the Real: Cultural and Personal Transformations of Archaeological Research on Groote Eylandt, Northern Australia." *World Archaeology* 34, no. 2 (2002): 249–264.

Clarke, A., and U. Frederick. "Closing the Distance: Interpreting Cross-Cultural Engagements through Indigenous Rock Art." In *The Archaeology of Oceania: Australia and the Pacific Islands*, ed. I. Lilley, 116–133. Oxford: Blackwell, 2004.

Cobb, C. R. *Stone Tool Traditions in the Contact Era*. Tuscaloosa: University of Alabama Press, 2003.

Colley, S. M., and A. Bickford. "'Real' Aborigines and 'Real' Archaeology: Aboriginal Places and Australian Historical Archaeology." *World Archaeological Bulletin* 7 (1996): 5–21.

Connah, G. *The Archaeology of Benin: Excavations and Other Researches in and around Benin City, Nigeria.* Oxford: Clarendon Press, 1975.

Coutts, P. J. F. "An Approach to the Investigation of Colonial Settlement Patterns: Whaling in Southern New Zealand." *World Archaeology* 7, no. 3 (1976): 291–305.

Cox, S. "A Norse Penny from Maine." In *Vikings: The North Atlantic Saga*, ed. W. R. Fitzgerald and E. I. Ward, 206–207. Washington, DC: Smithsonian Institution Press, 2000.

Crosby, A. W. *Ecological Imperialism: The Biological Expansion of Europe, 900–1900.* Studies in Environment and History. Cambridge/New York: Cambridge University Press, 1986.

———. *The Columbian Exchange: Biological and Cultural Consequences of 1492.* 30th Anniversary ed. Westport, CT/London: Praeger, 2003.

Crossman, C. L. *The China Trade: Export Paintings, Furniture, Silver and Other Objects.* Princeton: Pyne Press, 1972.

Curtin, P. D. *The Atlantic Slave Trade: A Census.* Madison: University of Wisconsin Press, 1969.

———. *Cross-Cultural Trade in World History.* New York: Cambridge University Press, 1984.

———. *The Rise and Fall of the Plantation Complex, Essays in Atlantic History.* Cambridge: Cambridge University Press, 1999.

Cusick, J. G., ed. *Studies in Culture Contact: Interaction, Culture Change, and Archaeology.* Carbondale: Center for Archaeological Investigations, Southern Illinois University, 1998.

Dalton, T. R., and R. M. Coats. "Could Institutional Reform Have Saved Easter Island?" *Journal of Evolutionary Economics* 10 (2000): 489.

Darwin, C. *The Voyage of the Beagle.* London: Dent, 1959.

David, B., and M. Wilson. "Spaces of Resistance: Graffiti and Indigenous Place Markings in the Early European Contact Period of Northern Australia." In *Inscribed Landscapes: Marking and Making Place*, ed. B. David and M. Wilson, 42–60. Honolulu: University of Hawai'i Press, 2002.

Davidson, B. *Old Africa Rediscovered.* London: Victor Gollancz, 1961.

Davidson, I., C. Lovell-Jones, and R. Bancroft. *Archaeologists and Aborigines Working Together.* Armidale, N.S.W.: University of New England Press, 1995.

de Barros, P. L. "The Effect of the Slave Trade on the Bassar Ironworking Society, Togo." In *West Africa during the Atlantic Slave Trade: Archaeological Perspectives*, ed. C. R. DeCorse, 59–80. London: Leicester University Press, 2001.

De Meulemeester, J. "Islamic Archaeology in the Iberian Peninsula and Morocco." *Antiquity* 79, no. 306 (2005): 837–843.

Deagan, K. A. "Spanish-Indian Interaction in Sixteenth-Century Florida and Hispaniola." In *Cultures in Contact: The Impact of European Contacts on Native American Cultural Institutions A.D. 1000–1800*, ed. W. W. Fitzhugh, 281–318. Washington, DC: Smithsonian Institution Press, 1985.

———. "Neither History nor Prehistory: The Questions That Count in Historical Archaeology." *Historical Archaeology* 22 (1988): 7–12.

———. "The Historical Archaeology of the Impact of Colonialism in Seventeenth-Century South Africa." In *Historical Archaeology in Global Perspective*, ed. L. Falk, 69–95. Washington, DC: Smithsonian Institution Press, 1991.

———.*Puerto Real: The Archaeology of a Sixteenth-Century Spanish Town in Hispaniola*. The Ripley P. Bullen Series. Gainesville: University Press of Florida, 1995.

———. "Colonial Transformations: Euro-American Cultural Genesis in the Early Spanish-American Colonies." *Journal of Anthropological Research* 52, no. 2 (1996): 135–160.

———. "Transculturation and Spanish American Ethnogenesis: The Archaeological Legacy of the Quincentenary." In *Studies in Culture Contact: Interaction, Culture Change, and Archaeology*, ed. J. G. Cusick, 23–43. Carbondale: Southern Illinois University, 1998.

Deagan, K., and J. M. Cruxent. *Archaeology at La Isabela: America's First European Town*. New Haven/London: Yale University Press, 2002.

———.*Columbus's Outpost among the Taínos: Spain and America at La Isabela, 1493–1498*. New Haven/London: Yale University Press, 2002.

Deagan, K. A., and J. K. Koch. *Spanish St. Augustine: The Archaeology of a Colonial Creole Community*. Studies in Historical Archaeology. New York: Academic Press, 1983.

Deagan, K. A., and D. A. MacMahon. *Fort Mose: Colonial America's Black Fortress of Freedom*. Gainesville: University Press of Florida, 1995.

Deagan, K. A., D. H. Thomas, K. H. Ashley, C. B. DePratter, R. Saunders, G. J. Waters, J. M. Williams, and J. E. Worth. *From Santa Elena to St. Augustine: Indigenous Ceramic Variability (A.D. 1400–1700): Proceedings of the Second Caldwell Conference, St. Catherines Island, Georgia, March 30–April 1, 2007*. Anthropological Papers of the American Museum of Natural History, no. 90. New York: American Museum of Natural History, 2009.

DeCorse, C. R. "Archaeological Perspectives of Culture Contact and Trade in West Africa." In *Aspects of African Archaeology: Papers from the 10th Congress of the PanAfrican Association for Prehistory and Related Studies*, ed. G. Pwiti and R. Soper, 681–686. Harare: University of Zimbabwe Publications, 1996.

———. "Culture Contact and Change in West Africa." In *Studies in Culture Contact: Interaction, Culture Change, and Archaeology*, ed. J. G. Cusick, 358–377. Carbondale: Center for Archaeological Investigations, Southern Illinois University, 1998.

———.*An Archaeology of Elmina: Africans and Europeans on the Gold Coast, 1400–1900*. Washington, DC: Smithsonian Institution Press, 2001.

———.*West Africa during the Atlantic Slave Trade: Archaeological Perspectives*. New Approaches to Anthropological Archaeology. New York: Leicester University Press, 2001.

———. "Culture Contact, Continuity, and Change on the Gold Coast, AD 1400–1900." *African Archaeological Review* 10, no. 1 (2005): 163–196.

Deetz, J. *In Small Things Forgotten: The Archaeology of Early American Life*. Garden City, NJ: Anchor Press/Doubleday, 1977.

———. "Archaeological Investigations at La Purísima Mission." In *Historical Archaeology: A Guide to Substantive and Theoretical Contributions*, ed. R. L. Schuyler. Farmingdale, NY: Baywood Press, 1978 [1963].

Dening, G. *Islands and Beaches: Discourse on a Silent Land, Marquesas, 1774–1880*. Honolulu: University of Hawai'i Press, 1980.

———. "Towards an Anthropology of Performance in Encounters in Place." In *Pacific History: Papers from the 8th Pacific History Association Conference*, ed. D. H. Rubinstein, 3–6. Mangilao, Guam: University of Guam Press and Micronesian Area Research Center, 1992.

Diamond, J. M. *Guns, Germs and Steel: The Fates of Human Societies*. London: Jonathan Cape, 1997.

———.*Collapse: How Societies Choose to Fail or Survive*. London: Allen Lane, 2005.

Ditchburn, D., S. MacLean, and A. MacKay, eds. *Atlas of Medieval Europe*. London: Routledge, 2007.

Dobyns, H. F. *Their Number Become Thinned: Native American Population Dynamics in Eastern North America*. Knoxville: University of Tennessee Press, 1983.

Dodds, J. D. *Architecture and Ideology in Early Medieval Spain*. University Park: Pennsylvania State University Press, 1990.

Doggett, R., M. Hulvey, and J. Ainsworth, eds. *New World of Wonders: European Images of the Americas 1492–1700*. Seattle: University of Washington Press, 1992.

Dowson, T. A., and J. D. Lewis-Williams. *Contested Images: Diversity in Southern African Rock Art Research*. Johannesburg: Witwatersrand University Press, 1994.

Earl, G. W. *The Eastern Seas, or Voyages and Adventures in the Indian Archipelago, in 1882–83–84, Comprising A Tour of the Island of Java—Visits to Borneo, The Malay Peninsula, Siam, &c.* Oxford University Press, 1974 [1837].

Eccles, W. "The Fur Trade in the Colonial Northeast." In *The Handbook of North American Indians*, vol. 4, *History of Indian–White Relations*, ed. W. E. Washburn, 324–334. Washington, DC: Smithsonian Institution, 1988.

Elisseeff, V., ed. *The Silk Roads: Highways of Culture and Commerce*. New York: Berghahn Books, 2000.

English, A. *The Sea and the Rock Gives Us a Feed. Mapping and Managing Gumbaingirr Wild Resource Use Places*. Sydney: NSW National Parks and Wildlife Service, 2002.

Evans, D., C. Pottier, R. Fletcher, S. Hensley, I. Tapley, A. Milne, and M. Barbetti. "A Comprehensive Archaeological Map of the World's Largest Preindustrial Settlement Complex at Angkor, Cambodia." *Proceedings of the Natural Academy of Sciences* 104 (2007): 14277–14282.

Ewen, C. R. *The Archaeology of Spanish Colonialism in the Southeastern United States and the Caribbean*. Guides to the Archaeological Literature of the Immigrant Experience in America, no. 1. Gainesville: Society for Historical Archaeology, 1990.

———.*From Spaniard to Creole: The Archaeology of Cultural Formation at Puerto Real, Haiti*. Tuscaloosa: University of Alabama Press, 1991.

———. "Continuity and Change: De Soto and the Apalachee." *Historical Archaeology* 30, no. 2 (1996): 41–53.

———. "The Archaeology of La Florida." In *International Handbook of Historical Archaeology*, ed. T. Majewski and D. Gaimster, 383–398. New York: Springer, 2009.

Falk, L., ed. *Historical Archaeology in Global Perspective*. Washington, DC: Smithsonian Institution Press, 1991.

Farnsworth, P. "Native American Acculturation in the Spanish Colonial Empire: The Franciscan Missions of Alta California." In *Centre and Periphery*, ed. T. C. Champion, 186–206. London: Unwin Hyman, 1989.

———. "Missions, Indians and Cultural Continuity." *Historical Archaeology* 26, no. 1 (1992): 22–36.

Fiske, J. *The Discovery of America with Some Account of Ancient America and the Spanish Conquest.* Boston/New York: Houghton Mifflin, 1893.

Fitzgerald, C. P. *China: A Short Cultural History.* Sydney: Cresset Library, 1986 [first published 1935].

Fitzhugh, W. W., ed. *Cultures in Contact: The Impact of European Contacts on Native American Cultural Institutions A.D. 1000–1800.* Anthropological Society of Washington Series. Washington, DC: Smithsonian Institution Press, 1985.

Fitzhugh, W. W., and E. I. Ward. *Vikings: The North Atlantic Saga.* Washington/London: Smithsonian Institution Press and National Museum of Natural History, 2000.

Fleisher, J. "Beyond the Sultan of Kilwa's 'Rebellious Conduct': Local Perspectives on an International East African Town." In *African Historical Archaeologies*, ed. A. M. Reid and P. J. Lane. New York: Kluwer Academic/Plenum Publishers, 2004.

Flenley, J. R., and S. M. King. "Late Quaternary Pollen Records from Easter Island." *Nature* 307 (1984): 47.

Flinders, M. *Voyage to Terra Australis.* London: G. W. Nicol, 1814.

Foster, G. M. *Culture and Conquest: America's Spanish Heritage.* Chicago: Quadrangle Books, 1960.

Fowler, W. R. "Historical Archaeology in Yucatan and Central America." *International Handbook of Historical Archaeology* (2009): 429–447.

Fowler, W. R., F. Estrada-Belli, J. Bales, M. D. Reynolds, and K. L. Kvamme. "Landscape Archaeology and Remote Sensing of a Spanish-Conquest Town: Ciudad Vieja, El Salvador." In *Remote Sensing in Archaeology*, ed. J. Wiseman and F. El-Baz, 395–421. New York: Springer, 2007.

Frederick, U. "At the Centre of It All: Constructing Contact through Rock Art of Watarrka National Park, Central Australia." *Archaeology in Oceania* 34 (1999): 132–144.

———. "Keeping the Land Alive: Changing Social Contexts of Landscape and Rock Art Production." In *The Archaeology of Difference. Negotiating Cross-Cultural Engagements in Oceania*, ed. R. Torrence and A. Clarke, 300–330. London: Routledge, 2000.

Freedman, P. *Out of the East: Spices and the Medieval Imagination.* New Haven: Yale University Press, 2008.

Fried, M. H. "On the Concepts of 'Tribe' and 'Tribal Society.'" In *Essays on the Problem of Tribe*, ed. J. Helm, 3–20. Seattle: University of Washington Press, 1967.

Friesen, M. T. "Analogues at Iqaluktuuq: The Social Context of Archaeological Inference in Nunavut, Arctic Canada." *World Archaeology* 34, no. 2 (2002): 330–345.

Funari, P. P. "Archaeology, History, and Historical Archaeology in South America." *International Journal of Historical Archaeology* 1, no. 3 (1997): 189–206.

Gaborit-Chopin, D. "Walrus Ivory in Western Europe." In *From Viking to Crusader: The Scandinavians and Europe 800–1200*, ed. E. Roesdahl and D. M. Wilson, 204–205. Uddevalla: The 22nd Council of Europe Exhibition, 1992.

Galloway, P. K. *Choctaw Genesis, 1500–1700, Indians of the Southeast.* Lincoln: University of Nebraska Press, 1995.

————.*Practicing Ethnohistory: Mining Archives, Hearing Testimony, Constructing Narrative*. Lincoln: University of Nebraska Press, 2006.

Gara, T., S. Colley, S. Brockwell, and S. Cane. "The History and Archaeology of Ooldea Soak and Mission." *Australian Archaeology* 28 (1989).

Garlake, P. S. *The Early Islamic Architecture of the East African Coast*. British Institute of History and Archaeology in East Africa, Memoir no. 1. Nairobi/London: Oxford University Press, 1966.

————. "Seventeeth Century Portuguese Earthworks in Rhodesia." *South African Archaeological Bulletin* 21 (1967): 157–170.

Gasco, J., G. C. Smith, and P. F. García. *Approaches to the Historical Archaeology of Mexico, Central and South America*. Los Angeles: Institute of Archaeology, University of California, Los Angeles, 1997.

Gibson, J. R. "The Maritime Trade of the North Pacific Coast." *Handbook of North American Indians*, vol. 4: *History of Indian-WhiteRelations*, ed. W. E. Washburn. Washington, DC: Smithsonian Institution, 1988.

Gibson, R., ed. *Exchanges: Cross Cultural Encounters in Australia and the Pacific*. Sydney: Museum of Sydney, 1996.

Gill, N., and A. G. Paterson. "A Work in Progress: Aboriginal People and Pastoral Cultural Heritage in Australia." In *Loving a Sunburned Country? Geographies of Australian Heritages*, ed. R. Jones and B. Shaw, 113–131. Aldershot: Ashgate, 2007.

Glick, T. F. *From Muslim Fortress to Christian Castle: Social and Cultural Change in Medieval Spain*. Manchester/New York: Manchester University Press, 1995.

Gosden, C. "Transformations: History and Prehistory in Hawaii." *Archaeology in Oceania* 31 (1996): 165–172.

————. *Archaeology and Colonialism: Cultural Contact from 5000 B.C. to the Present*. Cambridge: Cambridge University Press, 2004.

Graham-Campbell, J., and C. E. Batey. *Cultural Atlas of the Viking World*. New York: Facts on File, 1994.

Graham-Campbell, J., and M. Valor. *The Archaeology of Medieval Europe*. Aarhus: Aarhus University Press, 2007.

Green, R. C. "The Conquest of the Conquistadors." *World Archaeology* 5, no. 1 (1973): 14–31.

Greer, S., R. Harrison, and S. McIntyre-Tamwoy. "Community-Based Archaeology in Australia." *World Archaeology* 34, no. 2 (2002): 265–287.

Grønnow, B., M. Meldgaard, and J. B. Nielsen. *The Great Summer Camp. Archaeological, Ethnographical and Zoo-Archaeological Studies of a Caribou-Hunting Site in West Greenland*. Meddelelser om Grønland, Man and Society, no. 5. Copenhagen: National Museum of Denmark, 1983.

Gulløv, H. C. "The Eskimo's View of the European: The So-Called Norse Dolls and Other Questionable Carvings." *Arctic Anthropology* 20, no. 2 (1982): 121–129.

————. "Whales, Whalers, and Eskimos: The Impact of European Whaling on the Demography and Economy of Eskimo Society in West Greenland." In *Culture in Contact: The European Impact on Native Cultural Institutions in Eastern North America, A.D.*

1000–1800, ed. W. W. Fitzhugh, 71–96. Washington, DC: Smithsonian Institution Press, 1985.

———.*From Middle Ages to Colonial Times: Archaeological and Ethnohistorical Studies of the Thule Culture in South West Greenland 1300–1800 A.D.* Meddelelser om Grønland, Man and Society, no. 23. Copenhagen: Commission for Scientific Research in Greenland, 1997.

———. "On Depopulation—A Case Study from South East Greenland." In *Identities and Cultural Contacts in the Arctic: Proceedings from a Conference at the Danish National Museum, Copenhagen November 30 to December 2, 1999*, ed. M. Appelt, J. Berglund, and H. C. Gulløv, 43–54. Copenhagen: Danish National Museum and Danish Polar Center, 2000.

———. "Aasiviit as Focal Places in Historical Greenland." In *Dynamics of Northern Societies: Proceedings of the SILA/NABO Conference on Arctic and North Atlantic Archaeology, Copenhagen, May 10th–14th, 2004*, ed. J. Arneborg and B. Grønnow, 209–214. Copenhagen: National Museum Studies in Archaeology and History, 2006.

Gulløv, H. C., and M. Appelt. "Social Bonding and Shamanism among Late Dorset Groups in High Arctic Greenland." In *The Archaeology of Shamanism*, ed. N. S. Price, 146–162. London: Routledge, 2001.

Gulløv, H. C., and H. Kapel. *Haabetz Colonie 1721–1728: A Historical-Archaeological Investigation of the Danish-Norwegian Colonization of Greenland*, Vol. I: *Ethnohistorical Studies of the Meeting of Eskimo and European Cultures*. Copenhagen: National Museum of Denmark, 1979.

Gulløv, H. C., C. Andreasen, B. Grønnow, J. F. Jensen, M. Appelt, J. Arneborg, and J. Berglund. *Grønlands Forhistorie*. Copenhagen: Gyldenhal, 2005.

Hackett, C. W. *Pichardos' Treatise on the Limits of Louisiana and Texas,* Vol. 5. Austin: University of Texas Press, 1934.

Hacquebord, L., and R. Vaughan. *Between Greenland and America: Cross-Cultural Contacts and the Environment in the Baffin Bay Area*. Groningen: Arctic Centre, University of Groningen, 1987.

Haines, F. "The Northward Spread of Horses among the Plains Indians." *American Anthropologist* 40 (1938): 429–437.

———. "Where Did the Plains Indians Get Their Horses?" *American Anthropologist* 40 (1938): 112–117.

Hall, M. "The Archaeology of Colonial Settlement in Southern Africa." *Annual Review of Anthropology* 22 (1993): 177–200.

Hamilton, S. "Dynamics of Social Complexity in Early Nineteenth-Century British Fur-Trade Posts." *International Journal of Historical Archaeology* 4, no. 3 (2000): 217–273.

Hamilton, S., and B. A. Nicholson. "The Middleman Fur Trade and Slot Knives: Selective Integration of European Technology at the Mortlach Twin Fawns Site (DiMe-23)." *Canadian Journal of Archaeology* 31, no. 3 (2007): 137–162.

Hansen, I. L., and C. Wickham. *The Long Eighth Century*. Leiden/Boston: Brill, 2000.

Harper, R. P., and D. Pringle. *Belmont Castle: The Excavation of a Crusader Stronghold in the Kingdom of Jerusalem*. Oxford: British Research in the Levant and Oxford University Press, 2000.

Harriot, T. and T. de Bry. *A Briefe and True Report of the New Found Land of Virginia.* Charlottesville: Library at the Mariners' Museum and University of Virginia Press, 2007.

Harrison, Rodney. "'Nowadays with Glass': Regional Variation in Aboriginal Bottle Glass Artefacts from Western Australia." *Archaeology in Oceania* 35, no. 1 (2000): 34–47.

———. "Australia's Iron Age: Aboriginal Post-Contact Metal Artefacts from Old Lamboo Station, Southeast Kimberley, Western Australia." *Australasian Historical Archaeology* 20 (2002): 67–76.

———.*Shared Landscapes: Archaeologies of Attachment and the Pastoral Industry in New South Wales.* Studies in the Cultural Construction of Open Space. Sydney: UNSW Press, 2004.

———. "An Artefact of Colonial Desire? Kimberley Points and the Technologies of Enchantment." *Current Anthropology* 47, no. 1 (2006): 63–88.

Harrison, R., and C. Williamson, eds. *After Captain Cook: The Archaeology of the Recent Indigenous Past in Australia.* Walnut Creek, CA: AltaMira Press, 2004.

Head, L., and R. Fullagar. "Hunter-Gatherer Archaeology and Pastoral Contact: Perspectives from the Northwest Northern Territory, Australia." *World Archaeology* 28 (1997): 418–428.

———. "Exploring the Prehistory of Hunter-Gatherer Attachments to Place: An Example from the Keep River Area, Northern Territory, Australia." In *The Archaeology and Anthropology of Landscape,* ed. P. Ucko and R. Layton, 322–335. London: Routledge, 1999.

Heeres, J. E., ed. *Abel Janszoon Tasman's Journal of His Discovery of Van Diemens Land and New Zealand in 1642....* Los Angeles: Kovach, 1965.

Hester, T. R. "Texas and Northeastern Mexico: An Overview." In *Columbian Consequences,* Vol. 1: *Archaeological and Historical Perspectives on the Spanish Borderlands West,* ed. D. H. Thomas, 191–211. Washington, DC: Smithsonian Institution Press, 1989.

Hirth, F., and W. W. Rockhill. *Chau Ju-kua. His Work on the Chinese and Arab Trade in the Twelfth and Thirteenth Centuries, Entitled Chu-fan-chï.* St. Petersburg: Imperial Academy of Sciences, 1911.

Hoover, R. L. "Spanish-Native Interaction and Acculturation in the Alta California Missions." In *Columbian Consequences,* Vol. 1: *Archaeological and Historical Perspectives on the Spanish Borderlands West,* ed. D. H. Thomas, 395–406. Washington, DC: Smithsonian Institution Press, 1989.

Horton, D., ed. *The Encyclopedia of Aboriginal Australia: Aboriginal and Torres Strait Islander History, Society and Culture.* Canberra: Aboriginal Studies Press and the Australian Institute of Aboriginal and Torres Strait Islander Studies, 1994.

Horton, M., and C. Clark. "Archaeological Survey of Zanzibar." *Azania* 20 (1985): 115–123.

Horton, M., and J. Middleton. *The Swahili.* Oxford: Blackwell, 2000.

Horton, M., H. W. Brown, and N. Mudida. *Shanga: The Archaeology of a Muslim Trading Community on the Coast of East Africa.* London: British Institute in Eastern Africa, 1996.

Hull, K. L. *Pestilence and Persistence: Yosemite Indian Demography and Culture in Colonial California*. Berkeley: University of California Press, 2009.

Hutchinson, D. L. *Tatham Mound and the Bioarchaeology of European Contact: Disease and Depopulation in Central Gulf Coast Florida*. Ripley P. Bullen Series. Gainesville: University Press of Florida, 2006.

Insoll, T. *The Archaeology of Islam*. Malden, MA: Blackwell Publishers, 1999.

——. *The Archaeology of Islam in Sub-Saharan Africa*. Cambridge World Archaeology. Cambridge/New York: Cambridge University Press, 2003.

Jamieson, R. W. "Colonialism, Social Archaeology and lo Adino: Historical Archaeology in the Andes." *World Archaeology* 37, no. 3 (2005): 352–372.

Jennings, F. *The Invasion of America: Indians, Colonialism, and the Cant of Conquest*. New York: Norton, 1976.

Jensen, E. L. "Uiarnerit—Migrations from Southeast to Southwest Greenland in the 19th Century." In *Dynamics of Northern Societies: Proceedings of the SILA/NABO Conference on Arctic and North Atlantic Archaeology, Copenhagen, May 10th–14th, 2004*, ed. J. Arneborg and B. Grønnow, 225–234. Copenhagen: National Museum Studies in Archaeology and History, 2006.

Johns, C. N., and D. Pringle. *Pilgrims' Castle ('Atlit), David's Tower (Jerusalem), and Qal'a tar-Rabad ('Ajlun): Three Middle Eastern Castles from the Time of the Crusades*. Aldershot: Ashgate, 1997.

Jones, P. G. *Ochre and Rust: Artefacts and Encounters on Australian Frontiers*. Kent Town: Wakefield Press, 2007.

Jordan, K. A. *The Seneca Restoration, 1715–1754: An Iroquois Local Political Economy*. Gainesville: University Press of Florida, 2008.

Jordan, S., and C. Schrire. "Material Culture and the Roots of Colonial Society at the South African Cape of Good Hope." In *The Archaeology of Colonialism*, ed. C. L. Lyons and J. K. Papadopoulos, 241–272. Los Angeles: Getty Research Institute, 2002.

Junker, L. L. "Integrating History and Archaeology in the Study of Contact Period Philippine Chiefdoms." *International Journal of Historical Archaeology* 2, no. 4 (1998): 291–320.

Kaplan, S. A. "European Goods and Socio-Economic Change in Early Labrador Inuit Society." In *Culture in Contact: The European Impact on Native Cultural Institutions in Eastern North America, A.D. 1000–1800*, ed. W. W. Fitzhugh, 45–69. Washington, DC: Smithsonian Institution Press, 1985.

Karg, S., and P. Lafuente. "Food." In *The Archaeology of Medieval Europe*, ed. J. Graham-Campbell and M. Valor, 181–207. Aarhus: Aarhus University Press, 2007.

Kathirithamby-Wells, J., and J. Villiers, eds. *The Southeast Asian Port and Polity: Rise and Demise*. Singapore: Singapore University Press, 1990.

Keen, I. "Aboriginal Economy and Society at the Threshold of Colonisation: A Comparative Study." *Before Farming* 3, no. 2 (2003): 1–24.

Kelly, K. G. "The Archaeology of African-European Interaction: Investigating the Social Roles of Trade, Traders, and the Use of Space in the Seventeenth- and Eighteenth-Century *Hueda* Kingdom, Republic of Benin." *World Archaeology* 28, no. 3 (1997): 351–369.

———. "Indigenous Responses to Colonial Encounters on the West African Coast: Hueda and Dahomey from the Seventeenth through Nineteenth Century." In *The Archaeology of Colonialism*, ed. C. L. Lyons and J. K. Papadopoulos, 96–120. Los Angeles: Getty Research Institute, 2002.

———. "Creole Cultures of the Caribbean: Historical Archaeology in the French West Indies." *International Journal of Historical Archaeology* 12 (2008): 388–402.

Kennedy, H. "From Polis to Madina: Urban Change in Late Antique and Early Islamic Syria." *Past and Present* 106 (1985): 3–27.

———.*The Prophet and the Age of the Caliphates: The Islamic Near East from the Sixth to the Eleventh Century, A History of the Near East*. London: Longman, 1986.

———.*Crusader Castles*. Cambridge: Cambridge University Press, 1994.

———.*Muslim Spain and Portugal: A Political History of Al-Andalus*. London: Longman, 1996.

Kent, S., ed., *Ethnicity, Hunter-Gatherers, and the "Other": Association and Assimilation in Africa*. Washington, DC: Smithsonian Institution Press, 2002.

Kepecs, S., and R. T. Alexander. *The Postclassic to Spanish-Era Transition in Mesoamerica: Archaeological Perspectives*. Albuquerque: University of New Mexico Press, 2005.

Kerber, J. E. *Cross-Cultural Collaboration: Native Peoples and Archaeology in the Northeastern United States*. Lincoln: University of Nebraska Press, 2006.

Keyser, J. D. "Writing-On-Stone: Rock Art on the Northwestern Plains." *Canadian Journal of Archaeology* 1 (1977): 15–80.

Keyser, J. D., and M. A. Klassen. *Plains Indian Rock Art*. Seattle: University of Washington Press, 2001.

Kinahan, J. *Cattle for Beads: The Archaeology of Historical Contact and Trade on the Namib Coast*. Studies in African Archaeology. Windhoek/Uppsala: Namibia Archaeological Trust and the Department of Archaeology and Ancient History, University of Uppsala, Sweden, 2000.

King, M. L., ed. *Western Civilisation: A Social and Cultural History*. 2nd ed. Upper Saddle River, NJ: Prentice Hall, 2003.

Kirch, P. V., and J.-L. Rallu. *The Growth and Collapse of Pacific Island Communities: Archaeological and Demographic Perspectives*. Honolulu: University of Hawai'i Press, 2007.

Kirch, P. V., and M. D. Sahlins. *Anahulu: The Anthropology of History in the Kingdom of Hawaii*. 2 vols. Chicago: University of Chicago Press, 1992.

Kirkman, J. S. *Fort Jesus, Mombasa*. 9th ed. Mombasa: Museum Trustees of Kenya, 1981.

Klassen, M. "Icon and Narrative in Transition: Contact-Period Rock-Art at Writing-On-Stone, Southern Alberta, Canada." In *The Archaeology of Rock-Art*, ed. C. Chippindale and P. S. C. Taçon, 64. Cambridge: Cambridge University Press, 1998.

Klein, H. S. *The Atlantic Slave Trade*. Cambridge: Cambridge University Press, 1999.

Klimko, O. "Fur Trade Archaeology in Western Canada: Who is Digging up the Forts?" In *The Archaeology of Contact in Settler Societies*, ed. T. Murray, 157–175. Cambridge: Cambridge University Press, 2004.

Krogh, K. J. *Qallunaatsiaaqarfik Grønland*. Copenhagen: Nationalmuseets Forlag, 1982.

Kunin, D., trans., and C. Phelpstead, ed. *A History of Norway and the Passion and Miracles of the Blessed Óláfr.* London: Viking Society for Northern Research, University College London, 2001.

Lane, P. "Whither Historical Archaeology in Africa?" *Review of Archaeology* 28, no. 2 (2007): 1–24.

Lape, P. V. "Political Dynamics and Religious Change in the Late Pre-Colonial Banda Islands, Eastern Indonesia." *World Archaeology* 32, no. 1 (2000): 138–155.

———. "Historic Maps and Archaeology as a Means of Understanding Late Precolonial Settlement in the Banda Islands, Indonesia." *Asian Perspectives* 41, no. 1 (2002): 43–70.

———. "A Highway and a Crossroads: Island Southeast Asia and Culture Contact Archaeology." *Archaeology in Oceania* 38 (2003): 102.

———. "Focus on Islam IV: Archaeological Approaches to the Study of Islam in Island Southeast Asia." *Antiquity* 79 (2005): 829–836.

Larsen, C. S. *The Archaeology of Mission Santa Catalina de Guale: 2. Biocultural Interpretations of a Population in Transition.* Anthropological Papers of the American Museum of Natural History, no. 68. New York: American Museum of Natural History, 1990.

———. *Bioarchaeology of the Late Prehistoric Guale: South End Mound I, St. Catherines Island, Georgia.* Anthropological Papers of the American Museum of Natural History, no. 84. New York: American Museum of Natural History, 1994.

LaViolette, A. "Swahili Cosmopolitanism in Africa and the Indian Ocean World, A.D. 600–1500." *Archaeologies: Journal of the World Archaeological Congress* 4, no. 1 (2008): 24–49.

Law, R. *The Impact of the Atlantic Slave Trade upon Africa.* Vienna: Lit. Verlag, 2008.

Lawrence, S. *Archaeologies of the British: Explorations of Identity in Great Britain and Its Colonies, 1600–1945.* One World Archaeology, no. 46. London/New York: Routledge, 2003.

———. *Whalers and Free Men: Life on Tasmania's Colonial Whaling Stations.* North Melbourne: Australian Scholarly Publishing, 2007.

Leciejewicz, L., and M. Valor. "Peoples and Environments." In *The Archaeology of Medieval Europe,* ed. J. Graham-Campbell and M. Valor, 46–75. Aarhus: Aarhus University Press, 2007.

Lee, G. *Rock Art of Easter Island: Symbols of Power, Prayers to the Gods.* Los Angeles: Institute of Archaeology, University of California, 1992.

Leichhardt, L. *Journal of an Overland Expedition in Australia, from Moreton Bay to Port Essington.* London: T. & W. Boone, 1847.

Liebmann, M. "The Innovative Materiality of Revitalization Movements: Lessons from the Pueblo Revolt of 1680." *American Anthropologist* 110, no. 3 (2008): 360–372.

Lightfoot, K. G. "Culture Contact Studies: Redefining the Relationship between Prehistoric and Historical Archaeology." *American Antiquity* 60, no. 2 (1995): 199–217.

———. *Indians, Missionaries, and Merchants: The Legacy of Colonial Encounters on the Californian Frontiers.* Berkeley: University of California Press, 2005.

Lightfoot, K. G., and A. Martinez. "Frontiers and Boundaries in Archaeological Perspective." *Annual Review of Anthropology* 24 (1995): 471–492.

Lightfoot, K. G., A. Martinez, and A. M. Schiff. "Daily Practice and Material Culture in Pluralistic Social Settings: An Archaeological Study of Culture Change and Persistence from Fort Ross, California." *American Antiquity* 63, no. 2 (1998): 199–122.

Lightfoot, K. G., T. A. Wake, and A. M. Schiff. "Native Responses to the Russian Mercantile Colony of Fort Ross, Northern California." *Journal of Field Archaeology* 20 (1993): 159–175.

Lilley, I. *Native Title and the Transformation of Archaeology in the Postcolonial World*. Oceania Monograph, no. 50. Sydney: University of Sydney, 2000.

Lohse, E. S. "Trade Goods." In *Handbook of North American Indians*, vol. 4: *History of Indian-White Relations*, ed. W. E. Washburn. Washington, DC: Smithsonian Institution, 1988.

López, J. C. Carvajal. "Pottery Production and Islam in South-East Spain: A Social Model." *Antiquity* 83, no. 320 (2009): 388–398.

Loren, D. D. "Creolization in the French and Spanish Colonies." In *North American Archaeology*, ed. T. R. Pauketat and D. D. Loren, 297–318. Malden, MA: Blackwell Publishing, 2005.

———.*In Contact: Bodies and Spaces in the Sixteenth- and Seventeenth-Century Eastern Woodlands*. Lanham, MD: AltaMira Press, 2008.

Lovejoy, P. E. *Transformations in Slavery: A History of Slavery in Africa*. 2nd ed. Cambridge: Cambridge University Press, 2000.

Lydon, J. *Eye Contact: Photographing Indigenous Australians*. Durham, NC: Duke University Press, 2005.

———. "Pacific Encounters, or Beyond the Islands of History." In *Historical Archaeology*, ed. M. Hall and S. Silliman, 293–312. Oxford: Blackwell Studies in Global Archaeology, 2006.

———. "'Men in Black': The Blacktown Native Institution and the Origins of the 'Stolen Generation.'" In *Object Lessons: Archaeology and Heritage in Australia*, ed. J. Lydon and T. Ireland, 201–224. Melbourne: Australian Scholarly Publishing, 2005.

———. "'Fantastic Dreaming': Ebenezer Mission as Moravian Utopia and Wotjobaluk Responses." In *Making Space: Settler-Colonial Perspectives on Land, Place and Identity*, ed. P. Edmonds and T. Banivanua Mar. London: Palgrave Macmillan, 2009.

———.*Fantastic Dreaming: The Archaeology of an Australian Aboriginal Mission*. Lanham, MD: AltaMira, 2009.

———. "Imagining the Moravian Mission: Space and Surveillance at the Former Ebenezer Mission, Victoria, South-Eastern Australia." *Historical Archaeology* 43, no. 1 (2009).

Lynnerup, N. "Palaeodemography of the Greenland Norse." *Arctic Anthropology* 33, no. 2 (1996): 122–136.

Lyons, C. L., and J. K. Papadopoulos, eds. *The Archaeology of Colonialism*. Los Angeles: Getty Research Institute, 2002.

Macintyre, S., and A. Clark. *The History Wars*. Carlton: Melbourne University Press, 2003.

Macknight, C. *The Voyage to Marege*. Melbourne: Melbourne University Press, 1976.

Malinowski, B. *The Dynamics of Culture Change: An Inquiry into Race Relations in Africa*. New Haven: Yale University Press, 1945.

Manguin, P.-Y. "Palembang and Sriwijaya: An Early Malay Harbour-City Rediscovered." *Journal of the Malaysian Branch of the Royal Asiatic Society* 66, pt. 1 (1993): 23–46.

Manne, R. *Whitewash: On Keith Windschuttle's Fabrication of Aboriginal History, Agenda*. Melbourne, Victoria: Black Inc., 2003.

Marquette, J. *The Mississippi Voyage of Jolliet and Marquette, 1673*. AJ-051, Wisconsin Historical Society, 1673.

Massola, A. *Aboriginal Mission Stations in Victoria*. Melbourne: Hawthorn Press, 1970.

Mathew, K. M. *History of the Portuguese Navigation in India, 1497–1600*. Delhi: Mittal Publications, 1988.

Mathew, K. S., and J. Varkey. *Winds of Spices: Essays on Portuguese Establishments in Medieval India with Special Reference to Cannanore*. Tellicherry: Institute for Research in Social Sciences and Humanities, 2006.

McBryde, I. "Goods from Another Country: Exchange Networks and the People of the Lake Eyre Basin." In *Australians to 1788*, ed. D. J. Mulvaney and J. P. White, 253–274. Broadway, NSW: Fairfax Syme & Weldon Associates, 1987.

———.*Guests of the Governor—Aboriginal Residents of the First Government House*. Sydney: Friends of the First Government House Site, 1989.

———. "'.... to establish a commerce of this sort': Cross Cultural Exchange at the Port Jackson Settlement." In *Studies from Terra Australis to Australia*, ed. J. Hardy and A. Frost, 169–182. Canberra: Australian Academy of the Humanities, 1989.

McDonald, J. "Rock Art and Cross-Cultural Interaction in Sydney: How Did Both Sides Perceive the Other?" In *Strangers on the Shore: Early Coastal Contact in Australia,* ed. P. Veth, P. Sutton, and M. Neale, 46–89. Canberra: National Museum of Australia, 2008.

McEwan, B. G. *The Spanish Missions of La Florida*. Gainesville: University of Florida Press, 1993.

———. "San Luís de Tamali: The Archaeology of Spanish-Indian Relations at a Florida Mission." *Historical Archaeology* 25, no. 3 (1991): 36–60.

———, ed. *Indians of the Greater Southeast*. Gainesville: University Press of Florida, 2000.

McGee, W. J. "Piratical Acculturation." *American Anthropologist* 11 (1898): 243–249.

McGee, W. J., and B. L. Fontana. *Trails to Tiburón: The 1894 and 1895 Field Diaries of W. J. McGee*. Tucson: University of Arizona Press, 2000.

McGhee, R. "Contact between Native North Americans and The Medieval Norse: A Review of Evidence." *American Antiquity* 49, no. 1 (1984): 4–26.

———. "Epilogue: Was There Continuity from Norse to Post-Medieval Explorations of the New World?" In *Contact, Continuity, and Collapse: The Norse Colonization of the North Atlantic*, ed. J. H. Barrett, 239–248. Turnhout: Brepols, 2003.

McGovern, T. H. "The Arctic Frontier of Norse Greenland." In *The Archaeology of Frontiers and Boundaries*, ed. S. W. Green and S. M. Perlman, 275–323. Orlando: Academic Press, 1985.

McManamon, F. P., gen. ed. *Archaeology in America: An Encyclopedia*. 4-vol. set. Westport, CT: Greenwood Press, 2008.

McNiven, I., and L. Russell. *Appropriated Pasts: Indigenous Peoples and the Colonial Culture of Archaeology*. Walnut Creek, CA: AltaMira Press, 2005.

Menta, J. *The Quinnipiac: Cultural Conflict in Southern New England*. Yale University Publications in Anthropology, no. 86. New Haven: Yale Peabody Museum, 2003.

Meskell, L., ed. *Archaeologies of Materiality*. London: Blackwell, 2005.

Middleton, A. *Te Puna—A New Zealand Mission Station. Historical Archaeology in New Zealand*. Contributions to Global Historical Archaeology. New York: Springer, 2008.

Miksic, J. N. "Recent Archaeological Excavations in Singapore: A Comparison of Three Fourteenth-Century Sites." *Bulletin of the Indo-Pacific Prehistory Association* 20 (2000): 48–55.

Milanich, J. T. *Laboring in the Fields of the Lord: Spanish Missions and Southeastern Indians*. Gainesville: University Press of Florida, 2006.

Milanich, J. T., and S. Milbrath. *First Encounters: Spanish Explorations in the Caribbean and the United States, 1492–1570*. Ripley P. Bullen Monographs in Anthropology and History. Gainesville: University of Florida Press and Florida Museum of Natural History, 1989.

Miller, D. *Materiality*. Durham, NC: Duke University Press, 2005.

Mills, P. "European Exploration and Colonization of the Hawaiian Islands." In *Archaeology in America*, ed. F. P. McManamon, 131–134. Greenwood Press, 2008.

Milton, G. *Big Chief Elizabeth: How England's Adventurers Gambled and Won the New World*. London: Hodder and Stoughton, 2000.

Mitchell, M. D. "Tracing Comanche History: Eighteenth-Century Rock Art Depictions of Leather Armoured Horses from the Arkansas River Basin, South-Eastern Colorado, USA." *Antiquity* 78 (2004): 115–126.

Mitchell, P. *The Archaeology of Southern Africa*. Cambridge World Archaeology. Cambridge: Cambridge University Press, 2002.

———*African Connections: Archaeological Perspectives on Africa and the Wider World*. Walnut Creek, CA: AltaMira, 2005.

Mitchell, S. "Dugongs and Dugouts, Sharp Tacks and Shellbacks: Macassan Contact and Aboriginal Marine Hunting on the Cobourg Peninsula, Northwestern Arnhem Land." *Bulletin of the Indo-Pacific Prehistory Association* 15, no. 2 (1996): 181–191.

Møbjerg, T. "The Saqqaq Culture in the Sisimiut Municipality Elucidated by the Two Sites Nipisat and Asummiut." In *Man, Culture and Environment in Ancient Greenland: Report on a Research Program*, ed. J. Arneborg and H. C. Gulløv, 98–118. Copenhagen: Danish National Museum and Danish Polar Center, 1998.

Moorehead, A. *The Fatal Impact: An Account of the Invasion of the South Pacific, 1767–1840*. London: Hamish Hamilton, 1966.

Morrison, K. D., and L. L. Junker. *Forager-Traders in South and Southeast Asia: Long Term Histories*. Cambridge: Cambridge University Press, 2002.

Morwood, M. J., and D. R. Hobbs. "The Asian Connection: Preliminary Report on Indonesian Trepang Sites on the Kimberley Coast, N.W. Australia." *Archaeology in Oceania* 32, no. 3 (1997): 197–206.

Mulvaney, D. J., and J. P. White. *Australians to 1788*. Broadway, NSW: Fairfax Syme & Weldon Associates, 1987.

Murray, T. "The Childhood of William Lanne: Contact Archaeology and Aboriginality in Tasmania." *Antiquity* 67 (1993): 507–519.

———ed. *The Archaeology of Contact in Settler Societies*. Cambridge: Cambridge University Press, 2004.

Mytum, H. "The Vikings and Ireland: Ethnicity, Identity, and Culture Change." In *Contact, Continuity, and Collapse: The Norse Colonization of the North Atlantic*, ed. J. H. Barrett, 113–137. Turnhout: Brepols, 2003.

Nassaney, M. S. "Identity Formation at a French Colonial Outpost in the North American Interior." *International Journal of Historical Archaeology* 12, no. 4 (2008): 297–318.

Nassaney, M. S., and E. S. Johnson. *Interpretations of Native North American Life: Material Contributions to Ethnohistory.* Gainesville: University Press of Florida, 2000.

Newman, M. "Contact Period Houses from the Lake Rotoaira Area, Taupo." *Archaeology in New Zealand* 32, no. 1 (1989): 17–25.

Nichols, M. "The Spanish Horse of the Pampas." *American Anthropologist* 41, no. 1 (1939): 119–129.

Oastler, John. "The Honorary Magistrate." Manuscript in the Mortlock Library of South Australiana, Adelaide, 1908.

Odess, D., S. Loring, and W. W. Fitzhugh. "*Skraeling*: First People of Helliland, Markland, and Vinland." In *Vikings: The North Atlantic Saga*, ed. W. W. Fitzhugh and E. I. Ward, 193–205. Washington, DC: Smithsonian Institution Press, 2000.

Ogundiran, A. "Of Small Things Remembered: Beads, Cowries, and Cultural Translations of the Atlantic Experience in Yorubaland." *International Journal of African Historical Studies* 35 (2002): 427–457.

———. "Four Millennia of Cultural History in Nigeria (ca. 2000 B.C.–A.D. 1900): Archaeological Perspectives." *Journal of World Prehistory* 19, no. 2 (2005): 133–168.

Orser Jr, C. E. "Historical Archaeology as Modern-World Archaeology in Argentina." *International Journal of Historical Archaeology* 13, no. 3 (2008): 181–194.

Orser, C. E., and Pedro P. A. Funari. "Archaeology and Slave Resistance and Rebellion." *World Archaeology* 33, no. 1 (2001): 61–72.

Ouzman, S. "Indigenous Images of a Colonial Exotic: Imaginings from Bushman Southern Africa." *Before Farming* 1, no. 6 (2003): 1–17.

Parker Pearson, M. "Reassessing *Robert Drury's Journal* as a Historical Source for Southern Madagascar." *History in Africa* 23 (1996): 233–256.

Parkington, J. "Soaqua and Bushmen: Hunters and Robbers." In *Past and Present in Hunter Gatherer Studies*, ed. C. Schrire, 151–174. Orlando: Academic Press, 1984.

Paterson, Alistair G. "The Texture of Agency: An Example of Culture-Contact in Central Australia." *Archaeology in Oceania* 38, no. 2 (2003): 52–65.

———. "Hunter-Gatherer Interactions with Sheep and Cattle Pastoralists from the Australian Arid Zone." In *Desert Peoples: Archaeological Perspectives*, ed. M. A. Smith and P. Veth, 276–292. Oxford: Blackwell, 2005.

———. "Towards a Historical Archaeology of Western Australia's Northwest." *Australasian Historical Archaeology* 24 (2006): 99–111.

———. *The Lost Legions: Culture Contact in Colonial Australia*, Indigenous Archaeologies Series. Lanham, MD: AltaMira Press, 2008.

Paterson, A. G., and A. Wilson. "Indigenous Perceptions of Contact at Inthanoona, Northwest Western Australia." *Archaeology in Oceania* 44 (2009): 98–110.

Pauketat, T. R. *The Archaeology of Traditions: Agency and History Before and After Columbus.* The Ripley P. Bullen Series. Gainesville: University Press of Florida, 2001.

Pegolotti, F. B. *La pratica della mercatura.* Ed. A. Evans. Cambridge, MA: Mediaeval Academy of America, 1936.

Phillips, C. "Post-Contact Landscapes of Change in Hauraki, New Zealand." In *The Archaeology of Difference: Negotiating Cross-Cultural Engagements in Oceania*, ed. R. Torrence and A. Clarke, 79–103. London: Routledge, 2000.

——. *Waihou Journeys: The Archaeology of 400 Years of Maori Settlement*. Auckland: Auckland University Press, 2000.

Phillipson, D. W. *African Archaeology*. 2nd ed. Cambridge: Cambridge University Press, 1993.

Piana, M. *Burgen und Städte der Kreuzzugszeit*. Petersberg: Imhof, 2008.

Pikirayi, I. *The Archaeological Identity of the Mutapa State: Towards an Historical Archaeology of Northern Zimbabwe*. Studies in African Archaeology, no. 6. Uppsala: Societas Archaeologica Upsaliensis, 1993.

Pires, T. *The Suma Oriental of Tomé Pires: An Account of the East, from the Red Sea to Japan, Written in Malacca and India in 1512–1515*. Trans. Armando Cortesão. Nendeln: Kraus Reprint Limited, 1967.

Plato. *Dialogues of Plato: Laws*. Trans. B. Jowett. Oxford: Oxford University Press, 1892.

Plomley, N. J. B. *Weep in Silence: A History of the Flinders Island Aboriginal Settlement*. Netley: Blubber Head Press, 1987.

Polo, Marco. Translated by H. Yule; ed. Henri Cordier. *The Travels of Marco Polo: The Complete Yule-Cordier Edition: Including the Unabridged Third Edition (1903) of Henry Yule's Annotated Translation, as Revised by Henri Cordier, Together with Cordier's Later Volume of Notes and Addenda (1920)*. New York/London: Dover Publications Constable, 1993.

Posnansky, M. "Toward an Archaeology of the Black Diaspora." *Journal of Black Studies* 15, no. 2 (1984): 195–205.

Posnansky, M., and C. R. DeCorse. "Historical Archaeology in Sub-Saharan Africa: A Review." *Journal of Historical Archaeology* 20, no. 1 (1986): 1–14.

Powell, J. W. "Human Evolution: Annual Address of the President, J. W. Powell, Delivered November 6, 1883." *Transactions of the Anthropological Society of Washington* 2 (1883): 176–208.

——. *Introduction to the Study of Indian Languages*. Washington, DC: U.S. Government Printing Office, 1880.

Power, D. *The Central Middle Ages: Europe 950–1320*. The Short Oxford History of Europe. Oxford: Oxford University Press, 2006.

Preucel, R. W. *Archaeologies of the Pueblo Revolt: Identity, Meaning, and Renewal in the Pueblo World*. 1st ed. Albuquerque: University of New Mexico Press, 2002.

Prickett, N. "The Archaeology of the New Zealand Wars." *Australasian Historical Archaeology* 10 (1992): 3–14.

Prince, P. "Cultural Coherence and Resistance in Historic-Period Northwest Coast Mortuary Practices at Kimsquit." *Historical Archaeology* 36, no. 4 (2002): 50–65.

Proust, K. "Public Archaeology and the Physical Legacy of European Colonisation in South East Asia." *Australasian Historical Archaeology* 11 (1993): 108–117.

Pwiti, G., and R. Soper, eds. *Aspects of African Archaeology: Papers from the 10th Congress of the PanAfrican Association for Prehistory and Related Studies*. Harare: University of Zimbabwe Publications, 1996.

Pyszczyk, H. W. "The Use of Fur Trade Goods by the Plains Indians, Central and Southern Alberta, Canada." *Canadian Journal of Archaeology* 21, no. 1 (1997): 45–84.

Quimby, G. I. *Indian Culture and European Trade Goods: The Archaeology of the Historic Period in the Western Great Lakes Region.* Madison: University of Wisconsin Press, 1966.

Quimby, G. I., and A. Spoehr. "Acculturation and Material Culture." *Fieldiana: Anthropology* 36, no. 6 (1951): 107–147.

Quinn, D., ed. *New American World: A Documentary History of North America to 1612.* New York: Arno Press, 1979.

Rainbird, P. "A Message for our Future? The Rapa Nui (Easter Island) Ecodisaster and Pacific Island Environments." *World Archaeology* 33, no. 3 (2002): 436–451.

Ramenofsky, A. F. "Historical Science and Contact Period Studies." In *Columbian Consequences.* Vol. 3: *The Spanish Borderlands in Pan-American Perspective,* ed. D. H. Thomas, 437–452. Washington, DC: Smithsonian Institution Press, 1991.

Ramenofsky A. F., A. K. Wilbur, and A. C. Stone. "Native American Disease History: Past, Present and Future Directions." *World Archaeology* 35, no. 2 (2003): 241–257.

Ray, A. J. *Indians in the Fur Trade: Their Role as Trappers, Hunters, and Middlemen in the Lands Southwest of Hudson Bay, 1660–1870.* Toronto/Buffalo: University of Toronto Press, 1974.

———. "The Hudson's Bay Company and Native People." In *Handbook of North American Indians,* vol. 4: *History of Indian–White Relations,* ed. W. E. Washburn. Washington, DC: Smithsonian Institution, 1988.

Redfield, R., R. Linton, and M. J. Herskovits. "Memorandum for the Study of Acculturation." *American Anthropologist* 38 (1936): 149–152.

Reid, A., and P. J. Lane, eds. *African Historical Archaeologies.* London: Kluwer Acadmic/Plenum, 2004.

Reynolds, H. *With the White People.* Ringwood: Penguin, 1990.

Rhodes, D., and R. Stocks. "Excavations at Lake Condah Mission 1984–1985." *Historic Environment* 4 (1985): 4.

Ridinger, R. B. M. *African Archaeology: A Selected Bibliography.* New York: G. K. Hall, 1993.

Robinson, E. J. *Interaction on the Southeast Mesoamerican Frontier: Prehistoric and Historic Honduras and El Salvador.* BAR International Series. Oxford: B.A.R., 1987.

Robinson, G. A., and N. J. B. Plomley. *Friendly Mission: The Tasmanian Journals and Papers of George Augustus Robinson, 1829–1834.* Launceston: Queen Victoria Museum and Art Gallery, 2008.

Robinson, P. A., M. Kelley, and P. E. Rubertone. "Preliminary Biocultural Interpretations from a Seventeenth-Century Narragansett Indian Cemetery in Rhode Island." In *Cultures in Contact: The Impact of European Contacts on Native American Cultural Institutions, A.D. 1000–1800,* ed. William Fitzhugh, 107–130. Washington, DC: Smithsonian Institution, 1985.

Rodriguez-Alegria, E. "Narratives of Conquest, Colonialism, and Cutting-Edge Technology." *American Anthropologist* 110, no. 1 (2008): 33–44.

Roesdahl, E. *The Vikings.* London: Allen Lane, 1991.

Roesdahl, E., and B. Scholkmann. "Housing Culture." In *The Archaeology of Medieval Europe*, ed. J. Graham-Campbell and M. Valor, 154–180. Aarhus: Aarhus University Press, 2007.

Rogers, J. D., and S. M. Wilson, eds. *Ethnohistory and Archaeology: Approaches to Post-contact Change in the Americas.* New York: Plenum Press, 1993.

Rogers, P. W. "The Raw Materials of Textiles from GUS—With a Note on Fragments of Fleece and Animal Pelts from the Same Site." In *Man, Culture and Environment in Ancient Greenland: Report on a Research Programme*, ed. J. Arneborg and H. C. Gulløv, 66–73. Copenhagen: Danish National Museum and Danish Polar Center, 1998.

Rose, D. B. *Hidden Histories: Black Stories from Victoria River Downs, Humbert River and Wave Hill Stations.* Canberra: Aboriginal Studies Press, 1991.

———. *Nourishing Terrains: Australian Aboriginal Views of Landscape and Wilderness.* Canberra: Australian Heritage Commission, 1996.

Rothschild, N. A. *Colonial Encounters in a Native American Landscape: The Spanish and Dutch in North America.* Washington, DC: Smithsonian Books, 2003.

Rowlands, M. J. "The Archaeology of Colonialism and Constituting the African Peasantry." In *Domination and Resistance*, ed. D. Miller, M. J. Rowlands, and C. Y. Tilley, 375–395. London: Routledge, 1998.

———. "Ritual Killing and Historical Transformation in a West African Kingdom." In *Social Transformations in Archaeology: Global and Local Perspectives*, ed. K. Kristiansen and M. J. Rowlands, 397–409. London: Routledge, 1998.

Rubertone, P. E. "Matters of Inclusion: Historical Archaeology and Native Americans." *World Archaeological Bulletin* 7 (1996): 77–86.

———. "The Historical Archaeology of Native Americans." *Annual Review of Anthropology* 29 (2000): 425–446.

———. *Grave Undertakings: An Archaeology of Roger Williams and the Narragansett Indians.* Washington, DC: Smithsonian Institution Press, 2001.

Rudmin, F. W. 2003. "Catalogue of Acculturation Constructs: Descriptions of 126 Taxonomies, 1918–2003." In *Online Readings in Psychology and Culture,* ed. W. V. Lonner, D. L. Dinnel, S. A. Hayes, and D. N. Sattler. Bellingham, WA: Center for Cross-Cultural Research, Western Washington University, *http://www.wwu.edu/culture* (accessed 1 January 2009).

Russell, L. "Kangaroo Island Sealers and Their Descendants: Ethnic and Gender Ambiguities in the Archaeology of a Creolised Community." *Australian Archaeology* 60 (2005): 1–5.

———. "'Dirty Domestics and Worse Cooks': Aboriginal Women's Agency and Domestic Frontiers, Southern Australia, 1800–1850." *Frontiers: A Journal of Women Studies* 28, nos. 1–2 (2007): 18–46.

Russell, L., ed. *Colonial Frontiers: Indigenous–European Encounters in Settler Societies.* Manchester: Manchester University Press, 2001.

Sadr, K., and I. Plug. "Faunal Remains in the Transition from Hunting to Herding in Southeastern Botswana." *South African Archaeological Bulletin* 56, nos. 173–174 (2001): 76–82.

Sagan, C. *Contact.* New York: Simon and Schuster, 1985.

Sahlins, M. D. *Historical Metaphors and Mythical Realities: Structure in the Early History of the Sandwich Islands Kingdom*. Association for Social Anthropology in Oceania Special Publications, no. 1. Ann Arbor: University of Michigan Press, 1981.

———.*How "Natives" Think: About Captain Cook, For Example*. Chicago: University of Chicago Press, 1995.

Said, E. W. *Orientalism*. London: Routledge and Kegan Paul, 1978.

Salmond, A. *Between Worlds: Early Exchanges Between Maori and Europeans, 1773–1815*. Auckland: Viking, 1997.

———.*The Trial of the Cannibal Dog; Captain Cook in the South Seas*. London/Auckland: Penguin, 2004.

Scheiber, L. L., and M. D. Mitchell. *Across a Great Divide: Continuity and Change in Native North American Societies, 1400–1900*. Tucson: University of Arizona Press, 2010.

Schledermann, P. "A.D. 1000: East Meets West." In *Vikings: The North Atlantic Saga*, ed. W. R. Fitzgerald and E. I. Ward, 189–192. Washington, DC: Smithsonian Institution Press, 2000.

Schmidt, P. R. *Historical Archaeology: A Structural Approach in an African Culture*. Westport, CT: Greenwood Press, 1978.

———.*Historical Archaeology in Africa: Representation, Social Memory, and Oral Traditions*. Lanham, MD: AltaMira, 2006.

Schofield, J., and H. Steuer. "Urban Settlement." In *The Archaeology of Medieval Europe*, ed. J. Graham-Campbell and M. Valor, 111–154. Aarhus: Aarhus University Press, 2007.

Schrire, C. "Wild Surmises on Savage Thoughts." In *Past and Present in Hunter-Gatherer Studies*, ed. C. Schrire, 1–25. London: Academic Press, 1984.

———.ed. *Past and Present in Hunter-Gatherer Studies*. London: Academic Press, 1984.

———. "The Historical Archaeology of Colonial–Indigenous Interaction in South Africa." In *Papers in the Prehistory of the Western Cape, South Africa*, ed. J. Parkington and M. Hall, 424–461. British Archaeological Report Series. Oxford: B.A.R., 1987.

———. "The Historical Archaeology of the Impact of Colonialism in 17th Century South Africa." *Antiquity* 62 (1988): 211–225.

———. "The Historical Archaeology of the Impact of Colonialism in Seventeenth-Century South Africa." In *Historical Archaeology in Global Perspective*, ed. L. Falk, 69–96. Washington, DC: Smithsonian Institution Press, 1991.

———.*Digging through Darkness: Chronicles of an Archaeologist*. Charlottesville: University Press of Virginia, 1995.

Schrire, C., and J. Deacon. "The Indigenous Artefacts from Oudepost I, a Colonial Outpost of the VOC at Saldanha Bay, Cape." *South African Archaeological Bulletin* 44 (1989): 105–113.

———. "Digging Archives at Oudepost I, Cape, South Africa." In *The Art and Mystery of Historical Archaeology*, ed. A. E. Yentsch and M. C. Beaudry, 361–372. Boca Raton, FL: CRC Press, 1992.

Schrire, C., and D. Merwick. "Dutch–Indigenous Relations in New Netherland and the Cape in the Seventeenth Century." In *Historical Archaeology in Global Perspective*, ed. L. Falk, 11–20. Washington, DC: Smithsonian Institution Press, 1991.

Schwartz, S. B. *Implicit Understandings: Observing, Reporting, and Reflecting on the Encounters between Europeans and Other Peoples in the Early Modern Era*. Cambridge: Cambridge University Press, 1994.

Scott, D. D., R. A. Fox, M. A. Connor, and D. Harmon. *Archaeological Perspectives on the Battle of Little Big Horn*. Norman: University of Oklahoma Press, 1989.

Secher, K. "Stone Finds from the Hall (XVII) and Their Functions—Geological Commentary." In *Man, Culture and Environment in Ancient Greenland: Report on a Research Programme*, ed. J. Arneborg and H. C. Gulløv, 45–47. Copenhagen: Danish National Museum and Danish Polar Center, 1998.

Service, E. R. *Primitive Social Organization: An Evolutionary Perspective*. New York: Random House, 1962.

Sharp, L. "Steel Axes for Stone Age Australians." In *Human Problems in Technological Change: A Casebook*, ed. E. H. Spicer, 69–90. New York: Russell Sage Foundation, 1952.

Sigurðsson, G. "The Quest for Vinland in Saga Scholarship." In *Vikings: The North Atlantic Saga*, ed. W. R. Fitzgerald and E. I. Ward, 232–237. Washington, DC: Smithsonian Institution Press, 2000.

———. "An Introduction to the Vinland Sagas." In *Vikings: The North Atlantic Saga*, ed. W. R. Fitzgerald and E. I. Ward, 218–224. Washington, DC: Smithsonian Institution Press, 2000.

Silliman, S. "Theoretical Perspectives on Labour and Colonialism: Reconsidering Californian Missions." *Journal of Anthropological Archaeology* 20 (2001): 379–407.

———. *Lost Laborers in Colonial California: Native Americans and the Archaeology of Rancho Petaluma*. Tucson: University of Arizona Press, 2004.

———. "Social and Physical Landscapes of Contact." In *North American Archaeology*, ed. T. R. Pauketat and D. DiPaolo Loren, 273–296. London/Malden, MA: Blackwell Publishing, 2004.

———. "Culture Contact or Colonialism? Challenges in the Archaeology of Native North America." *American Antiquity* 70, no. 1 (2005): 55–74.

———. *Collaborating at the Trowel's Edge: Teaching and Learning in Indigenous Archaeology*. Tucson: University of Arizona Press, 2008.

———. "Change and Continuity, Practice and Memory: Native American Persistence in Colonial New England." *American Antiquity* 74, no. 2 (2009): 211–230.

Singleton, T. A., and M. Bograd. *The Archaeology of the African Diaspora in the Americas*. Guides to the Archaeological Literature of the Immigrant Experience in America, no. 2. Tucson: Society for Historical Archaeology, 1995.

Singleton, T. A., and M. A. Torres de Souza. "Archaeologies of the African Diaspora: Brazil, Cuba, and the United States." In *International Handbook of Historical Archaeology*, ed. T. Majewski and D. Gaimster, 449–469. New York: Springer, 2009.

Skelton, R. A. *Explorer's Maps: Chapters in the Cartographic Record of Geographical Discovery*. London: Spring Books, 1958.

Skowronek, R. K. "On the Fringes of New Spain: The Northern Borderlands and the Pacific." In *International Handbook of Historical Archaeology*, ed. T. Majewski and D. Gaimster, 471–505. New York: Springer, 2009.

———. "The Spanish Philippines: Archaeological Perspectives on Colonial Economics and Society." *International Journal of Historical Archaeology* 2, no. 1 (1998): 45–71.

Slupecki, L., and M. Valor. "Religions." In *The Archaeology of Medieval Europe*, ed. J. Graham-Campbell and M. Valor, 366–397. Aarhus: Aarhus University Press, 2007.

Smith, A. B. "Keeping People on the Periphery: The Ideology of Social Hierarchies between Hunters and Herders." *Journal of Anthropological Archaeology* 17, no. 2 (1998): 201–215.

———. "The Archaeology of Hunter–Herder Interaction in the Drylands of Southern Africa." In *23 Degrees South: Archaeology and Natural History of the Southern Deserts*, ed. M. Smith and P. Hesse, 250–266. Canberra: National Museum of Australia Press, 2005.

Smith, L., A. Morgan, and A. van der Meer. "Community-Driven Research in Cultural Heritage Management: The Waanyi Women's History Project." *International Journal of Heritage Studies* 9, no. 1 (2003): 65–80.

Solomidou-Ieronymidou, M. "The Crusaders, Sugar Mills and Sugar Production in Medieval Cyprus." In *Archaeology and the Crusades*, ed. P. Edbury and S. Kalopissi-Verti, 63–81. Athens: Pierides Foundation, 2007.

Spector, J. "What This Awl Means: Towards a Feminist Archaeology." In *Engendering Archaeology: Women and Prehistory*, ed. J. Gero and M. Conkey, 388–406. Oxford: Blackwell, 1991.

———. *What This Awl Means: Feminist Archaeology at a Wahpeton Dakota Village*. St. Paul: Minnesota Historical Society Press, 1993.

Spicer, E. H. *Perspectives in American Indian Culture Change*. Chicago: University of Chicago Press, 1961.

———. *Cycles of Conquest: The Impact of Spain, Mexico, and the United States on the Indians of the Southwest, 1533–1960*. Tucson: University of Arizona Press, 1962.

Spielmann, K. A., T. Clark, D. Hawkey, K. Rainey, and S. K. Fish. "'...being weary, they had rebelled': Pueblo Subsistence and Labor under Spanish Colonialism." *Journal of Anthropological Archaeology* 28 (2009): 102–125.

Stahl, A. B. "Concepts of Time and Approaches to Analogical Reasoning in Historical Perspective." *American Antiquity* 58, no. 2 (1993): 235–260.

———. "Change and Continuity in the Banda Area, Ghana: The Direct Historical Approach." *Journal of Field Archaeology* 21 (1994): 181–203.

———. "The Archaeology of Global Encounters Viewed from Banda, Ghana." *African Archaeological Review* 16, no. 5 (1999).

———. *Making History in Banda: Anthropological Visions of Africa's Past*. New Studies in Archaeology. New York: Cambridge University Press, 2001.

———. "Political Economic Mosaics: Archaeology of the Last Two Millennia in Tropical Sub-Saharan Africa." *Annual Review of Anthropology* 33, no. 1 (2004): 145–172.

———. *African Archaeology: A Critical Introduction*. Malden, MA: Blackwell, 2005.

———. "The Slave Trade as Practice and Memory: What Are the Issues for Archaeologists?" In *Invisible Citizens: Captives and Their Consequences*, ed. C. M. Cameron, 25–56. Salt Lake City: University of Utah Press, 2008.

———. "Material Histories." In *Oxford Handbook of Material Culture Studies*, ed. D. Hicks and M. C. Beaudry. Oxford: Oxford University Press, 2010.

Stark, M. T. "Early Mainland Southeast Asian Landscapes in the First Millennium A.D." *Annual Review of Anthropology* 35, no. 1 (2006): 407–432.

Stark, M. T., and S. J. Allen. "The Transition to History in Southeast Asia: An Introduction." *International Journal of Historical Archaeology* 2, no. 3 (1998): 161–174.

Staski, E. "Change and Inertia on the Frontier: Archaeology at the Paraje de San Diego, Camino Real, in Southern New Mexico." *International Journal of Historical Archaeology* 2, no. 1 (1998): 21–44.

Stein, G. *The Archaeology of Colonial Encounters: Comparative Perspectives.* 1st ed. School of American Research Advanced Seminar Series. Santa Fe/Oxford: School of American Research Press, 2005.

Stoklund, M. "Greenland Runes: Isolation or Culture Change." In *The Viking Age in Caithness, Orkney and the North Atlantic*, ed. C. E. Batey, J. Jesch, and C. D. B. A. Morris, 528–543. Edinburgh: Edinburgh University Press, 1993.

Stumman Hansen, S. "The Early Settlement of the Faroe Islands: The Creation of Cultural Identity." In *Contact, Continuity, and Collapse: The Norse Colonization of the North Atlantic*, ed. J. H. Barrett, 33–71. Turnhout: Brepols, 2003.

Sturt, Charles. *Two Expeditions into the Interior of Southern Australia during the Years 1828, 1829, 1830, 1831: With Observations on the Soil, Climate, and General Resources of the Colony of New South Wales.* Canberra: Petherick Reading Room, National Library of Australia. E-book published by eBooks@Adelaide, *http://ebooks.adelaide.edu.au/s/sturt/charles/s93t/.*

Sturtevant, W. C., gen. ed. *The Handbook of North American Indians.* 17 vols. Washington, DC: Smithsonian Institution, 1978–2006.

Sutherland, P. "The Norse and Native Americans." In *Vikings: The North Atlantic Saga*, ed. W. R. Fitzgerald and E. I. Ward, 238–247. Washington, DC: Smithsonian Institution Press, 2000.

———. "Strands of Culture Contact: Dorset-Norse Interactions in the Canadian Eastern Arctic." In *Identities and Cultural Contacts in the Arctic: Proceedings from a Conference at the Danish National Museum, Copenhagen November 30 to December 2, 1999*, ed. M. Appelt, J. Berglund, and H. C. Gulløv, 159–169. Copenhagen: Danish National Museum and Danish Polar Center, 2000.

Swadling, P., R. Wagner, and B. Laba. *Plumes from Paradise: Trade Cycles in Outer Southeast Asia and Their Impact on New Guinea and Nearby Islands until 1920.* Coorparoo, Queensland: Papua New Guinea National Museum in association with Robert Brown & Associates, 1996.

Swanepoel, S. "The Practice and Substance of Historical Archaeology in Sub-Saharan Africa." In *International Handbook of Historical Archaeology*, ed. T. Majewski and D. Gaimster, 565–581. New York: Springer, 2009.

Swanepoel, N., A. Esterhuysen, and P. Bonner, eds. *Five Hundred Years Rediscovered: Southern African Precedents and Prospects.* Johannesburg: Wits University Press, 2008.

Sweet, J. *Recreating Africa: Culture, Kinship, and Religion in the African-Portuguese World, 1441–1770.* Chapel Hill: University of North Carolina Press, 2003.

Taçon, P. S. C., B. South, and S. Hooper. "Depicting Cross-Cultural Interaction: Figurative Designs in Wood, Earth and Stone from South-East Australia." *Archaeology in Oceania* 38, no. 2 (2003): 89–101.

Taçon, P. S. C., S. K. May, S. J. Fallon, M. Travers, D. Wesley, and R. Lamilami. "A Minimum Age for Early Depictions of Southeast Asian Praus in the Rock Art of Arnhem Land, Northern Territory." *Australian Archaeology* 71 (2010): 1–9.

Taylor, J. G. "Meditations on a Portrait from Seventeenth-Century Batavia." *Journal of Southeast Asian Studies* 23, no. 1 (2006): 23–31.

Tench, W. *A Complete Account of the Settlement at Port Jackson.* Pall Mall: G. Nichol, 1793.

Thomas, D. H. *Exploring Native North America, Places in Time.* Oxford/New York: Oxford University Press, 2000.

———.*Native American Landscapes of St. Catherines Island, Georgia.* 3 vols. American Museum of Natural History, Anthropological Papers. New York: American Museum of Natural History, 2008.

Thomas, D. H., ed. *Columbian Consequences.*3 vols. Washington, DC:Smithsonian Institution Press, 1989, 1990, 1991.

Thomas, D. H., and L. S. A. Pendleton. *The Archaeology of Mission Santa Catalina de Guale: 1. Search and Discovery.* Anthropological Papers of the American Museum of Natural History no. 63, pt. 2, New York: American Museum of Natural History, 1987.

Thomas, N. *Entangled Objects: Exchange, Material Culture, and Colonialism in the Pacific.* Cambridge, MA: Harvard University Press, 1991.

———. *Colonialism's Culture: Anthropology, Travel and Government.* Princeton: Princeton University Press, 1994.

———. "Tabooed Ground: Augustus Earle in New Zealand and Australia." In *Exchanges: Cross Cultural Encounters in Australia and the Pacific,* ed. R. Gibson, 143–162. Sydney: Museum of Sydney, Historical House Trust of New South Wales, 1996.

———. *Cook: The Extraordinary Voyages of Captain James Cook.* New York: Walker & Company, 2003.

Thompson, D. *David Thompson's Narrative of his Explorations in Western America 1784–1812.* Ed. J. B. Tyrrell. Toronto: Champlain Society, 1916.

Torrence, R., and A. Clarke. *The Archaeology of Difference: Negotiating Cross-Cultural Engagements in Oceania.* One World Archaeology, no. 38. London: Routledge, 2000.

Trigger, B. G. *Time and Traditions: Essays in Archaeological Interpretation.* Edinburgh: Edinburgh University Press, 1978.

———.*Natives and Newcomers: Canada's "Heroic Age" Reconsidered.* Kingston: McGill-Queen's University Press, 1985.

———. *The Children of Aataentsic: A History of the Huron People to 1660.* Kingston: McGill-Queen's University Press, 1987.

Tuck, J. A. "European-Native Contacts in the Strait of Belle Isle, Labrador." In *Between Greenland and America: Cross-Cultural Contacts and the Environment in the Baffin Bay Area,* ed. L. Hacquebord and R. Vaughan, 61–74. Groningen: Arctic Centre, University of Groningen, 1987.

Turgeon, L. "Beads, Bodies and Regimes of Value: From France to North America, c. 1500–c. 1650." In *The Archaeology of Contact in Settler Societies,* ed. T. Murray, 19–47. Cambridge: Cambridge University Press, 2004.

Turpin, S. A. "The Iconography of Contact: Spanish Influences in the Rock Art of the Middle Rio Grande." In *Columbian Consequences,* Vol. 1: *Archaeological and Historical Perspectives on the Spanish Borderlands West,* ed. D. H. Thomas, 277–299. Washington, DC: Smithsonian Institution Press, 1989.

UNESCO. *General History of Africa.* 8 vols. London: Heinemann Educational Books, 1981–1985.

Van Tilburg, J.-A. *Easter Island: Archaeology, Ecology and Culture.* Washington, DC: Smithsonian Institution Press, 1994.

Veth, P., P. Sutton, and M. Neale, eds. *Strangers on the Shore: Early Coastal Contact in Australia.* Canberra: National Museum of Australia Press, 2008.

Voss, B. L. "From Casta to Californio: Social Identity and the Archaeology of Culture Contact." *American Anthropologist* 107, no. 3 (2005): 461–474.

———. "The Archaeology of Overseas Chinese Communities." *World Archaeology* 37, no. 3 (2005): 424–439.

———. *The Archaeology of Ethnogenesis: Race and Sexuality in Colonial San Francisco.* Berkeley: University of California Press, 2008.

———. "Gender, Race, and Labor in the Archaeology of the Spanish Colonial Americas." *Current Anthropology* 49, no. 5 (2008): 861–893.

Voss, B. L., and R. Allen. "Overseas Chinese Archaeology: Historical Foundations, Current Reflections, and New Directions." *Historical Archaeology* 42, no. 3 (2008): 5–28.

Wallace, B. L. "An Archaeologist's Interpretation of the Vinland Sagas." In *Vikings: The North Atlantic Saga,* ed. W. R. Fitzgerald and E. I. Ward, 225–231. Washington, DC: Smithsonian Institution Press, 2000.

———. "The Viking Settlement at L'Anse Aux Meadows." In *Vikings: The North Atlantic Saga,* ed. W. R. Fitzgerald and E. I. Ward, 208–216. Washington, DC: Smithsonian Institution Press, 2000.

———. "L'Anse aux Meadows and Vinland: An Abandoned Experiment." In *Contact, Continuity, and Collapse: The Norse Colonization of the North Atlantic,* ed. J. H. Barrett, 207–237. Turnhout: Brepols, 2003.

Wallerstein, I. *The Modern World-System I: Capitalist Agriculture and the Origins of the European World-Economy in the Sixteenth Century.* Studies in Social Discontinuity. New York: Academic Press, 1974.

———. *The Modern World-System II: Mercantilism and the Consolidation of the European World-Economy, 1600–1750.* New York: Academic Press, 1980.

———. *The Modern World-System III: The Second Great Expansion of the Capitalist World-Economy, 1730–1840's.* San Diego: Academic Press, 1989.

Wartburg, M.-L. von. "Production du sucre de canne a Chypre: Un chapitre de technologie medievale." In *Coliniser au Moyen Age,* ed. M. Balard and A. Ducellier, 126–131. Paris, 1995.

Watkins, J. *American Indian Values and Scientific Practice.* Indigenous Archaeology. Walnut Creek, CA: AltaMira Press, 2000.

Wells, H.G. *War of the Worlds.* London: Heineman, 1898.

Wegars, P. *Hidden Heritage: Historical Archaeology of the Overseas Chinese.* Baywood Monographs in Archaeology Series. Amityville: Baywood Publishing Co., 1993.

Wesler, K. *Historical Archaeology in Nigeria*. Trenton, NJ: World Press, 1998.

White, R. *The Middle Ground: Indians, Empires, and Republics in the Great Lakes Region, 1650–1815*. Cambridge Studies in North American Indian History. Cambridge/New York: Cambridge University Press, 1991.

Wilcox, M. V. *The Pueblo Revolt and the Mythology of Conquest: An Indigenous Archaeology of Contact*. Berkeley: University of California Press, 2009.

Williamson, C. "Finding Meaning in the Patterns: The Analysis of Material Culture from a Contact Site in Tasmania". In *After Captain Cook: The Archaeology of the Recent Indigenous Past in Australia*, ed. R. Harrison and C. Williamson, 76–101. Sydney: Sydney University Archaeological Methods Series, 2002.

Wilson, R. *Bringing Them Home: Report of the National Inquiry into the Separation of Aboriginal and Torres Strait Islander Children from their Families*. Sydney: Human Rights and Equal Opportunity Commission, 1997.

Wilson, S. M. *Hispaniola: Caribbean Chiefdoms in the Age of Columbus*. Tuscaloosa: University of Alabama Press, 1990.

———. "From Spaniard to Creole: The Archaeology of Cultural Formation at Puerto Real, Haiti." *American Anthropologist* 94, no. 3 (1992): 755–756.

Wilson, S. M., and J. D. Rogers. "Historical Dynamics in the Contact Era." In *Ethnohistory and Archaeology: Approaches to Postcontact Change in the Americas*, ed. J. D. Rogers and S. M. Wilson, 3–15. New York: Plenum Press, 1993.

Windschuttle, K. *The Fabrication of Aboriginal History*. Reprinted with corrections ed. Sydney: Macleay Press, 2003.

Wolf, E. R. *Europe and the People without History*. Berkeley: University of California Press, 1982.

Woollett, J. M. "Living in the Narrows: Subsistence Economy and Culture Change in Labrador Inuit Society during the Contact Period." *World Archaeology* 30, no. 3 (1999): 370–387.

Worth, J. E. *The Struggle for the Georgia Coast: An 18th-Century Spanish Retrospective on Guale and Mocama*. Anthropological Papers of the American Museum of Natural History, no. 75. Athens, GA: American Museum of Natural History, 1995.

Wright, Ronald. *Stolen Continents: The "New World" through Indian Eyes*. New York: Houghton Mifflin, 1992.

Wylie, A. "The Reaction against Analogy." *Advances in Archaeological Method and Theory* 8 (1985): 63–111.

———. "'Simple' Analogy and the Role of Relevance Assumptions: Implications of Archaeological Practice." *International Studies in the Philosophy of Science* 2 (1988): 134–150.

INDEX

ABOUT THE AUTHOR

Alistair Paterson is Associate Professor and Discipline Chair of Archaeology at the University of Western Australia. His research and teaching covers culture contact, historical archaeology in maritime and terrestrial settings, sheep and cattle pastoralism, European colonization, historical rock art, and archaeological and historical methodology. Much of his work is now located in Western Australia, including regional studies of Australia's Northwest, the uses of coast and offshore islands in colonial and precolonial settings (in collaboration with the Western Australian Museum), and early colonial settlements across the state. He is the author of *The Lost Legions: Culture Contact in Colonial Australia* (AltaMira, 2008) and editor, with Jane Balme, of *Archaeology in Practice: A Student Guide to Archaeological Analyses* (Blackwell Publishing, 2006). In 2009, he was based in Copenhagen as Honorary Visiting Fellow at the University of Copenhagen and at the National Museum. He is past President of the Australian Archaeological Association (2005-2007) and has been involved with editing for, and publishing in, key *Australian archaeology journals, including Archaeology in Oceania, Australasian Historical Archaeology, and Australian Archaeology.*